THE
USENET
HANDBOOK

A User's Guide to Netnews

THE
USENET
HANDBOOK

A User's Guide to Netnews

Mark Harrison

O'Reilly & Associates, Inc.
103 Morris Street, Suite A
Sebastopol, CA 95472
(800) 998-9938 • (707) 829-0515

The USENET Handbook: A User's Guide to Netnews
by Mark Harrison

Editor: Mike Loukides

Production Editor: Mary Anne Weeks Mayo

Printing History:

>   May 1995:   First Edition.

ISBN: 1-56592-101-1

TABLE OF CONTENTS

CHAPTER FOUR

READING NEWS WITH THE TIN NEWSREADER _____ 63

CHAPTER FIVE

READING NEWS WITH EMACS AND GNUS _____ 99

PREFACE

Why I Am Excited About USENET

These days, it's hard to turn around without hearing something about the information superhighway. There is no shortage of pundits offering their predictions about the direction it will take, what will be on it, and who will be footing the bill.

Since there doesn't seem to be anyone *not* making confident and profound predictions as to the future, I would like to get my two cents in and tell you what I think is in store, and why this strange amorphous blob called the USENET will play an important role in the days to come.

The Public Square of the Internet

There are several computer networks that receive a lot of press (both good and bad) these days. The one that seems to garner the most attention is the Internet, a worldwide network of computer networks. It has appeared in everything from Doonesbury cartoons to the television show *Seaquest: DSV*, where it was interrupted by space aliens. With a connection to the Internet, you can download files, send electronic mail, interact with other users in real time, read (and publish) *home pages* on every topic under the sun, and interact with other users in message areas or *newsgroups*.

This last item is the area that USENET covers. It is unique because it is public, widespread, and designed around interacting with other people. The other activities are mostly performed on an individual basis—you read a technical paper, search the network, and download the source code. But if you want to share opinions, solicit input, or just engage in conversation, you need the USENET. The USENET has thousands of newsgroups, with millions of readers.

From the very first time I posted an article and received a reply, I have been excited about this extraordinary communications channel. I hope that this book gives a taste of some of that excitement, and that it helps you get the most out of

USENET. If you have any comments, please send them to *usenet-hand-book@ora.com*. See you on the Net!

How to Read This Book

- *If you have never read USENET news:*

  Read Chapter 2, *Reading News: Getting Started*, for more details and information on the Net. Then, read one of the newsreader chapters (Chapters 3 through 6), which will cover the operation of the software and step you through a sample session.

  Which newsreader should you use? Ask other users at your site to see which is more popular (there's safety in numbers!). It's never a bad idea to use the same one as your news administrator; you can always be sure it will be up and running.

  Once you are familiar with your newsreader and comfortable in reading news, continue with the next bullet item, which covers the casual Net user.

- *If you are a casual user and are already familiar with a newsreader:*

  Read the chapter on your preferred newsreader and experiment with a few unfamiliar features. Or, peruse the other newsreader chapters if you wish to try out another newsreader.

  Then, feel free to browse any of the later chapters. There's no special order, but if you plan on posting an article, be sure to read Chapter 7, *Posting Articles to the Net*, which discusses posting etiquette.

- *If you are an experienced user:*

  Look at some of the advanced features in the newsreader chapters. It's been my experience that there are quite a few longtime users of the Net who haven't bothered to figure out how to use kill files, macro programming, or automatic unpacking of articles.

  Be sure also to check out later chapters for numerous tidbits and interesting topics.

- *If you are impatient to get started and hate to read:*

  OK, so you're a busy type-A person who doesn't want to waste time reading the documentation. No problem: you're probably going to like the Net and its quick pace.

  Skim Chapter 2, *Reading News: Getting Started*, to get an idea of what's behind the Net and then skip to one of the newsreader chapters. Glance over the chapter and then start right in on one of the sample sessions. Don't post messages until you read Chapter 7, *Posting Articles to the Net*. The other chapters have examples on how get software, decode files, etc. Look them over when you've got a minute.

The appendixes cover a variety of miscellaneous topics:

- Appendix A covers geographic distributions.
- Appendix B contains various classic USENET documents.
- Appendix C summarizes the newsreaders' wildcards and regular expressions.
- Appendix D tells you where to get news software if you don't already have it.
- Appendixes E and F list the newsgroups. If you haven't read news before, this is a good introduction to the wide variety of topics covered.

Typographical Conventions

We will use the following conventions in the body of this book:

- Filenames, newsgroups, and command names are in *italics*.
- Computer output is in courier.
- User commands are in **bold courier**.
- In Chapter 6, any menu/button actions are in **bold**.
- Command-line variables are in *italic courier*; the reader should replace them with actual values.

Acknowledgments

Like the USENET itself, this book would not have been possible without the generous assistance of many people. First, I owe a special debt to my wife Ellen and children Allegra and Alexander for their enthusiasm and kind forbearance. John Ho had the original idea to contact O'Reilly & Associates about a book on the USENET. His infectious enthusiasm forced me to agree to give it a try when I Newsmeisters extraordinaire Cornell Kinderknecht and Ying-Da Lee helped in more ways than I can say.

Professor Eugene "Spaf" Spafford provided enthusiastic support and the critical eye only a teacher can provide.

I have always wondered why authors always take such pains to thank their editors; buttering them up for the next book, etc. Mike Loukides disabused me of that idea by his careful reading, critical eye, and constant encouragement.

For their expertise in newsreaders and critical comments, I am especially grateful to Ethan Bradford, Mark Engelthaler, Iain Lea, and Bill Wohler.

For allowing me to quote material or comments, thanks to Chris Lewis, Jonathan I. Kamens, David C. Lawrence, John Levine, John K. Ousterhout, Rob Pike, Dennis Ritchie, and Gene Spafford.

These pages reveal a few additional voices: Valerie Quercia provides color commentary in a number of sidebars throughout the book; Clairemarie Fisher O'Leary describes her USENET revels in "A Good Time Was Virtually Had By All" in Chapter 9; Joe Ilacqua wrote the *newsindex* script and contributed to the section describing it in Chapter 8; and Stephen Spainhour helped research and write the section "Using *Netscape* To Read News," also in Chapter 8.

The staff at O'Reilly & Associates has been a pleasure to work with. Mary Anne Weeks Mayo served as project manager/copyeditor and was ably assisted by Stephen Spainhour in the final stages of production. Both exercised great patience in waiting for last minute additions, deciphering hand-written scribbles, and generally smoothing out and improving the text. Thanks to Michael Sierra, O'Reilly's resident FrameMaker expert, for tool tweaking and formatting expertise; to Kismet McDonough and Sheryl Avruch for their talented proofreading; and to Donna Woonteiler for indexing. Jen Niederst was responsible for the original book design. Hanna Dyer created the original design for the Appendixes E and F as well as the sidebars; fine-tuned the book design; and, along with Chris Reilley, turned my rough sketches into real illustrations.

Finally, I would like to thank the people who worked so hard to make the USENET a reality, and the millions of people who each day make it an interesting and exciting place to visit. Thank you all, and see you on the Net!

INTRODUCTION

What Is USENET?

Have you ever wanted to

- Get free software?

- Ask a question about a software package?

- Discuss a new computer language, or an antique computer system?

- Get advice on your finances?

- Discuss political and social issues with people of all viewpoints?

- Talk about your favorite hobbies?

One place you can go for all of these is to the USENET. What's the USENET?

The USENET news network, variously referred to as "news," "USENET news," "Netnews," or sometimes just "the Net," is a worldwide network of cooperating computer sites that exchange public user messages, known as *articles* or *postings*. These postings are an eclectic mix of questions, commentary, hints, and ideas of all kinds, expressing the views of the thousands of participants at these sites. They often contain free software, more or less intelligent discussion on various topics including recipes, help sheets and reference material, sounds and pictures, and just about anything else that can be put into a file.

These postings are sorted into categories that are collectively known as *newsgroups*. Each of these newsgroups (see Appendix E, *Newsgroups*, and Appendix F, *Alternative Newsgroups*, for more or less complete newsgroup listings) is devoted to a certain topic, ranging from computer languages to woodworking.

What Can It Do for Me?

This is a tough question, since the Net means so many things to so many people. Here's a few of the most popular things people do.

- *Access free software.* There are over twenty groups devoted to distributing software in both source and executable forms. There are groups for specific computer systems, such as IBM PCs, Macs, and NeXT machines. There are groups devoted to particular operating systems or environments, including UNIX, the X Window System, Microsoft Windows, etc. There are also groups devoted to particular kinds of software, such as graphics algorithms and compression techniques as well as groups that provide software for such venerable computers and operating systems as the Apple II and CP/M.

- *Discuss technical topics.* If you are interested in computers, there are literally hundreds of groups devoted to every aspect of computing, everything from specialized topics like telecommunications standards, to popular topics such as using UNIX and programming in C. There is speculation on new topics such as the future of UNIX and what Windows-NT will do to the operating-systems world.

  One of the most exciting aspects of the Net is that every discussion group has at least a few wizards who don't mind sharing their experience and helping others. For example, you might have some questions about the most efficient way to manipulate memory in a certain programming language. You may not have access to many experts in your company or school, but by participating in the Net, you can discuss and share opinions with many experienced people, some of whom have probably faced (and already solved!) the problems you are working with.

- *Keep current on a hobby or special interest, or learn about new ones.* There may not be many people on your block who enjoy discussing your favorite hobby, but chances are you'll find a lot of like-minded people on the Net. Topics range from cooking and woodworking to hi-fi audio and backpacking. There are groups for virtually all professional sports teams, popular television shows and music groups, cultures, and religious faiths.

The Proof Is in the Posting

USENET participants can provide knowledge and assistance in a wide variety of areas. I've benefited from these resources many times, particularly to aid me in my work. For instance:

```
Newsgroups: comp.lang.postscript
Path: amber.ora.com!noc.near.net!news2.near.net!. . .
From: mh@ora.com
Subject: Need Blue Book* routines
```

```
Message-ID: <Ai3LkWXi1ix5070yn@ora.com>
Lines: 28

Sender: mh@ora.com (Mark Harrison)
Organization: O'Reilly & Associates, Inc.
Date: Fri, 18 Nov 1994 05:54:34 EST

Hi. I would like to use some routines from the PostScript Blue Book
for a project I'm working on...If anyone has typed in these
routines and would be willing to mail me a copy, I would be very
grateful.

Thanks in advance.

Mark H.

mh@ora.com --> Mark Harrison at O'Reilly and Associates

Newsgroups: comp.lang.postscript
Subject: RE: Need Blue Book routines
Sender: helper@nice.com (Jerry Helper)
Organization: Nice Guys Are Netters Too, Ltd
Date: Mon, 21 Nov 1994 11:32:21 EST

In article <Ai3LkWXi1ix5070yn@ora.com> Mark Harrison writes:
> Hi.  I would like to use some routines from the PostScript Blue Book
> for a project I'm working on...

Hi, Mark.  Adobe has included the routines you're talking about in
their collection of release PostScript code.  Here's how to retrieve
them....

Jerry, aka The Helpmeister
```

The fictionalized Mr. Helper (whose name is appropriated from the old *Dick Van Dyke Show*) was only one of several knowledgeable users who responded to my query.

I had a similarly positive USENET experience while researching this book. In Chapter 7, *Posting Articles to the Net*, there's a small four-line C program. The program is unusual because when run, it prints its own source code, and I thought it would be an interesting example to use. Unfortunately, I lost my only copy of the program shortly before we sent in the chapter for review. So, I posted to the Net, asking for someone to send me a copy of the file. I received a reply the same evening and over the next day or so, received nearly a dozen different programs. One respondent sent an entire collection of self-replicating programs with the request that I forward any others received to add to his collection.

One last example involves a nest of hornets that my editor, Mike Loukides, found near his house. He wanted to get rid of the nest, and being a good guy, he didn't want to run out and pour gasoline on it. He posted to the group *misc.rural* and asked for advice. He received over a dozen replies and suggestions, from "go ahead and pour the gasoline" to freezing them out with dry ice. He ended up not doing anything, and a hurricane came along and flooded the bugs out. If he sees another request about getting rid of hornets, he'll probably pass along that advice as well.

What Makes USENET Unique?

There are several aspects of USENET that make it unique among computer networks.

- It is totally voluntary and cooperative in nature. There is no centralized governing board and no "USENET, Inc." that controls what topics can be discussed or who can participate. Nearly all software used in the daily operation of the Net is free, and has been written and maintained solely by volunteers, mostly on their own time. This has its advantages and disadvantages. You don't have to pay for it, but you can't complain very loudly if there's a problem. Fortunately, support for this Net software is excellent, and reported bugs are usually fixed very quickly.

- There are no restrictions as to who can participate. Although it was originally developed for UNIX, news software is available for many machines and operating systems, including MS-DOS, Windows, VMS, and the Macintosh. The only requirements are that you obtain and install the necessary software, and find another computer site willing to exchange news articles with you. If you can't find such a site, there are several excellent commercial services that can provide a newsfeed for a reasonable monthly rate. See "How Can I Connect?" later in this chapter, for details.

  One side effect of this (good or bad, according to your point of view) is that there are no minimum standards of politeness or reasonableness that can be imposed on users. There is a general consensus as to what constitutes reasonable behavior, and the great majority of users adhere to these standards. For those who diverge from the norm, there are very few ways to "punish" the behavior other than ignoring them.* As a result, although most of the Net participants are reasonably well behaved, some newsgroups veer towards a state of barely controlled anarchy.

- It is global network, with sites on all seven inhabited continents. You can exchange messages with a student in Chicago, an engineer in Paris, or a computer researcher in Moscow. Most of the Net conversations are carried on

---

* Occasionally you will see someone telling one of these people "I'm going to have a word with your system administrator." This generally serves only to amuse and encourage the miscreant.

in English. In addition, many countries have their own regionally distributed newsgroups in their native languages.[*]

Not Just Another Pretty BBS

In some ways, the USENET is similar to personal-computer bulletin-board systems (BBS) such as FidoNet. They both have public and private messaging capabilities,[†] and the capacity to exchange messages among systems.

Like BBS systems, USENET is based on cooperative effort between systems, and is run largely by volunteers. Both have grown from relatively small efforts to become popular and even respected methods of communications.

The primary difference between the USENET and BBS systems is that USENET's main focus is in transporting messages between machines, whereas most BBS systems are usually more focused around particular machines or sites. Networking between machines came later, and is still not a fundamental requirement for a BBS. Most of the message groups on a typical BBS are local, which means you have to dial into that system to post and read messages. So, if you're interested in a particular topic, you have to find a particular BBS to discuss it. There may be different groups on different systems that you are interested in, or two systems discussing the same topic in isolation. With USENET, it's all there at once. If you become interested in a particular newsgroup or topic on the Net, you can jump to that newsgroup and start reading right away.

In addition to local messaging areas, many BBSs also have echo mail sections that will transfer messages among participating BBS systems. Interestingly enough, several of these echo mail systems are gatewayed to USENET newsgroups!

Not the Internet, Either...

This is a source of confusion to many users, especially those at sites connected to the Internet. This confusion generally comes about because USENET is presented as one of the networking facilities available on their machine, along with FTP, telnet, and other Internet capabilities, these things all being lumped together as the Net.[‡]

So to clarify: USENET is not the Internet, and the Internet is not USENET. The Internet is primarily concerned with connecting computers together and with

---

[*] It's widely believed that there is a base in Antarctica that receives a USENET feed. We haven't found any hard evidence, but it's probably true.

[†] Actually, USENET doesn't have private messaging capabilities, but almost every system that exchanges news also exchanges Internet mail. Most of the newsreader programs also have an interface to mail.

[‡] For more information on the Internet, see Ed Krol's *Whole Internet User's Guide & Catalog*, also published by O'Reilly & Associates.

providing a standard communications protocol for those computers. Facilities like FTP and telnet are "real" Internet facilities that can't operate without the Internet communications protocol.

Things like news and mail, however, are at a higher level of abstraction and don't require the Internet as such. USENET was created using modems and dial-up telephone lines, and can be adapted to just about any transportation medium, including satellite and CD.

So, you can have one without the other. Having said that, however, we should note that many Internet sites are also USENET sites. They share and transfer news just like non-Internet sites, but typically use Internet networking capabilities rather than the modem-based dial-up networking software used at non-Internet sites.

A Little History

Recently, it was estimated that there were in excess of six million people who read news around the world. This section covers a little bit of the history behind the USENET.

Pre-History

In order to understand the context in which the USENET was created, we have to go back to the 1960s. The Department of Defense, through the Advanced Research Projects Agency, was investigating the use of large-scale networks to connect computers from various manufacturers over large distances and to optimize computer-resource use by making it feasible to share resources at remote sites. The company Bolt, Beranek and Newman (BBN) was chosen to build the network, with AT&T supplying the leased computer lines. This experiment, called the ARPAnet, proved to be very successful, connecting over 50 sites throughout the United States.

One of the surprising aspects of the ARPAnet was the enthusiastic adoption of *electronic mail* (*email*) as the primary means of communications. It combined the immediacy of a telephone call with the permanence of a written letter, with the added benefit of being in an electronic format that could easily be edited, stored, and forwarded. It made collaboration possible between people who had never met and who were thousands of miles apart.

In addition to messages from one individual to another, mailing lists soon sprang up. Sending a message to a mailing list alias would forward the message to all the individuals who had subscribed to the list. This rapidly became a popular and effective means of communication between groups of like-minded individuals.[*]

The ARPAnet quickly grew to over 50 nodes, including sites in Hawaii and Europe. Over the next several years, it proved the feasibility of connecting computers and sharing resources over great distances.

The Start

While the ARPAnet was a successful and popular project, there was one problem with it. In order to participate, you had to be working on a Department of Defense related project at one of the large universities that were on the ARPAnet. This meant that there were plenty of people and sites that wanted to participate but could not.

Duke University and the University of North Carolina at Chapel Hill were two sites that were not on the ARPAnet. Graduate students Tom Truscott and James Ellis (of Duke) and Steve Bellovin (of UNC) wanted to have access to this kind of networking, and saw a possibility of doing this using some software which had recently been distributed with the UNIX operating system. The UUCP (UNIX to UNIX copy) program was designed to use low-cost telephone lines and modems to provide a method of transferring files and executing commands between computers.

The original version of Netnews, written in 1979, was a three-page shell script that handled newsgroup subscriptions and the interface to the UUCP program. It was rewritten in C and set up between Duke and UNC (another version, written by Stephen Daniel, replaced this version after a short time). Another site at Duke was added, as well as a site at Bell Labs, where UNIX originated.[†] Truscott and Ellis gave an informal presentation at the Winter 1980 Usenix technical conference, and distributed a flyer describing the system (which they described as a "poor man's ARPAnet"), and applications for connections to Duke's dial-up system.[‡]

---

[*] Mailing lists also heralded the birth of two themes that are with us to this day. The first came about when one of the mailing lists exceeded 100 subscribers, prompting concern about overloading the network. The second was when the "powers-that-be" grew concerned over the WINE-LOVERS list and issued a memorandum concerning the appropriate use of computer resources.

[†] In a joke posted in the newsgroup *rec.humor.funny*, Dennis Ritchie presented a guide for differentiating himself, UNIX coauthor Ken Thompson, and Brian Kernighan. One of the items reads "Dennis reads more news than is good for him, Brian has *misc.invest* secretly mailed to him, and Ken wouldn't touch news with a ten-foot pole."

[‡] These are reproduced in Appendix B, *USENET Articles*.

That year, USENET grew to about 15 sites and averaged about 10 articles per day. A large portion of this traffic was related to UNIX bug reports and fixes, since UNIX was still not officially supported by AT&T at that time.

By this time, the University of California at Berkeley (which was already on the ARPAnet) had connected to the USENET, and graduate student Mark Horton had the idea to bridge the gap between the USENET newsgroups and the ARPA mailing lists. This was a significant contribution because for the first time, sites not on the ARPAnet could participate in discussions taking place in the mailing lists. This event provided a ready source of material and USENET began to grow rapidly.

The very first news groups had the prefix *net*, signifying that these messages were received over the UUCP network and did not originate locally. Newsgroups that were gatewayed from the ARPAnet mailing lists were given the prefix *fa*, which stood, naturally enough, for "from ARPAnet." Some of the most popular groups at this timer were *fa.sf-lovers* (for science-fiction fans) and *fa.human-nets* (discussing cognitive science). *Moderated* newsgroups, where all postings were forwarded to a moderator for approval and posting, were added, using the prefix *mod*.

The USENET continued to expand across the United States and in May 1981, became an international network with the addition of the University of Toronto zoology department. Sites soon appeared in Europe and Australia. A very special moment for the Net was the first site in the Soviet Union, which was established in Moscow in 1990. At the time of this writing, there are over 50,000 sites participating in the USENET on all seven continents.

Some larger corporations helped immeasurably by footing the bill for many of the long-distance calls. AT&T sponsored the first cross-country connections, between Duke and Bell Labs, and between Bell Labs and UC Berkeley. Later, Digital Equipment Corp. became a major USENET carrier, transmitting articles between its sites in New England, California, and Europe. This was not a trivial proposition. Some sources estimate that DEC's annual expenses on this operation exceeded $250,000 per year.

By 1985, it was becoming apparent that the number of groups was growing large enough to overload the naming scheme then in use (*net*, *fa*, and *mod*). This led to the epochal event known as "The Great Renaming," in which the old groups were replaced by the top-level hierarchy that we have today (see "A Quick Newsgroup Overview" in Chapter 2). This was preceded by a lengthy period of debate, and more than a few *flame wars*. In addition to the new hierarchy, a democratic process was created to foster the orderly creation and management of newsgroups. (In the earliest days you could create a group merely by posting a message to it.) Details of this more orderly process can be found in Appendix B, *USENET Articles*.

Along the way, several other top-level hierarchies have been put into place. In one sense they are not properly a part of the USENET, since they don't fall into one of the seven official categories. They have, however, become part of the *de facto* USENET and are carried at most sites. These groups are also described in Chapter 2.

The Net has continued to grow steadily, stubbornly refusing to yield to predictions of its imminent collapse due to its expansion. It has grown from a handful of computers linked by 300-baud modems to an international phenomenon with participants numbering in the millions. It was at one time considered fast to get a one-day turnaround on posted articles. Now it's common at many sites for a posting to travel thousands of miles to hundreds of machines within seconds of posting. Will the USENET be able to absorb this ever-increasing traffic with its network bandwidth and disk storage requirements? We think Brad Templeton has the definitive answer for this question: "If there is a gigabit network with bandwidth to spare that is willing to carry USENET, it has plenty of growth left."

Table 1-1 summarizes ten years of USENET growth. A recent weekly summary from UUNET Technologies gives a dry summary of the phenomenal success and growth of the Net: "925,834 articles, totaling 1,857 megabytes (2,363 including headers), were submitted from 57,889 different USENET sites by 180,351 different users to 9,887 different newsgroups for an average of 133 megabytes (169 including headers) per day."[*]

This seemingly unstoppable growth has caused people to predict over and over the imminent death of the Net from sheer overload. The popular slogan of several years ago, "imminent death of the Net predicted, /news at 11 meg!" has been recently updated to "imminent death of the Net predicted, /news at 11 gig!"

Table 1-1. USENET Traffic Summary (courtesy of Gene Spafford)

Year	# of Sites	Articles/Day	Megabytes/Day
1979	3	2	< 1
1980	15	10	< 1
1981	150	20	< 1
1982	400	50	< 1
1983	600	120	< 1
1984	900	225	< 1
1985	1,300	375	1+

---

[*] This figure is almost certainly out of date by the time you read this. As a measure of how quickly the network is growing, the original draft of this chapter quoted the following weekly summary: "319,446 articles, totaling 589.229392 megabytes (753.128485 including headers), were submitted from 27,699 different USENET sites by 75,906 different users to 4,526 different newsgroups for an average of 42.087814 megabytes (53.794892 including headers) per day."

Table 1-1. USENET Traffic Summary (courtesy of Gene Spafford) (Continued)

Year	# of Sites	Articles/Day	Megabytes/Day
1986	2,500	500,	2+
1987	5,000	1000	2.5+
1988	11,000	1800	4+

How Do I Get USENET?

This is probably the most frequently asked question I receive whenever I describe the Net to someone who doesn't have it. In some ways, USENET access is like electricity or running water. Once you have it, it's hard to imagine not having it, and you don't give it a second thought until it breaks. Fortunately, it's becoming easier and easier to get access.

Do I Already Have It?

The easiest way to find out if your system is connected to the USENET is to ask your system administrator. If he or she is not handy at this time, here are a few things you can try.

- *Look for some news software.* Try looking for two of the most common *newsreaders*, *nn* and *tin*. On many systems, you can do this by typing the command:

  `% which nn tin`

  If these programs are available on your system, you will see a message like this:

  `/usr/local/bin/nn`

  If this is the case, you can run the software by typing the program name; you don't need to type the whole pathname. If you don't have this software in your execution path, you will receive a message:

  `no nn in ...`

  And a listing of the directories in your search path.

  If you do not have the *which* command, try:

  `% ls -l /usr/local/bin/nn`

  or

  `% ls -l /bin/tin`

  If you see a directory listing of any of these programs, the software is at least installed, and you are halfway there.

- *Look for news-related files in the following directories:*

```
% ls -ld /usr/spool/bin/nn
% ls -l /usr/lib/news
% ls -l /usr/local/lib/news
```

If any of these directories exist, and they have a recent modification date, there is a good chance your site is receiving news. If not, there may still be hope: your site may be using a news server on your local network.

- *You can also try just running the software.* Type **nn** or **tin** at the system prompt. If the news is installed and running on your system, and your path is properly set according to your local customs, this should be all that is needed.

  If you try this and suddenly find yourself in either *nn* or *tin*, turn to Chapter 3 or Chapter 4, respectively, to find out what to do next.

How Can I Connect?

There are a number of ways to connect to the USENET. Here are a few ideas for finding connections in your part of the world:

- Check with any universities and colleges in your area. Their system administrators will probably be aware of nearby network resources.

- Take a class at a school that is connected to the Net. Many schools have USENET and email access for all students.

- Check out local computer clubs or professional organizations. Many such groups either run sites themselves or have made arrangements for their members to have access at other sites.

- Look into paying for an account with one of the commercial Internet service providers. This has become a hot industry and many providers advertise their services in both local and national publications.

  If you want a news feed for your site, you'll have more flexibility, but you'll also have administrative overhead (and cost—if nothing else, you'll be using a lot more disk space to store articles). Any of the sources above can probably provide information about getting a news feed as well as an account for reading news.

- You may also want to take a look at Susan Estrada's *Connecting to the Internet*, also published by O'Reilly & Associates. It is a comprehensive source for USENET information.

- Most other commercial network, services, like America Online, Delphi, also provide access to USENET. If you choose one of these services, you'll probably have to use a custom newsreader rather than the software described in Chapters 3 through 6. However, the general information in this book will still apply.

## CHAPTER TWO

READING NEWS: GETTING STARTED

How USENET Is Organized
Anatomy of an Article
First Groups to Read
Newsreaders
Controlling What You Read
How USENET Works
Cryptic Articles

A rmed with Chapter 1's background on the USENET, we can now explore what is needed to start reading news. First, you need to get a general feel for how the Net is organized and what software is required to read the news. We'll also take a quick glance at how messages are distributed and stored on your system.

How USENET Is Organized

This section discusses the logical organization of USENET, showing how topics and subjects are divided and organized.

Newsgroups

Articles posted on the Net are organized by topic into newsgroups, each of which is devoted to a particular topic. There are a dozen or so top-level categories, each divided into many subtopics. Many of the subtopics are further divided, and so on. As a result, although thousands of messages flow through USENET every day, there's probably only a few new messages in most categories. If you know how USENET is organized and what you're interested in, it's easy to find what you need. USENET is organized like a tree. Think of a tree trunk spreading into large limbs (top-level categories), which divide into branches, which divide into smaller branches, and finally into twigs.

For example, Figure 2-1 shows that the *invest* group (where people discuss investments) is inside the *misc* group; likewise, the *c++* group (which discusses the C++ programming language) is a subtopic within *lang* (computer languages), which is a subtopic within *comp* (computer-related topics). The seven categories in the diagram are the standard top-level categories. Other categories have been added, as mentioned below.

To talk about this tree, we need to introduce a little notation. People write news-group names from left to right, starting with the highest level, and using periods (dots) to separate each name. Therefore, we'd refer to the C++ group as *comp.lang.c++*, and to the invest group as *misc.invest*. The importance of this notation is that it allows two groups to have the same name. For example, in addition to *comp.sources*, there's also *alt.sources*—a related topic, but a different newsgroup.

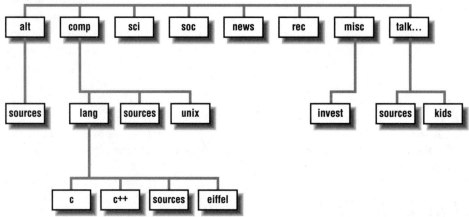

Figure 2-1. A partial breakdown of the newsgroup hierarchy. Two of the groups shown here are comp.lang.c *and* misc.invest.

A Quick Newsgroup Overview

Here's an overview of the top-level categories, which should give you a feel for some of the newsgroups available on the Net. An annotated listing of all the news-groups can be found in Appendixes E and F.

comp: computer-related topics
As you might imagine, this is one of the largest categories with over 400[*] groups. The groups range from computer-science and engineering topics such as *comp.ai* (artificial intelligence), *comp.lang* (computer languages—nearly 40 groups), and *comp.theory* (theoretical computer science), to software and hardware related groups such as *comp.sys* (over 100 groups, covering nearly every computer ever made), *comp.unix* (32 groups devoted to discussing

---

[*] These numbers are current at the time of writing. They will certainly be greater by the time you read this.

UNIX), and *comp.os* (36 groups discussing all manner of other operating systems, including Windows).

This is also where to look for a *lot* of free software. Check out the groups under *comp.binaries* (10 groups, devoted to distributing binary and executable files) and *comp.sources* (18 groups, distributing program source code).

sci: matters relating to science
About 60 groups, covering most areas of science. *sci.math* (mathematics) and *sci.space* (astronomical matters) are a few of the groups here.

soc: social groups and issues
There are about 80 groups here, most of them under the *soc.culture* umbrella, which are devoted mainly to different ethnic or national groups, such as *soc.culture.hongkong* or *soc.culture.india*. Other groups discuss varied social topics, include *soc.college* (social aspects of the college life) and *soc.feminism* (the social aspects of feminism).

news: issues relating to USENET news administration
About two dozen groups, many of which are rather dry postings of network statistics, etc. One of the really important USENET groups, *news.newusers.questions*, hides in here. The various news-reading programs are also discussed under *news.software*.

rec: recreational activities
Over 250 groups, devoted to all kinds of recreational activities. Some of the larger subgroups are *rec.arts* (44 groups, discussing the fine arts), *rec.music* (28 groups, everything from *Ars Nova* to Frank Zappa) and *rec.sport* (27 groups, discussing different sports). Most of the other groups discuss various hobbies, ranging from bicycling to woodworking to brewing beer.

misc: miscellaneous topics
About three dozen miscellaneous groups, ranging from home maintenance to education to the ultimate miscellaneous group, *misc.misc*. One of the most popular groups on the Net is here: *misc.jobs.offered*, where employers can post job openings and receive almost immediate feedback from prospective employees.

talk: chatty topics
About 20 groups, most of which discuss controversial topics such as politics, religion, and current affairs. This is a good place to visit if you need to build up your blood pressure. Be warned, though: it can get mean and nasty, and no holds are barred.

biz: business-related activities
Topics related to business. This is one of the few area where advertising is tolerated.

gnu: Free Software Foundation and Project GNU-related topics
The 28 groups here are dedicated to the support of the various GNU programs and utilities. There is a dedicated newsgroup for most of the GNU

utilities, where questions can be asked and bugs reported. New GNU software announcements are made here, and various aspects of the free software movement are discussed.

bionet: biology network

If terms such as *bionet.genome.arabidopsis* or *bionet.molbio.proteins* are meaningful to you, these 33 groups could change your life.

alt: alternative groups

This hierarchy is somewhat unique. It is not properly a part of USENET, but, as the name implies, offers alternative groups. Unlike the other areas discussed here, there are no guidelines for group creation or any voting procedures for adding new groups. As you can imagine, this leads to some unusual groups being created. There are about 20 groups in *alt.tv* (discussions pertaining to various television shows such as *The Simpsons*) and about a dozen in *alt.politics*. If you ever start to think that the USENET is dry and boring, check out *alt.bizarre* or *alt.flame*.

There are a few "normal" groups here, such as *alt.folklore* (all kinds of folklore), *alt.sewing* (sewing and textiles) and *alt.cobol* (the COBOL language). Many of these are groups where the volume of postings is too low to justify creating a group in one of other hierarchies. It also includes groups where the participants don't want to bother with the rigmarole of formal newsgroup creation and groups that are created to discuss late-breaking current events. There are also a number of groups that were created primarily for shock value.

regional hierarchies, such as *tx* (texas), *ca* (california), or *ne* (northeast)

These regional hierachies often feature such groups as *politics* (regional politics), *for-sale* (items for sale or trade), and *news* (regional news statistics and administration). Various announcements of regional interest (meetings, rallies, etc.) are made here.

local hierarchies, such as *dfw* (Dallas/Ft. Worth), or *ba* (San Francisco Bay Area)

Similar to the regional hierarchies, but on an even smaller scale.

native language hierarchies, such as *fj* (Japanese) and *de* (German).

These usually mirror the normal USENET groups, but discussions are carried on in languages other than English.

organization-wide hierarchies

Many sites set up groups specifically for internal use. These range from project related groups (*local.admin*, which discusses computer-administration items such as downtime schedules) to social groups (*local.lunch*, discussing that all-important question, "Where are we going for lunch?").

If Madonna Were a Newsgroup, She'd Be an Alt

But so would Donna Woonteiler for that matter. (No, you're not supposed to know who that is.)

I mentioned the title of this section to a friend of mine, and he said "But Madonna is an alt group." I pointed out that this might upset Madonna's father who has always thought of her as a person. Obviously, my friend meant that there's an alt (or alternative) newsgroup devoted to discussion about Madonna. What I meant was that if a topic is offbeat, it generally winds up in the alt dimension of the USENET universe.

You don't have to do a lot of news reading to notice that the unusual, bizarre, and even scary interests converge under the umbrella of alt. Just take a look in your .newsrc or other comparable file.

But there's more to alt than funk, camp, and perversion—and that's where Donna Woonteiler comes in. (Sorry, Donna.) Who is she? Well, she's a friend (and also a co-worker) of mine. Although she's important to me, in the *Encyclopaedia Britannica*, Donna wouldn't even merit a footnote.

But in USENET, Donna can create an *alt* group about herself. Heck, she can start a league of groups, all dedicated to the pursuit of Woonteilerness. (James "Kibo" Parry, yet another *Britannica* reject, has done just that, spawning several groups that sport the pseudoscience "kibology" in their names. See "Alchemy, FidoDidoism, and Kibology" in Chapter 9.) Because alt newsgroups don't have to go through the same approval process as groups under other categories, anything goes. Anyone can create a group at any time, about anything, or nothing.

What is the result of this, um, system? Well, some people create nonsense groups the way kids make prank phone calls. You want to start *alt.rubbermaid.die.die.die*? Hey, you got it. You want *alt.gardenhose.eat.it.up.yum*? Go nuts! There are plenty of ridiculously named groups like these that (gratefully) will never have a line of traffic.

And, of course, this free-for-all is also a breeding ground for the kinkier and weirder subjects you'll find in USENET. But even these cover a broad spectrum. Some *alt* groups seem to exist in a high school locker room, where kids talk about sex, drugs, and rock 'n roll. Only this is an electronic locker room where they can also swap GIF and JPEG centerfolds. In the farthest reaches of the *alt* fun house, the truly deviant interests of USENET converge.

—continued—

The FBI would be doing a public service if they monitored *alt.evil* where some truly sick minds share warped and horrible fantasies, which we can only hope remain so.

Yet among the wacky, lusty, lewd, and even downright frightening groups are a large number of low-profile, extremely ordinary groups that focus on perfectly mundane subjects: television shows, history, politics, music, science, the Internet, etc. The same free-for-all system that lets people get into spats about Spam also allows people with more serious common interests to create a forum for discussion without going through an involved procedure, or having to drum up widespread support. In fact, the *alt* hierarchy is a valuable entry-point for lots of groups who don't have the energy, time, or visibility to start up under one of the mainstream branches. Some groups that start in *alt* do so with the intention of establishing themselves, getting a good dialog going, generating wider interest, and then going through the formal process needed to move into another hierarchy.

— Valerie Quercia

Anatomy of an Article

Figure 2-2 shows a typical article on the Net. It consists of three components: the header, the body, and (optionally) the signature.

The Header

The header contains all the administrative information necessary to process your article. It is generated by your newsreader and the various news-processing programs. Some of the headers (such as the subject) consist of text which you enter at the time you post your message. Other headers (such as the message id) are put there by the system. The message in Figure 2-2 contains most of the typical headers that you will see in most messages. Here are quick explanations of what they mean:

Newsgroups:

> What newsgroups this article has been posted to. The example article was posted to the newsgroup *news.software.nn*. Note that an article can be posted to more than one group.

Path:

> The path the message has taken from the poster's machine to your machine. The rightmost item on the list is the account name of the user that posted the

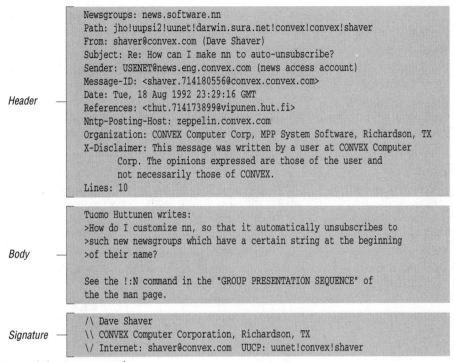

Header —

```
Newsgroups: news.software.nn
Path: jho!uupsi2!uunet!darwin.sura.net!convex!convex!shaver
From: shaver@convex.com (Dave Shaver)
Subject: Re: How can I make nn to auto-unsubscribe?
Sender: USENET@news.eng.convex.com (news access account)
Message-ID: <shaver.714180556@convex.convex.com>
Date: Tue, 18 Aug 1992 23:29:16 GMT
References: <thut.714173899@vipunen.hut.fi>
Nntp-Posting-Host: zeppelin.convex.com
Organization: CONVEX Computer Corp, MPP System Software, Richardson, TX
X-Disclaimer: This message was written by a user at CONVEX Computer
        Corp. The opinions expressed are those of the user and
        not necessarily those of CONVEX.
Lines: 10
```

Body —

```
Tuomo Huttunen writes:
>How do I customize nn, so that it automatically unsubscribes to
>such new newsgroups which have a certain string at the beginning
>of their name?

See the !:N command in the "GROUP PRESENTATION SEQUENCE" of
the the man page.
```

Signature —

```
/\ Dave Shaver
\\ CONVEX Computer Corporation, Richardson, TX
\/ Internet: shaver@convex.com  UUCP: uunet!convex!shaver
```

Figure 2-2. A news article

message. As each machine receives and processes the message, it inserts the machine name at the head of the list.

From:

This is the name and login of the person posting the message. The person's name is usually taken from the person's login entry, although most newsreaders allow this to be overridden.

Subject:

The subject of the message. When you follow up a message, the newsreader will default to inserting "Re:" (short for "reference" or "regarding") and the subject of the original message. In the example, the poster used this default.

Sender:

This field is usually filled in with the account name that the news software is run under.

Message-ID:

Every message on USENET is given a unique message-identification string, usually some combination of the posting machine's name, the user's name, the date, and a sequence number. This can be used to identify messages for cross-referencing purposes.

Date:

The time and date the message was posted. Some sites use the local time, while some sites add the Greenwich Mean Time.

Reference:

A reference to any previous postings with the same topic. Some newsreaders use this information to group articles together for viewing.

Nntp-Posting-Host:

The name of the machine running the Net News Transport Protocol (NNTP) news software at the sender's site. Of some possible use in debugging news software.

Organization:

The organization (i.e., the company, school, or whatever) that the user is affiliated with. Some humorists fill this field with witty sayings, such as "Organization, noun. The state of being organized."

X-Disclaimer:

An "X-" header is a header that is not specifically used in the official news protocol, but is reserved for user-defined headers. If a user or a company wishes to add a header of their own, they can usually preface it with the string "X-". In this case, it is a disclaimer disassociating the posted message from any company policy, a common practice at many sites.

The Body

As in a letter, the body is the main part of the message and consists of the text that you enter. This message quotes another message. The first line introduces the quoted party, and indicates the quoted portion of text by preceding each line with a ">". A subsequent poster might quote both previous posters, causing the quoted lines to have another series of ">". When a popular or controversial topic is discussed, quoting can be nested to a confusing degree.

In this example, the poster (Dave Shaver) is replying to a question posted by Tuomo Huttunen.

The Signature

Although not required, nearly all messages end with a signature. It is usually not typed by the user, but is appended to the message by the news-posting software. The text of the message is usually stored in the user's home directory in the file-name *.signature*. The format varies, but it usually has one or more of the following: user's name, email address, company or project, job title, and a telephone or fax number. Many people also include an entertaining message, a plug for their particular company or project, or some other kind of informational message.

Signatures can be very elaborate, but it's considered in good taste to keep yours to four lines or less. Some people pay by the character for their newsreading. Even a small signature, like the one in the example, is 10% of the message. Toss in a few thousand 20-line signatures, and you can soon be talking real money! For more information on signatures, see "Signature Files" in Chapter 9.

First Groups to Read

USENET currently has over 9,000 newsgroups. After reading the previous section, you've probably got a general idea of some of the topics available, but the question remains: which to read first? Here are a few of my favorite newsgroups, as well as some groups I've observed to be helpful to others. Again, you can browse Appendixes E and F for comprehensive newsgroup listings.

One of the most important groups you can read is one designed especially for new USENET users, *news.newusers.questions*. In addition to regularly posting introductory messages, there is plenty of advice, help, and support for new users.

Of course, every area of computing is well covered. If you are interested in computer languages, look at the groups *comp.lang.**, which discuss everything from Ada to Xlisp.* The groups under *comp.sys.** and *comp.os.** discuss virtually every computer and operating system still in use (and maybe even a couple that aren't). A few of the more popular groups are *comp.sys.ibm.pc*, *comp.sys.apple*, *comp.os.windows*, and *comp.unix.questions*.

The *rec.** hierarchy covers nearly every recreational activity known to humankind. Music, sports, the arts, television shows, games, and hobbies are just the beginning. I personally recommend *rec.woodworking* and *rec.humor.funny*.

A wide range of scientific topics are covered under *sci.**. The group *sci.space* is fascinating reading for anyone interested in space research or the space program.

Are you interested in the cultures of different countries? Almost every country has a newsgroup devoted to its culture. These are in the *soc.culture* hierarchy. As an example, *soc.culture.hongkong* discusses all kinds of topics related to Hong Kong.

Some topics generate so much discussion that they have been placed in the *talk* hierarchy. Many of the topics discussed here are too controversial to even mention, but *talk.rumors* can be very entertaining.

You will notice that there are **.announce* groups scattered throughout the various hierarchies. As you might guess, these are for important or interesting announce-

---

* The asterisk (*) is a wildcard character, which indicates multiple newsgroups. This shorthand is commonly used on the Net.

ments about the group's particular topic. If the topic is interesting to you, you will almost certainly get some benefit from subscribing to its *announce* group.

Likewise, there are *.d* groups (discussion groups) for topics like *alt.binaries.pictures.fine-arts. fine-arts* is for posting pictures (and nothing else); *fine-arts.d* is for discussing those pictures. Similarly, there are *.advocacy* groups (like *comp.unix.advocacy*) that are intended for debate, while other groups are for factual discussion.

So, pick some newsgroups that sound interesting, and let's get on with it!

Newsreaders

The actual piece of software you use to read news is called, appropriately enough, a *newsreader*. Newsreaders come in all shapes and sizes, but all of them have a few things in common. They keep track of your subscribed groups and what articles you have read. They present new articles to you, and allow you to read, save, and respond to them.

How do they differ? Some are simple, with just enough functionality to read messages and reply to them. Others feature a full-blown macro language with hundreds of functions that allow you to customize every aspect of the newsreader's operation. Some are written for particular environments such as the X Window System, or to be run from within other environments, such as *Emacs*.

Which newsreader is right for you? All have the same basic features, but vary widely in their advanced options and in their interface. Most people use either *nn* or *tin*. *gnus* has a strong following among *Emacs* users. *Trumpet* is the most popular newsreader among Windows users. My best advice is to try several of the newsreaders installed at your site. Talk to your friends and see what they like. Try one or two and see which ones agree with you. It's never a bad idea to use the same software as your system administrator; you know it will be well maintained! If one of the above newsreaders sounds appealing, but your site doesn't have it, ask your news administrator. All of the packages mentioned here are freely available in source form from various places. Most of them have been posted at various times onto some of the USENET source groups.[*]

Here is a brief overview of some of the available newsreaders. We cover four of the most common—*nn, tin, gnus,* and *Trumpet*—in depth. The others either have similar features or are not as widely used.

---

[*] One of the groups created especially for the posting of messages containing source code for a particular system. The group *comp.unix.sources* is a prime example.

nn   *nn* is a full screen-oriented reader designed to make it easier to cope with the large number of messages posted to the Net. Its main feature is the way it displays messages. Instead of stepping sequentially through all the messages in a group, it presents a list of unread messages, allowing the user to select by subject which messages are to be displayed. It has the ability to follow message "threads" (groups of related messages).

tin   *tin* is another full-screen newsreader that is rapidly becoming the newsreader of choice. It has the ability to follow message threads. At many sites, both *tin* and *nn* are installed: *tin* is considered the standard newsreader, with *nn* provided for people who want a more advanced macro language, etc.

gnus

> *gnus* is a set of LISP functions that implements a news-reading mode within Gnu *Emacs*. If you're an *Emacs* enthusiast, this may be for you.

Trumpet

> *Trumpet* is the most popular newsreader for Windows. It's part of a free software package, also called *Trumpet,* that includes everything you need to get on the Net. It doesn't have a lot of features, but it's very easy to use; ideal for a beginner.

Miscellaneous Newsreaders

In addition to the newsreaders mentioned above, there are many other readers in existence. Some of them were written with a specific set of features in mind, while others were written in order to exercise a particular language.[*] We don't cover them in detail here, but if you see one that looks interesting, your news administrator can probably get some more information for you.

readnews

> This is one of the original newsreaders. It's pretty much obsolete by now, and we mention it for historical purposes. If this is the only newsreader on your system, talk to your administrator.

rn   Dated *readnews* written by Larry Wall (of Perl fame) and one of the most popular newsreaders for several years. Its features have been incorporated into several other newsreaders. Although it still has some fans, *rn* should be considered obsolete.

trn   A threaded news reader based on *rn*, developed and maintained by Wayne Davidson. *trn*'s main addition to *rn* is the ability to follow threads

---

[*] In fact, writing a newsreader is a good way to become familiar with a new language, or to improve your programming skills in general, since it involves a broad range of programming skills and techniques. Looking at a newsreader written in a particular language will also give you a feel about how various tasks (such as accessing files or displaying text) can be handled in the language.

of conversation in a newsgroup. *trn* probably has the most advanced thread concept of any of the newsreaders, since it uses the information in the news header to reconstruct the stream of conversation, rather than relying upon changes in the subject line. Although this book does not describe *trn*, it is very popular and a good choice.

xrn   A newsreader for the X Windows System. It is not related to *rn*.

vnews

Visual news: one of the original simple, full-screen newsreaders.

Netscape

A World Wide Web browser, important because it's the first to include a full-featured newsreader. A free version is available for Windows, Macintosh, and UNIX systems. For more information, see "Using *Netscape* to Read News" in Chapter 8.

Controlling What You Read

As we mentioned previously, there are literally thousands of messages being posted every day on the Net. Clearly, it is impossible to read this many messages every day.[*] This section discusses how to bring this down to a manageable number.

The Groups Carried at Your Site

The number of groups you see when you open a newsreader is determined by your news administrator (also, your feeder sites may not carry every group). The news administrator subscribes and unsubscribes to groups by editing a configuration file.[†]

There are many local and regional newsgroups, and it probably isn't useful for a site in Australia to carry a newsgroup offering items for sale in Boston. Likewise, there isn't much need to carry articles written in German or Japanese if no one at your site can read them.

Finally, there are probably a lot of specialized newsgroups (such as the *bionet.* * hierarchy) that your site may not carry simply because no one is interested in reading them.

---

[*] Although I know a few people who have tried!

[†] Occasionally you may wish to look at a group to which your site does not subscribe. To do so is an easy task for your news administrator. We have seen some instances where a lazy "admin" will try to offer some kind of technical reason for not bringing a group on site. There are occasions where this might be true (some groups eat up a lot of disk space, for example), but in general, there shouldn't be a technical problem with subscribing to a new group.

The .newsrc Initialization File

This file (pronounced either "news are see" or "dot news are see") is located in your home directory and is the primary method for controlling the articles you read. This file originated with the early news software, and is now used by all newsreaders. The name of the file derives from the UNIX tradition of naming configuration programs by using the program name followed by the initials "rc" (run commands).

The *newsrc* file keeps track of two things: the newsgroups you are subscribed to and what articles in the newsgroups you have read.

The actual format of the .*newsrc* file is simple. There is one line in the file for every newsgroup on the system. The first item on the line is the group name, followed by either a colon (:) or by an exclamation point (!). If the name is followed by a colon, you are subscribed to that group and will see the articles in that group when you read news. If the name is followed by an exclamation point, you are not subscribed to that group and will not see new articles as they arrive.

Following the group name is a list of numbers. These are the numbers of the articles you have already seen. This list is updated each time you read news.

The example below shows an excerpt from my .*newsrc* files. Several of the groups (such as *news.sysadmin* and *comp.lang.c*) are unsubscribed. I have subscribed to the group *comp.lang.perl*, and have read (or skipped) the articles through number 7829.

```
news.announce.newusers: 1-4957
news.admin!
news.announce.conferences:
news.announce.important: 1-46
news.groups!
news.lists:
news.lists.ps-maps!
news.misc:
news.newusers.questions: 1-7105
news.software.nn!
news.sysadmin!
comp.ai: 1-5513
comp.ai.neural-nets!
comp.lang.pascal!
comp.lang.c++: 1-9531
comp.lang.perl: 1-7829
```

Most newsreaders have commands that allow you to subscribe and unsubscribe to groups, but you can also edit the .*newsrc* file with your favorite editor, which can sometimes be a little easier when making many changes.

Finally, you can use some of the UNIX utilities to get a few statistics on your news-reading. The command

```
% wc -l .newsrc
```

will show the number of groups (more or less) that are carried at your site, and the commands

```
% grep : .newsrc | wc -l
% grep \! .newsrc | wc -l
```

will show the number of groups to which you are and are not subscribed, respectively. The backslash prevents the C shell from interpreting the **!** as a special character. If you use the Bourne shell, the **** isn't needed.

expiry, or News Article Expiration

It's obvious that you can't receive several megabytes of news every day without running out of disk space very quickly. To keep this from happening, the news-administration software deletes, or "expires," news articles on a regular basis. This is done on an "oldest file first" basis, and different groups can be expired at different rates.

This has an additional benefit besides conserving disk space. When you don't read news for even a few days or a week, the backlog of unread articles can really start to build up. Having these old articles deleted on a regular basis can make it a lot easier to resume news reading when you return.

Expiration schedules vary a lot, according to disk space, newsgroup popularity (popular groups are usually kept longer), and the nature of the group (non-serious groups are usually expired pretty quickly). In the good old days it was common to keep news articles for a month. Now that news traffic more than 150 MB a day, few sites keep anything for more than three days. Your news administrator can provide you with details on the expiration schedule at your site.

Kill Files

In addition to the *.newsrc* file, many newsreaders have another mechanism to control what articles you will see, called the *kill file*. This file is used to filter out (*kill*) articles that you know in advance that you know you won't want to see. This can be done by subject ("I don't want to read anything with the subject 'Disco Revival'") or by person ("I don't want to read anything posted by Joe Obnoxious"). Kill files are also used to automatically *select* articles you are interested in. Each newsreader has a different method for dealing with kill files; we will cover the operational details in the newsreader chapters. The following list presents a few tips on how to use kill files to maximize your efficiency in reading news.

Use the kill file to select topics and authors
>   I use the kill file almost exclusively to select articles, mostly by name. There are some people whose opinions I admire so much that I'd like to see everything they post! I also select any articles that I have posted (to double-check what I wrote), and any articles that mention me by name.*

Don't bother killing articles to annoy people
>   One of the ultimate Net putdowns is "OK, you're going into my kill file!" This may relieve your stress in the short term, but it has two drawbacks. First, the other person will think that you are surrendering and that he has won some kind of moral victory. Second, unless you can get *everyone* in the group to ignore the person as well, you are going to be reading the miscreant's opinions anyway, as people quote him in follow-up articles.

Use the 30-day kill feature
>   Most newsreaders support a "30-day kill" whereby the topic or author is "black-listed" for 30 days, after which the articles will be seen again. This is a good idea. Most discussion threads die down in that time frame. In the future, interesting discussions may start that would otherwise be screened out by the kill file entry.

Don't put common phrases in your kill file
>   You may kill more than you intended. Avoid phrases such as "FAQ," "Answers," or "Important! Please Read!"

Review your kill file occasionally
>   Just in case you change your mind!

Selection by Subject or Thread

Finally, almost all newsreaders have the ability to select or skip articles by subject or by thread (a series of related articles). This makes it easy to pass over groups of articles you aren't interested in.

How USENET Works

The material we have presented so far discusses what an individual needs in order to read news. It can be useful to know a little bit of the mechanism by which articles are posted and transferred between machines.

---

* This has had an interesting side effect. I've found two other "Mark Harrisons" on the Net and found out that another netter has written a novel where the main character's name is Mark Harrison!

The Short Answer

- When you post an article (using the newsreader software), it is stored as a file on your computer. Everyone at your site can read it almost immediately.

- Additionally, your article will be transferred to USENET sites all over the world, usually within hours. You specify the group and the geographic distribution[*] using the newsreader program and the networking software your system administrator has set up.

- Everyone else on the Net can read your article, post follow-up articles, or reply directly to you.

The Long Answer

When you post an article to a group on the Net, it is stored in a file on a machine at your site. It could be on your local machine, in which case it's probably somewhere under the directory */usr/spool/news*. If your machine is on a local area network (LAN), it might also be stored on another machine (no use duplicating thousands of articles on every machine, unless you own stock in a disk-drive company). If this is the case, that machine is called the *news server*, and other machines on the network transfer articles using NNTP. Anyone reading the article at your site will be accessing that file or talking to that server.

In addition, your site has agreed with one or more other sites to cooperatively exchange news. This means that two sites will make periodic connections (generally at least once per day—usually more) and exchange any messages that have been posted to one site but not the other. When this takes place, your message will be distributed to the next site.

As an example, consider the hypothetical network in Figure 2-3. When a message is posted at site A, it is transferred to its immediate network neighbors, B and C. These sites likewise pass the message along to their neighbors, until the message has been propagated to all the sites in the network. Note that site G could receive the message from either site B or site E. When this is the case, it will accept the message from the first site that passes it on, and reject it from other sites.

Since this is taking place between all the machines on the network, your message will eventually arrive at all the member systems of the USENET. This may sound like it takes a long time, but most messages are completely propagated within a

---

[*] After all, it's pretty useless to post an article trying to sell your car to another country.

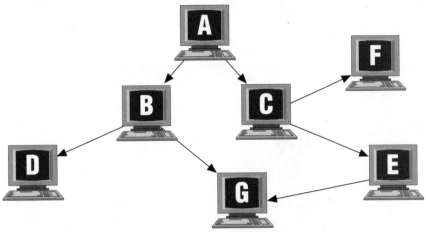

Figure 2-3. How articles are transferred

day, and once a message reaches a *backbone** site, it will be propagated to a good percentage of USENET sites within 10-15 minutes!

Figure 2-4 depicts the USENET network. Individual sites are represented by dots, and connections between sites by lines. The thicker the line, the higher the volume of messages being transmitted. As you can see, the United States and Europe are pretty well covered. New editions of this and other maps are posted to the group *news.lists.ps-maps* every month.

Cryptic Articles

Here's an advance warning as you start to read news. You may occasionally see strangely formatted articles that don't look like they were typed by human beings. Most probably, they are postings of software, pictures, or some other sort of computer data. Details on these formats and how to decrypt them are found in Chapter 10.

---

* In USENET terminology, a backbone site is generally a large system with multiple high-speed network connections. These are usually universities or large corporations that have significant computing resources that forward mail and news as a public service. This is different from the stricter definition of an Internet backbone site.

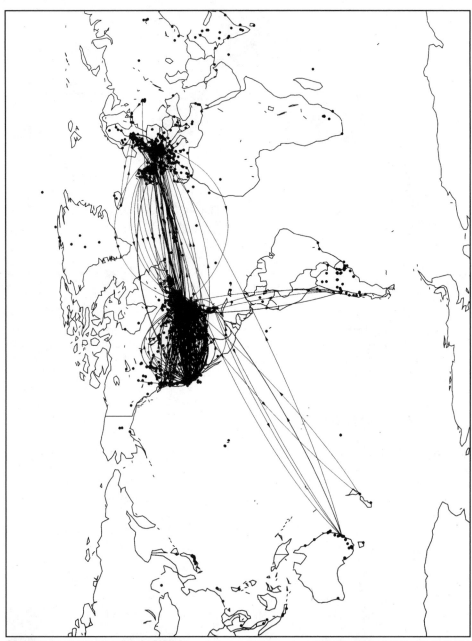

Complete aggregate news flow, worldwide
Line width proportional to directional effective flow volume

DECWRL netmap-2.1 by Brien Reid at Sat Feb12 15:48:47 1994
Gall Stereographic Projection, Map Center:[15°N, 88°W]

Figure 2-4. The USENET network

## CHAPTER THREE

READING NEWS WITH THE NN NEWSREADER

No News Is Good News?

nn is the popular newsreader written by Kim Storm. It was first released in Denmark in 1984. It was released in Europe in 1988, and released to the rest of the world in June 1989. Since then, it has become the newsreader of choice at many organizations, vying with other packages for the title of most popular newsreader. Kim's philosophy of reading news can be seen from the title of his program: "No news is good news, but *nn* is better." *nn* was designed to minimize the time required to read news by helping you ignore articles that are uninteresting. Now that thousands of articles are posted every day, the ability to ignore what you don't want can be lifesaving.

A few of *nn*'s key features are:

- A full-screen point-and-shoot interface that allows the user to navigate quickly through large numbers of articles. Most commands are entered with a single keystroke.

- Fast response time. *nn* speeds up its operation by keeping a database of all online articles. (Some other newsreaders such as *tin* use a similar approach).

- A powerful and easy-to-use kill file system. This feature lets you automatically screen out messages of little interest and automatically select preferred articles.

- Automatic handling of news digests. Digests are automatically split and presented as ordinary articles.

- Extensive online help and reference manual.

- Built-in facilities for unpacking, decoding, and unsharing postings.

nn is well supported by an active community of users. The newsgroup *news.software.nn* is very dynamic, discussing all aspects of installing, using, and supporting *nn*. An *nn* FAQ[*] list is posted there regularly. Bug reports and suggestions may be sent to *nn-bugs@dkuug.dk*. You can even send messages there automatically from within *nn* by using the **:bug** command.

The rest of this chapter is organized as follows:

- How to start *nn*
- Selecting articles you wish to read
- Reading selected articles
- Basic commands
- A sample *nn* session. If you have never used a newsreader before, this section walks you through reading news step by step.
- Posting articles and sending mail
- Automatically selecting and screening out (killing) articles
- Customizing *nn*

Getting Started

To start *nn*, simply run the command **nn**. If this is your first time reading news, or if you have not read news for some time, it is handy to be able to discard the thousands of messages that have accumulated on the system in your absence. To do this, start *nn* with the command

```
% nn -anumber
```

where *number* is the number of articles you wish to see in each group. (The rest are silently discarded). For beginners, **-a30** is a reasonable value to pick. To automatically discard all articles, use **-a0** (in this case, you are prompted for confirmation).

---

[*] FAQs are frequently asked questions lists. See "Frequently Asked Questions" in Chapter 7 for details.

Modes

nn has two modes for reading news. The first is *article-selection* mode–used to pick articles; the second is *reading* mode–used to read selected articles.

nn starts up in article-selection mode, placing you in the first[*] group that contains unread articles. You then select the articles you wish to read, either by author or topic. After you have selected articles, *nn* enters reading mode, which displays the articles one at a time, allowing you to scroll through them, save them, etc.

When you have finished reading the selected articles in that group, you are placed in article-selection mode for the next group. This sequence repeats until you have been presented with all unread articles.

The distinction between these two modes is a key *nn* concept; make sure you understand it!

Selecting Articles

When you first enter a newsgroup, you are placed in article-selection mode, where you select the articles you wish to view. A typical selection screen is shown below.

```
Newsgroup: comp.lang.c                    Articles: 463 of 5635/48

a Alan Bowler       20   >>>array element swap help
b Lars Wirzenius    28   >linking gcc code with CC code
c A. Kardanev       58   >
d Wayne Throop      107  >>>Editor mined (pointer declaration snafu)
e Thomas Wolff      75   >>>>
f Tim Pierce        56   >>>
g beshir@vax1       11   HELP!!with wordprocessor font
h Mary Wyllie       59   Looking for ideas to tran<>trings to function calls in C.
i T S Thompson      17   >good memory allocation strategies?
j John Anderson      9   PC Based C Compiler targeted to Mips R3000
k Deepak            44   Function name : C preprocessor question
l Dave Schaumann    30   >
m Dave Sisson       24   Here's some pointers for TV and TMenuItems
n William Kaufman   30   >>>Pointers to freed memory

-- 20:01 -- SELECT -- help:? -----24%-----
```

---

[*] Your news administrator has probably set up a default ordering for newsgroups at your site. See "Newsgroup Sequencing" later in this chapter for details on how you can customize the order of the groups you wish to read.

The header at the top shows the newsgroup (*comp.lang.c*, discussing the C programming language) and some statistics as to the number of articles left to read (463 unread articles in this newsgroup, 5,635 articles to be read in all groups,[*] and 48 groups left to read).

The bottom line shows the time, the mode (article selection), how far along we are in the list of articles (roughly 24%), and a reminder that pressing "?" displays the help screen.

All other lines on the screen describe news articles. Each line consists of a selection letter (on the left), the name of the article's poster, the number of lines in the article, and the article's subject. If the article's subject begins with a greater-than sign (>), the article is a reply to a prior article; two greater-than signs (>>) indicate replies to replies, and so on. If the "subject" field only contains greater-than signs but no text, the article has the same subject as the previous one. Hence in the display above, articles d through f all have the same subject: "Editor mined (pointer declaration snafu)". *nn* sorts its selection-mode display by conversation (or thread); the display makes it easy to see where threads begin and end.

To select an article for viewing, type its selection letter (the letter on the left). Often, you want to select a group of consecutive articles: for example, you might want to select one article, plus all of its replies. To do so, type a range of letters (two letters separated by a dash). For example, **d-f** selects all the articles with the subject "Editor Mined" (articles d, e, and f). It's also possible to select all articles with the same subject by typing a letter, followed by an asterisk. For example, **d*** also selects the articles with the subject "Editor Mined."

Obviously, if there are 463 unread articles in this newsgroup, there are many more articles to select than the ones we've shown here. Pressing the space bar moves you to the next screen of articles. (Typing **>** also moves you to the next screen, while **<** moves you to the previous screen.) If you are looking at the last screen of articles, pressing the space bar moves you into reading mode. You can also type **Z** or **X** to enter reading mode immediately, without waiting until you have looked at the entire selection menu.[†]

Typing **N** takes you directly to the selection-mode menu for the next subscribed newsgroup, without reading the articles you have selected; likewise, **P** takes you to the previous newsgroup.

---

[*] This could possibly be the reason for Kim's thinking, "No news is good news!"

[†] **Z** and **X** differ only in what happens when you finish reading articles. With **Z**, after reading you return to the selection menu you just left; with **X**, you go to the selection menu for your next newsgroup.

Reading Articles

When you reach the end of a selection menu, *nn* places you in reading mode, in which you view your selected articles. Here is a typical screen in reading mode:

```
Jonathan Kamens: Welcome to news.newusers.questions! (weekly posting)993 01:00
Archive-name: news-newusers-intro
Version: $Id: news-newusers-intro,v 1.20 1993/06/09 15:43:35 jik Exp $

  Welcome to the news.newusers.questions newsgroup!  According to the
"List of Active Newsgroups" posting in news.announce.newusers, the
purpose of this newsgroup is "Q & A for users new to the Usenet."  So
if you've got questions about the USENET, this is the place to post
them!

          Get to know news.announce.newusers.

  However, before you do that, there is another newsgroup with which
you should become acquainted. The news.announce.newusers newsgroup
contains (once again according to the "List of Active Newsgroups"
posting) "Explanatory postings for new users."  Its purpose is to
provide a base set of information with which all participants in the
USENET should be familiar in order to make the USENET a better place
for all of us.
-- 05:03 --.questions-- LAST --help:?--Top 6%--
```

The top line shows the article's author (Jonathan Kamens), subject (Welcome...), the number of lines in the posting (993), and the time it was posted (1:00). The bottom line is similar to that of the article-selection screen. The name of the current newsgroup (truncated to save space) has replaced the selection-mode indicator, and a count of remaining articles is displayed (on this screen, LAST is displayed because there are no more selected articles to read).

Reading mode should come fairly naturally if you're familiar with the UNIX *more* utility. If not, here's a very quick summary. Pressing the space bar gets you to the next screen of the article; if you're already on the last screen, it takes you to the next article you've selected. (And if you haven't selected any more articles in this newsgroup, pressing the space bar takes you to article-selection mode for the next group). Pressing the Delete or Backspace keys (they may be named something different on your computer) takes you to the previous page. Typing an **n** at any time takes you to the next article; as you'd expect, **p** takes you to the previous article.

There are a lot of other commands—for saving articles, decoding articles, and so on. We'll cover many of these commands later in this section; so far, you should have enough to get started. All you really need to know about is your space bar; whatever you want to do, pressing the space bar usually does it for you. Again, you can type **?** to get help.

A Few Essentials

Although *nn* has well over a hundred commands, to get going you don't need much more than the ability to select and read articles, which we've already covered. There are a few other essential commands, though, which we'll cover in this section. Take a moment to glance through it, and then proceed to the next section, where we will step through a sample *nn* session. Afterwards, we'll proceed to some of *nn*'s more advanced features.

Quitting nn

To exit *nn*, issue the quit command by typing a single uppercase **Q**. This command updates your configuration files, records which articles you have read, and performs several other bookkeeping chores that speed up *nn*'s operation the next time you read news.

If you wish to quit *nn* and restore the configuration file to the state it was in before you started, use the **quit!** command by typing **:q!** and pressing the Enter key. You are prompted for confirmation, and *nn* then exits and restores your files to their previous condition. You can think of **quit!** as an emergency escape. Use it if something goes wrong: for example, if you accidentally select a thousand articles and can't figure out how to unselect them.

The two quit commands work in both reading and article-selection modes.

Getting Help

nn provides several ways to get help. Both selection and reading mode have help screens; to display the help screen for the mode you're using, type a question mark (**?**). The article-selection mode screen is shown below. If you want more detailed help, try the extended command **:help**. This gives you information about the help features available, in addition to a list of specific topics for which you can get further help. To get further information on those topics, type **:help** *topic*.

```
SELECT (toggle)                             MOVE
a-z0-9   Specified article                  ,        Next menu line
x-y      Range x to y                       /        Previous menu line
x*       Same subject as x                  SPACE    Next menu page (if any)
. Current article                           < >      Prev/Next menu page
@ ~      Reverse/Undo all selections        ^ $      First/Last menu page
=regexp Matching subjects (=. selects all)
L/JJJJ   Leave/Change attributes
SHOW SELECTED ARTICLES
SPACE    Show (only when on last menu page)
Z        Show NOW, and return to this group afterwards
```

```
X         Show NOW, and continue with next group
GOTO OTHER GROUPS
X         Update current group, skip to next.      Y    Group overview
N P       Goto next/previous group.                ~/.nn/init:
G         Goto named group or open a folder.             Defines group
B A       Go back/forward in groups already read.        presentation sequence.
MISCELLANEOUS
U C       (Un)subscribe / Cancel                   :man    Online manual
F R M     Follow-up/Reply/Mail                     :help   More online help
S O W     Save articles                            !       Shell escape
:post     Post new article                         "       Change menu layout
:unshar :decode :patch  Unpack articles            Q       Quit nn
Hit any key to continue
```

Finally, you can type **:man** to read the online version of the manual. This is a neat feature: the manual is presented in newsgroup format, with each section presented as an article.

Emergencies

Typing **CTRL-G** cancels whatever operation is in progress and returns you to whatever you were previously doing. This is handy if you become confused about what you have typed or if you accidentally type a command you don't want (saving an article, for example). It's not extremely useful because most commands are executed quickly; by the time you realize you made a mistake, it's too late to go back. But it can be helpful, particularly if you do a lot of customization.

Typing **CTRL-L** refreshes (redisplays) the screen. This is handy if the screen is garbled for some reason.

As stated earlier, **:q!** is the emergency escape hatch; use it if you want to quit immediately, without updating any of the status files.

Navigating

If you want to read a particular newsgroup right away, rather than politely wading through all your newsgroups, you use the **G** (goto) command, in either selection or reading mode. When you type **G**, *nn* prompts you for the name of a newsgroup. In this example, we'll jump directly to the newsgroup *rec.music.folk*.

```
Group or Folder (+./~ %=sneN) rec.music.folk
```

After you type the name of the newsgroup, *nn* prompts you for the number of articles you wish to read:

```
Number of articles (uasne) (a) 30
Use: j)ump u)nread a)ll @)archive s)ubject n)ame e)either or number
```

This looks a lot more confusing than it really is.* Pressing the Return key accepts the default: **a**, or all, which says you want to read all of the articles in the new group. If you choose this option, *nn* places you in article-selection mode, with a menu including all of the articles in the newsgroup. As seen previously, this can be a huge number; in this case, we chose to specify the number of articles to read (30). Alternatively, you can choose **s**, in which case *nn* prompts you for a subject, and only presents you with articles that match. (This is less useful than it sounds; if you haven't been reading the newsgroup, it's not easy to pick good subjects.) **n** lets you select postings sent by a given person. If you're already subscribed to the newsgroup, you can select **u**, which presents you with all unread articles; or **j**, which goes directly (jumps) to the group. New articles are displayed as if you had entered it normally. When you respond to this prompt, *nn* puts you into article-selection mode for the new group.

Another handy feature is that *nn* can process news and mail files in the same way it processes newsgroups. At the "Group or Folder" prompt, enter a filename rather than a group name. The file is then opened and presented to you in the same format as a newsgroup. This is a very nice way to browse saved news messages. It's also a handy way to look at mail without leaving *nn*. To specify a folder (file), enter the filename at the "Group or Folder" prompt. To distinguish a filename from a newsgroup name, the name you enter must begin with either a dot "**.**" (if the file is relative to the current directory, e.g., *./unix*), a tilde "**~**" (if it's relative to your home directory, e.g., *~/mbox*), or a slash "**/**" (if it's relative to the root directory, e.g., */usr/spool/mail/mharriso*, my own incoming mail directory).

If these commands don't quite make sense yet, don't worry. We'll go over them in more detail in a moment. If these commands do make some sense, you're well on your way to using *nn*!

An nn session

NOTE

If you need to exit this session at any time, type an uppercase **Q** and answer yes (by typing a lowercase **y**) to any questions you may be asked.

Now that some of the basics out of the way, let's step through an *nn* session. This is what you see the first time you run *nn*. Later invocations are pretty much the same, only you won't see the initial welcome screen. Remember the difference between article-selection and reading modes.

---

* The manpage says, "...very powerful, but unfortunately also a little bit tricky at first sight...."

First, you need to start *nn*. Use the **-a30** option in order to keep from being swamped with articles. So, at the prompt, type:

    % nn -a30

As this is our first time using *nn*, we receive the welcome screen and message of the day. Again, you only see these items once. After that, you are placed directly in article-selection mode for the first newsgroup.

```
Welcome to the nn news reader                    Release 6.4.16

Unlike the other news readers you might be familiar with, the ultimate
goal of nn is "not to read news"; actually, "nn" is an acronym for "No
News", and the motto of nn is:

        No news is good news, but nn is better.

I hope that you will enjoy using nn.

Three levels of online help is available:
 ? gives a quick reference guide for the current mode.
 :help     explains how to get help on specific subjects.
 :man      opens the online manual.

Use Q to quit nn.

Have fun,

Kim Fabricius Storm
Texas Instruments A/S
Denmark

Hit any key to continue
```

Pressing any key takes us to the message of the day. This file is maintained by your news administrator. Like all messages of the day, ours has an urgent plea from the system administrator to conserve disk space. At any rate, it's certainly more informative than the default message, which tersely states, "Hi. Welcome to *nn*."

```
Release 6.4.16,  Kim F. Storm, 1991

Welcome to nn on jho.com. PLEASE try to keep your News/ directory cleaned
up. In particular, if you save some uuencoded files and then
uudecode them, be sure and DELETE the uuencoded originals!
Thanks, and have fun.
Please send all news problems to mail alias "news".

Hit any key to continue
```

Type any key, and you are in *nn*. This is the article-selection mode for the first group containing articles. The first group you see varies from system to system, so let's go to a newsgroup that should be available from just about anywhere, *news.newusers.questions.* This is an excellent group for learning your way around the Net; I strongly suggest you subscribe to it for awhile. Many questions that draw sharp answers[†] in other groups receive patient and comprehensive explanations here.

First, invoke the group by typing an uppercase **G**. You are then prompted for the group you wish to view. Type *news.newusers.questions* and press the Return key. You are then presented with the "Number of articles" prompt. Select the jump option to go directly to the newsgroup by typing **j**. You soon get into the habit of pressing the space bar to use *nn*'s defaults, which are generally good.

```
Group or Folder (+./~ %=sneN) news.newusers.questions
Number of articles (juasne)  (j) space
Use: j)ump u)nread a)ll @)archive s)ubject n)ame e)ither or number
```

You should now be viewing the selection screen for *news.newusers.questions.*

```
Newsgroup: news.newusers.questions        Articles: 30(L-395) of 2264/10 NEW

a Craig Amundsen    11  America Online
b Crossly Bear       ?  >
c Will Leland       16  >>Please Respond
d Rune Bang Lyngs|   5  HELP! UNIX to Macintosh how is it done (bin to mac?)
e Jonathan Kamens  512  FAQ: How to find people's E-mail addresses
f Jonathan Kamens  294  Welcome to news.newusers.questions! (weekly posting)
g Emilio Grimaldo   25  Help!!! missing postings
h jmoulder@mis       9  >>Test Message
i Allen R Sparks    15  >Internet History?
j Mary E S Morris    ?  >
k Marshall G. Flax  15  >
l Stan Hall          ?  >
m Jon Bell          13  >>
n Tim Pierce        22  >>
o Ricardo N Silva   13  BIONET.MOLBIO.AGEING: Is it dead ?
p Jack Carbaugh      ?  Access to the Internet in SC + questions
q William L. Urton   ?  >
r Alex Brozan        ?  Gen. Info on Networks
s Mary E S Morris    ?  >unsolicited junk email - what do I do ?

-- 20:26 -- SELECT -- help:? -----Top 62%-----
Q & A for users new to the Usenet.
```

---

* If this group isn't on your system, see your system administrator.
† See "What to Post" in Chapter 7.

Let's take a minute and review a few things. First, there are 19 articles on the screen, labeled a through s. If your terminal has more lines, *nn* displays up to 36 articles per screen (labelled a through z, then 0 through 9).

The top line reminds you which group you are looking at, and the number of articles. (There are 425 unread articles in this newsgroup. 395 articles were killed, leaving 30 to be read. This is why you need to be careful and specify the **-a30** option on the command line.) The bottom of the screen shows a brief description of the newsgroup. The status line directly above that presents the time, the mode you are in, a reminder on how to get help, and the fact that you are 62% of the way through the article selections.

The articles are grouped by subject, oldest articles first. Only the first article displays the text of the subject. Subsequent follow-up articles are denoted by the greater-than sign (>). Articles with two greater-than signs (>>) are follow ups to follow ups, and so on.

Now let's select some articles that we want to read. Article f ("Welcome to *news.newusers.questions!*") looks interesting, so let's select it by typing a lower-case **f**. That line is highlighted to indicate its selection. If you change your mind, typing **f** again deselects it. This is the only article we are going to view, so press the space bar to see the next screen of articles.

Continue hitting the space bar until you have seen all the unread articles in that group. You are then placed in reading mode, looking at the first article selected. It is by Jonathan Kamens, who regularly posts an introductory article to this group:

```
Jonathan Kamens: Welcome to news.newusers.questions! (weekly posting)992 05:01
Archive-name: news-newusersfintro
Version: $Id: news-newusers-intro,v 1.12 1992/03/16 15:38:59 jik Exp $

   Welcome to the news.newusers.questions newsgroup!  According to the
"List of Active Newsgroups" posting in news.announce.newusers, the
purpose of this newsgroup is "Q & A for users new to the Usenet."  So
if you've got questions about the USENET, this is the place to post
them!

               Get to know news.announce.newusers.

   However, before you do that, there is another newsgroup with which
you should become acquainted. The news.announce.newusers newsgroup
contains (once again according to the "List of Active Newsgroups"
posting) "Explanatory postings for new users."  Its purpose is to
provide a base set of information with which all participants in the
USENET should be familiar in order to make the USENET a better place
for all of us.
-- 20:37 --.questions-- 11 MORE --help:?--Top 6%--
```

Most of the commands in reading mode deal with moving around in the article. Pressing the space bar displays the next screenful of text. Typing **u** scrolls up a screen, **CTRL-L** refreshs the display and **n** proceeds to the next message or group, as will pressing the space bar on the last screen of the message.

Now press the space bar to see the next screen of the article.

```
USENET should be familiar in order to make the USENET a better place
for all of us.

If you have not already done so, you are strongly encouraged to read
the introductory postings in news.announce.newusers before posting any
messages to any newsgroup. In particular, the following postings in
that newsgroup might be considered the "mandatory course" for new
users:

        A Primer on How to Work With the Usenet Community
        Answers to Frequently Asked Questions
        Emily Postnews Answers Your Questions on Netiquette
        Hints on writing style for Usenet
        Rules for posting to Usenet
        What is Usenet?

Furthermore, you should be aware that the following articles exist in
the newsgroup so that you can use them for reference in the future
(you might want to glance at them now so you have a slight familiarity
with their contents):

        A Guide to Social Newsgroups and Mailing Lists
-- 20:38 --.questions-- 11 MORE --help:?--12%--
```

This looks like some pretty interesting stuff that we'll want to read carefully. Instead of reading it right now, save the file and read it later, when there's more time. To save the file, type **s**. You are then prompted for a name for the saved article; press the Enter key to use the default filename. The default filename is *~/ News/group-name,*[*] where *group-name* is constructed by replacing the dots in the newsgroup name with slashes. For example, articles from the group *comp.newusers.questions* are saved in the file *questions* in the directory *News/ comp/newusers*. Remember that all articles from this newsgroup are saved in the same file!

As the file does not exist, you are asked to confirm the creation of the file (type **y** to do so). If the file already exists, you won't be prompted. After the file is written, you see a confirmation message. These files are normal text files; you can

---

[*] The tilde ("~") is your home directory. It's possible to change the default filename; how to do so is described later in this chapter.

print them, read them with your favorite editor, or even read them with *nn* itself by using the group command, **G**.[*]

```
Save on (+~|) +news/newusers/questions enter
Create /home/harrison/News/news/newusers/"questions2" ? y
/home/vivaldi/harrison/News/news/newusers/questions2 created: 295 lines written
```

Because this is the last selected article in the group, pressing the space bar takes you to the next newsgroup, where you can repeat the previous steps. Instead, type **Q** to quit and look at a few of the files that *nn* has created.

```
% cd
% ls .n*
.newsrc       .newsrc.bak

.nn:
./      ../      .motd   .param  LAST    NEXTG
```

First, *nn* has created the *.newsrc* file, which keeps track of which groups you are subscribed to and which articles you have read.

Additionally, *nn* has created a *.nn* directory, in which it keeps miscellaneous administrative information about your session. The file *NEXTG*, for example, keeps track of the next group you view. If you decide to customize any *nn* options, you do so by creating a file called *init* in this directory.[†]

Finally, let's take a look at your news directory, where you saved the article from *news.newusers.questions*. It is right where expected, in the file *News/news/ newusers/questions*.

```
% ls -R News
News/news:
./          ../          newusers/

News/news/newusers:
./          ../          questions
```

Make sure you read this article. It's highly recommended and the "Emily Post-news" section is very amusing.

More Commands

Before we cover some of the more advanced *nn* commands, we should point out the distinction between basic commands, which can be bound to keystrokes, and

---

[*] These files can also be viewed with *nn*. Use the "goto group" (**G**) command, and just enter a plus sign (+) followed by the name of the file you wish to view instead of the newsgroup name.

[†] See "The Initialization File" later in this chapter.

extended commands, which must be invoked directly. Extended commands are invoked by pressing the colon (:) key, typing the command, and pressing the Enter key. We've already seen a few extended commands: :q! (quit!) and :help.

Working with Newsgroups

Often, you'll decide that some newsgroup you're reading is too boring for words, and you don't want to bother with it again. (Yes, this is decidedly a negative way to look at it. If you'd like something more cheerful, maybe your company has finally gotten rid of their mainframe, and you no longer have to worry about keeping up with *comp.sys.mvs.*) To do so, just type **U** when you're in the group— either in article-selection mode or reading mode. As a side effect, you'll automatically proceed to the next newsgroup. This is called *unsubscribing*. You can reverse your decision by going back to the newsgroup and typing **U** again. (You'll have to type **G** to return to the newsgroup, since **U** automatically takes you to a new group.)

Somewhat confusingly, the unsubscribe command is also used to subscribe to a newsgroup. If you are reading a group that you have not subscribed to (you had to type **G**, the goto group command, to get there), typing **U** subscribes to it.

Automatically Decoding Articles

One of *nn*'s strengths is the ease in which it can unpack and decode software posted to the Net. The commands supported are:

:unshar
> Decode source code and other files that have been packed in *shar* format

:decode
> Decode binary files that have been uuencoded

:patch
> Automatically apply software patches that have been posted in *patch* format

The operation of these commands is similar. We'll use :unshar to illustrate.

From reading mode, you can unpack the current article by typing the extended command :unshar.

You are prompted for the directory where you want the unshar command to take place. If the directory does not exist, *nn* asks for confirmation before creating it. The file is unencoded in that directory, and a status report is displayed when the operation is completed. Two files are created: *Unshar.headers*, which contains all of the preliminary parts of the article, and *Unshar.results*, which has a log and final results of the unshar operation.

There is a little more flexibility in article-selection mode, where you can decode multipart postings. Select the articles you wish to unpack, and issue the :unshar command. As in reading mode, *nn* prompts you for a directory, and (if it does not exist) asks whether you want to create it.

You are then asked if you wish to unpack only the selected articles on the current screen (type *****), or all the selected articles in the newsgroup (type **+**). Use the second option if the articles you wish to unpack span two or more screens.

Once you make this selection, the articles are unpacked. Articles that are unpacked successfully are automatically unselected. This makes it easy to double-check that everything has gone well.

The following is an example of unsharing a multipart posting from article-selection mode. We are interested in getting a copy of *gtetris* from the group *comp.sources.games.*

```
Newsgroup: comp.sources.games          Articles: 31 of 1043/33

a v15INF1: intro15 - Introduction to comp.sources.games
b v15INF2: num-idx15a - Ind<>rces.games postings by volume/issue number, Part1/
c v15INF3: num-idx15b - Ind<>rces.games postings by volume/issue number, Part2/
d v15INF4: alpha-idx15a - Index of comp.sources.games postings by name, Part1/3
e v15INF5: alpha-idx15b - Index of comp.sources.games postings by name, Part2/3
f v15INF6: alpha-idx15c - Index of comp.sources.games postings by name, Part3/3
g v15INF7: patchlog15 - Index of patches posted to comp.sources.games
h v15INF8: saab-idx15a - Index of games in the archive on saab, Part1/2
i v15INF10: archivers15 - Listing of archive sites
j v15INF9: saab-idx15b - Index of games in the archive on saab, Part2/2
k v15i001: gtetris - Generic Tetris for X11, Part01/02
l v15i002: gtetris - Generic Tetris for X11, Part02/02

-- 20:47 -- SELECT -- help:? -----Bot-----<level 2>--
```

First, select the articles by using *nn*'s selection command (**=**) and enter the string you wish to select, **tetris**:

    =tetris

Next, invoke the unshar command:

    :unshar

and answer a few questions.

You should save this program in its own directory under your source directory. Since this directory does not exist, you are asked to confirm the creation of the directory:

```
Unshar Directory: ~/src/gtetris
Create /home/vivaldi/harrison/"src/gtetris/" ? y
```

Next, you are asked how many articles to unshar. Packages are usually unpacked one at a time, in order to put each in a separate directory, so the usual response is to type **∗**, and only unshar the selected articles on the current page. The most common reason to select **+** is when a particular package spans more than one selection screen.

```
Unshar /home/vivaldi/harrison/src/gtetris/ Article (* +): *

* selected articles on this page, + all selected articles
```

Finally, *nn* starts the unshar process and displays its output. Some shar files are less informative than others, so don't be alarmed if your output doesn't correspond to our example. Sometimes you won't see any output until the end of the process. The archive we're unpacking is fairly verbose:

```
UNPACKING v15i001: gtetris - Generic Tetris for X11, Part01/02
shar: Extracting "README" (2210 characters)
shar: Extracting "MANIFEST" (393 characters)
shar: Extracting "COPYRIGHT" (848 characters)
shar: Extracting "data.h" (19903 characters)
shar: Extracting "tetris.c" (23128 characters)
shar: Extracting "tetris.h" (4639 characters)
shar: End of archive 1 (of 2).
You still need to unpack the following archives:
        2

UNPACKING v15i002: gtetris - Generic Tetris for X11, Part02/02
shar: Extracting "Makefile" (2093 characters)
shar: Extracting "die.c" (4448 characters)
shar: Extracting "tscores.c" (1474 characters)
shar: End of archive 2 (of 2).
You have unpacked both archives.
```

To confirm that the posting has been unpacked, use the shell (**!**) command to check the newly created directory.

```
!ls -FC ~/src/gtetris
  ./          MANIFEST     Unshar.Headers  die.c       tscores.c
  ../         Makefile     Unshar.Result   tetris.c
  COPYRIGHT   README       data.h          tetris.h
```

Now, all you have to do is complete the game and start playing. But that's not a news problem; you're on your own.

NOTE

Occasionally, you get an error in unpacking or decoding because the articles reached your site in the wrong order. To rectify this situation, issue
the command :sort lexical, which sorts the articles alphabetically. In
nearly every case, this reorders the articles in an manner that decodes
properly. There's no good reason why, but some people have reported
that :sort sender also seems to help sometimes.

Command-Line Article Selection

One of *nn*'s unique features is the ability to select articles from the command line
based on the sender's name or subject. You can

- Collect articles by subject
- Collect articles by sender's name
- Merge all found articles into one "meta" group
- Scan unsubscribed as well as subscribed groups

The option **-s** *word* selects articles in which the subject contains *word*. Similarly, **-n** *name* selects articles whose author has the given *name*. For example, the
command below finds all articles that contain the string "nn"[*] in their subject:

```
% nn -s" nn "
```

Not surprisingly, when you try this, most of the articles you find are in *news.soft-
ware.nn*. By default, the search is *case-insensitive*, meaning that nn doesn't
differentiate between uppercase and lowercase letters: in our example, nN and
Nn would be equivalent to nn. If you want a case-sensitive search, add the **-i**
option. The following command only finds articles that contain a lowercase nn:

```
% nn -i -s" nn "
```

If you precede your search string with a slash, you can search for a regular expression. Regular expressions allow much more complex searches.[†] For example, let's
start by searching for all articles written by John:

```
% nn -n"/john"
```

This is helpful, but not quite what we want: in addition to finding articles by John
Fredrickson, it also finds articles by Fred Johnson. However, you do want the
search to be case-insensitive; there's no guarantee how people on the Net will

---

[*] Putting the spaces around "nn" keeps it from matching words such as "planning" that have an embedded "nn."

[†] See Appendix C for a fuller discussion of regular expressions.

capitalize their names. To search for the first name John, precede the name with a caret (^), a regular-expression character that says "only match at the beginning of a line:"

```
% nn -n"/^john"
```

To find authors named Mark or John, use an "or" operation, expressed by the vertical bar (|) character:

```
% nn -n"/^john|^mark"
```

This should do the trick. Note that the vertical bar has to be within the quotes. The quotes weren't strictly necessary in our previous examples, but they are here; without them, the UNIX operating system would interpret the vertical bar as its "pipe" character.

You can only give one **-s** or **-n** option on the command line; that is, you can't search for a particular subject and a particular author, and you can't search for two different authors (except by using the regular-expression mechanism we just described). If two or more **-s** and **-n** options appear on the command line, *nn* uses the last one, and ignores the earlier options.

In many cases, you don't care which group the articles you find are from. If this is the case, you can collect all the found articles into one large "meta" group by specifying the **-m** option on the command line; for example:

```
% nn -m -n"/^john|^mark"
```

Making the search wider

By default, when you use **-s** and **-m**, nn only searches for unread articles in the newsgroups to which you have subscribed. Often, you want a wider search. The **-X** option causes *nn* to search all groups that are available, including those to which you haven't subscribed. This is very useful for scouring all the newsgroups your site receives for relevant news. For example, let's search for articles about the Free Software Foundation (FSF) or its GNU project in all groups:

```
% nn -s"/GNU|fsf|free software foundation" -X
```

You can go even farther. **-X** only searches for articles that haven't been read yet. If you want to search all the articles available to you, both read and unread, use the **-x** option in addition. The following command searches for immortal words of wisdom in all groups, including articles that have already been read, and presents the articles as one group:

```
% nn -n"/Dennis Ritchie|Mark Harrison|Don Knuth" -mxX
```

Decrypting ROT13 Articles

As discussed previously, someone occasionally posts an article others may not wish to see. These are posted in ROT13 format, and look like this:

```
Ubj qb lbh gryy vg'f n pbzchgre ercnvezna gung unf n syng gver
orfvqr gur ebnq?  Ur'f gur bar punatvat bhg gverf gb frr jung'f gur
ceboyrz.
```

```
Ubj qb lbh gryy vg'f n pbzchgre ercnvezna gung'f bhg bs tnf?  Ur'f
gur bar punatvat bhg gverf gb frr jung'f gur ceboyrz.
```

Follow this two-step procedure to read the encrypted posting:

1. Make sure that you really want to read the post. If the subject says "offensive to IBM salesmen," and you are particularly sensitive about IBM salesmen, don't read the post! If you do read the post and are offended, don't complain. You were warned.

2. Execute the decrypt command by typing **D**. If you save the article while it is decrypted, the file will be in decrypted form as well.

```
How do you tell it's a computer repairman that has a flat tire
beside the road?  He's the one changing out tires to see what's the
problem.
```

```
How do you tell it's a computer repairman that's out of gas?  He's
the one changing out tires to see what's the problem.
```

Filename and Command Completion

nn supports *Emacs*-style command and filename completion. When you enter a command, newsgroup name, or filename, there are several shortcut keys you can use:

- Typing **?** displays a list of possible completions. If the list is too long to fit on one screen, pressing **?** repeatedly cycles through the list.

- When you enter a command, pressing the space bar completes the command for you. If you are entering a filename or newsgroup name, *nn* completes the current component (for example, the "lang" part in *comp.lang.postscript*). If there are several possibilities, pressing the space bar repeatedly cycles through the possible alternatives.

- Pressing the Tab key completes the current component and presents the first possibility for the next component.

Posting Messages

CAUTION

A posted message is seen by tens of thousands of people all over the world. Keep this in mind when you are posting! The group *misc.test* is designated for test postings. Try posting there a few times before posting somewhere else.

There are two ways to post messages in *nn*. You can either post an original message using the :post command, or you can answer someone else's posting with the f (follow-up) command. These commands can be executed in either selection or reading mode. When you choose to follow up from article-selection mode, *nn* asks you which article you wish to answer.

Posting New Articles

When you issue the **:post** command, *nn* asks you a few questions, and then places you in your editor so you can write the text of the message. Here's a quick example. Let's post a small message to the group *misc.test*.

> **:post**

Start the posting process.

> POST to group: **misc.test**

Enter the group you wish to post to. Pressing the Enter key selects the default, which means to post a message to the current group–the group whose articles you are either reading or selecting.

> Subject: **test post**

Enter a brief subject line here. Try to be as specific as possible. For example, if you are posting a question on *comp.unix.questions*, avoid subjects like "unix question." Why else would you be posting there?

> Keywords: *enter*

The text you enter here is placed in the keyword field of the message header. Keywords can be used to search for related messages by topic, or to build indices into news archives. This doesn't really apply to our small test message, so just press the Enter key and leave it blank.

> Summary: **this is a test**

Enter a quick summary of your message.

```
Distribution: (default 'world') enter
```

This field controls the geographic distribution of your message. See Appendix A for more information on distributions. We'll distribute our test message worldwide.

Once you have answered these questions, you are placed in the editor to type your message. The headers at the top reflect the answers you gave to the questions previously. You may edit the contents of the header, but don't change any of the keywords at the beginning of the line. Be sure and leave the blank line between the header and the message body. The news-posting software depends on this to tell where the header ends. If you delete this blank line, the results can be spectacular.

```
Newsgroups: misc.test
Distribution: world
Subject: test post
Summary: this is a test

Do not be alarmed, this is only a test!
```

Once you finish typing your posting, save the temporary file and exit from the editor. You then have the chance to:

- *abort* the posting; nothing is posted. Your posting is then saved in a temporary file, *~/dead.article.*

- *mail* (send) the article to an individual rather than posting it

- *edit* (re-edit) the posting

- *view* the article as it will appear to others

- *write* the file to disk without posting

- *post* the article. This is the default action.

```
a)bort e)dit m)ail r)eedit s)end v)iew w)rite
Action: (post article) p
```

Depending on your system, it takes anywhere from a few minutes to over a day for a posting to start propagating to other sites. Expect to see replies and follow ups soon after. See "Test Messages" in Chapter 7 for an example of what to expect when posting to *misc.test.*

If you decide too late that the posting was inappropriate, there's a partly effective way to back out. Wait for the article to appear on your server (i.e., on your selection-mode screen). Select it and type the command **C** to cancel it. It's impossible to cancel an article completely, but this limits the damage. You can still expect to see some replies. You can only cancel your own articles.

Following Up Another Article

The procedure for answering another person's post is essentially the same as for posting a new article. The differences are:

- Type an **F** to post a follow up to an article.

- If you are in article-selection mode, *nn* asks you which article you want to answer. If you're in reading mode, *nn* assumes you want to follow up to the article you're reading.

- You are given the chance to include the original message in your article.

- You won't be asked for a newsgroup, a subject line, or keywords; these are all taken from the article to which you're replying. However, once you've started the editor, you may change any of these fields, if you wish.

After you have responded to these questions, just follow the steps outlined in the previous "Posting New Articles" section.

Sending Mail

nn provides some basic services for sending regular electronic mail. You can use *nn* to originate new mail messages, though it's rarely used that way. More commonly, you will use the mail facilities to reply to the author of a particular article, or to forward an interesting article to others who may not read news. In this section, we'll discuss replying and forwarding.

Reply

The most common reason for using mail within *nn* is to reply to the author of an article without sending a message to the entire newsgroup. We'll discuss network etiquette more thoroughly in Chapter 7, but for now, just note that mail should be used whenever a network-wide response is inappropriate. For example, if you want to buy someone's used car, you obviously wouldn't post your offer to all of *misc.forsale*. Etiquette aside, such a posting would be counterproductive: you might lead someone to make a better offer.

To send a reply, type **R** or use the command `:reply` in either reading mode or article-selection mode. If you are in selection mode when you give the reply command, *nn* asks you to which article you wish to reply:

```
Reply to author of article:
```

Answer with the selection letter of the article. If you choose to reply from reading mode, *nn* assumes you want to reply to the author of the current article.

You are then asked whether or not you wish to include the text of the posted message:

    Include original article?

If you answer **y**, *nn* includes the original article in the message. If you do this, be sure to delete any unnecessary lines. Be kind to the other guy's mailbox!

You are then placed in the editor. From this point on, just follow the steps outlined in the previous section, "Posting New Articles."

Forwarding a Post via Mail

You may want to forward an interesting article to friends and associates, particularly if you have friends who don't read news. This feature is also a handy way to save articles or give yourself a reminder about something that strikes you: just mail the article to yourself. You'll save yourself the trouble of deleting it from the folder where it was saved. As an example of how this can be used, I usually forward notices of interesting software to myself. The article hanging around in my mailbox reminds me to go out and get the software.

To forward an article, follow these steps:

- Invoke the mail command using **M** or `:mail`.

- If you are in reading mode, type **y** to the "forward article?" query. If you are in article-selection mode, indicate which article you wish to forward by answering the "Article to be forwarded" prompt.

- Press the Enter key when prompted for the subject line.

- Answer **n** when asked if you wish to edit the forwarded message.

- *nn* then asks if you wish to append your signature to the message. Go ahead and type **y** if you are bouncing the article to someone else. Your signature reminds the recipient that you forwarded the article.

Killing and Selecting Articles

As you read news, you will often find particular subjects or authors to be very interesting, very boring, or very offensive. *nn* makes it easy to *auto kill* such articles and *auto select* interesting ones. This can be done in a particular newsgroup or globally across all newsgroups, on a permanent or temporary basis.

To auto kill or auto select articles, press **K** in either the article-selection or reading modes. *nn* then asks you a series of questions, as follows. In this example, choose to permanently kill articles with the subject "boring post" in the group *misc.test*. The prompts you see vary according to the options you choose.

    AUTO (k)ill or (s)elect (CR => Kill subject 30 days) **k**

Do you want to automatically kill or automatically select articles? Pressing the Return key kills a particular subject for 30 days. You are prompted for the letter of the article containing the subject that you don't want to see for a while. **k** (for a permanent kill) and **s** (for automatic selection) are a bit more complicated. If you pick kill or select, you are asked several more questions.

    AUTO KILL on (s)ubject or (n)ame (s) **s**

Do you want to kill (select) by subject or by name? We've chosen to kill all articles with a particular subject, but you can also kill articles based on the sender.

    KILL Subject: (=/) **boring post**

What subject do you wish to kill or select? In addition to typing a simple search string, as we gave here, you can search for a UNIX regular expression by preceding your search string with a slash (/). (We touched on regular expressions very briefly earlier.) You can also select a subject by typing an equal sign (**=**), followed by an article letter; this selects (or kills) articles with the same subject as the article you choose. If you're killing articles based on their author, you'll see the same set of choices.

    KILL in (g)roup 'misc.test' or in (a)ll groups (g) **g**

You can choose to kill (or select) articles in the current group by typing **g**, or in all groups by typing **a**. In this case, kill articles in the current group only; this means that if the subject "boring post" turns up in some other newsgroup, we'll see it.

    Lifetime of entry in days (p)ermanent (30) **p**

You can make the entry permanent, or specify the number of days for the selection to have effect. The latter option is handy when someone starts a minor flame-fest on a topic that you might be interested in reading about once everyone has calmed down. Most flame-fests subside eventually, so reserve "permanent" for topics that you are completely uninterested in.

    CONFIRM KILL Subject Permanent: boring post **y**

You're given a last chance to review and confirm your choice: type **y** or **n**.

Unkilling

Unfortunately, there is no built-in command to undo a kill or select command. Fortunately, it is still not difficult to edit the kill file with a text editor.

If you wish to view or modify your kill-file selections, edit the file *~/.nn/kill.* There is one kill or select specification per line. Find the subject or name you wish to unkill and delete it. *nn* reads this file every time it starts, so the edited kill file takes effect the next time you run *nn.* If you have edited the file without stopping *nn*, you can cause the changes to take effect by issuing the :compile command, which causes *nn* to re-read the kill file.

Searching Through Subjects, Senders, and Messages

One of the less obvious, but extremely useful, features of *nn* is that it allows you to perform searches at both the article-selection level (through subject text or senders' names), and at the message level (within the contents of a particular posting). No matter what type of search you are doing, searching is case-insensitive. This means that it doesn't matter whether you use upper- or lowercase letters; *nn* will match characters regardless of case.

At the article-selection level, when you match one or more subject lines or senders, those postings are automatically selected, and you can view them if you choose. For some reason, *nn* treats searching through senders' names differently than through subjects; before you can search through senders' names, you actually need to perform a simple customization. More about that later.

When you're viewing a list of the messages in a particular group, you can search through subject lines by typing an equal sign and then entering the text to find. The equal sign signals *nn* to provide a search prompt, "Select regexp" (Select regular expression), at the bottom of the screen, and also to move the text cursor there. You enter the text you want to search for and press the Return key. In the following figure, the user is searching for "mac." (Since this is a group about things for sale, there are frequent postings about Macintosh software and equipment.)

```
Newsgroup: ne.forsale                        Articles: 63 of 163/2

a Bob Wright                         1   new 40 Gal. gas water hea<> $125
firm
b Efthymios Kiafoulis               22   DISCOUNT HEALTH CLUB
MEMBERSHIPS!!!!!
c Steve Collins                     15   Free Sealpoint Siamese Cats
d R.C. Mitchell                     66   >ZX-6R parts for sale
e John A. Flood                     10   >Mitsubishi 20" TV for sale
f comments@farley.com               48   >Business Opportunity
g ALAN BRONSTEIN                    20   87 Cavalier ($500 obo)
h The Saint                         21   WANTED: 60" x 75" Truck Cap
i Jeff Nowak                         7   WTB: Land in or near Littleman, MA
j john lamson                       19   House for Sale - Dracut, MA
```

```
k Yoky Matsuoka                    12   For Sale: Snowboarding Boots
l Brian D. Goodman                 32   FS -- 486sx 25mhz PC -- LOADED!
m ACTION                           24   CHEAP
n What're You Lookin' At           16   fs: Hell (oem) & Xwing (3.5")
p Anne Harley                       1   BMW 530i, 1978, 4-dr w/sunroof
q Anne Harley                      22   -
r cconroy                           5   Gadget CD-ROM
s cconroy                           5   Mac Classic II


Select regexp mac
```

In this case, when the user initiates the search (by hitting the Return key), a single subject line on the current screen is highlighted:

```
s   cconroy                             5 Mac Classic II
```

However, a message at the bottom of the screen indicates that two other articles in the current group have also matched:

```
Selected 3 articles
```

(If you were to page through the group, you would see that those two articles are also highlighted.) You can view each of the selected articles sequentially by first pressing the Return key; then page through the text of each message by pressing the space bar.

In order to search through the names of senders, which also appear on the subject line, you need to map a key. You can do this so that it works every time you start up *nn* by mapping the key in your *nn init* file, which generally lives in the directory *~/.nn*. (If you need to create an *init* file from scratch, do it there. See "Customizing nn" for more information.) The following text lets you initiate a search through senders' names using the underscore character (_). The first three lines are comments.

```
# Add the following macro to your init file (~/.nn/init) and invoke
# via '_' (underscore).
# _ does search on sender (as = does a search on subject)
map menu _ (
    :set select-on-sender
    find input
    :unset select-on-sender
    message
)
```

Once this map is entered into your *init* file, when you start up *nn* you can search through posters' names as easily as through subjects; just begin the search with an underscore rather than a forward slash. Again, you can view any postings selected in this way by hitting the Return key, and then paging through using the space bar. Regardless of how articles are selected, you can clear all selections by typing the tilde character (~) twice.

You can also search for text within an individual posted message. While viewing the message, type a forward slash (/), which will then appear as a prompt at the bottom of the window. Enter the text to search for after the slash and press the Return key. All instances of the text string found will be highlighted. In the following posting from the same "for sale" group, we've searched for any instance of the word "bedroom" in an ad for a house:

```
john lamson: House for Sale - Dracut, MA              14 Mar 1995 13:49
HOUSE FOR SALE
DRACUT, MASSACHUSETTS

Spectacular 20x20 fireplaced family room featuring cathedral ceiling,
skylights, bay window and french doors is the centerpiece of this 8
room, 2275 sq. ft. gambrel with attached 2 car garage.  3/4 bedrooms,
2 1/2 baths, eat-in kitchen with Jenn-Air grill, formal dining room,
front to back master bedroom, 12x24 living room, two fireplaces.
Extraordinary guest suite/office with full bath and private entrance.
Many top-quality extras.

Impeccably maintained home is situated on 40,000+ sq. ft. corner lot.
Professionally landscaped with more than 70 flowering trees and
evergreens.  Convenient to shopping and Rt. 93.  Well-know East Dracut,
Old Parker Village neighborhood.  Offered at $187,500.
7 Lexington Road, Dracut, Massachusetts

No brokers please.  For appointment, call owner @ 508-555-1212.

-- 13:26 --ne.forsale-- LAST  --help:?--All--
```

Customizing nn

nn has many features that can be customized to your preference. These include the newsgroup presentation sequence, keyboard remapping, macro definitions, and many internal commands. I will introduce a few commands and syntax as needed to demonstrate some useful *nn* customizations. I won't try to give a comprehensive discussion of *nn* customization; complete coverage could easily require an entire book, and most of the features aren't really relevant to everyday use. A comprehensive list of commands, macro conditionals, and so forth can be found in the manpage.

Files

This section summarizes the files that are of interest to the general user. There are several other files that are used internally by *nn*, or are of interest primarily to the news administrator. They are documented in the *nn* manual.

~/.nn/init

> This is your personal configuration file. Any customizations you make go here, and will override the sitewide initialization (init) file. It is described in more detail below.

$lib/init

> This is the sitewide init file set up by your news administrator. It is the first file read by *nn*. (*$lib* is the location of the *nn* library directory. The default is */usr/lib/news/nn*.)

~/.nn/kill

> This is the kill file. Each time *nn* starts up, it compiles this into the file *~/.nn/KILL.COMP*.

~/.newsrc

> The standard news init file. It keeps track of what groups you are subscribed to and which articles you have read in each group.

The Initialization File

When *nn* starts, it reads several init files. The first file is the systemwide init file, set up by your system administrator. This file is usually in */usr/local/lib/nn/init.** After the global init file has been read, *nn* reads your personal init file, *~/.nn/init*. Put your own modifications and customizations here.

The comments in this section apply to both files. Anything in your personal init file overrides the systemwide init file.

Comments

> Blank lines and any lines starting with a pound sign (#) are ignored. Comments can also appear on the same line as a command if the pound sign is preceded by a space.

> ```
> # this is a comment
> cd ~  # change to home directory
> cd ~# this isn't a comment -- no space!
> ```

Commands

> Any *nn* command can be placed in the init file. For example, if you want to clear the screen and change to your news directory:

> ```
> clear # not really necessary, since nn also clears the screen
> cd ~/News
> ```

---

* It's a good idea to check this file before doing any extensive customization of your own, as many news administrators have made many local customizations. If you can't find it, ask your administrator. Also note that any customizations the news administrator made may cause *nn* to behave differently than that described here.

Variables

You can also set any variables you like. Numeric or text variables are set to the value specified in the command. Boolean variables are set to "true" by using the set command and to "false" by using the unset command.

```
set expert            # turn off a few prompts
unset confirm-create  # don't ask for confirmation when creating files
set overlap 0         # when paging, don't show any lines from the
                      # previous screen
set spell-checker /usr/gnu/bin/ispell
```

Save-files section

Whenever you save an article, *nn* suggests a filename. By default, this file name is the newsgroup name, with the periods (.) replaced by slashes (/). Thus, the group *comp.unix.questions* would be stored in *~/News/comp/unix/questions*. You can specify new defaults in the save-files section. The same file can be specified for multiple groups, and you can use wildcards to name groups. The syntax is:

```
save-files
    newsgroup name filename
    newsgroup name filename
    ...
end
```

If the filename starts with a plus sign (+), it is placed in your news directory (default *~/News*). If it begins with *~/*, it is placed relative to your home directory. Otherwise, it is written relative to the current directory. Here's an example:

```
save-files
        # let's see what we'll be reading today
        comp.unix*    +unix
        comp.mac*     +mac
        comp.lang.c   +c
        comp.lang.c++ +c
        rec.humor*    ~/funny-stuff
end
```

This save-files block says that, by default, all postings you save from newsgroups underneath *comp.unix* should be saved in the single file *~/News/unix*, even though *comp.unix* consists of many newsgroups. Likewise, all subgroups of *comp.mac* should be saved in the file *~/News/mac*. Articles from the two groups *comp.lang.c* and *comp.lang.c++* are, by default, saved in the file *~/News/c*; and articles from the *rec.humor* newsgroups are saved in the file *funny-stuff*, in your home directory.

Command Groups

Sets of commands can be conditionally executed by using command groups. Conditions can include shell commands, host names, terminal types, and various things such as running on a slow terminal. See below for an example.

Newsgroup Sequencing

The final thing to appear in the init file is the article-presentation sequence. Unlike many newsreaders, *nn* does not rely on the order of the *.newsrc* file to determine the order in which to display newsgroups. Instead, this is specified in the sequence section of the init file.

The sequence section is the last section in the init file and follows this syntax:

```
sequence
     group-specification  [save-file] [entry-action]
     ...
(continues to end of file)
```

The sequence continues to the end of the file. Group-specification can either be the name of a single newsgroup (such as *comp.lang.c*) or a wildcard (such as *comp.lang.**). If save-file is specified, that file is used as though it had been specified in the save-files section. Finally, one or more *nn* commands can be specified (in parentheses). These commands are executed each time *nn* enters that particular group.

nn presents the groups in the order specified. Groups not mentioned in the sequence list are displayed after the groups in the sequence list.

As an example, this sequence first displays any new groups (via the NEW pseudonym, then *rec.humor.funny, comp.lang.tcl,* subscribed *comp* groups, subscribed *rec* groups, and (finally) anything else.

```
sequence
     NEW              # a synonym for all new groups
     rec.humor.funny  # get some jokes to tell at lunch
     comp.lang.tcl    # then catch up on the latest tcl information
     comp             # serious stuff
     rec              # non-serious stuff
# end of .nn/init file
```

Note that the sequence section is the only section that must be placed in a particular part of the init file. Since there is no keyword to end the section, it must be placed at the end of the file. The other sections can be placed anywhere you like.

Environment Variables

nn uses the following environment variables, which are usually set in your shell initialization file (usually *.login* or *.profile*).

EDITOR
     The editor is invoked to compose postings, responses, and follow ups. If this is not specified, *vi* is the default.

LOGNAME

> Your login id. This is used to return mail *nn* cannot deliver. It is set by the system when you log in, and you normally shouldn't have to change it.

PAGER

> This can be used to specify a particular paging program, such as *more* or *less*. If you don't specify this variable, *nn*'s internal pager is used. Note that *nn*'s internal article pager cannot be overridden, since it needs to support the various article-reading commands.

SHELL

> The program specified by this variable is used to execute shell commands. It is usually set automatically by the system.

TERM

> The type of terminal you are using. Depending on your version of UNIX, *nn* uses either the *termcap* or *terminfo* terminal database to provide full-screen capabilities.

Slow Terminals

It is feasible to use a full-screen program such as *nn* with a slow terminal (a dial-up line with a 1200- or 2400-bps modem, for example). In fact, I did this for quite some time. Use these options to make it easier:

```
set confirm-entry-limit 10
set confirm-entry
```

> These options cause *nn* to prompt you before entering any group with more than 10 articles. confirm-entry prevents *nn* from displaying large selection menus (in this case, menus with more than 10 items) unless you really want to read the group.

```
set slow-mode
```

> When slow-mode is set, *nn* tries to minimize screen output in several ways. First, it indicates selected articles with an asterisk (*) rather than by highlighting the line. Second, it avoids automatically redrawing the screen when you respond to an article. You can use **CTRL-L** to redraw the screen if desired.

```
set delay-redraw
```

> When delay-redraw is set, *nn* doesn't redraw the screen after extended commands. Again, you can use **CTRL-L** to redraw the screen as desired.

```
set compress
```

> When compress is set, *nn* compresses multiple spaces and tabs to one space. If you wish to see the original spacing or indentation, you can toggle between compressed and uncompressed mode with the compress (**c**) command.

unset header-lines

When header-lines is not set, *nn* doesn't display article headers unless you request them explicitly. Instead, you get a one-line summary at the top of the screen, showing the sender, the subject, and the date. If you wish to see the headers for a particular article, use the header (**h**) command when you're reading the article.

set stop 5

When stop is set to *n*, *nn* only displays the first *n* lines of each new article. This makes it easy to skip uninteresting articles without waiting for the first screen of the article to be displayed.

You can set these values in every *nn* session by adding these lines to your init file:

```
set slow-speed 2400
on slow
    set confirm-entry
    set confirm-entry-limit 10
    set slow-mode
    set delay-redraw
    set compress
    unset header-lines
    set stop 5
end
```

Recommended Options

So, after all that, what options should you really use? Here is a copy of the init file I use; it's what I give people when they ask my advice. It's simple compared to others, but it's a reasonable start. For more ideas on what to customize, read the manpages. Experiment and find what suits you.

```
set confirm-junk-seen
set auto-select-subject
set header-lines =F=SPGfDdOB
set mark-overlap
set show-purpose-mode 2
set re-layout 1
set confirm-junk-seen
```

## CHAPTER FOUR

READING NEWS WITH THE TIN NEWSREADER

Introducing tin

tin was developed by Iain Lea in Germany. It was based on the *tass* newsreader by Rich Skrenta, and first released publicly in 1991. It has been regularly maintained and upgraded and has been ported to UNIX, AmigaDOS, OS/2, and Windows/NT. This chapter covers *tin* version 1.3 and above.

A short, unscientific scan through a few thousand news articles showed that *tin* is, by far, the most popular newsreader currently in use. For many people, *tin* has become the newsreader of choice because of its blend of practical features and an elegant, easy-to-use human interface. It is one of the few pieces of software that is attractive to new users, but doesn't sacrifice any of the power old timers have come to appreciate. If you're new to USENET, I strongly recommend that you give *tin* a try. Even if you've been reading news for years, *tin* is still worth checking out; you may become a convert!

Some of *tin*'s key features are:

- An intuitive, easy-to-use interface. *tin* has become the standard newsreader at many sites because its simplicity helps to relieve the support burden from the news administrator.

- A simple kill-file system. This feature lets you automatically screen out messages of little interest and select preferred articles.
- The ability to group articles by subject
- The ability to tag and operate on groups of articles. Groups of articles can be saved, printed, mailed, etc.
- Excellent on-screen help
- Built-in facilities for unpacking, decoding, and unsharing postings

The only drawback to *tin* is that it redraws the screen a lot—probably more than any other UNIX newsreader. If you have a slow modem (i.e., 2400 baud), it can be uncomfortable; and even if you have a faster modem, you may become impatient with it.

tin is well supported by an active community of users. It does not have a dedicated newsgroup, but is discussed in the newsgroup *news.software.readers*. Bug reports and any suggestions may be sent directly to the author of *tin* (*iain.lea@erlm.siemens.de*) by typing **R** from just about any prompt.

The rest of this chapter is organized as follows:

- How to start *tin*
- Navigating among newsgroups
- Navigating within a newsgroup (selecting articles to read)
- Basic commands for reading articles
- A sample *tin* session. If you have never used a newsreader before, this section walks you through the process step by step.
- Posting articles and sending mail
- Automatically selecting and screening out (killing) articles
- Customizing *tin*

Getting Started

You have several choices when you start *tin*. Most often you'll use one of the following commands:

tin
>   Starts *tin* using local */usr/spool/news* directory

rtin or *tin -r*
>   Starts *tin* using NNTP (network news transport protocol)

You can check with your system administrator about which is the best choice for your site. If you want to experiment, try *tin* first. If that doesn't work, then most likely *tin -r* will. If you use *tin -r*, the NNTPSERVER environment variable must be set to the name of your news server. If you need to use another server, your system administrator probably set your account up with NNTPSERVER defined correctly to start with. However, if you run into problems or don't know which news server to use, ask your system administrator for help.

If this is your first time reading news, or if you have not read news for some time, it is handy to be able to discard the thousands of messages that have accumulated on the system in your absence. To do this, start *tin* with the command

```
% tin -c
```

to catch up on all unread news.

Levels

Like most newsreaders, *tin* has a concept of levels or modes for looking at group lists, article lists, and the articles themselves. In fact, *tin* has more modes than any other newsreader we know about. However, rather than complicating matters, the levels provide a well-thought-out approach to reading news. They are:

Group selection
> This level navigates among the groups you have subscribed to. When you pick a group, you move to the article-selection level.

Article selection[*]
> This level navigates among the unread articles and threads in the newsgroup. Each thread is only listed once, no matter how many articles it has. (Of course, there's no difference between an individual article and a thread that contains only one article). From this level, you can proceed to the thread-browsing level, or jump directly to the article-browsing level.

Thread browsing
> This level is similar to the article-selection level, except that it operates on conversation threads. It shows you each article in the thread. On this level, you can select individual articles in a thread, and proceed to the article-browsing level.

Article browsing
> This is the level where you actually read the articles you have selected. Other article-level operations, such as saving and replying to messages, are performed here.

---

[*] This is referred to as the group level in the *tin* manpage. I think that the term "Article selection" is a little more consistent and makes it easier to explain navigation between the various levels.

Spooling directory selection

This level lets you choose different news-spooling directories. It's only valuable if you have different spooling directories to choose from. In all probability this would be the case only if you bought a news distribution on CD-ROM. We won't discuss the spooling directory level any further.

Selecting Articles

When you first start *tin*, you are placed at the group-selection level, which lists the various newsgroups to which you've subscribed. A typical selection screen is shown below:

```
    Group Selection (news.utdallas.edu 32)      h=help

-> 1   148 bit.listserv.christia
   2     3 dfw.eats
   3       dfw.flame
   4    15 dfw.forsale
   5   178 comp.lang.c++
   6    49 comp.object
   7   225 comp.lang.c
   8    97 news.newusers.questions
   9     6 dfw.general
  10   216 misc.jobs.offered
  11     3 rec.humor.funny
  12   256 soc.culture.asian.american
  13     2 tx.general
  14    13 tx.jobs
  15       utd.acc.announce
  16       utd.acc.downtime

    <n>=set current to n, TAB=next unread, /=search pattern, c)atchup,
   g)oto, j=line down, k=line up, h)elp, m)ove, q)uit, r=toggle all/unread,
   s)ubscribe, S)ub pattern, u)nsubscribe, U)nsub pattern, y)ank in/out
```

The header at the top tells us that we are at the group-selection level, the name of the news server, and a reminder on how to get help. Following that is a list of subscribed newsgroups and a count of the number of unread articles in each one (178 in *comp.lang.c++*, for example).

At the bottom of every screen, *tin* always gives a short summary of the most important commands you can give at your current level. This screen is no exception. While you're learning *tin*, get used to looking for these cues.

Depending on how *tin* is configured, the newsgroup currently selected is either highlighted or has an arrow (->) in the left margin. To select a group, either type its number and press the Enter key; use the arrow keys to move up and down; or use the **h** and **j** keys to move up and down. To enter the group and see the articles for reading, press the Enter key or the right arrow. You can also use **CTRL-F** and **CTRL-B** to page forwards and backwards a screen at a time. A useful shortcut is the Tab key, which takes you to the next group with unread articles.

When a group is selected, a list of unread articles is presented on the article-selection level. A typical article-selection screen is shown below:

```
comp.lang.c++ (128T 178A 0K 11H R)            h=help

-> 1 +   char *x Vs char* x                    James Kanze
   2 +   Union member with user-def = op. forbidden!  W  Peter Jacobsen
   3 +   Everything Virtual !!!!!               Robert Martin
   4 + 3 Witty definition of your programming language  Sami Nieminen
   5 +   Project deadlines [8/7 is important!]  Raj Rao
   6 +   Pointer to an array of objects         Andreas Balogh
   7 + 3 Class design: Member vs. Pointer       Robert Martin
   8 +   Q: a way to use strings in switch-statement?  Paul J Lucas
   9 +   Static Inheritance                     Paul J Lucas
  10 *   Forward declaration of typedef via "class T;"  John Polstra
  11 *   Default Argument if Arg is class object??  Edgar Holcomb
  12 +   main ... :-)                           James Kanze
  13 +   argument conversion problem?           Gnanasekaran Swam
  14 * 2 string class: is it part of ANSI C++?  Eric Roode
  15 +   Multiply Overloaded Operators?         Ellster
  16 +   How can I get a signal when data arrives on a  Jon Olav Linde 121

<n>=set current to n, TAB=next unread, /=search pattern, ^K)ill/select,
a)uthor search, c)atchup, j=line down, k=line up, K=mark read, l)ist thread,
|=pipe, m)ail, o=print, q)uit, r=toggle all/unread, s)ave, t)ag, w=post
```

The header at the top displays the group name, the number of conversation threads (128), unread articles (178), automatically killed articles (0), automatically selected "hot" articles (11), and an indication that we are viewing only unread articles ("R"). As usual, a help reminder is also displayed.

Following that is a list of the unread article threads in the newsgroup. Each line shows the thread number, its status (**+** means unread; ***** means that the article is "hot," i.e., automatically selected), the number of articles in the thread (blank when there is just one article in the thread), and the subject and author of the first unread article in the thread.

The navigation keys are the same as for the newsgroup-selection screen. To select any article or thread, type its number and press the Return key; or use the up and down arrow keys or type **h** to move up, and **j** to move down. Once you select an article, press the Return key or the right arrow key to display it. You can use *tin* effectively with just the arrow keys: the up and down arrows move up and down on the current screen, while the left and right arrows move up a menu level and down a menu level, respectively. Pressing the Tab key displays the next unread article. This is a really handy feature; you can view every new article on the system with nothing more than the Tab key.

Like the other levels, the bottom of the screen offers a quick summary of the most frequently used commands at this level.

Finally, you can list the articles in a particular conversation thread by selecting the thread and pressing a lowercase **1** (letter ell). This isn't necessary to view the articles—you can read individual articles and threads directly from the article selection menu—but it is useful for viewing the history of a thread that interests you, or for selecting individual articles from a thread. If you read a thread from the article level, you have to start with the first unread article, and work from there to the end—or until you get tired, whichever comes first. The thread selector lets you choose parts of the conversation that seem interesting. A typical thread listing is shown below:

```
       Thread (Witty definition of your programming language)    h=help

   16    [ 19]   Lennart Benschop (lennart@blade.stack.urc.tue.nl)
   17    [ 38]   David Brabant (David.Brabant@csl.sni.be)
   18    [ 16]   Greg Goodman (gregg@sugar.NeoSoft.COM)
   19    [ 83]   Dr Henry Brancik (henryb@aix00.csd.unsw.OZ.AU)
   20    [  4]   Benjamin Ketcham (bketcham@u.washington.edu)
   21    [ 14]   Job Honig (joho@dutiag.twi.tudelft.nl)
   22    [ 102]  Thurman (cs1jd@herts.ac.uk)
   23    [ 10]   Xian the Desk Lizard (C.D.A.Hellon@bradford.ac.uk)
   24    [ 27]   Mark J. Bobak (bobak@tr0210.to.ford.com)
   25    [ 11]   Gavin Russell Baker (gavinb@ariel.ucs.unimelb.EDU.AU)
   26    [ 13]   Domenico De Vitto (devitto@spearmint)
-> 27 + [ 23]    Pete Clinch (pjclinch@dux.dundee.ac.uk)
   28    [ 24]   randy baer (randy.baer@310.mechanic.fidonet.org)
   29    [ 20]   Ellster (COATES@UMUC.UMD.EDU)
   30 + [ 25]    Rick Stanley (stanleyr@acf4.nyu.edu)
   31 + [ 16]    Paul Ward (ward@appliedmicro.ns.ca)

    <n>=set current to n, TAB=next unread, c)atchup, d)isplay toggle,
       h)elp, j=line down, k=line up, q)uit, t)ag, z=mark unread
```

This is a listing of the fourth thread of the previous example. In addition to the three new articles (marked with a **+**), the articles that you have already seen are also displayed. This is somewhat of a departure from other newsreaders, which usually don't display articles you have already read. The topic is displayed in the heading, and each article shows author's name and the number of lines in the article.

Searching Through Subject Lines

One of the less obvious, but extremely useful, features of *tin* is that it allows you to search (either forward or backward) through subject lines. Searching is case-insensitive, which means it doesn't matter whether you use upper- or lowercase letters; *tin* will match characters regardless of case.

When you're viewing a particular group, and you're at the subject-line level (i.e., not viewing a specific message), you can search forward through subject lines by typing a forward slash (/) and then entering the text to find. When you type the slash, *tin* provides a search prompt at the bottom of the screen and moves the text cursor there. You enter the text you want to search for and press the Return key. In the following figure, the user is searching for "rail." (Since this is a European travel group, there are frequent postings about rail travel.)

```
            rec.travel.europe (342T 502A OK OH R)              h=help

-> 1  + 3   Scenic Rail Trips in Europe              Pertti Tapola
    2  + 3   Non-smokers: Avoid Air France            W. Henry
    3  +     Hotel in Schipol Airport, Amsterdam      henry mensch
    4  +     Video Tape Conversion (PAL/SECAM/NTSC)   Vasily Nasedkin
    5  +     Directory of travel information available via  Brian Lucas
    6  +     Directory of tourist information offics world  Brian Lucas
    7  +     Index to rec.travel ftp archive          Brian Lucas
    8  +     Internet Travel Info.--25 October GNN Travele  Allen Noren
    9  +     Chunnel Info                             Erik Evrard
   10  +     Antique shops in Strasbourg, France--where?  Erik Evrard
   11  + 2   Beerhalls in Munich                      Franz Betzel
   12  + 3   Cheapest Air Fares!                      Holger Groth
   13  + 2   Day trips from London                    edente@pearl.tufts
   14  +     Carte Musee (Paris)                      Richard M. West
   15  + 2   Hiking in Ireland (Inishowen)            Sean Fitzpatrick
   16  +     Guidebooks covering all of East Europe   Sean Fitzpatrick
   17  + 5   Fast car for the autobahn?               Markus Imhof
   18  + 2   BritRail luggage storage?                Mark Brader
   19  +     WWII Museums (France/Eng/Ger)            M.A.Hearnden@lut.a
   20  +     test                                     abal@msg.ti.com

Search forwards [london]> rail
```

In this case, when the user initiates the search (by hitting Return), the highlighting bar skips to the subject line:

```
   18  +  BritRail luggage storage?                Mark Brader
```

Looking back at our sample screen, notice that the previous text searched for ("london") appears as part of the prompt. This feature allows someone to search multiple times for the same text, without entering it over and over. Now that the user has entered "rail" once, she can simply type a slash and then hit the Return key to find the next occurrence.

If you suspect that searching backwards would be faster in some cases, you can perform the same kind of search in that direction simply by initiating the procedure with a question mark (?) rather than a forward slash.

Reading Articles

When you select an article for reading from the article-selection or thread-browsing levels, you are placed in the article-browsing level, where you can view the selected article and perform other operations, such as saving it and replying to it. The example below shows a typical screen in reading mode:

```
Sun, 12 Jun 1994 03:00:32  news.announce.newusers     Thread 14 of 21
Lines 816    Answers to Frequently Asked Questions    No responses
netannounce@deshaw.com                          Mark Moraes


Archive-name: usenet-faq/part1
Original-author: jerry@eagle.UUCP (Jerry Schwarz)
Comment: enhanced & edited until 5/93 by spaf@cs.purdue.edu (Gene Spafford)
Last-change: 23 Mar 1994 by moraes@deshaw.com (Mark Moraes)


              Frequently Submitted/Asked Items

This document discusses some questions and topics that occur
repeatedly on USENET. They frequently are submitted by new users, and
result in many followups, sometimes swamping groups for weeks. The
purpose of this note is to head off these annoying events by answering
some questions and warning about the inevitable consequence of asking
others. If you don't like these answers, let the poster of thie
article know.

   <n>=set current to n, TAB=next unread, /=search pattern, ^K)ill/select,
     a)uthor search, B)ody search, c)atchup, f)ollowup, K=mark read,
     |=pipe, m)ail, o=print, q)uit, r)eply mail, s)ave, t)ag, w=post
```

The header shows several pieces of information, starting at the top line of the screen: The date and time the message was posted, the newsgroup (*news.announce.newusers*), the thread number, the number of lines in the posting (816), the subject (Answers to Frequently...), and the number of response to this article (none). The third line identifies the author (Mark Moraes).

Paging through the article is straightforward. Pressing the space bar or the down arrow pages through the article a screen at a time; if you're on the last screen, this proceeds to the next article. Typing **b** or the up arrow pages backwards one screen, and typing **n**, the right arrow, or the Tab key takes you to the next article.

p takes you to the previous article. The left arrow takes you back to the article or thread-selection menu.

We've spent a lot of time detailing the arrow keys. Particularly for new users, the arrow keys are one of *tin*'s most attractive features; you can do all your basic newsreading with these four keys. Not only that, the interface is fairly intuitive: the right arrow takes you "in" to the next level, the left arrow takes you "out," and down arrows move around vertically at the current level. There's no other news reader where you can accomplish so much with so little.

There are a lot of other commands–for saving articles, decoding articles, and so on. We'll cover many of these commands later in this chapter; so far, you should have enough to get started. The two essential keys are the Tab key and the space bar. Pressing the Tab key takes you to the next unread article; pressing the space bar pages through the article. Again, you can type **h** to see the help screens, and **H** to turn the on-screen help reminders on and off.

A Few Essentials

Although *tin* has quite a few commands, all you need to get going is the ability to select and read articles, and you can do that with the arrow keys. There are a few other essential commands that we'll cover in this section. Take a moment to glance through it, and then proceed to the next section, where we will step through a sample *tin* session. Afterwards, we'll proceed to some of *tin*'s more advanced features.

Quitting tin

To exit any level of *tin*, issue the quit command by typing either an uppercase or lowercase **Q**. An uppercase **Q** exits *tin* immediately; a lowercase **q** takes you to the next higher level in the newsreading hierarchy. When you quit, *tin* updates your configuration files, records articles you have read, and performs other necessary bookkeeping chores.

You can also use the left-arrow key to exit from any level of *tin*. If you're at the top level, you exit from *tin* as described above.

Getting Help

tin provides two ways to get help online. First, as mentioned previously, a brief help message appears at the bottom of every screen. If you don't see this message, type **H**. (If the message is already visible, typing **H** again turns it off; once you're experienced, you may prefer to save the screen space.) In addition, each level has several help screens associated with it. Typing **h** displays the help

screen for your current level. The example below shows the first help screen for
the group-selection level.

```
        Group Selection Commands (page 1 of 2)

^D^U       Down (^U = up) one page
^F^B       Down (^B = up) one page
<SPACE>b   Down (b = back up) one page
jk         Down (k = up) one line (vi style)
4$         Choose group 4 ($ = choose last group)
g          Choose group by name
n<TAB>     Choose next group with unread news and enter it
N          Choose next group with unread news
/?         Choose group by group name string forward (? = backward) search
           (all searches are case-insensitive and wrap around to all groups)
#          Choose range of groups to be affected by following command
<CR>       Read chosen group
w          Write (post article to) chosen group
cC         Mark all articles in chosen group read (C = and choose next unread)
z          Mark all articles in chosen group unread
^R         Reset .newsrc so all articles are unread
y          Yank in/out unsubscribed groups from .newsrc
Y          Yank in active file to see any new news
  PgDn,End,<SPACE>,^D - page down. PgUp,Home,b,^U - page up. <CR>,q - quit
```

Emergencies

Pressing the Escape key cancels whatever operation is in progress and returns
you to whatever you were doing previously. This is handy if you become
confused about what you have typed, or if you accidentally type a command you
don't want (saving an article or posting a message, for example).

Typing **CTRL-L** refreshes (redisplays) the screen. This is handy if the screen is
garbled for some reason.

Navigating

If you want to jump directly to a particular newsgroup, use the **g** (goto)
command. This is done from either the group-selection or article-selection level.
When you type **g**, *tin* prompts you for the name of a newsgroup. If you have
subscribed to the newsgroup, the cursor is placed on the newsgroup. If you are
not already subscribed to the group, you are asked where you would like to
place it in the list. In this example, let's jump directly to the newsgroup
rec.music.folk, to which you are not currently subscribed.

```
    Goto newsgroup []> rec.music.folk
```

After you type the name of the newsgroup, *tin* asks you where in the newsgroup list you would like to place the newsgroup. Selecting **$** puts the newsgroup at the end of the newsgroup list. Typing a number means to place the newsgroup in that position in the list (i.e., **1** means place it first in the list, **2** means second, etc.). The default is the current position in the newsgroup list. We'll take this default by pressing the Enter key.

```
Position rec.music.folk in group list (1,2,..,$) [10]> enter
```

We discuss more newsgroup commands in the section, "Working with Newsgroups," which appears later in this chapter.

A tin Session

NOTE

If you need to exit this session at any time, type **q** to exit the various menu levels. If you are ever stuck at a prompt, press the Escape key to return to command mode.

Now that we have some of the basics out of the way, let's step through a *tin* session. The following screen is what you see the first time you run *tin*. Later invocations are pretty much the same, only you won't see the initial welcome screen. Remember the various levels we've discussed.

First, we need to start *tin*. From the UNIX command prompt type:[*]

```
% tin
```

As this is our first time using *tin*, we receive the welcome screen, which only appears this one time. From now on, when opening *tin*, you are placed directly in the group-selection screen.

```
tin 1.3 310394BETA PL0 [UNIX ISO2ASC] (c) Copyright 1991-94 Iain Lea.

Welcome to tin, a full screen threaded Netnews reader. It can read news locally
(ie. <spool>/news) or remotely (-r option) from a NNTP (Network News Transport
Protocol) server. tin -h lists the available command line options.

Tin has five newsreading levels, the newsgroup selection page, the spooldir
selection page, the group index page, the thread listing page and the article
viewer. Help is available at each level by pressing the 'h' command.
```

---

[*] If this doesn't work, check with your administrator. Depending on how *tin* is configured at your site, you may have to type **tin -r** to connect to your news server.

Move up/down by using the terminal arrow keys or 'j' and 'k'. Use PgUp/PgDn or
Ctrl-U and Ctrl-D to page up/down. Enter a newsgroup by pressing RETURN/TAB.

Articles, threads, tagged articles or articles matching a pattern can be mailed
('m' command), printed ('o' command), saved ('s' command), piped ('|' command).
Use the 'w' command to post a news article, the 'f'/'F' commands to post a
follow-up to an existing news article and the 'r'/'R' commands to reply via
mail to an existing news articles author. The 'M' command allows the operation
of tin to be configured via a menu.

For more information read the manual page, README, INSTALL, TODO and FTP files.
Please send bug reports/comments to the programs author with the 'R' command.

Typing any key takes you to the group-selection screen. If you have read news
before, you will see your subscribed newsgroups. If you have never read news
before, you are automatically shown a list of all newsgroups on the system.

```
            Group Selection (news.utdallas.edu 32)        h=help

 ->  1  148  bit.listserv.christia
      2    3  dfw.eats
      3       dfw.flame
      4   15  dfw.forsale
      5  178  comp.lang.c++
      6   49  comp.object
      7  225  comp.lang.c
      8   97  news.newusers.questions
      9    6  dfw.general
     10  216  misc.jobs.offered
     11    3  rec.humor.funny
     12  256  soc.culture.asian.american
     13    2  tx.general
     14   13  tx.jobs
     15       utd.acc.announce
     16       utd.acc.downtime

     <n>=set current to n, TAB=next unread, /=search pattern, c)atchup,
  g)oto, j=line down, k=line up, h)elp, m)ove, q)uit, r=toggle all/unread,
  s)ubscribe, S)ub pattern, u)nsubscribe, U)nsub pattern, y)ank in/out
```

The available newsgroups vary from system to system, so let's go to a group that
should be on just about all systems: *news.newusers.questions.*[*] This is an excellent
group for learning your way around the Net; I strongly suggest you subscribe to it
for a while. Many questions that draw sharp answers[†] in other groups receive
patient and comprehensive explanations here.

---

[*] If this group isn't on your system, complain to your system administrator!
[†] See Chapter 7 for details on posting etiquette.

To get to *news.newusers.questions*, type **g**. You are then prompted for the group you wish to view. Type **news.newusers.questions** and press the Return key.

    Goto newsgroup []> **news.newusers.questions**

If you are not subscribed to this group, you are asked where to place it in the newsgroup list. Press the Enter key to accept the default, which is to place it at the current position. If you haven't moved the cursor around, you will still be at the top of the newsgroup list and your current position is "1".

    Position news.newusers.questions in group list (1,2,..,$) [1]> *enter*

To view the article-selection screen for *news.newusers.questions*, press Enter again.

```
        news.newusers.questions (13T 31A 0K 0H R)        h=help

-> 1 +    remote access to a file ?F+
   2 + 4 Dumb Newbie-esque Question                  James "Kibo" Parry
   3 +    This is a test                             Amy K. Smith
   4 +    Wingohper Question...                       Tom Malone
   5 + 5 America Online -worth it??                  Fred Carter
   6 +    Getting Cursor to Move in Edit             Ellen Bell
   7 +    Please help for decompression              Jeffrey Hall Jenni
   8 +    nn problem HELP!!!!!                        steve drennan
   9 + 7 In an old house in Paris...                 Allegra Chan Harrison
  10 +    FAQ on making and using a .signature file  Britt
  11 + 2 Test - Please Read and Respond              John J Kane
  12 +    Answers to Frequently Asked Questions about U  Mark Moraes
  13 + 2 FTP reading at the site?                    Jeffrey Hall Jenni

<n>=set current to n, TAB=next unread, /=search pattern, ^K)ill/select,
a)uthor search, c)atchup, j=line down, k=line up, K=mark read, l)ist thread,
|=pipe, m)ail, o=print, q)uit, r=toggle all/unread, s)ave, t)ag, w=post
```

Let's take a minute and review a few things. First, there are 13 threads of conversation on the screen, labeled 1 through 13. The top line reminds us which group we are looking at, and the number of unread articles (31 articles in 13 threads), and a brief reminder on how to view the help screens. The bottom of the screen presents a brief summary of some frequently used commands:

The articles are grouped by conversation thread. All of the threads are marked by a plus sign (**+**), indicating that the articles in the threads have not been read. The threads with a number to the right of the plus sign have more than one unread article. For example, the second thread (Dumb Newbie-esque Question) has four unread articles.

Now let's read some articles. Article 10 ("FAQ on making and using a *.signature* file") looks interesting, so let's read it by moving the cursor down to the article by typing the **j** key or the down-arrow key. When the cursor is positioned on that article, press the Enter key or the right arrow key to read the article. You could also have gone directly to the article by typing its number (**10**) and pressing the Enter key twice: once to select the article; the second time to read it.

After you select an article, *tin* places you in reading mode:

```
Sun, 12 Jun 1994 03:00:32  news.announce.newusers    Thread 10 of  21
Lines 102    FAQ on making and using a .signature file
tierna@agora.rdrop.com                        Britt Klein

Archive-name: usenet/signature-faq
News-newusers-questions-archive-name: signature-faq
Last-modified: 1994/12/1
Author: tierna@agora.rdrop.com - with tips gathered from posts
        and submissions and credited wherever possible
Comment: Available for FTP from rtfm.mit.edu in usenet/news/newusers/questions
        and by email from tierna@agora.rdrop.com.


              FAQ on making and using a .signature file
                        by Britt Klein

Last updated: 1 December 1994

What follows are the bare basics on how to create a .signature file and get
it to append to your news posts and email.  It *should* work for most users.

  <n>=set current to n, TAB=next unread, /=search pattern, ^K)ill/select,
  a)uthor search, B)ody search, c)atchup, f)ollowup, K=mark read,
   |=pipe, m)ail, o=print, q)uit, r)eply mail, s)ave, t)ag, w=post
```

Most of the commands in reading mode deal with moving around in the article. Pressing the space bar or **CTRL-F** displays the next screenful of text; **CTRL-B** scrolls up a screen; **CTRL-L** refreshes the display. Typing **n** proceeds to the next message or group, as does pressing the space bar on the last screen of the message. Pressing the Tab key proceeds to the next unread article.

For now press the space bar to see the next screen of the article.

```
Thread 10 of 21 (page 2): FAQ on making and using a .signature file

I'm going to try and pop this thing off every 4 days or so, just to keep
it in people's faces and possibly eliminate the constant-request syndrome.
Therefore this might be repeated twice in some postings:
        Available for FTP from rtfm.mit.edu in usenet/news/newusers/questions
        by email from tierna@agora.rdrop.com.

Anything in quotes is a prompt-line command and should work verbatim.
(Also, the terminology herein is quite near the lowest level of enduser.
This is on purpose, as the last thing new users need is to be confused by
too much technicalese.)
```

This is formulated for *nix-based systems, outside of that realm I'm
out of my level of expertise big-time. I never claimed to know everything,
just enough to get around.

Yes, DO email for clarification or further information or advice. I'm
perfectly willing to help people if they ask.

```
<n>=set current to n, TAB=next unread, /=search pattern, ^K)ill/select,
   a)uthor search, B)ody search, c)atchup, f)ollowup, K=mark read,
   |=pipe, m)ail, o=print, q)uit, r)eply mail, s)ave, t)ag, w=post
```

This looks like some interesting stuff that requires careful reading. Instead of
reading it right now, save the file for later, when there's more time. To save the
file, type **s**. You receive several prompts. We'll cover the simplest responses now
and other options later in this chapter.

```
Save a)rticle, t)hread, h)ot, p)attern, T)agged articles, q)uit: a
```

Type **a** to save an individual article.

```
Save filename []> news.announce.newusers
```

You can type any filename here. It's convenient to pick filenames that reflect the
group the article was posted to.[*]

```
Process n)one, s)har, u)ud, l)ist zoo, e)xt zoo, L)ist zip, E)xt zip, q)uit: n
```

tin wants to know whether to apply any special processing to the file after saving
it. For now, type **n** to indicate no special processing; we'll cover other options
later. *tin* displays:

```
Saving...
```

to indicate that it is saving the file. If the file exists, *tin* asks for confirmation
before saving the file by appending it (adding it to the end) to the existing file.

```
File /ruby/home/mharriso/News/news.announce.questions exists. Append? (y/n): y
```

If you wish to append the article to the file, type **y**. If you don't want to save the
article, type **n**. If you save the article, *tin* gives you confirmation:

```
-- 1 Article(s) saved --
```

The saved file is a normal ASCII text file; you can print it or read it with your
favorite editor.

From this point, you have several options: you can continue paging through the
article by pressing the space bar; you can go to the next article by typing **n**; or

---

[*] If your system doesn't support long filenames, try saving the article in *news/newusers/questions*.

you can type **q** to return to the article-selection level. For now, exit *tin* to take a look at what news files *tin* has created. Type **q** three times: once to return to the article selection level, again to return to the group selection level, and once more to exit *tin*.

Now, let's take a look at the files *tin* has created.

```
% cd
% ls -aF .newsrc .tin News
.newsrc

.tin:
./        .mail/       .save/        attributes    posted
../       .mailidx/    active        filter        tinrc
.index/   .news/       active.mail   kill

News:
./        ../       news.newusers.questions
```

First, *tin* has created the *.newsrc* file, which keeps track of your subscribed groups and articles you have read. Additionally, *tin* has created a *.tin* directory, in which it keeps miscellaneous administrative information about your session (you may see different files here, depending on your version of *tin* and the customizations you have made). The file *tinrc*, for example, keeps track of any customizations you make to *tin*.*

Finally, let's take a look at our news directory, where we saved the article from *news.announce.newusers*. It is right where we expected it to be, in the file *News/ news.announce.newusers*.

```
% ls News
news.announce.newusers
```

More Commands

This section covers some more of *tin*'s useful features. We'll start with some commands that deal with newsgroups and files.

Working with Newsgroups

The group-selection screen has several commands for working with newsgroups.

y "Yank in" all newsgroups. This includes unsubscribed newsgroups on the group-selection screen. Typing **y** again yanks out the unsubscribed newsgroups or removes them from the selection screen.

---

* See "Customizing tin" later in this chapter.

This is a very useful feature; it allows you to browse the master newsgroup list, reading groups that might be interesting without having to subscribe to them.

s   Subscribe to the current newsgroup

u   Unsubscribe to the current newsgroup. Unsubscribed newsgroups are marked by a "u" in the newsgroup list. The next time you run *tin*, the unsubscribed newsgroups are not shown in the list.

S   Wildcard* subscription. Any groups matching the given wildcard are subscribed to. For example, entering the wildcard "*apple*" would subscribe to any newsgroup containing "apple" as part of its name, such as *comp.sources.apple2* and *comp.protocols.appletalk*. Be sure and "yank in" unsubscribed newsgroups before you run this command.

U   Wildcard unsubscription. This unsubscribes any groups matching the given wildcard. For example, entering the wildcard "*apple*" would unsubscribe to the newsgroups subscribed to in the previous example.

m   Move the newsgroup. This command lets you rearrange the newsgroup list to your liking.

/   Search for string. This command searches forward in the list to find the next newsgroup with the specified string in its name or description.

The wildcard subscribe and unsubscribe commands (**S** and **U**) are incredibly useful; it's too bad we had to wait until *tin* was released to have them! They solve very nicely the nasty startup problem: trimming down your subscription list from the thousands of groups that may be present on your news server. For example, if you're not interested in the *talk* hierarchy, you can quickly get rid of all the *talk* groups by unsubscribing to *talk.*; if you are interested in all newsgroups devoted to security, you can subscribe to **security**; and so on. With a few operations, you can quickly trim your subscriptions down to a reasonable list.

Seeing Old Articles

A standard feature of all newsreaders is the ability to keep track of previously read articles, so that you don't have to see them each time you read news. It's usually a good feature, keeping you from having to page through tons of old stuff you don't want to see.

Occasionally, you will want to go back and look for a particular article or topic. You can easily recall all messages in a newsgroup by typing **r**. This toggles between reading all messages in the group and reading only unread messages in

---

* *tin* does not use standard regular expressions for matching. It uses shell-like wildcard notation where an asterisk (*****) matches any sequence of characters and a question mark (**?**) matches any single character.

the group. Of course, once an article has been "expired" (i.e., deleted from your server), it's gone permanently.

Articles: Current, Hot, Tagged, and Otherwise

Most of *tin*'s commands for working with individual articles (such as saving, mailing, printing, etc.) can also deal with groups of articles. For example, whenever you save an article, you see the prompt:

```
Save a)rticle, t)hread, h)ot, p)attern, T)agged articles, q)uit:
```

Rather than going through the details of this menu for each of the commands that use it, we'll cover it here once and not mention it in the remaining sections.

a)rticle
Refers to the current article, the one you were reading when you typed the command.

t)hread
Refers to all the articles in the current conversation thread. If you want to see the articles that are a part of the thread, go to the article-selection level (press **q** once to return to the article, and **q** again to return to the article-selection screen) and press **l** (lowercase L) to see the thread.

h)ot
"Hot" articles are articles that have been automatically selected. See the section "Killing and Selecting Articles" later in this chapter.

p)attern
Prompts you for a wildcard text pattern and selects all articles with subject lines that match.

T)agged articles
Tag interesting articles by typing **t** from the article-browsing or article-selection levels. When you select this option, the requested operation is performed on all the tagged articles in the order you tagged them. Tagging is a great way to get a sequence of messages that have arrived out of order into the correct order for printing, decoding, saving, or whatever.

q)uit
Quits the menu; you can also press the Escape key.

These options give you a great deal of flexibility when saving or printing articles. The most commonly used option is **a**, which operates on just the current article. If you wanted to print the article you are reading, you would type **o** (output) followed by **a** (article). To print all the articles in the thread, you would type **o** **t** (thread).

Gone Fishing

If you're going to be away from your terminal for a while, and don't feel like toting a laptop and modem to Caracas, Morocco, Tibet, or your mom's, *tin* offers a couple of ways to save your news for later.

The *-M* option specifies that new articles will be mailed to you. Receiving articles by mail is a reasonable alternative if you anticipate a very limited amount of traffic. Perhaps you only want to monitor a single newsgroup and the number of postings to that group is generally moderate. Using the command:

```
% tin -M val@ora.com -c
```

I had some news from *rec.travel.europe* mailed to me:

```
N185 singsai@hal.com  Thu Mar  2 18:15 26/720   The address of Norwegian Tour
N186 shef@vms.cis.pitt.edu Thu Mar  2 18:15  19/937   Seder in England?
N187 kmk2@Lehigh.EDU   Thu Mar  2 18:15  34/1356  Organic Farms/work in europe
N188 shef@vms.cis.pitt.edu Thu Mar  2 18:15  22/874   Daytrips from Edinburgh
N189 pbt@mail.ast.cam.ac.uk Thu Mar  2 18:15  34/1467  Re: How crowded is europe
N190 jorge.andres@canrem.com Thu Mar  2 18:15  47/2152 Spanish,English,French
N191 robb@argus.co.za  Thu Mar  2 18:15  45/1842  Is there a euro rail tick
N192 dswayze@is.dal.ca Thu Mar  2 18:15  71/3670  Re: Come on! Will my came
N193 lairg@lairg.win-uk.net Thu Mar  2 18:15  59/2716  Re: Daytrips from Edinbur
N194 Jens@INFORM.inform-bbs.dk Thu Mar  2 18:15  24/976   Irish Folk-festivals?
N195 lairg@lairg.win-uk.net Thu Mar  2 18:15  37/1467  Re: Ireland --> England
N196 rbrown@vaxa.stevens-tech.edu Thu Mar  2 18:15  41/1262  Re: Air Fares
N197 den@oakwood.win-uk.net Thu Mar  2 18:15 26/961   Specific UK travel newsgr
```

This can be a neat way to go through older news because it mimics the experience of getting it in a more timely fashion using a newsreader. You just browse the subject lines and read what you want. However, newshounds should beware. If you request a lot of news by this method, your mailbox will be flooded. In testing, I almost brought our system to its knees.

If you want to receive postings from several groups or even one or two popular ones, or you'll be away for an extended period, have *tin* save your postings in a directory. The *-S* option specifies that tin should save postings under *~/News,* or you can supply an alternate parent directory using the *-f* option.

When you request your news to be saved, *tin* creates a subdirectory tree that mirrors the newsgroup hierarchy. What does this mean? Well, say you're monitoring the newsgroup *rec.travel.europe*, postings will be saved in the directory *~/News/rec/travel/europe*. According to this scheme, under *~/News* you might have *comp*, *rec*, and *alt* subdirectories. Under *comp*, you might have subdirectories for *mail, sys, sources, windows,* etc. Under *rec*, I have *pets* and *travel*. Under *travel*, I have *europe*.

—continued—

Postings are saved in individual files that are named for the group-specific message number. In order to read news you have saved by this method, start tin up with the *-R* option. Saved messages for each newsgroup will be prepended to any new messages. In order to read them, you must currently be subscribed to the groups in question.

tin also sends you an email catalog of the messages saved—basically a list of message numbers and their corresponding subject lines. (You also get a catalog when you use *-M* to have messages mailed to you.) Here's a sample catalog:

```
To: val
Subject: NEWS LOG Thu Mar 2 18:15:33 1995
Status: R

Saved rec.travel.europe...
[12239]  The address of Norwegian Tourist Office in US
[12241]  Seder in England?
[12244]  Daytrips from Edinburgh
[12216]  Is there a euro rail ticket - unlimited travel?
[12245]  Air Fares
[12228]  Spanish,English,French
[12213]  Come on! Will my camera really get stolen?
[12240]  Sicily
[12248]  Re(2): Where should I go?
[12209]  Daytrips from Edinburgh
[12210]  Ireland --> England
[12225]  Irish Folk-festivals?
[12220]  Specific UK travel newsgroup?
```

Whether you decide to have *tin* mail or save your news, it's a good idea to run it automatically on a fairly frequent basis while you're away. This will minimize the amount of traffic at any one time. In most UNIX environments, you should be able to automate this process using a *crontab* file. (If you're not familiar with the *cron* mechanism, this may get a little confusing, but hang in there.) Here's a sample file I'll call *cron1*:

```
15 6 * * 1,2,3,4,5 /home/val/bin/cronme
```

I will give this one-line script as an argument to the *crontab* command. The line specifies that at 15 minutes past the hour of 6:00 A.M., on each of the five weekdays (1, 2, 3, 4, 5), *cron* will run my script */home/val/bin/cronme*.

Why can't I just give my *tin* command at the end of this line? Why do I need to nest this script in here? This is the only tricky part. tin requires that you pass it a terminal setting or it dies. The only way for me to do this in my environment and also automate the process is to create a script. Here's the very simple script */home/val/bin/cronme*:

—continued—

```
    #!/bin/sh TERM=vt100 /usr/local/bin/tin -S -c exit 0
```

This script tells *tin* what the terminal setting is and it asks *tin* to save my news postings. Period. If I want my news mailed instead, I would replace the third line with:

```
    /usr/local/bin/tin -M val@ora.com -c
```

To automate this process, I run the original *cron1* file (that calls */home/val/bin/ cronme*), using *crontab*.

```
    Bcrontab cron1
```

How do you turn this business off when you get back from vacation? The easiest way is to run *crontab* again, this time without any arguments:

```
    crontab
```

Press the Return key and type **CTRL-D**. To make sure your *crontab* process is gone, enter **crontab -1**. You should get no output.

— *Valerie Quercia*

Automatically Decoding Articles

In the previous section, we saw how to save articles to disk using the **s** (save) command. In addition to handling normal text files, *tin* can automatically decode files that have been posted in a variety of formats.[*] These include multipart shar files and uuencoded binary files. *tin* also supports automatically extracting and listing the table of contents of *zoo* and *zip* files.

As an example of how to do this, we'll unpack some software shipped as a binary *zip* file.

There are several groups where binary files are regularly posted. One of the most common hierarchies is *comp.binaries.*[*,†] where packages are posted for various computers and operating systems. In this example, let's unpack a posting from the group *comp.binaries.ms-windows*.

```
    comp.binaries.ms-windows (10T 10A 0K 0H)        h=help

-> 1    v7i66: music.zip (part 01/06), Windows MIDI S  Sonja Struben 257-
   2    v7i67: music.zip (part 02/06), Windows MIDI S  Sonja Struben 257-
   3    v7i68: music.zip (part 03/06), Windows MIDI S  Sonja Struben 257-
   4    v7i69: music.zip (part 04/06), Windows MIDI S  Sonja Struben 257-
```

---

[*] See Chapter 7 for a discussion of these formats.

[†] One nice feature about most of the groups in this hierarchy is that they are moderated, so you don't have a lot of "noise" messages to wade through.

```
 5    v7i70: music.zip (part 05/06), Windows MIDI S  Sonja Struben 257-
 6    v7i71: music.zip (part 06/06), Windows MIDI S  Sonja Struben 257-
 7 +  v7i72: seahaven.zip (part 01/03), Seahaven To  Cary Farrier
 8 +  v7i73: seahaven.zip (part 02/03), Seahaven To  Cary Farrier
 9 +  v7i74: seahaven.zip (part 03/03), Seahaven To  Cary Farrier
10 +  v7inf3: cbmsw.faq (part 01/01), Informational  cbmsw@Saigon.COM
```

Start by taking a look at message 1, to see if this looks like an interesting package and to make a note of the file's checksum.

```
Fri, 08 Apr 1994 01:15:35  comp.binaries.ms-windows   Thread  1 of  10
Lines 1055   v7i66: music.zip (part 01/06), Windows MIDI No responses
strubens@cuug.ab.ca Sonja Struben 257-0261 at TL Consulting - Saigon.COM (Viet

Music Sculptor for Windows v1.2
by Aleph Omega Software

Very easy to use MIDI sequencer with
music keyboard window.

Record, edit, and play music.
Use with either external MIDI keyboard
or music keyboard window which
can be played using mouse or computer
keyboard.

[...]
[Checksums obtained with the 4.3BSD "sum" or System V "sum -r" command.]
[...]

checksum   size (bytes) file
  1106   228502    music.zip
```

Now return to the article-selection menu and issue the save command by typing **s**. We want to save all the articles that have the pattern *music.zip* in the subject line, so we type **p** and press the Enter key to enter the subject.

```
    Save a)rticle, t)hread, h)ot, p)attern, T)agged articles, q)uit: p
    Enter regex pattern []> *music.zip*
```

Choose a temporary filename; it doesn't matter what it is as long as the name is unique, since you will delete the intermediate files after unpacking the file. Specify your wish to uudecode the article by typing **u**.

```
Save filename []> music-tmp
Process n)one, s)har, u)ud, l)ist zoo, e)xt zoo, L)ist zip, E)xt zip, q)uit: u
```

You could also have typed **L** to list the contents of the file or **E** to extract the files from the archive. *tin* displays several messages detailing its progress, and then displays the file's checksum, so you can verify that the file was uncorrupted in transit. The file size is displayed both in blocks and bytes, since both values are used by various versions of the checksum program.

```
Saving...4
Post processing...
Uudecoding...
Checksum of /home/zul/mharriso/News/music.zip...

01106  224  228502 bytes
```

Finally, you can delete the saved article files, since you've extracted the desired uuencoded file:

```
Delete saved files that have been post processed? (y/n): y
```

Now you're left with the desired binary *music.zip* file. If you had selected the *extract zip* option, *tin* would also have extracted the components of the *zip* file as well. Since most *zip* files posted to the Net are MS-DOS related, they are destined to be downloaded to a PC and it is not necessary to extract the files on the UNIX box where *tin* is running.

Occasionally, the postings are received at your site out of order (e.g., the third article is before the second article), which causes problems when you try to unpack a file. An easy way to work around this problem is to use the tagging mechanism: select the first article, tag it by typing **t**, select the second, tag it, and so on. Since tagged files are saved in the order in which they were tagged, you can tag the articles in the proper order (e.g., tag the first article first, second article second, etc.). When you save the tagged articles, they are unpacked in the proper order.

Decrypting ROT13 Articles

As discussed previously, someone occasionally posts an article others may not wish to see. These are posted in ROT13 format, and look like this:

```
Ubj qb lbh gryy vg'f n pbzchgre ercnvezna gung unf n syag gver
orfvqr gur ebnq? Ur'f gur bar punatvat bhg gverf gb frr jung'f gur
ceboyrz.

Ubj qb lbh gryy vg'f n pbzchgre ercnvezna gung'f bhg bs tnf? Ur'f
gur bar punatvat bhg gverf gb frr jung'f gur ceboyrz.
```

Follow this two-step procedure to read the encrypted posting:

1. Make sure that you really want to read the post. If the subject says "offensive to IBM salesmen," and you are particularly sensitive about IBM salesmen,

don't read the post! If you do read the post and are offended, don't complain. You were warned.

2. Execute the decrypt command by typing **d**.

    > How do you tell it's a computer repairman that has a flat tire beside the road? He's the one changing out tires to see what's the problem.

    > How do you tell it's a computer repairman that's out of gas? He's the one changing out tires to see what's the problem.

Posting Messages

CAUTION

A posted message is seen by tens of thousands of people all over the world. Keep this in mind when you are posting! The group *misc.test* is designated for test postings. Try posting there a few times before posting somewhere else.

There are two ways to post messages in *tin*. You can either post an original message using the **w** (write) command, or you can follow up to someone else's posting with the **f** (follow up) command. The write command can be issued from any level; the follow-up command can be issued while browsing an article.

Posting New Articles

When you type **w**, *tin* asks you the subject and then places you in your editor so you can write the text of the message. Here's a quick example. Let's post a small message to the group *misc.test*. Begin by entering **misc.test*** and typing **w** to start the posting process.

```
Post subject []> test post
```

Enter a brief subject line here. Try to be as specific as possible. For example, if you are posting a question on *comp.unix.questions*, avoid subjects like "unix question." What else would you be posting there?

When you answer this question, you are placed in the editor for you to type your message. The headers at the top show the subject and newsgroup. You may edit the contents of the header, but don't change any of the keywords at the beginning of the line. Be sure to leave the blank line between the header and the message body; the news posting software uses the blank line to tell where the header ends. *tin* will reject your message if the blank line isn't there.

---

* You can use the **g** (goto) command to do this as described in the previous section.

```
Subject: test post
Newsgroups: misc.test
Summary:
Keywords:

test post
--
Mark Harrison
```

Once you finish typing your posting, save the temporary file and exit from the editor. You then have the chance to:

- Quit; nothing is posted, and your article will be lost.

- Edit (re-edit) the posting. You are then placed back in the editor.

- Post the article. This is the default action.

```
                    Check Prepared Article

Your article will be posted to the following newsgroup:
  misc.test   For testing of network software. Very boring.



q)uit, e)dit, p)ost: p
a)bort e)dit m)ail r)eedit s)end v)iew w)rite
Action: (post article)
```

Depending on your system, it takes anywhere from a few minutes to over a day for your message to start propagating to other sites. You can expect to see replies or follow ups soon after this. See "Test Messages" in Chapter 7 for an example of what to expect when posting to *misc.test*.

Following Up Another Article

The procedure for following up another person's posting is essentially the same as for posting a new article. The differences are:

- Type an **f** to post a follow-up to the article you are reading. The text of the article you are responding to is included in your response; type an **F** to follow up an article without quoting it.

- You won't be asked for a subject line; it's taken from the article to which you're replying.

After you have responded to these questions, just follow the steps outlined in the previous "Posting New Articles" section.

If you suddenly regret having sent a message, wait until the message appears in your article-selection menu; select it; and type **D**. You may only cancel your own postings. It is impossible to cancel the message completely, but this will limit its circulation. You will probably still see some responses.

Sending Mail

tin provides some basic services for sending regular electronic mail. You can reply to the author of a particular article, or forward an interesting article to others who may not read news.

Reply

The most common reason for using mail from within *tin* is to reply to the author of an article without sending a message to the entire newsgroup. We'll discuss network etiquette more thoroughly in Chapter 7, but for now we'll note that mail should be used whenever a network-wide response is inappropriate. For example, if you want to buy someone's comic book collection, you obviously wouldn't post your offer to all of *misc.forsale*. Etiquette aside, such a posting could be counterproductive: you might lead someone to make a better offer.

To send a reply, type **r** or **R** while reading the article (**r** includes the text of the original article in your reply; **R** does not). *tin* then places you in the editor where you can edit your message. When you exit your editor, you are given the choice of quitting, re-editing your message, or sending it to the recipient.

Forwarding a Post via Mail

You may want to forward an interesting article to friends and associates, particularly if you have friends who don't read news. This feature is also a handy way to save articles or give yourself a reminder about something that strikes you: just mail the article to yourself. You'll save yourself the trouble of deleting it from the folder where it was saved. As an example of how this can be used, I usually forward notices of interesting software to myself. The article hanging around in my mailbox reminds me to go out and get the software.

To forward an article, invoke the mail command using **m**, which gives you a prompt with the usual options:

```
Mail a)rticle, t)hread, h)ot, p)attern, T)agged articles, q)uit:
```

You can choose any of these options as described above. You are queried for the recipient's address, and given the choice of quitting, editing the message, or sending it to the recipient.

Killing and Selecting Articles

As you read news, you will often find particular subjects or authors to be very interesting, very boring, or very offensive. *tin* makes it easy to *auto-kill* uninteresting and offensive articles and *auto-select* interesting ones. This can be done in either a particular newsgroup or globally across all newsgroups, on a permanent or temporary basis.

To kill articles, type **CTRL-K** from either the article-selection or article-browsing levels. Press **CTRL-A** to auto-select articles. *tin* displays a screen that allows you to specify which you would like to kill or select. We'll look at the kill screen for in this section; the automatic selection screen is identical except for the heading.

```
                Kill Article Menu

Kill text pattern  :
Apply pattern to   :

Kill Subject: [a test for tin -- ignore        ] (y/n):
Kill From:    [mh@ora.com (Mark A Harrison)     ] (y/n):

Kill Msg-Id:  [<2uu9gp$hge@news.ora.com>        ] (y/n):

Kill Lines: (</>num):
Kill time in days  :

Kill pattern scope : misc.test
Enter text pattern to filter if Subject: & From: lines are not what you want.
```

All you have to do is fill in the screen. Some of the items require you to type text (e.g., the subject of the articles you want to kill); others are a set of options you can circulate through by pressing the space bar. In either case, pressing the Return key sets the current value and moves you to the next line. The bottom line of the screen gives you some help; it explains the line you're on and tells you what your options are.

When you have filled in the screen, you are given the chance to confirm your choices. There's no way to back up to prior fields, so if you wish to correct a mistake, press the Escape key to exit the screen and start over. This is a quick screen to fill out, so it's not as inconvenient as it sounds. Let's go through the items on the screen and see what they do:

Kill text pattern

The wildcard that you want to use as the criterion for the article to be killed or selected. This is used in conjunction with the next field to screen the articles. For example, if you wanted to skip all articles posted by *joe@somewhere.com*, you would enter **joe@somewhere.com** in this field and select one of the "From:" line options in the next field.

Apply pattern to
   You can apply the pattern to any of these choices:

   - Subject: line (case sensitive)

   - Subject: line (ignore case)

   - From: line (case sensitive)

   - From: line (ignore case)

   - Message-Id: line

   It should be obvious how the subject and from lines would be used, but why select on the message ID? The message ID usually contains the name of the site from which the message was posted, so it's a handy way to include or exclude people from a particular site. For example, you could kill all articles posted from the site *total.idiots.com*, or automatically select all articles posted from *total.geniuses.com*.

   Pressing the space bar toggles between the choices.

Kill Subject, Kill From, Kill Msg-Id
   If you did not fill in the Kill text pattern field, you can select one of these fields. Pressing the space bar toggles each field between "yes" and "no."[*]

Kill Lines: (+/-num
   This field kills any articles over or under a certain line count. If you enter a greater-than sign and a number, you can kill or select all articles that have more than that number of lines. If you enter a less-than sign, you can kill or select all articles that have less than that number of lines. This is good for the various source and binary groups, where people frequently make inappropriate postings (i.e., posting questions to a group designated for binaries or source code). For example, to skip over most non-source postings in *comp.sources.misc*, you could kill articles with less than 20 lines (enter **<20**) in the group; virtually any software is longer than this.

Kill time in days
   This can be toggled between "Unlimited" (the default) and "28 days." Twenty-eight days is the default; it can be modified in the *~/.tin/tinrc* file by setting the variable *default_filter_days*.

Kill pattern scope
   This can be toggled to kill/select from either the current group, all groups, or groups in a particular hierarchy (e.g., *misc.*,* or all groups under the *misc* hierarchy).

---

[*] If you select yes for more than one option, *tin* uses the first option selected.

Once you've filled in all the entries, you are given the chance to confirm your selection.

```
q)uit e)dit s)ave kill description: s
```

s saves your kill entry, which takes effect immediately; **q** abandons the entry; and **e** lets you edit or revise it. If you choose to revise your entry, *tin* invokes your editor so you can edit *~/.tin/filter*, where *tin* stores the kill and selection entries. Details on this file are in the next section.

Unkilling

There is no built-in command to undo a kill or select command. Fortunately, it is not difficult to edit the kill file with a text editor. If you wish to view or modify your kill file selections, edit the file *~/.tin/filter.* [*] The following is an example of the *.filter* file, including the comments that are automatically included at the beginning of the file to describe the format.

```
# Global & local filter file for the TIN v1.3 310394 PL0 newsreader
#
# Global format:
#  scope=STRING   Newsgroups (ie. comp.*)  [mandatory]
#  type=NUM       0=kill 1=auto-select (hot) [mandatory]
#  case=NUM       Compare=0 / ignore=1 case when filtering
#  subj=STRING    Subject: line (ie. How to be a wizard)
#  from=STRING    From: line (ie. *Craig Shergold*)
#  msgid=STRING   Message-ID: line (ie. <123@ether.net>)
#  lines=NUM      Lines: line (default 0)
#  time=NUM       Filter period in days (default 28)
#
# Local format:
#  group=STRING   Newsgroup (ie. alt.flame) [mandatory]
#  type=NUM       0=kill 1=auto-select (hot) [mandatory]
#  case=NUM       Compare=0 / ignore=1 case when filtering
#  subj=STRING    Subject: line
#  from=STRING    From: line
#  msgid=STRING   Message-ID: line
#  lines=NUM      Lines: line
#  time=NUM       Filter period in days
#
#  type=...

scope=*
type=1
case=0
from=*Mark Harrison*
time=775392673
```

---

[*] Older versions of *tin* use *~/.tin*/kill.

The comment lines all begin with #. Each kill or auto-select entry is a block of lines, with a blank line before and after. This example shows an auto-select entry beginning with the line scope=* (meaning that the entry applies to all news-groups), and ending with time=77539267 (*tin*'s equivalent to "forever"). type=1 means that this is an auto-select entry, and case=0 means that the auto-select criterion is case-insensitive. from=*Mark Harrison* is the actual selection criterion; articles with "Mark Harrison" anywhere in the "From:" header are elected.

To delete an entry from the kill file, delete these lines; to modify an entry, edit the fields as you like. *tin* reads this file every time it starts up, so these changes will take effect in your next newsreading session.

Customizing tin

tin is one of the few newsreaders with a customization screen. This global-options menu is accessed from any of the other menus by typing **M**. In addition to the options that can be set on this screen, we'll look at other features, which can be specified via *tin*'s configuration files.

The example below shows the customization (global-options) screen. To change a particular option, type its corresponding number and press the Enter key. Pressing the space bar rotates through various options; pressing the Enter key sets the option. Pressing any non-numeric character exits from the setup screen.

```
                          Options Menu

1. Auto save       : ON    2. Editor Offset   : ON    3. Mark saved read : ON
4. Confirm command : ON    5. Draw arrow      : ON    6. Print header    : OFF
7. Goto 1st unread : ON    8. Scroll full page: ON    9. Catchup on quit : OFF
10 Thread articles : ON    11 Show only unread: ON    12 Show description: ON
13 Show author     : Name  14 Process type    : None
15 Sort article by : Date: field (ascending)
16 Save directory  : ~/News
17 Mail directory  : ~/Mail
18 Printer         : /usr/ucb/lpr

     Select option by entering number before text. Any other key to save.
```

Here's what the options mean:

1. Auto save
    If this flag is on, *tin* automatically use the "Archive-name:" header line to determine the filename when you save a file. This is useful when unpacking postings from one of the moderated newsgroups, where the moderator assigns an archive name to each posting. The "Archive-name:" header must be in one of the two formats

    Archive-name: xyz/part01

or

Archive-name: abc/patch01

which is usually the case in the source groups. *tin* validates the archive name by checking for a "/" and "part" or "patch" in the name.

2. Editor Offset
    This flag should be on if your default text editor can place the cursor at a particular line using the command line option "+*lineno*". Almost all editors honor this option.

3. Mark saved read
    If this option is on, any articles saved are automatically marked as being read. This is useful for source groups, since it lets you skip over multiple part postings easily.

4. Confirm command
    If this flag is on, *tin* prompts for confirmation before executing commands such as catching up on unread news. It's added safety for new users; when you get used to using *tin*, you may find all these confirmations annoying and wish to turn them off.

5. Draw arrow
    This option affects the article-selection and thread-browsing menus. If this option is off, *tin* highlights the current article in reverse video. If it is set, *tin* draws an arrow to the left of the article number. The setting you should choose depends on the capabilities of your display. Some very old displays can't handle reverse video; some new versions don't always do it correctly. The arrow is also useful if you use *tin* over a low-speed modem; redrawing the screen will be quicker.

6. Print header
    If this option is set, *tin* includes the complete article header when printing files. If this option is not set, only the "Subject:" and "From:" lines are printed.

7. Goto 1st unread
    This option causes *tin* to display the first unread article automatically upon entering a newsgroup.

8. Scroll full page
    This option controls whether *tin* scrolls the screen in full-page or half-page increments. Half page is usually more convenient, but full page is better if you have a slow terminal.

9. Catchup on quit
    If set, *tin* asks if you wish to mark unviewed articles as being read when you leave each newsgroup.

10. Thread articles
    If this option is set, *tin* displays the articles by thread. If it is not set, *tin* displays all articles on the article selection screen.

11. Show only unread
    If this option is set, *tin* will not show previously read messages.

12. Show description
    Setting this option displays a description for each newsgroup in the group-selection screen.

13. Show author

    This option controls what author information is displayed when the article is read. It can be set to one of the following values:

    None: The author's name will not be displayed

    Addr: Only the author's email address will be displayed

    Name: Only the author's "real" name will be displayed

    Both: Both the author's name and email address will be displayed

14. Process type
    This specifies the default processing (e.g., uudecoding, unsharing) that is applied to saved articles.

15. Sort article by
    This specifies how articles are to be sorted on the article-selection screen. Articles can be either unsorted, or sorted by the "Subject:", "Date:", or "From:" lines, in either ascending or descending order.

16. Save directory
    This is the default directory for saving news articles.

17. Mail directory
    This is the default directory for saving pieces of mail.

18. Printer
    This option specifies the command line used for sending an article to the printer. On a UNIX system, you would probably use something like *lpr*, although your site may require something different.

tin Variables

In addition to the options that can be set from the menu, *tin* supports the setting of some options in the file *~/.tin/tinrc*. The format of each entry in the file is a line of the form:

    option=value

Comments are specified by lines starting with a pound sign. For example, here is the line in the default *tinrc* file that corresponds to menu item 11 above.

    # if ON show only new/unread articles otherwise show all.
    show_only_unread=ON

As usual, we'll touch upon just a few of the most important variables that can be set. The manpage has a full listing of all the variables that can be set:

- *mail_quote_format*
  news_quote_format

  When replying or following up to an article, you can include the body of the original message. These two variables set the header for these quoted pieces of text.

  You can place these special characters in the variable:

  %A: The original poster's email address

  %D: Date the original article was posted

  %F: Original poster's full name and address (%N (%A))

  %G: The group the article was posted to

  %M: The original article's message ID

  %N: The original poster's name

  The manpage gives these examples for setting the quote format. If you have these variable definitions in your *tinrc* file:

  ```
  mail_quote_format=On %D in %G you wrote:
  news_quote_format=In %M, %F wrote:
  ```

  Replies to other posters' messages would be prefixed with:

  ```
  On 21 Jul 1992 09:45:51 -0400 in alt.sources you wrote:
  ```

  And follow ups would be prefixed with:

  ```
  In <abcINN123@anl433.uucp>, Iain Lea (iain@erlm.siemens.de) wrote:
  ```

- *quote_chars*

  This variable is used to set the prefix used in quoting the body of other people's articles. An underscore character ("_") can be used to represent a blank. The default quoting string is (":_"), which means that each line in the quoted article is prefixed with a colon and a space, like this:

  ```
  : This is what the
  : original poster
  : posted.
  ```

  According to news guru Henry Spencer, the only proper quoting string is a greater-than sign (>). I set my *quote_chars* variable to **>_** and recommend that you do as well.

Environment Variables

tin also uses some environment variables to customize its settings. Many of these variables are used for historical reasons, to maintain compatibility with other older newsreaders. Environment variables are usually defined in your shell initialization files (usually *.login* or *.profile*).

VISUAL

> This variable can be used to set the editor *tin* invokes to compose messages and replies. The default editor is *vi*.

NNTPSERVER

> Depending on how your site has configured *tin*, you may need to set this variable to inform *tin* of the machine that is acting as your site's news server. For example, if your site uses the machine *news.yoursite.com* as its news server, you should add the command

```
setenv NNTPSERVER news.yoursite.com
```

> to your *.login* file if you use the C shell, or

```
NNTPSERVER=news.yoursite.com; export NNTPSERVER
```

> to your *.profile* file if you use the Bourne shell.

REPLYTO

> This variable overrides the "Reply-To:" field in the message header. You can use it to correct a bad address that is generated because of an incorrect network configuration.

Group Attributes

Attributes can also be set on a per-group basis, allowing you to specify customized settings for each group. These group attributes are specified in the file *~/.tin/attributes*. The syntax is the same as for global variable settings, with the exception that a "newsgroup=" line precedes the customization section for each newsgroup. The global defaults are used for any of the parameters not specified.

This example is given in the *tin* manpage.

```
group=alt.sources
maildir=/usr/iain/Mail/sources
savedir=/usr/iain/News/alt.sources
sigfile=/usr/iain/.funny_sig
organization=Wacky Bits Inc.
followup_to=alt.sources.d
printer=/usr/local/bin/a2ps -nn | /bin/lpr
auto_save=ON
batch_save=OFF
delete_tmp_files=ON
show_only_unread=OFF
thread_arts=ON
show_author=1
sort_art_type=5
post_proc_type=1
```

It sets various attributes for the newsgroup *alt.sources*. Some of the parameters are specified as strings (such as organization or printer). Boolean values (such as auto_save) are specified as being either ON or OFF. The values of the remaining fields are as follows:

show_author: controls how *tin* displays the author's name in an article list
    0 = none: don't show the article's author
    1 = username: show author's username
    2 = network address: show author's network address
    3 = both: show both username and address

sort_art_type: controls how *tin* sorts the articles
    0 = none: no sort, articles appear in the order they arrive
    1 = subject descending: alpha sort by subject, z-a
    2 = subject ascending: alpha sort by subject, a-z
    3 = from descending: alpha sort by author name, z-a
    4 = from ascending: alpha sort by author name, a-z
    5 = date descending: sort by posting date, most recent first
    6 = date ascending: sort by posting date, oldest first

post_proc_type: determines the default post processing applied to saved articles
    0 = none: no processing (appropriate for "text groups")
    1 = unshar: appropriate for source code groups
    2 = uudecode: appropriate for binary groups
    3 = uudecode and list zoo archive: appropriate for binary groups
    4 = uudecode and extract zoo archive: appropriate for binary groups
    5 = uudecode and list zip archive: appropriate for binary groups
    6 = uudecode and extract zip archive: appropriate for binary groups

There's a lot of value in having the ability to configure defaults on a per-newsgroup basis. For example, you probably don't want any post processing (post_proc_type=0) for a discussion group (like *soc.singles*); as this file suggests, you probably do want some default post processing for a binaries group (like *alt.sources*). You probably want your organization and signature to represent your employer for postings to work-related groups; you probably *don't* want it to represent your employer in certain more recreational groups!

One other interesting feature: this example automatically directs any follow-up messages to the discussion group *alt.sources.d*, thus enforcing an all-too-frequently unobserved rule of netiquette: a source group should be reserved for the sources themselves; conversations about the sources (bug reports, complaints, software reviews, etc.) should take place in the discussion (.d) group. Similar rules hold for binaries groups and other groups designated for particular types of postings. Use this feature, and you'll never send a posting to an inappropriate place!

Files

This section summarizes the files that are of interest to the general user. There are several other files which are used internally by *tin*, or are of interest primarily to the news administrator. They are documented in the *tin* manual.

~/.tin/tinrc
> Your personal configuration file. Any customizations you make go here.

~/.tin/filter
> The kill file. Each time *tin* starts up, it reads this file to determine which articles to automatically kill and select.

~/.tin/kill
> The kill file for older versions of *tin*

~/.tin/attributes
> The per-group attribute customization file, as described earlier

~/.tin/posted
> A very handy file unique to *tin*. It keeps a list of all your posted messages. It doesn't keep the message text, but does store the date posted, the subject line, and the newsgroup the message was posted to.

~/.newsrc
> The standard news-initialization file. It keeps track of what groups you are subscribed to and which articles you have read in each group.

Recommended Options

So, after all that, what options should you really use? These are the changes that I made to my *tinrc*, and the ones that I recommend to people when they ask for my advice. Feel free to experiment and find what suits you.

```
mail_quote_format=On %D in %G you wrote:
news_quote_format=In %M, %F wrote:
quote_chars=>
```

READING NEWS WITH EMACS AND GNUS

What's GNU?

gnus is a newsreading package for the popular GNU *Emacs* editor. It provides full newsreading functionality from within *Emacs*, which is one of its greatest strengths. All of *Emacs'* features are available from within *gnus*. There's no need for special macro languages, commands to save or copy files, or any of the other features that must be provided by other newsreaders. If you know how to use *Emacs*, learning *gnus* should come easily.

A few of *gnus'* key features are:

- Full integration into *Emacs*
- A familiar look and feel for current *Emacs* users
- Easy customization
- Easy integration with *Emacs* mail programs

gnus is supported by its author, Mananobu Umeda, and by participants in the newsgroup *gnu.emacs.gnus*. A FAQ[*] list is posted there regularly. Bug reports and suggestions may be sent to the author at *umerin@mse.kyutech.ac.jp*.

The rest of this chapter is organized as follows:

- How to start *gnus*
- Selecting articles you wish to read
- Reading the selected articles
- Basic commands
- A sample *gnus* session. If you have never used a newsreader before, this section walks you through reading news step by step.
- Posting articles and sending mail
- Automatically screening out (killing) articles
- Customizing *gnus*

GNU Redux

Because *gnus* is part of the *Emacs* editor, let's take a moment and review a few aspects of *Emacs*. If you're already an *Emacs* user, you can skip this section; your fingers will intuitively reach for the right keys. If you don't use *Emacs*, here's a quick summary of the terms we'll use in this chapter.[†]

Keystrokes

Emacs makes extensive use of both control keys and "meta" keys. *Emacs* has the usual concept of control keys. To type Control-A, you type the "A" key while holding down the Control key. In this chapter, we'll use **CTRL-x** to mean "press Control and x simultaneously." In addition, *Emacs* has the concept of a meta key (or the Alt key on some systems). Typing Meta-x or Alt-x means the same as typing Control-x, only holding down the meta/Alt key instead of the Control key. The meta/Alt key is like the Control key, in that you can hold it down while pressing a sequence of other keys.

Many keyboards do not have a meta key, so there's an alternative. The sequence **ESC-x** (Escape followed by any key) is equivalent to Meta/Alt-x (pressing any key while holding down Meta/Alt). The only difference is that you can't hold Escape down while pressing a sequence of other keys. We'll use the Escape key

---

[*] FAQs are frequently asked questions lists. See "Frequently Asked Questions" in Chapter 7 for details.

[†] If you're interested in learning more about *Emacs*, check out *Learning GNU Emacs* by Debra Cameron and Bill Rosenblatt, O'Reilly & Associates Inc., 1992.

notation in our examples. If you have a meta/Alt key on your keyboard, you can use either the Escape- or meta-key methods. *Emacs* documentation is written in terms of the meta/Alt key.

Buffers

When you're using *Emacs*, every file you edit is associated with a buffer. Like most editors, the changes you make while typing a document affect the buffer only, and do not modify the disk file until the buffer is saved. Buffers under *Emacs* are much more powerful, however. They can be created dynamically, and not assigned to any particular file. Whenever you view the help screen, for example, you are viewing a dynamically created buffer. And when you're looking at a list of articles in *gnus*, you're also viewing a dynamically created buffer, and there may be special commands that work only when you're in that buffer. There-fore, you don't bounce between "reading modes" and "selection modes," as you do with other newsreaders; you move your cursor between different buffers that *Emacs* creates as you need them. We'll discuss the particular buffers *gnus* uses below.

Getting Started

gnus runs inside of *Emacs,* so before you can use it, you must start *Emacs.* To do so, give the command:

    % emacs

This will bring up *Emacs*, either on the screen where you started it or in a sepa-rate window (if you are using a windowing system). If this does not work, or if you have problems, contact your system administrator.

Once you are in *Emacs*, you can start *gnus* by typing **ESC-x gnus Return.**[*] *gnus* will display an introductory screen, and print several messages while it initializes. After it has initialized, it will display the group-selection screen.

It's possible to start *gnus* directly from the command line, though that's not normally how you would use it; it's more typical to drop into *gnus* while you're performing some other editing task. To bring up *gnus* from the command line, give this command:

    % emacs -f gnus

---

[*] **ESC-x** is bound to the **execute-extended-command** function. We then type the extended command *gnus* and press the Enter key.

Reading Articles

gnus has three main buffers. The first, which I mentioned above, is the *News-group* buffer; it lists the newsgroups you're subscribed to that have articles waiting to be read, and shows you how many articles are waiting in each group. It's essentially a menu for selecting newsgroups. The other *Summary* buffer displays a list of unread articles in the current newsgroup; the *Article* buffer displays articles (one at a time) for reading.

When you first start *gnus*, you are placed in the *Newsgroup* buffer, shown below:

```
      5: comp.lang.tcl
    111: comp.lang.c++
     23: comp.object
      2: dfw.eats
      5: dfw.forsale
      2: dfw.general
    361: gnu.emacs.gnus
    144: misc.jobs.offered
      3: tx.general
     19: tx.jobs
     47: alt.lefthanders


  --- GNUS: List of Newsgroups        (Newsgroup {news.utdallas.edu})--All-----
  SPC:Select  n:Forward  p:Backward  q:Exit  C-c TAB:Run Info  ?:This help
```

You will use this buffer for navigating to various newsgroups, as well as for subscribing and unsubscribing to newsgroups. You can use *Emacs'* usual scrolling and searching commands to navigate in this buffer. In addition, this mode adds a few extra key bindings. Typing **n** moves the cursor to the next news-group with unread news. **p** moves to the previous newsgroup with unread news. Typing **?** in any *gnus* buffer displays a one-line command summary at the bottom of the screen. Typing **CTRL-C TAB** puts you into the "info" documentation browser, reading *gnus'* online documentation.

Pressing the space bar selects a newsgroup for reading. If the newsgroup has more than 50 unread articles, *gnus* asks you how many articles you want listed in the newsgroup summary; after you respond (pressing the Return key accepts their default), you'll see the *Summary* buffer, with a one-line summary for each article in the group. *Emacs* also displays the *Article* buffer, which contains the text of the current article (both buffers are shown below).

```
D 47294:+[ 20:robert@steffi] Binary operator question
  47295: [ 46:kanze@us-es.s] Re: Equalities of doubles (IEEE equality)
  47296: [  9:roth@oasys.dt] pascal to c translator? (I missed it)
  47297: [ 46:kanze@us-es.s] Re: Nested friend classes
--- GNUS: comp.lang.c++/47294 {110 more}      (Summary Thread)--Top--------
From: robert@steffi.demon.co.uk (Robert Nicholson)
Newsgroups: comp.lang.c++
Subject: Binary operator question
Date: 22 Nov 1993 13:43:51 -0000
Organization: me organized? That's a joke!
NNTP-Posting-Host: steffi.demon.co.uk

I've forgotten where I read in the RM where it defines the reason
behind.


"String" == "String"
(This is probably ambiguous if it were allowed anyway)
never matching to any functions whilst
"String" == aStringType
--- GNUS: comp.lang.c++/47294 Binary operator...      (Article)--Top-------
```

Now that you're reading an article, there isn't much more to say! There are relatively few *gnus* commands; you can do most of what you want with *Emacs*. For example, you can use the editor's search commands to find interesting articles; you can use the regular commands for moving on the screen to navigate; and so on. Pressing the space bar selects the current article (the article on which the cursor is resting) for reading, and displays it in the *Article* buffer. Continuing to press the space bar pages through all the articles in the currently selected group. Typing **n** displays the next article in the list; typing **p** displays the previous unread article.

To move between the *Article* and *Summary* buffers, you use the normal commands for moving between windows (**CTRL-x o**). When you're in either the *Article* or *Summary* buffer, you can press the space bar to page down, and the Delete key to move back.

We'll cover specifics on the other commands later. For now, you should have enough to get started. All you really need to know about is your space bar: whatever you want to do, pressing the space bar will usually do it for you. Again, you can type **?** to see a short command summary, and **CTRL-c TAB** to view the *gnus* info file. Typing **CTRL-h m** will give a list of commands available in the current mode. In particular, it will list all the special Newsgroup, Article, and Summary commands when typed in the appropriate buffer.

A Few Essentials

Although *gnus* has several dozen commands, you don't need much more than the ability to select and read articles to get started. There are a few other essentials, though, which we'll cover in this section. Take a moment to glance through it, and then proceed to the next section, where we will step through a sample *gnus* session. Afterwards, we'll proceed to the more advanced things you can do.

Quitting gnus

The normal way to exit *gnus* is to type **q** in the *Newsgroup* buffer. You will be asked to confirm that you want to exit *gnus*. If you respond by typing **y**, *gnus* will update your configuration files, delete its internal buffers, and close its news connections. To exit from *Emacs*, type **CTRL-x CTRL-c**.

To quit *gnus* and restore the configuration file to the state it was in before you started, type **Q**. This is an emergency escape; it's useful if you've made a mistake, like accidentally unsubscribing to your favorite groups. You will be prompted for confirmation (you may have to type **yes** twice, if the *.newsrc* buffer has been modified); after you confirm, *gnus* exits and restores your files to their previous condition. Any changes you've made during this session will be forgotten.

If you type **q** from the *Summary* or *Article* buffers, you will be placed in the *Newsgroup* buffer. At that point, you can either quit or select another newsgroup to read.

Getting Help

gnus provides several kinds of help. The simplest way to get help is to type **?**, which displays a one-line help message at the bottom of the screen. The message isn't elaborate, but it's good for basic navigation, and it tells you how to get more detailed help. For a quick summary of the commands available in a particular mode, type **CTRL-h m**. To get detailed help, type **CTRL-c TAB**; this displays the online documentation using the built-in "info" reader. The example below shows the top level of the *gnus* info file.

```
File: gnus,  Node: Top,  Next: Starting Up,  Prev: (DIR),  Up: (DIR)

The GNUS News Reader
********************

   You can read netnews within Emacs using the GNUS package.  GNUS uses
the NNTP protocol to communicate with a news server, which is a
repository of news articles.  This need not be the same computer you
are logged in on.

   While the author of GNUS recommends pronouncing it as "news", we
recommend pronouncing it as "gnoose", to avoid confusion.

* Menu:

* Starting Up::
* Buffers of GNUS::
* Newsgroup Commands::
* Summary Commands::
* Article Commands::
* Startup File::
* Kill File::
* Troubleshooting::
* Customization::
* Reporting Bugs::
* Index::
--%%-Info:   (gnus)Top        (Info Narrow)--Bot----------------------------
```

Emacs documentation is actually in an early form of hypertext. So this page looks more like a "table of contents" or a menu—which it really is—than a typical help file. The starred items are menu entries, or links to other topics. To read a link, type the command **m**. You'll see a "menu item" prompt at the bottom of the screen. Then type the first few letters of the topic that interests you and then press the Return key. *Emacs* then displays a help file discussing that topic; the help file may contain further links to other help topics. Type **q** to quit the info reader, and return to *gnus*. When you return to *gnus*, *Emacs* redisplays the buffers you were reading when you left.

If you would like help with info mode, type **?**. If you would like to step through the online info mode tutorial, type **?h**. Working through the tutorial is a good idea; the info reader has a lot of features.

Emergencies

Like all other *Emacs* commands, typing **CTRL-g** cancels whatever operation is in progress, and returns you to whatever you were doing previously. This is handy if you become confused about what you have typed, or if you accidentally type a command you don't want. It's probably not as useful as you'd think, though; on modern systems, most commands are executed so quickly that they're finished before you can cancel them.

Typing **CTRL-l** (that's an el) refreshes (redisplays) the screen. This is handy if the screen is garbled for some reason.

Navigating

If you want to read some particular newsgroup right away, rather than politely wading through all your newsgroups, you use the **j** (jump) command from the *Newsgroup* buffer. When you type **j**, *gnus* prompts you for the name of a news-group; type the name, and press the Return key. You can use *Emacs'* name completion feature to avoid typing a full name; after you've typed a few letters, press the Tab key and *Emacs* will complete as much of the name as possible. If there's only one unambiguous choice, *Emacs* fills in the entire newsgroup name; if there are several choices, *Emacs* creates a new buffer with a list of possible completions. Pressing the space bar does the same thing, but only to the next dot in the group name.

In this example, we'll jump directly to the newsgroup *rec.music.folk*.

```
--- GNUS: List of Newsgroups      (Newsgroup {news.ora.com})--Top----------
Newsgroup: rec.music.folk
```

After you type the name of the newsgroup, *gnus* places it in the *Newsgroup* buffer. If you are not subscribed to the group, you will see a "U" in the left column. To subscribe to the group, type **u** to subscribe to the group. If you later wish to unsubscribe to the group, simply type **u** again.

If these commands don't quite make sense yet, don't worry. We'll go over them in more detail in a moment. If these commands do make some sense, you're well on your way to using *gnus*!

A gnus Session

NOTE

If you need to exit this session at any time, type a lowercase **q** and an-swer **yes** to any questions you may be asked. To exit *Emacs*, type **CTRL-x CTRL-c** and answer **yes** to any questions.

Now that we have some of the basics out of the way, let's step through a *gnus* session. First, we need to start *gnus*. Normally, you'd start *gnus* in the middle of an editing session, but we'll take the shortcut and start it directly from the UNIX command line:

```
% emacs -f gnus
```

Emacs starts and loads *gnus*, which then initializes itself and displays its introductory screen:

```
                              GNUS 4.1

                   NNTP-based News Reader for GNU Emacs

        If you have any trouble with this software, please let me
        know. I will fix your problems in the next release.

        Comments, suggestions, and bug fixes are welcome.

        Masanobu UMEDA
        umerin@mse.kyutech.ac.jp

--- GNUS: List of Newsgroups        (Newsgroup {news.utdallas.edu})--All-----
Checking new news...
```

You'll see lots of messages flashing across the bottom of the screen while this process is taking place. After initializing, *gnus* places you in the *Newsgroup* buffer. If you haven't read news before, *gnus* automatically subscribes you to all the groups available from your news server. Let's go to a group that should be on just about all systems, *news.newusers.questions.* [*] This is an excellent group for learning your way around the Net; I strongly suggest you subscribe to it for awhile. Many questions that draw sharp answers[†] in other groups receive patient and comprehensive explanations here.

First, invoke the jump command by typing **j**. You are then prompted for the group you wish to view.

```
--- GNUS: List of Newsgroups        (Newsgroup {news.utdallas.edu})--All---------
Newsgroup: news.newusers.questions
```

Type *news.newusers.questions* and press the Return key. *gnus* places your cursor on the entry for *news.newusers.questions* in the list of newsgroups. To read the articles in this group, press the space bar to select it. If there are many unread articles, you are asked how many articles you wish to read. Press the Return key to read all the articles in the group or type a number to limit the damage.

---

[*] If this group isn't on your system, complain to your system administrator!

[†] See Chapter 7 for details on posting etiquette.

When you specify the number of articles to read, *gnus* splits the screen and displays the *Summary* and *Article* buffers for *news.newusers.questions.*

```
D 14801:+[  7:antonio@garfi] Re: What does :-) means?
  14802: [206:elhaag@sun1.r] Re: What does :-) means?
  14803: [ 19:afc@cs.nott.a] Re: What does :-) means?
--- GNUS: news.newusers.questions/14801 {482 more}  (Summary Thread)-- 1%--
From: antonio@garfield.fe.up.pt (Antonio Barros Ferreira)
Newsgroups: news.newusers.questions
Subject: Re: What does :-) means?
Date: 10 Nov 1993 08:51:10 GMT
Organization: Universidade do Porto
NNTP-Posting-Host: garfield.fe.up.pt
X-Newsreader: TIN [version 1.1 PL9]

Thanks for all answers (:-)).

: "When working toward the solution of a problem it always helps if you
: know the answer" (Murphy's Laws of computers).
: ################################################################
:

--- GNUS: news.newusers.questions/14801 Re: What does :...  (Article)--All-
```

Let's take a minute and review a few things. The *Summary* buffer, in the top window, summarizes the articles that are available for reading. The current article is displayed in the bottom window (the *Article* buffer).

The *Summary* buffer contains several pieces of information about the articles in the group. The leftmost column is the article status. A space indicates an unread article, and a "D" indicates an article that has been read and will be deleted after this newsreading session.[*] The second item is the article number, which is assigned when the article reaches your system. Following that, in square brackets, are the number of lines in the article, and the author's ID (this is truncated to fit on the line). Finally, *gnus* displays the subject line of the article.

The first few lines of the *Article* buffer are the current news article's headers, showing various pieces of information related to the article (the time it was posted, the newsgroup it was posted to, etc.). Following the headers, you see the actual message the poster entered.

---

[*] "Deleted" in the *Emacs* sense, meaning that you won't be presented with this article the next time you read news. Of course, *gnus* does not delete the actual article.

You might notice that this screen is a little cramped; it shows only four articles in the *Summary* buffer. There are several things you can do about this:

- If you are working on a workstation or other terminal where you can resize the screen, you can make your *Emacs* window larger.

- You can increase the size of the top window (the *Summary* buffer) by typing either **CTRL-x ^** (which increases the size of the current window by one line) or **CTRL-x +** (to split the screen evenly between the two windows).

- Type **=** to expand the *Summary* buffer to fill the entire screen. The *Article* buffer will be redisplayed as soon as you select an article for reading.

We'll take the last option and enlarge the summary screen by typing **=**. We can now browse the messages posted to this group.

```
26973: [ 34:dave@frackit.] Re: Forwarding with Elm and Pine
26974: [ 22:dave@frackit.] Re: 2
26975: [ 18:dave@frackit.] Re: Howard Stern
26976: [ 69:ts@chyde.uwas] The Weekly FAQ on test postings
26977: [  6:david.morse@d] Mailing Lists
    27027: [  8:edmoore@vcd.h]
    27051: [ 36:partl@hp01.bo]
26978: [  6:hammonds@olym] Second Hand Smoke
    26994: [ 10:grobe@ins.inf]
26979: [ 23:mark@overture] Re: List of Newsgroup names?
26980: [ 20:alant24fps@ao] Re: Hero's Dad Dis's Clinton
26981: [ 10:jamz@valinor.] Re: Death to AOL! was: F\377\377\377\377\377
26982: [ 17:dqle@netcom.c] HELP! How to set Distribution?
    27062: [ 18:partl@hp01.bo]
    27141: [ 10:bmarcum@iglou]
26984: [  4:chrisr9044@ao] Re: Test
    27052: [ 20:partl@hp01.bo]
26985: [ 22:dsmith@inmos.] Re: Can you read files while in FTP?
26986: [ 17:Bill.Yeakel@d] FTP via Email: How?
    27012: [ 16:rathinam@ins.]
26987: [  7:m-tg0017@barn] Where to post job question
    26995: [ 16:grobe@ins.inf]
--- GNUS: news.newusers.questions/26960 {198(+14419) more}   (Summary Thread
```

Now let's select some articles to read. Article 26976 ("The Weekly FAQ on test postings") looks interesting, so let's select it. Move the cursor to the article, using *Emacs'* **CTRL-n** (next line) and **CTRL-p** (previous line) commands, and press the space bar. The screen splits again, showing the beginning of the article.

```
   26975: [ 18:dave@frackit.] Re: Howard Stern
D 26976:+[ 69:ts@chyde.uwas] The Weekly FAQ on test postings
   26977: [  6:david.morse@d] Mailing Lists
      27027: [  8:edmoore@vcd.h]
--- GNUS: news.newusers.questions/26976 {197(+14419) more}   (Summary Thread
From: ts@chyde.uwasa.fi (Timo Salmi)
Newsgroups: news.newusers.questions
Subject: The Weekly FAQ on test postings
Date: Thu, 30 Jun 1994 02:10:00 GMT
Organization: University of Vaasa, Finland
NNTP-Posting-Host: uwasa.fi
Summary: Posted automatically each Thursday
Originator: ts@uwasa.fi

-From: garbo.uwasa.fi:/pc/ts/tsfaqn41.zip Frequently Asked Questions
-Subject: Where to put test postings

17. *****
 Q: Where to put test postings?

 A: Let me try to give hopefully helpful information about how best
go about making test postings. Please don't take offense by this
--- GNUS: news.newusers.questions/26976 The Weekly FAQ ...  (Article)--Top-
```

Your cursor is now in the *Article* buffer. You can use most of the standard *Emacs* commands, like **ESC v** and **CTRL-v**, to move around in this buffer. You can also press the space bar to display the next screenful of text, and automatically jump to the next unread article when you're through with the current one. Press **n** at any time to reach the next unread article.

Now press the space bar to see the next screen of the article.

```
   26975: [ 18:dave@frackit.] Re: Howard Stern
 D 26976:+[ 69:ts@chyde.uwas] The Weekly FAQ on test postings
   26977: [  6:david.morse@d] Mailing Lists
     27027: [  8:edmoore@vcd.h]
--- GNUS: news.newusers.questions/26976 {197(+14419) more}  (Summary Thread
 A: Let me try to give hopefully helpful information about how best
go about making test postings. Please don't take offense by this
item. It is solely meant as friendly guidance so that you can better
find your way on the net.
   Novice users, and sometimes even others, occasionally place these
"A test, please ignore" messages in discussion newsgroups. Please
don't do this. It is wasteful of the resources. These news reach
tens of thousands of readers, so a very wide distribution is
involved. Furthermore, many users find the test messages very
annoying in the discussion newsgroups, and you have a good chance of
getting some testy email.
   There is a much better solution for the testing. There are
special test newsgroups just for this purpose, such as alt.test and
misc.test. The misc.test is a good option, since there are several
test echos along the feed. They will automatically send you
email acknowledgements when your test posting reaches these sites.
   If you just wish to test posting without the automatic
--- GNUS: news.newusers.questions/26976 The Weekly FAQ ...  (Article)--11%-
```

This looks like some pretty interesting stuff, to be read carefully, so save the file for later viewing by typing **o**.[*] You will be prompted for a filename for the saved article; press the Enter key to use the default filename, which is just the name of the newsgroup, placed in the directory *~/News*. For example, articles saved in the group *comp.newusers.questions* are saved in the file *~/News/comp.newusers.questions*.[†] Since the file does not exist, we will be prompted to confirm its creation.

```
--- GNUS: news.newusers.questions/26976 The Weekly FAQ ...      (Article)--Top-
Save article in Rmail file: (default news.newusers.questions) ~/News/
```

Press the Return key to give *Emacs* the confirmation it wants; if you want to use a different filename, type your new filename and press Return. Once you're done, you can continue reading by pressing the space bar, or you can return to the *Summary* buffer to find more interesting articles. Instead, exit *gnus* and *Emacs*

---

[*] This saves the buffer in standard *rmail* (the default *gnus* mailer) format. If you want to save the article in standard UNIX mail (and news) format, type **CTRL-o**.

[†] If you are on a system that does not support long filenames, you can change this default by setting the variable **gnus-use-long-file-name** to nil. Your news administrator may already have done this. You can check the value of this variable by typing **CTRL-h v** and entering the name of the variable.

by typing **q** twice, answering **y** to confirm, and typing **CTRL-x CTRL-c** to terminate *Emacs.* Now, let's look at a few of the files that *gnus* has created:

```
% cd
% ls .newsrc*
.newsrc      .newsrc.el    .newsrc.el~     .newsrc~
```

First, *gnus* has created the *.newsrc* file, which keeps track of the groups you are subscribed to and the articles you have read. *gnus* has also created the file *.newsrc.el*, which is an *Emacs*-LISP version of the *.newsrc* file. *gnus* creates this to speed news processing.

Finally, let's take a look at our news directory, where we saved the article from *news.newusers.questions.* It is right where we expected it to be, in the file *News/ news.newusers.questions.*

```
% ls -R News
News/
news.newusers.questions
```

More Commands

This section discusses some more of the useful commands that *gnus* provides. Remember, you can use just about all the usual *Emacs* commands when working with *gnus* buffers.

Subscribing and Unsubscribing to Newsgroups

Often, you'll decide that some newsgroup you're reading has degenerated into mindless babbling (this is particularly common in the *alt* groups, some of which exist purely for mindless babbling). When a group no longer interests you, you can unsubscribe to it. To do so, go to the *Newsgroup* buffer and position your cursor on the newsgroup in question; then type **u**. The newsgroup will be marked with a "U" in the left-hand column, and you will not see the newsgroup the next time you read news.

Somewhat confusingly, the unsubscribe command is also used to subscribe to a newsgroup. To subscribe to the newsgroup, go to the *Newsgroup* buffer. Then you have to get the name of the group you want into the buffer (if you aren't subscribed, the group won't be listed there already). So use the **j** command to jump to the group. The newsgroup's name will appear in the group list with a U in the left margin to tell you that you haven't subscribed. Type **u** to subscribe. You don't have to subscribe immediately; you could read a few articles first to see whether you're really interested. When you've decided, return to the list of newsgroups, put the cursor on top of your new group, and subscribe.

You can also subscribe and unsubscribe to groups by typing **U** and the name of the group. The usual *Emacs* completion keys (typing a **?** to see completion options; pressing the Tab key completes to uniqueness) can be used here.

Catching Up

Often, you don't have time to read some newsgroups for an extended period; you may go on vacation for a week, or you may have a huge project at work (or even a domestic crisis) that keeps you from staying current. When you make the painful decision that you're never going to read these articles, you can "catch up" by marking the entire newsgroup as "read" (i.e., telling *gnus* to act as if you've already read all the articles). Catching up isn't the same as dropping your subscription to a newsgroup; you'll still see new articles as they arrive. You're just flushing the articles you won't have time to read.

There are two ways to catch up. When you're looking at the *Newsgroup* buffer, scan the listing to see what newsgroups contain huge numbers of articles that you're not likely to read. Use **CTRL-n** and **CTRL-p** to move to these newsgroups; then type the **c** command. Depending on some optional settings, *gnus* may prompt you for confirmation. After you've given it, you'll see the number of unread articles for that group set to zero. Catching up in the *Newsgroup* buffer is particularly convenient, because you can easily scan your entire subscription and catch up as many groups as you'd like.

You can also catch up when you're in a newsgroup's *Summary* buffer. Type **c**; when you confirm, *gnus* marks all the articles as read and puts you back in the *Newsgroup* buffer. Why do you return to the *Newsgroup* buffer? Easy; there are no articles left to read in the current newsgroup; that's what catch up means.

Decrypting ROT13 Articles

As discussed previously, someone occasionally posts an article others may not wish to see. These are posted in ROT13[*] format and look like this:

```
Ubj qb lbh gryy vg'f n pbzchgre ercnvezna gung unf n syng gver
orfvqr gur ebnq?  Ur'f gur bar punatvat bhg gverf gb frr jung'f gur
ceboyrz.
```

```
Ubj qb lbh gryy vg'f n pbzchgre ercnvezna gung'f bhg bs tnf?  Ur'f
gur bar punatvat bhg gverf gb frr jung'f gur ceboyrz.
```

---

[*] *gnus* also handles messages posted in ROT47 (Japanese) format.

Follow this three-step procedure to read the encrypted posting:

- Make sure that you really want to read the post. If the subject says "offensive to IBM salesmen," and you are particularly sensitive about IBM salesmen, don't read the post! If you do read the post and are offended, don't complain. You were warned.

- Find the article in the *Summary* buffer.

- Execute the decrypt command by typing **CTRL-c CTRL-r** in the *Summary* buffer. (You might expect this command to work in the *Article* buffer, but it doesn't). Here's the result:

```
How do you tell it's a computer repairman that has a flat tire
beside the road?  He's the one changing out tires to see what's the
problem.

How do you tell it's a computer repairman that's out of gas?  He's
the one changing out tires to see what's the problem.
```

Posting Messages

CAUTION

A posted message is seen by tens of thousands of people all over the world. Keep this in mind when you are posting! The group *misc.test* is designated for test postings. Try posting there a few times before posting somewhere else.

There are two ways to post messages in *gnus*. You can either post an original message by typing **a** (to author a new posting), or you can follow up to someone else's posting with either the **f** (follow up) or **F** (follow up with included message) command. The author command can be executed from either the *Newsgroup* buffer or the *Summary* buffer. If you execute the author command from the *Newsgroup* buffer, you will be asked which group you wish to post to. The follow-up commands must, of course, be executed from the *Summary* buffer. Your follow up will be to the currently displayed article.

Posting New Articles

NOTE

Typing **CTRL-g** at any prompt will get you out of posting mode.

When you issue the **a** command to post a new article, *gnus* asks you a few questions and then places you in an editing buffer so you can write the text of the message. Here's a quick example. Let's post a small message to the group *misc.test*. Text you type is shown in bold. Start the posting process from the *Newsgroup* buffer by typing **a**. *gnus* then replies:

```
Are you sure you want to post to all of USENET? (y or n) y
```

You're given a chance to change your mind. Typing **n** returns you to whatever you were doing before you pressed **a**. Instead, type **y**. (You'll get another chance to chicken out later.) Next, *gnus* prompts you for the newsgroup (or groups) you wish to post to. We'll post to *misc.test*.

```
Newsgroup: misc.test*
```

gnus then asks for the posting's subject. Be specific! For example, if you are posting a question on *comp.unix.questions*, avoid subjects like "unix question." What else would you be posting there? For this posting, the subject will be **test post**—not interesting, but descriptive:

```
Subject: test post
```

Next, *gnus* asks for the geographic region you wish to distribute your message to. On our system, the default is "local," meaning that the message will only go to computers inside of our office. Override that and enter **world**, which sends the message to USENET nodes everywhere.

```
Distribution: world
```

After these questions have been answered, *gnus* creates an editing buffer for typing the message. The headers at the top of the buffer reflect the answers given to the previous questions. It is OK to edit the header lines, but don't change any of the keywords at the beginning of the line. Be sure and leave the "text follows" line between the header and the message body; *gnus* depends on this to tell where the header ends!

```
Newsgroups: misc.test
Subject: test post
Distribution: world
--text follows this line--
Do not be alarmed, this is only a test!


--**-Emacs: *post-news*      (News)--All--------------------------------
```

---

* Some versions of *gnus* will keep prompting for newsgroups until you enter an empty line.

When finished with your message, type **CTRL-c CTRL-c**[*] to send it. Be careful! You don't have to save the file first and you will not be prompted with any kind of "are you sure?" message. The message will be sent as soon as you type these keys. If you change your mind at this point, delete the edit buffer[†] and you will be returned to the newsgroup you were reading.

Depending on your system, it will take anything from a few minutes to over a day for a posting to start propagating to other sites. Expect to see replies and follow ups soon after this. See "Test Messages" in Chapter 7 for an example of what to expect when posting to *misc.test.*

Following Up Another Article

The procedure for following up another person's posting is essentially the same as for posting a new article. The differences are:

- Type an **f** to post a follow up to an article. Type an **F** if you wish to include the article you are answering.

- You won't be asked for a newsgroup, a subject line, or keywords; these are all taken from the article to which you're replying. However, once you've started the editor, you may change any of these fields, if you wish.

After you have responded to these questions, just follow the steps outlined in the previous "Posting New Articles" section.

If you suddenly regret having sent a message, there is a remedy, albeit somewhat ineffective. Wait until the message appears in your *Summary* buffer; select it; and type **C** to cancel it. Unfortunately, the message will still be seen briefly on many sites, but the damage will be less.

Sending Mail

As previously discussed, one of *gnus'* best features is its tight integration with *Emacs*. Unlike the other newsreaders we have discussed, *gnus* does not provide its own mail interface, but instead uses the standard *Emacs* mailer. The process for sending mail and replying to articles is (intentionally) very similar to that of posting messages. I won't spend much time discussing *gnus* mail here, but will present a brief synopsis.

---

[*] Yes, that means type **CTRL-c** twice.

[†] You can delete the current buffer by typing **CTRL-x k**. It's not totally necessary, since your message won't be sent until you type **CTRL-c CTRL-c**, but deleting the buffer ensures you won't accidentally send the message by mistake at a later time.

Reply

To reply to the author of a particular article without sending the message to the newsgroup, go to the *Summary* buffer; put your cursor on top of the article you want to reply to; and type **r**. If you want to include the original article in your response, type **R** and the original text will be copied to your *Mail* buffer. If you do this, be sure to delete unnecessary lines. Be kind to the other guy's mailbox!

Emacs then places you in a new buffer for editing the reply. From this point on, just follow the steps outlined in the previous section, "Posting New Articles."

When you have finished your message, type **CTRL-c CTRL-c** to send it. If you change your mind about replying, you can delete the *Mail* buffer by typing **CTRL-x k** as mentioned above.

Mail

To send mail from within *gnus*, type an **m** from the *Summary* buffer. You will be placed in the *Mail* buffer, where you can enter the recipient's name and subject of the message on the "To:" and "Subject:" lines, respectively. As with the reply command, typing **CTRL-c CTRL-c** delivers the message after you have entered it.

Forwarding a Post via Mail

You may want to forward an interesting article to friends and associates, particularly if you have friends who don't read news. This feature is also a handy way to save articles or give yourself a reminder about something that strikes you: just mail the article to yourself. You'll save yourself the trouble of having to delete it from the folder where it was saved. As an example of how this can be used, I usually forward notices of interesting software to myself, so that I can pick up a copy later. Seeing the article hanging around in my mailbox serves as a reminder to go out and get the software.

You can automatically forward a posting via mail by typing **CTRL-c CTRL-f** in the *Summary* buffer.

Killing Articles

As you are reading news, you will often find particular subjects or authors to be either boring or irrelevant. *gnus* can auto-kill these uninteresting articles.[*] This can be done in a particular newsgroup or globally across all newsgroups. It's not as simple as with the other newsreaders, but it works.

---

[*] Unlike the other newsreaders we've discussed, *gnus* does not have a way to automatically select articles.

If someone has sent an objectionable article and you don't want to read the follow-up postings that have already arrived, go to the *Summary* buffer, put your cursor on top of that article and type **k**. This article, and any responses to it, will be marked with a **K** in the summary; *Emacs* treats the articles as if you've already read them. This is a pretty lightweight kill: it doesn't last permanently because you'll see any further responses in your next newsreading session.

To kill a subject or an author more permanently, go the *Newsgroup* or *Summary* buffer. Then decide if you want to kill the particular subject or author in one newsgroup or all newsgroups. To kill articles in the current newsgroup, type **ESC k**. For a global kill (all occurrences of any topic or any author in any newsgroup), type **ESC K**. Either command creates a new editing window in which you can edit a kill file. *gnus* kill files are lists of *Emacs*-LISP commands that are executed whenever *gnus* enters a new group.

So, how do you edit these strange files? Several special key bindings exist to make kill-file maintenance easier. Typing **CTRL-c CTRL-k CTRL-s** inserts an entry for killing the current article (the article displayed in the *Article* window) by subject. You can modify this entry if you want—though if you don't know what you're doing, it's better not to. Similarly, to insert a template for killing all postings by the author of the current article, type **CTRL-c CTRL-k CTRL-a**. In both cases, if you aren't currently viewing an article, *Emacs* inserts a template with the author or article name blank. You can fill it in yourself—though again, it's best not to, unless you're familiar with *Emacs*-LISP.

When you're finished, look at the end of the kill file and make sure that it ends with a line reading:

```
(gnus-expunge "X")
```

This command removes the articles that have been tagged with *gnus-kill*. If there isn't a line like this, add it yourself. If you omit this step, you will still see the article in the *Summary* buffer, although it will be marked with an "X" and will be deleted when you leave the newsgroup.

Now comes the acid test: making sure these changes worked. Type **CTRL-c CTRL-a** to apply the current kill file, with your changes. The objectionable articles should disappear from the summary list. When you have finished editing your kill file, type **CTRL-c CTRL-c** to return to normal newsreading.

In this example, you will choose to permanently kill articles with the subject "boring post" in the group *misc.test*. The prompts you see will of course vary according to the options you choose. Begin by pressing **ESC k** to edit the file *misc.test.KILL,*[*] which is the group-specific kill file for *misc.test.*

```
 D 35563:+[  1:cmcneil@mta.c] test
   35564: [  4:usenet.test@c] TEST FROM CANREM
   35565: [ 16:Pai-Satish@CS] testing followup-to: poster
   35566: [  1:cmcneil@mta.c] test
 --- GNUS: misc.test/35563 {19(+5467) more}      (Summary Thread)--Top------


 -----Emacs: misc.test.KILL      (KILL-File)--All-------------------------
 Editing a local KILL file (Type C-c C-c to exit)
```

You now have two choices: you can begin typing kill commands[†] directly into the buffer, or you can have *gnus* insert a template for you to follow. Let's do the latter, asking for a subject template by typing **CTRL-c CTRL-k CTRL-s**.

```
  D 35563:+[  1:cmcneil@mta.c] test
    35564: [  4:usenet.test@c] TEST FROM CANREM
    35565: [ 16:Pai-Satish@CS] testing followup-to: poster
    35566: [  1:cmcneil@mta.c] test
 --- GNUS: misc.test/35563 {19(+5467) more}      (Summary Thread)--Top------
 (gnus-kill "Subject" "test")

 --**-Emacs: misc.test.KILL      (KILL-File)--All-------------------------
```

This has inserted a *gnus-kill* command for the Subject "test". Edit this to reflect the subject you wish to avoid ("boring post"), and add the command *gnus-expunge* to the end of the file.

```
 D 35563:+[  1:cmcneil@mta.c] test
   35564: [  4:usenet.test@c] TEST FROM CANREM
   35565: [ 16:Pai-Satish@CS] testing followup-to: poster
   35566: [  1:cmcneil@mta.c] test
 --- GNUS: misc.test/35563 {19(+5467) more}      (Summary Thread)--Top------
 (gnus-kill "Subject" "boring post")
 (gnus-expunge "X")

 --**-Emacs: misc.test.KILL      (KILL-File)--All-------------------------
```

----

[*] Again, assuming that you have long filenames on your system. If you are on a system that does not support long filenames, you can change this default by setting the variable ***gnus-use-long-file-name*** to nil. Your news administrator may already have done this. You can check the value of this variable by typing **CTRL-h v** and entering the name of the variable.

[†] In fact, any *Emacs* LISP commands.

Finally, type **CTRL-c CTRL-c** to save the kill file and return to reading news.

Unkilling

There is no built-in command to undo a kill command. Perhaps there doesn't need to be. To undo a kill command, just edit the appropriate kill file and get rid of any *gnus-kill* commands you don't want. Type **ESC k** or **ESC K** to edit the appropriate file; delete any lines you don't want; and type **CTRL-c CTRL-c** to save your changes.

Customizing gnus

One of *gnus'* big advantages is that it is part of *Emacs*. This gives you more than the ability to read news without leaving your editor. It also means that you can customize *gnus* the same way as other *Emacs* packages. All the standard *Emacs* commands are available, and there is no special syntax to learn.

As you probably know, *Emacs* uses a version of LISP as its customization language. As a result, customization is incredibly flexible; in fact *gnus* itself is nothing more than a very complicated set of customizations. We can't cover LISP in this small section, but we'll give you enough to customize the predefined *gnus* settings. Of course, if you really get into it, you can add your own features, display modes, etc.

Files

With one exception, *gnus* employs the usual *Emacs* and news files:

.emacs
> The standard *Emacs* initialization file. It is read once when *Emacs* starts up. Put any of your *gnus* customizations here.

.newsrc
> The standard news-initialization file.

.newsrc.el
> The *.newsrc* file, stored in LISP format. *gnus* does this in order to make news startup faster.

Syntax

We won't discuss *Emacs*-LISP in any detail. If you already know any dialect of the LISP programming language, it should come easily to you. If you don't, a good introduction is in O'Reilly & Associates' Nutshell Handbook *Learning GNU Emacs*. However, for simple customization, you need only one LISP statement:

```
(setq variable value)
```

setq is the LISP command that sets a symbol to a particular value. `variable` is the name of the variable[*] you wish to set, and `value` is the value you wish to set. As with all LISP commands, the entire command is enclosed in parentheses. The following sections show a few examples of how variables can be set.

Variables

Like most *Emacs* packages, *gnus* has many variables to customize its operation. Fortunately, most of these have to do with various administrative tasks (specifying news-spool directories and news-server names) and don't need to be modified. What follows is a list of variables that determine how articles are presented and saved, and how newsgroups are processed. For a complete list of the variables that *gnus* uses, see the online *gnus* info file, or use the *Emacs* describe variable (**CTRL-h v**) command.

gnus-ignored-newsgroups

This variable is used to filter out newsgroups you do not wish to see. It is specified as a regular expression. *gnus* will ignore any newsgroups that match this regular expression while processing newsgroups. For example, if you don't want to read the newsgroups *alt.fan* and *misc.test*, and any subgroups underneath these, or any group that has the word "poetry" anywhere in its name, add this command to your *.emacs* file:

```
(setq gnus-ignored-newsgroups "^alt\\.fan\\|^misc\\.test\\|poetry")
```

This is similar to unsubscribing to these groups, except that it does a little more. It also prevents you from seeing any subgroups: both those that exist now and those that might be created at some time in the future. You can also use it for more general purposes.

If you're not familiar with regular expressions, here's a brief description of how the one above works. It's *not* a technical explanation of regular expressions. The two backslashes and the one vertical bar (\\|) divide the expression into three alternatives; if a newsgroup name matches any of the alternatives, it's considered a match (and therefore ignored). The two backslashes and the dot (\\.) match the dots (or periods) in the newsgroup names. A period has a special meaning in regular expressions; the double backslashes take away this special meaning, saying "this is just a period, only a period, and nothing more." The carets (^) mean "the following character must appear at the beginning of a newsgroup name." So the whole expres-

---

[*] "Symbol" is actually the proper term to use.

sion matches any newsgroup with a name beginning with *alt.fan,* any group with a name beginning *misc.test,* or any group with the word poetry anywhere.

gnus-ignored-headers

This is a list of header fields you don't wish to see when *gnus* displays an article. It's also a regular expression. You'd construct it just like the regular expression above, except that you'd build it from header items, rather than group names. Be careful, though; by default, gnus-ignored-headers has a long, rather complex value; it probably does what you want.

gnus-large-newsgroup

The value that *gnus* considers to be a large number of articles for a newsgroup. If the number of unread articles in a newsgroup is greater than this value, *gnus* will prompt you for the number of articles in the group you wish to read. For example, the following command says that all newsgroups with more than 10 articles are considered large:

```
(setq gnus-large-newsgroup 10)
```

gnus-nntp-server

This is the name of the news server for your site. If *gnus* has not been configured, you may need to set this variable.

```
(setq gnus-nntp-server "news.ora.com")
```

gnus-window-configuration

This variable specifies the configuration of the *gnus* windows when performing certain actions such as viewing the newsgroup or reading an article. It is specified as a list of items in the form *(action (g s a))*, where *action* is either summary, newsgroups, or article, and *g, s,* and *a* are the size of the *Newsgroup*, *Summary*, and *Article* buffers, respectively. If a window has a size of zero, it is not displayed.

This is how the default window configuration is specified

```
(setq gnus-window-configuration
  '((summary       (0 1 0))
    (newsgroups     (1 0 0))
    (article        (0 3 10))))
```

The summary line tells *gnus* to display at least one line of the *Summary* buffer whenever it enters the summary mode; the other buffers aren't displayed. When *gnus* enters the newsgroup mode, it displays at least one line of the *Newsgroup* buffer, and doesn't display the others. When it enters the article-reading mode, it displays at least three lines of the *Summary* buffer, and at least 10 lines of the *Article* buffer. If your screen is larger than the total numbers of lines specified, each buffer will be given correspondingly more space.

The *gnus* documentation gives several additional examples, including the one below, which keeps all three windows on the screen all the time. It is pretty tight on screen space, but it saves a lot of time in screen updating and is useful on a slow terminal.

```
(setq gnus-window-configuration
  '((summary      (1 4 0))
    (newsgroups   (1 1 3))
    (article      (1 1 3))))
```

One hint: if you type this and it doesn't work, make sure you have the right number of parentheses.

gnus-use-long-file-name

If this variable is non-nil, then the default filename for saving an article in a group is the name of the group (*e.g., ~/News/comp.lang.c* for the group *comp.lang.c*). If the value is nil, then the default filename is generated by turning the dots in the group name into slashes (i.e., turning the group name into a directory; *e.g.,~/News/comp/lang/c*). Here are the commands you'd use to set this variable:

```
(setq gnus-use-long-file-name nil)  ;; NIL--use directory-style names
(setq gnus-use-long-file-name t)    ;; TRUE (non-nil): use long name
```

gnus-novice-user

If this variable is non-nil, *gnus* displays more verbose messages and asks for confirmations before performing certain actions.

gnus-interactive-catchup

If this variable is non-nil, you will be prompted for confirmation when catching up with a newsgroup with the **c** command.

gnus-interactive-post

If this variable is non-nil, *gnus* prompts you for the newsgroup, subject, and distribution when composing a new article. Otherwise, you're expected to add these header lines yourself.

gnus-interactive-exit

If this variable is non-nil, *gnus* asks for confirmation when you exit.

gnus-user-full-name

This variable can be used to specify your name. It is handy in case you have a mass-generated account name, such as cs101467, and would prefer to be known by your real name.

gnus-show-all-headers

This variable controls how articles are displayed. If it is non-nil, *gnus* displays all of the article's header lines. Since news articles can have many headers, you usually don't want to display all of them, particularly if you're using a slow terminal.

gnus-save-all-headers

This variable controls what happens when you save an article. If it is non-nil, gnus saves all the article's headers. If the variable is nil or is not set, *gnus* only saves the headers that have been displayed. Saving a file doesn't take much time, and the headers can occasionally come in handy for reference. You're not too likely to need them, but saving them won't hurt.

gnus-show-threads

If this variable is non-nil, *gnus* uses the article list to display threads; it lists replies underneath the article being replied to, and indents the reply. If the variable is nil or is not set, the articles will be displayed as a simple list. The examples in this chapter have shown the articles in threaded mode, which is the default.

gnus-auto-select

If this variable is non-nil, the next article with the same subject as the current article will automatically be selected.

gnus-default-article-saver

This variable specifies the format that articles will be saved in. You should change this if you do not use the standard *rmail* format for your mail and news folders.

The possible values are:

gnus-summary-save-in-rmail

To save in standard rmail format

gnus-summary-save-in-mail

To save in standard UNIX mail format

gnus-summary-save-in-folder

To save in MH folder format

gnus-summary-save-in-file

To save in news article format

gnus-subscribe-newsgroup-method

This variable specifies a function that is called when a new newsgroup is found. To set this variable, add a line like the following to your *.emacs* file:

(setq gnus-subscribe-newsgroup-method 'gnus-subscribe-interactively)

Note the right single-quote before the function name; that's necessary because gnus-subscribe-interactively is a function name, not a simple value.

The online info file contains several examples of how to write your own functions for handling new group subscriptions.

gnus provides four functions you can specify; if you're a LISP programmer, you can write a function of your own. The functions that *gnus* provides are:

gnus-subscribe-randomly

The new newsgroup is inserted at the beginning of the newsgroup list.

gnus-subscribe-alphabetically

The newsgroup is inserted in the newsgroup list in alphabetical order.

`gnus-subscribe-hierarchically`

> The newsgroup is inserted in the hierarchical order specified in the group name.

`gnus-subscribe-interactively`

> *gnus* will ask you if you want to subscribe to the new group. If you answer affirmatively, it will be added to the newsgroup list in hierarchial order. This is probably the best alternative; weird new groups are being created all the time (*alt.tanya.harding.whack.whack.whack* appeared around the time of the Winter Olympics), and you don't want to subscribe to them by default.

Recommended Options

So, after all that, what options should you really use? *gnus'* defaults are pretty good "out of the box." The cases I know where people have made extensive modifications were:

- They needed to modify their NNTP news connection parameters. If this is the case for you, it is probably going to be a problem for everyone at your site. Try to talk your system administrator into fixing the problem globally.

- They were running one of the versions of *Emacs* that uses the X Window System, and were adding Windows-related features.

- They were true *Emacs* hackers, and couldn't bear the thought of using any off-the-shelf package without extensive customizations of their own.

Here is a copy of the *gnus* initialization file that I use, and the one that I give to people when they ask for my advice. It's simple as compared to others, but it's a reasonable start. Experiment and find out what suits you.

```
(setq gnus-novice-user t)
(setq gnus-interactive-catchup t)
(setq gnus-save-all-headers t)
(setq gnus-subscribe-newsgroup-method 'gnus-subscribe-interactively)
```

## CHAPTER SIX

TRUMPET: A NEWSREADER FOR WINDOWS

And Now, For Something Completely Different...

From the world of UNIX newsreaders, we turn our attention to a newsreader that runs under Microsoft Windows. When I was researching the other newsreaders for this book, some informal research (looking at the X-Newsreader headers in several groups) showed that *Trumpet* is by far the most popular newsreader for Windows and second only to *tin* overall.

It was written in 1991 by Peter R. Tattam, and is part of a comprehensive Windows TCP/IP suite that also includes FTP and Telnet. It is distributed as shareware; full details on licensing and payments are included with the distribution. Inquiries can be sent to the author at *peter@psychnet.psychol.utas.edu.au*.

Some of *Trumpet's* key features are:

- Runs under Microsoft Windows
- Is part of a complete suite of TCP/IP programs
- Includes support for electronic mail
- Includes support for Novell networks and dial-up SLIP connections

- Is simple and easy to use
- Provides excellent on-line help

The rest of this chapter is organized as follows:

- Getting started with *Trumpet*
- Working with newsgroups
- Working with articles
- A few essentials
- A sample *Trumpet* session. If you have never used a newsreader before, this section walks you through the process step by step.
- Posting articles and sending mail
- Customizing *Trumpet*

Getting Started

We'll assume that you have installed the networking portion of your *Trumpet* software.[*] If you have not installed this on your PC, then you need to do one of two things.

- If you are connected to a local area network (LAN), talk to your network administrator and ask to have *Trumpet* set up for your machine. It may be a simple matter of locating the software on the network.

- If you are not running from a LAN, you are probably using a dial-up SLIP connection. The connection may be provided by either your organization or by a commercial Internet service provider. In any case, you need to follow the directions given to you by your service provider for setting up your connection. A word of warning: this is not the easiest thing in the world, and there are plenty of parameters that need to be fiddled with in order to get things working. Pick a time when your service provider is available and allocate a couple of hours to getting things set up.

If you have followed the default installation procedure, your program manager will have a group that looks like that in Figure 6-1. To start the *Trumpet* newsreader, double-click on the **Usenet** icon. Depending on your particular setup, you may also need to double-click on the **Trumpet** icon and establish your network connection. When the newsreader starts, it displays a copyright notice and attempts to connect to the news server.

---

[*] The *Trumpet* newsreader should work with other Windows socket implementations, but it's safest to use the ones provided.

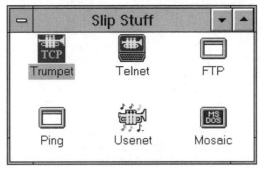

Figure 6-1. Trumpet group in program manager

Working with Newsgroups and Articles

The first screen *Trumpet* displays is the list of newsgroups to which you are subscribed. Figure 6-2 show this screen. If you haven't read news before, you won't have any subscriptions. I will discuss the process of subscribing to newsgroups when we run through a typical *Trumpet* session later in this chapter.

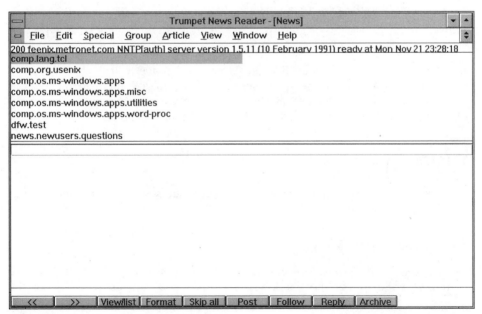

Figure 6-2. Trumpet's initial screen

One of *Trumpet*'s better features is the way that group selection and article viewing are integrated. They work together so well, in fact, that the two modes share many of the same commands. The most useful commands are available as buttons along the bottom of the window. They are:

<< and >>

> In group-selection mode, move to the previous (<<) or next (>>) group. When reading articles, read the previous or next article.

View/List

> Switch between the newsgroup view and article view.

Format

> In the newsgroup view, this toggles between various list formats. In article mode, it toggles between fixed- and variable-width fonts.

Skip all

> In both modes, move to the next newsgroup.

Post

> Post a message to the current newsgroup.

Follow

> Post a follow up to the current article. If you haven't selected an article, *Trumpet* will follow up the first article in the group.[*]

Reply

> Send a reply to the poster via email.

Archive

> Save a message in a folder.

To enter a newsgroup, double-click on its name. *Trumpet* will fetch a list of all unread news articles from the news server and summarize them in the bottom portion of the window. Figure 6-3 shows an article-selection screen. The group *comp.org.usenix* has been selected, and it contains four unread articles.

A Few Essentials

We'll cover more commands later in the chapter, but here are some good things to know about up front.

Quitting Trumpet

You can quit your *Trumpet* session at any time by selecting **File/Exit** from the menu bar at the top of the window. Of course, you can also use any of the

---

[*] Not particularly useful. Perhaps in a future version, this and the following buttons will be deactivated when an article is not selected.

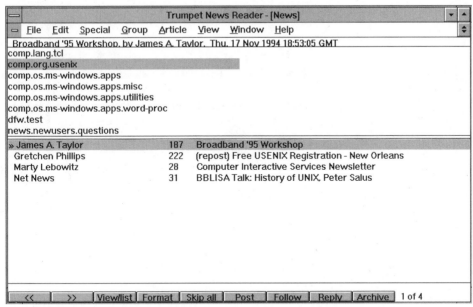

Figure 6-3. An article-selection screen

standard methods for exiting a Windows program, such as typing **Alt-F4** or selecting **Close task** from the Windows task list.

Getting Help

Trumpet has an excellent help system that uses the standard Windows help viewer. To get help, either type **F1** or select **Help** from the menu bar. You'll see the top-level help screen in Figure 6-4. For information on any topic, click on it.

A Trumpet Session

NOTE

If you need to exit this session at any time, simply select **File/Exit** from the menu bar.

With some of the basics out of the way, let's step through a *Trumpet* session.

First, start *Trumpet*. We've already discussed how to do this: double-click on the **Usenet** item in the **SLIP Communications** group. If you don't have this group installed in your program manager, you can use the file manager to launch your

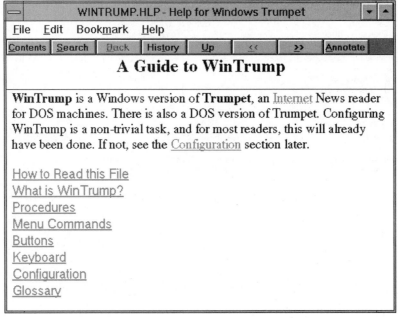

Figure 6-4. A top-level help screen

program. You may also need to launch the **Trumpet** item to initiate communications with your network host.* You'll temporarily see a "connecting" message that tells you *Trumpet* is establishing communications with your news server.

Once *Trumpet* has made the connection, it displays the group-selection screen, seen earlier in Figure 6-2. If this is your first time reading news, this screen will be blank; don't worry, the next step covers subscribing to new newsgroups.

The available newsgroups vary from system to system, so let's go to a group that should be on just about all systems: *news.newusers.questions.*[†] This is an excellent group for learning your way around the Net; I strongly suggest you subscribe to it for awhile. Many questions that will draw sharp answers in other groups will receive patient and comprehensive explanations here.[‡]

Our group-selection screen shows that you've already subscribed to the group *news.newusers.questions*, so all you need do to read the newsgroup is click on it. But what if you haven't subscribed to anything, and your selection menu is blank?

---

* Follow the instructions given to you by your service provider if this is the case.

† If this group isn't on your system, complain to your system administrator!

‡ See Chapter 7 for details on posting etiquette.

To get to *news.newusers.questions*, select the **Subscribe** option from the Group menu. You are then presented with the window in Figure 6-5.

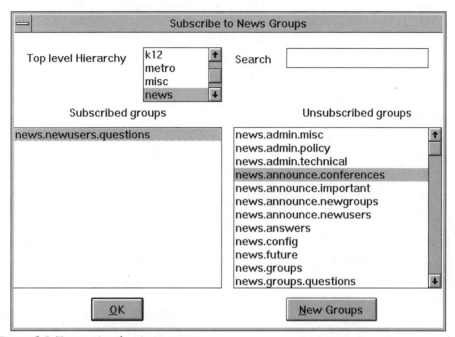

Figure 6-5. Trumpet's subscription screen

To subscribe to a group, first select the top-level hierarchy you are interested in. In this case, select **news**. The "unsubscribed" list box will then be populated with all the newsgroups within that hierarchy you do not wish to subscribe to. The list will be extremely long. Clicking on a newsgroup from this list adds the group to your list of subscribed newsgroups. Scroll down to *news.newusers.questions* (or use the search box) and click on that newsgroup. It will be placed in your subscription list. You can subscribe to as many groups as you like. When done, click the **OK** button and you'll go back to the group.

Now that you're back at the group-selection screen, double-click on *news.newusers.questions*. You are given a list of all unread articles. The list is generally long; use the scroll bar, the arrow keys, or the page-up and page-down keys to move through it (see Figure 6-6).

Now let's read some articles."The Weekly FAQ on test posting" looks interesting, so double-click on it or press the Enter key. You will now see the screen depicted in Figure 6-7.

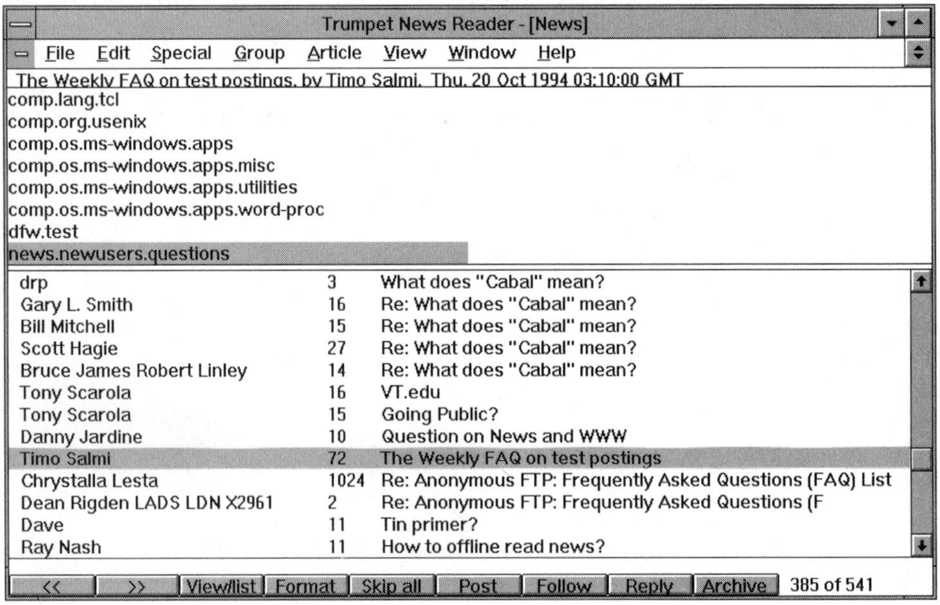

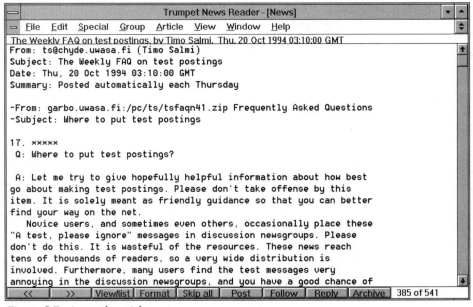

Figure 6-6. *Trumpet's group-selection screen*

Figure 6-7. *A sample article*

To move around in the article, use the scroll bar or the cursor key. Instead of reading the article now, you decide to save it for later. Select **Article/Save** from the menu bar, and a file-save dialog box pops up (see Figure 6-8).

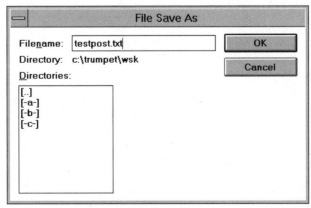

Figure 6-8. Trumpet's save dialog box

Enter the name of the file you wish to save the message to, and click on **OK**. The saved file is a normal ASCII text file; you can print it or read it with your favorite editor.

From this point, you can do several things. You can continue reading the current article; proceed to the next article by pressing the **>>** button; or you can quit. In this case, we'll quit for now and review the files *Trumpet* has created.

```
C:\TRUMPET\WSK>dir

 Volume in drive C is I_LUV_ELLEN
 Volume Serial Number is 18CD-8831
 Directory of C:\TRUMPET\WSK

 .            <DIR>      09-22-94   10:31p
 ..           <DIR>      09-22-94   10:31p
 WT_WSK   EXE   238080   08-28-93    7:36p
 WINTRUMP HLP    88154   05-05-93    5:00p
 README   TXT     3974   08-28-93    8:24p
 DISCLAIM TXT      621   08-28-93    7:57p
 WTDOC    DOC    40777   08-28-93    7:58p
 NEWS     INI     1522   11-22-94    8:01p
 NEWS     ID         3   11-18-94   12:32a
 NEWS     GRP    85703   11-17-94   11:18p
 NEWS     PRM      662   11-22-94    8:01p
 TESTPOST TXT     4298   11-22-94   12:37a
        15 file(s)      543121 bytes
                      13320192 bytes free
```

The first five files are from the *Trumpet* distribution and the next four files (*news.**) are configuration files. Finally, there is the file we saved, *testpost.txt.*

More Commands

This section covers some more of *Trumpet's* useful features.

Seeing Old Articles

Trumpet has several commands for viewing old articles. These are available under the Group menu and allow you to unread 10, 20, or all the articles in a group. There are also selections to catch up on newsgroups.

There are several reasons you might want to do this. Sometimes it's handy to view articles you've already read. There might be some old postings you want to reread, or you might want to review a prior post in an article thread. Additionally, when you browse a new group, you might want to sample a few articles in a group without wading through a ton of postings. You can do all this by selecting the **CatchUp** option from the Group menu, which marks all articles as "read"; then select **Unread 20** from the Group menu, which "unreads" the 20 most recent articles.

Decrypting ROT13 Articles

As mentioned earlier, someone occasionally posts an article others may not wish to see. These are posted in ROT13 format and look like this:

```
Ubj qb lbh gryy vg'f n pbzchgre ercnvezna gung unf n syng gver
orfvqr gur ebnq?  Ur'f gur bar punatvat bhg gverf gb frr jung'f gur
ceboyrz.

Ubj qb lbh gryy vg'f n pbzchgre ercnvezna gung'f bhg bs tnf?  Ur'f
gur bar punatvat bhg gverf gb frr jung'f gur ceboyrz.
```

Follow this two-step procedure to read the encrypted posting:

- Make sure that you really want to read the post. If the subject says "offensive to IBM salesmen," and you are particularly sensitive about IBM salesmen, don't read the post! If you do read the post and are offended, don't complain. You were warned.

- Execute the decrypt command by selecting **Rot13** from the View menu.

   ```
   How do you tell it's a computer repairman that has a flat tire
   beside the road?  He's the one changing out tires to see what's the
   problem.
   ```

How do you tell it's a computer repairman that's out of gas? He's
the one changing out tires to see what's the problem.

Posting Messages

CAUTION

A posted message is seen by tens of thousands of people all over the
world. Keep this in mind when you are posting! The group *misc.test* is
designated for test postings. Try posting there a few times before posting
somewhere else.

Posting New Articles

When you post a message to a newsgroup by either clicking on the **Post** button
or by selecting **Article/Post** from the menu bar. When you invoke the post
command, *Trumpet* displays a window for you to enter your post. As an example,
let's post a small message to the group *misc.test*. Begin by entering `misc.test`*
and clicking the **Post** button. Figure 6-9 shows the posting window.

The first line is the group to which the article will be posted. You can edit this if
you wish to change the group or add another group. The next line is the subject
line, which is filled in as "test post." The next two lines allow you to enter any
keywords or summaries you feel might be useful or informative to your readers.
Finally, you can enter a geographic distribution if you wish to restrict the transmission of your message to a certain area. Leaving it blank distributes the article to all
of USENET.

After you have finished editing your message and are satisfied with the contents,
click the **Post** button to send your message on its way.

Depending on your system, it will take anything from a few minutes to over a day
for your message to start propagating to other sites. You can expect to see replies
or follow ups soon after this. See "Test Messages" in Chapter 7 for an example of
what to expect when posting to *misc.test*.

If you have second thoughts after posting an article, you can cancel it. Select the
Cancel option from the Article menu. Canceling an article is not very effective, but
it will minimize the damage somewhat.

---

* You can use the **g** (goto) command to do this as described in the previous section.

```
┌─────────────────────────────────────────────────────────────────┐
│ ▬                        Post Article                          ▲ │
├─────────────┬─────────────────────────────────────────┬───────────┤
│ Newsgroups  │ misc.test                               │           │
│ Subject     │ test posting                            │  ┌──────┐ │
│ Keywords    │                                         │  │ Post │ │
│ Summary     │                                         │  └──────┘ │
│ Distribution│                                         │  ┌──────┐ │
│             │                                         │  │Cancel│ │
│             └─────────────────────────────────────────┘  └──────┘ │
├───────────────────────────────────────────────────────────────┬─┤
│ This is a test posting.|                                      │↑│
│                                                               │ │
│                                                               │ │
│                                                               │ │
│                                                               │ │
│                                                               │ │
│                                                               │ │
│                                                               │↓│
├─┬─────────────────────────────────────────────────────────┬───┤
│←│                                                         │ →│
└─┴─────────────────────────────────────────────────────────┴───┘
```

Figure 6-9. Posting a new article

Following Up Another Article

The procedure for following up another person's posting is essentially the same as for posting a new article. The differences are:

- You press the **Follow** button or select **Article/Follow** instead of using the posting commands.

- The subject and newsgroup lines are the same as the poster's.

- The poster's original message is included in the editing window, indented by ">" characters.

Sending Mail

Trumpet provides some basic services for sending regular electronic mail. You can reply to the author of a particular article or forward an interesting article to others who may not read news.

Reply

To reply to the article you are reading, click on the **Reply** button or select **Article/ Reply** from the menu bar. A window that is similar to the follow-up window is displayed. Edit your message as necessary and click the **Send** button to deliver it.

Forwarding a Post via Mail

You may want to forward an article to friends and associates, particularly if they don't read news. Selecting the **Forward** option from the Article menu pulls up the forward window. This is similar to the reply window; fill in the recipient's name and click the **Send** button to deliver.

Customizing Trumpet

Most of Trumpet's customization options deal with network-configuration and host parameters. Unlike the other newsreaders we have discussed, there are no special commands for binding new commands, creating macros, etc. If you desire to do these things, you can use the Windows macro recorder or one of the many commercial or shareware packages designed to do that.

Select the **Setup** option from the File menu, which then displays the customization screen as shown in Figure 6-10. Fill in the entries as described below.

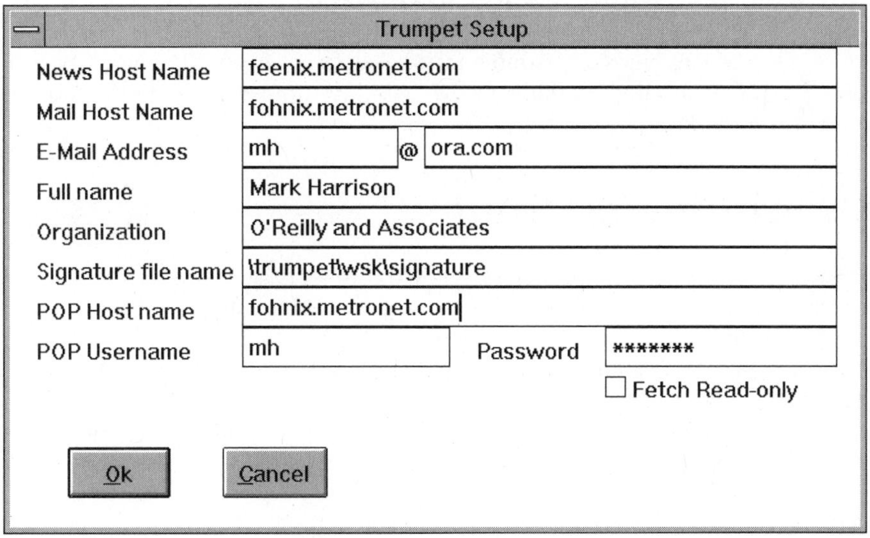

Trumpet Setup	
News Host Name	feenix.metronet.com
Mail Host Name	fohnix.metronet.com
E-Mail Address	mh @ ora.com
Full name	Mark Harrison
Organization	O'Reilly and Associates
Signature file name	\trumpet\wsk\signature
POP Host name	fohnix.metronet.com
POP Username	mh Password *******
	☐ Fetch Read-only

Ok   Cancel

Figure 6-10. Trumpet's customization screen

News Host Name and **Mail Host Name**

Once you've set up Trumpet, you shouldn't need to change these parameters. If you are working on a LAN, your network administrator should have set these up correctly. If you are using a commercial service provider, that provider will give you the names of the news server and mail host you should use; enter these names in the appropriate boxes. If you receive an error message "Can't connect to host..." or "Error connecting to NNTP", double-check these parameters. If these parameters are correct, there may be trouble with your host machines.

E-Mail Address

This is set to your usual email address. It is used as the default on some of the mail and reply screens.

Full name and **Organization**

These are used to fill in your name and organization when you post and reply. Fill these in as you prefer.

Signature file name

This is where your signature file is stored. Whenever you post or send mail, the contents of this file will be appended to your message. See "The Signature" in Chapter 2 for details as to what should go into this file.

POP Host name, **POP Username**, **Password**, and **Fetch Read-only**

POP stands for Post Office Protocol and is used at some sites to distribute mail. If your site or service provider uses POP, you will receive instructions on how to fill these in.

After setting these parameters up, click on **OK** to save the data.

There is also a **File/Network Configuration** selection from the menu bar. You shouldn't need to modify anything in that window unless instructed to do so by your service provider.

An Encouraging Word

Setting up a Windows SLIP connection to write this chapter was one of the trickiest aspects of writing this book. It took several evenings and several phone calls to my local service provider to get things working. I had to do a lot of fiddling with modem parameters and initialization strings, usually resetting my system after each attempt to get a clean start. Once you work out the kinks (I call this moment "SLIP epiphany") though, it's smooth sailing. Good luck, and don't hesitate to call your service provider.

## CHAPTER SEVEN

POSTING ARTICLES TO THE NET

What to Post
When to Post
What and When NOT to Post
Where to Post
Cancelling Articles
Multipart and Binary Postings

N ow that we've covered the mechanics of reading and posting messages, let's take a look at what we actually post. This is an important topic— after all, USENET is nothing more than the sum of its posted messages. Good messages make the Net more useful and enjoyable for everyone. Posting bad messages embarrasses only yourself (or maybe your employer), and can actually damage the newsgroup. After all, the regular participants in most newsgroups include several experts who really know their stuff, enjoy helping others out, and contribute greatly to the quality of the conversation. They aren't paid to do this– they do it because they enjoy it. When they cease to enjoy participating, they'll stop, and everybody loses. It's disheartening how many of the real experts have given up in the past few years. Do your part to make USENET a pleasant place.

What to Post

This section details a few guidelines about what to post. These guidelines have evolved over the years and represent the collective experience and common wisdom of the Net.

Posting your first message is a big step. Be conservative. Don't feel you have to solve all the world's problems in one fell stroke. After a few small questions or responses, you will get the feel for what is appropriate and inappropriate. If you don't, there will be plenty of people only too happy to let you know.

Most of the examples in this chapter relate to computers in some way. However, the same ideas apply to most non-technical groups as well. Being impolite or badly informed isn't any more acceptable in the group *rec.music* than it is in *comp.unix.wizards.*

Good Questions

Good questions are an integral part of the Net, serving to generate good answers and provide launching grounds for further discussions. Some of the attributes of good questions are:

- They are specific. Questions that are too general are hard to answer. "How can I remove a file whose name begins with a '-'?"[*] is better than "How do I remove files using the UNIX *rm* command?" Include details such as version numbers and model numbers where applicable. Give a specific idea of what you are trying to do. Remember that general, vague questions will usually receive general, vague answers.

- They are succinct. If you are posting concerning a problem or difficulty you are having, try and summarize it in a small example. Posting an example of several hundred lines with the comment "It doesn't seem to work" will garner neither sympathy or help.

- They are posted to the right place. Certain groups (such as *comp.unix.questions* and *news.newusers.answers*) are especially designated for "beginner" questions. Other groups (such as *comp.unix.wizards* and *comp.unix.internals*) are explicitly *not* for asking these kinds of questions.

- Finally, be sure that you have made an honest effort to find the answer yourself. Questions that are easily answered by a quick glance at the documentation don't get a very sympathetic response. Even worse is asking a question that is answered in the FAQ. Many old-timers have taken to answering such questions with a pointed reply saying something like "see question 12 in the FAQ."[†]

Good Answers

Good answers are the second part of the equation. If you know the answer to a question posted on the Net, don't feel shy in helping out. It's this spirit of cooperation that has made the Net what it is today. Here's a few guidelines as to what constitutes a good answer.

- It's correct. Remember the old adage to "measure twice and cut once." Double-check your answers. If it involves a command, try issuing it on your own system. If it's an address or a phone number, double-check it before posting. Imagine how you would feel if someone posted a message mentioning a free demo disk, and mistakenly gave *your* telephone number as the source.

---

[*] This question has been asked so often it has attained the status of being the canonical frequently asked question and appears on more than one FAQ list. The answer? To remove a file called *-f*, try `rm ./-f`.

[†] Sometimes not as politely as this, however.

- It takes into account differences between systems. Not everyone uses the same equipment you do. Make sure that you are not posting the correct answer for a Mac when the question was about a PC.

- It provides pointers to other sources of information. Technical documentation is not always a model of perfect clarity, and sometimes it's not very obvious where to look. A reference or two can be a really big help.

  Here's an example. I'm a classical-music aficionado, and a regular reader of *rec.music.classical*. Every so often, someone posts a request asking for a pointer to recordings of clavichord music. I've met several fellow clavichord enthusiasts by providing a reference to such a recording.[*]

Pertinent Observations

Everybody welcomes thoughtful input, especially when it is expressed in a hospitable and polite manner. Feel free to add your comments to a chain of messages, especially if you have some point or piece of information that has not yet been brought out.

Summaries of Answers You Have Received

It is common to get some very good replies by mail when you have posted a question. If you think that the topic might be of general interest, think about summarizing the responses and posting them back to the newsgroup where you originally posted. This doesn't mean to include all the answers, headers and all, but rather to edit and include the information that answers your question (perhaps in your own words), and publicly thanking those who sent answers. When you post your summary message, use the same subject line as when you posted, adding a "(SUMMARY)" to the end, like "Re: Best Stereo VCR? (SUMMARY)."

If you do plan on summarizing the answers you receive, mention it when you post. Sometimes people are more willing to help when their effort helps more than one person.

Test Messages

It's always good to try a test message or two before posting a real message, but be sure to post it to the right place. In this case, the right place is one of the test groups such as *misc.test*. *Don't* post a test message to a non-test group just to test the distribution of your article.

---

[*] If you are interested, it is Igor Kipnis' recording of *The Notebook of Anna Magdalena Bach*, Nonesuch 79020-2.

One interesting feature about *misc.test* is that several sites generate automatic replies to messages posted in this group. After posting a message there, you should soon expect to receive email replies from all over the world, containing variations of the following message:

```
This is an automatic reply to your test message, which recently arrived
here at news system "ee.und.ac.za", which is in the Electronic Engineering
department at the University of Natal, Durban, South Africa. If you need
to write to the human who administers the news system that generated this
message, the address <news@ee.und.ac.za> should work.
```

When checking out this feature for this book, I received about 20 confirmation responses, from sites as far away as South Africa (the response printed above). It's a good way to check how far your postings travel—and how fast. I received the first five replies within two minutes of posting.

If you don't want to receive these confirmations, put "ignore" somewhere in your subject line, as in "testing, please ignore." Most sites will not reply to such messages.

When to Post

In addition to knowing what to post, it's also important to know *when* to post. Here's a few guidelines for that as well.

When You Know What You're Talking About

Feel free to contribute to the conversation if you have some knowledge of the subject under discussion. Posting misleading information or idle conjectures is usually worse than posting nothing at all. When in doubt, remember the words of Solomon: "Even a fool is thought wise if he keeps silent, and discerning if he holds his tongue." (Proverbs 17:28)

After You've Checked Your Answers

As we discussed in the previous section, it doesn't help anybody to post bad information. At best it's useless, and at worst can waste other people's time and energy.

Even if you're a well-known authority in your field (*especially* if you're a well-known authority in your field!), it doesn't hurt to take a moment and double-check your answers. Everybody benefits, and you won't have to waste your time responding to people who complain that you don't know what you're talking about.

Once, I posted a response to a query for trivia concerning the number *pi* and quickly typed in a limerick I learned as a child:

'Tis a favorite project of mine
A new value of pi to assign
  I would set it at three,
  For it's simpler, you see,
Than three point one four one five nine.

Only I mistyped the last line as "three point one four five nine." I received several comments (mostly good-natured) about this. Probably the strongest comment was something to the effect that even if my mathematical knowledge was so limited as to let this mistake get by, surely my literary taste would have caused me to catch the error!

After You've Read the Group for a While

Sometimes it's best not to ask a question or jump into a discussion immediately. Just as in face-to-face interactions with other people, it's a good idea to listen for awhile just to get the general feel of the group and how it operates. It doesn't hurt to look at the FAQ.

Some reticence can also save you some embarrassment. Here's a real-life example. When I was first learning to program, someone showed me how to use the "exclusive or" operator to swap the contents of two variables without using an intermediate temporary variable. When I first started reading *comp.lang.c*, I thought this would be a really neat thing to post. Well, it turns out that this trick has been posted dozens of times, all with the same attitude of breathless wonder at such a neat trick, and regular readers were getting tired of hearing about it. These regular readers lost no time in letting me know that this was old news, and several of them also pointed out (quite correctly, and with various degrees of annoyance) that it wasn't really an appropriate subject for *comp.lang.c*, since it doesn't have anything to do with C programming other than the fact that it can be coded in C.[*]

After a time, I noticed a message with the subject "swapping two variables." Sure enough, it was the same thing. I sent a quick email to the poster, warning him of the flames to come, but reassuring him that he would only be toasted until lightly browned. The poster sent back a very nice note, confirming his level of doneness.

---

[*] If you are one of the few who *hasn't* heard about this neat trick, try this C program:
```
main(){int x=42,y=56;x^=y;y^=x;x^=y;printf("%d %d",x,y);}
```

How Not to Turn into a Pumpkin

Suppose you're invited to a party at a place you've never been, with a bunch of people you don't know. Now you might ask: "If I don't know anyone, how did I get invited?" Well, you have a point. So let's suppose instead that you want to crash said party, and at this particular shindig, crashing is OK.

You're setting off into uncharted social territory, and unless you're Madonna, or Newt Gingrich, you probably see some value in fitting in. And you probably have a lot of questions. What are all these people doing here? Does everybody know everybody else? What kind of conversation is acceptable? Can I talk business or will they think I'm boring? What about making jokes? Is this a serious crowd? How can I find out? Is there someone I can ask? Probably not that guy with the flame thrower. Maybe I'll just cruise around for a while, see what I can see, and do a little, um, eavesdropping.

Whether you're walking for the first time into a new crowd, a new neighborhood, or a new newsgroup, it's smart to scope things out. Different newsgroups have climates almost as diverse as different neighborhoods of New York City. And some are almost as dangerous to the sensitive of heart.

How do you judge the territory? Read postings for a while, at least a couple of days. Follow some threads. Notice people's level of knowledge and how they tend to treat each other. If you read news for expert bridge players and you don't know a spade from a club, think twice about jumping in. Unless, of course, you read postings that indicate that novices are welcome.

Some newsgroups are very receptive to people with all levels of knowledge in the particular subject area and very tolerant in general. Others will munch you up for fun. If you have a lot of confidence, the munching may not hurt, but netiquette still requires you to put your best possible foot forward into a new group.

So, test the waters for a while, until you feel comfortable that you understand the group's social climate. Besides this waiting and watching, it's not a bad idea to find out if the group has a list of Frequently Asked Questions, also known as an FAQ (an "F-A-Q" to some, a "fac" to others).

If a group has an FAQ, it will be posted periodically to the group. It may also be archived at a publicly accessible site, such as *rtfm.mit.edu*. (Check the */pub/ usenet* directory.) If you can't find it on your own, you can always post the question "where can I find the FAQ"? Keep in mind, however, that in some of the less friendly groups, this naive question might elicit a rebuff or two. ;-)

—continued—

Some FAQs present helpful information concisely, and you'll be thrilled to have them; some are long and full of arcane detail, and you'll want to pull your hair out immediately. But if you get ahold of a group's FAQ, read it in at least a cursory fashion because it can help you on a couple of levels. First, it can give you further clues as to the atmosphere within the group, the level of discussion, etc. Second, it can stop you from posting a question that's been asked hundreds of times before. Some groups take the reposting of a commonly asked question well and participants answer it happily no matter how often it crops up. In some groups, participants may bark "read the FAQ" at you. You might be helped, you might be ignored, you might be flamed, who knows. But if you have a question, it can only work in your favor to check the FAQ before posting.

The most important tip to remember in getting through the early days in a new newsgroup is just to hang in there. If the group is less than warm and fuzzy, and some barbs or arrows come your way, let them bounce off. It's only news, after all. And a little flaming never really hurt anyone.

— Valerie Quercia

After Checking to See If Someone Else Has Answered

Before answering a question, take a few moments to scan ahead and see if someone else has already answered the question. If so, don't bother to repeat the answer. This is especially pertinent to simple questions or requests for references, such as "How do I send a signal to a UNIX process?"[*] that doesn't need much discussion. Of course, this applies less to more complicated answers or answers that involve opinions or matters of taste.

Because of delays in transmission, some duplicate answers are unavoidable. But don't make the situation worse than it has to be; newsgroups filled with dozens of answers to one simple question are annoying, and making a newsgroup annoying is one way to drive out the *real* experts.

After You've Read the FAQ

We don't want to harp on this point, but there are so many people who ignore this that we feel it's really necessary. Many of the questions posted to different groups are directly answered in the FAQ, complete with explanations and samples. Take this advice before posting an answer, as well. Posted answers that appear in the FAQ waste just as much bandwidth and are just as annoying as the posted questions that are in the FAQ. Of course, if you can't find the FAQ or if

---

[*] Answer: use the *kill* command. Consult the its manpage for further information.

you're not sure one exists, it's always in good taste to post a message asking for a copy.*

After Taking a Few Deep Breaths

It's inevitable that some one at some time is going to say something that is going to really, deeply, thoroughly, 100% tick you off. Your first reaction is going to be to fire off a searing reply, slam-dunking him right into the ground, and causing him to forever repent of his ignorance and bad taste in choosing to disagree with you.

When this happens, lean back in your chair, close your eyes, and try to think rationally. What was the person really trying to say? Was the posting made in the person's second language? Starting a major quarrel over a minor misunderstanding wastes your time and everyone else's.

If it seems, however, that the person really is as ignorant as he seems, here are a few guidelines for handling the situation.

- Give yourself one last chance. Have you really understood what the poster is saying? Is he really serious? Have you overlooked a smiley somewhere in the message?

- Try replying via mail before you post. Sometimes it's easier to reach an agreement in private.

- Keep focused on the facts. Try to keep personalities in the background. This can be difficult if the other party is a total jerk and refuses to listen to your well-reasoned arguments and carefully packaged bits of wisdom, but do your best. To paraphrase Bill Wohler on this, "If he refuses to listen, just hang up the phone. You don't *need* to convince some random guy in some random office on some random planet that you're right."

- Be polite. Remember that onlookers will be judging you by your responses. Even though many other people on the Net aren't polite, that's no excuse.

- Very occasionally, these discourses will cause a consensus to be reached by all parties involved. In most cases, however, it's best to be ready to agree to disagree.

- When you finally become fed up with the whole matter, go get a copy of Bartlett's *Familiar Quotations* and read the sections discussing fools and foolishness. You'll feel much better knowing that the great minds of history experienced difficulties very similar to your own in dealing with the poor unenlightened souls of their generation.

---

* But first use anonymous FTP to check whether the FAQ is stored at the FAQ archive site *rtfm.mit.edu*. Anonymous FTP is described (briefly) in Chapter 10.

Do You Know the Way to San Jose?

USENET provides a wealth of valuable expertise and advice on all kinds of subjects. You'll find it in group after group. However, you should also keep in mind that a great deal of the "knowledge" available via USENET is no more than what another user tells you. Given this circumstance, there's a certain amount of misinformation. It's unavoidable. And information looks mighty convincing when it arrives via the USENET oracle.

That's not to say that there are lots of crackpots out there telling tales. Probably just a few. ;) But we are talking about millions of people here. And it's inevitable that some perfectly well-adjusted people with the best of intentions will still have absolutely no idea what they're talking about.

Much of the misinformation is fairly innocuous. No lives will be lost if someone looks in the wrong place for a file. Travelers wishing to get from London to Bath will probably make it, even if they follow Wrongway Feldman's directions:

```
From: Pimpernel@Tuilleries.Underground.org (The Purple Pimpernel)
Newsgroups: rec.travel.europe
Subject: Re: Day trips from London
Date: 23 Feb 1995 18:59:12 GMT
Organization: The Elusive Pimpernel\(tm, Inc.

Wrongway (Wrongway.Feldman@Gilligans.Isle.com) wrote:
> Bath and Straford are southwest of London and will take about 3 and 5 hours
> to reach respectively . . .
>
> Stonehenge is more due South of London and is worth a couple of hours visit.
>
> Happy Trails,
>
> Wrongway

Thanks, Wrongway, but I'm afraid that Bath is not southwest of London.
It's almost due west. And every time I've been to Stratford, it's been
northwest of London. And Stonehenge is southwest not south. But we
all appreciate your advice. My regards to the Professor and Mary Anne.

I remain as always,

Your Elusive You-Know-Who

Pimpernel@Tuilleries.Underground.org
"For a jester's chief employment is to kill himself for your enjoyment, and
a jester unemployed is nobody's fool!" -Giacomo, Court Jester
```

—continued—

If you were to follow Wrongway's advice, you might have ended up seeing a bit more of the countryside before reaching your destination. If you read in *rec.shopping.discounts* that there's a sale at Caldor, but it's really at Bradlees, you'll survive. But you certainly don't want to take it on the word of even the most knowledgeable person contributing to rec.pets.cats that your beloved kitty doesn't need to go to the vet.

USENET provides expertise of all kinds and that should not be discounted. On the contrary, take advantage of its extensive resources. Just don't believe everything you read. (Aw, you knew that anyway.)

— *Valerie Quercia*

It's tempting to make theories about why USENET disagreements become so vicious. Part of the problem is that news looks like something you do in the privacy of your own home; in other words, it appears to be a private form of communication. But it isn't; it's really the most public form of communication in existence. So, when you're tempted to nail someone to the wall, remember that you aren't having an argument in the privacy of your own home; you might as well be shouting your insults at the top of your voice in a crowded shopping mall. In fact, probably *more* people will hear you on USENET than would in the shopping mall. If that doesn't stop you, there's nothing I can say that will!

What and When NOT to Post

The Net is a valuable resource for everyone, but only if we can collectively keep discussion well focused and to the point. This section details the things you *don't* want to post to the Net. Take a moment to glance over the items mentioned here. It will save everybody's time and keep you from being embarrassed.

Late Breaking News Events

If you happen to be watching the headline news one evening and they announce some momentous event, don't run to your terminal to post a message "Have you heard about...?" The answer is "yes," and probably from watching the same channel you were watching. As fast and efficient as the Net is, you will only be repeating things everyone else has heard already. Of course, this doesn't apply to *discussing* the events (in the proper newsgroup, of course), but only to announcing the news events themselves.

Frequently Asked Questions

There are a number of questions that are asked so frequently that they have been collected into lists of Frequently Asked Questions (FAQ lists, or just the FAQ) that are regularly posted to appropriate newsgroups. Before posting a question to a newsgroup, check and see if the group has a FAQ list and if has already answered your question.

Asking a question that is on the FAQ list will generally draw a few well-deserved sharp comments, and usually a reference to one of the questions in the FAQ.

Another thing that tends to irritate people is to ask a question and then request that people send the answers to you via email, since you don't want to take the time to read the follow-up postings to your question.

Pointless Questions

Don't ask questions to which there are no answers. Posting a message asking "which is better, Apple or IBM?" will probably not add to your level of enlightenment. The sad part of the story is that there will always be a few people who won't just ignore the question, but will rise to the challenge with partisan cries of "IBM forever!" and "death to the non-Mac infidels!"

"What Time Is It?"

Try and avoid overly general questions. "Should I write my next program in C++ or in SmallTalk?" "Should I buy a Ford or a Chevy?" The answer to questions such as these is quite simple: It depends. It depends on many more variables than can reasonably be discussed, and no one is going to be able to help you without some specific information on your problem. For general questions like this, it's probably best to read a few books or magazine articles. Many of the FAQs have reading lists. It's also a very acceptable practice to ask for opinions on good reading material.

Likewise, don't ask questions that you can easily answer yourself by checking readily available reference material. You can easily answer questions such as "What was the 49th state?" and "What's the most recent version of Microsoft Windows?" without involving tens of thousands of people in your quest.

The question "Does anyone know what time it is?" was posted by Peter Honeyman (of HoneyDanBer UUCP fame), and has become the classic example of an overly general question. Be sure your questions don't fall into the same category!

What Is Cross-Posting, and How Can It Get Me in Trouble?

Well, it can't get you in real trouble. At least not real-time trouble.

If you've been reading news for a while, you've probably noticed that messages are often posted to multiple groups at once. Say you have a question about Macintosh software. There are at least a dozen groups that deal with some aspect of the Mac; you might post your query to a few of them. That might be perfectly appropriate, or it might be overkill. It depends on the situation.

Before you post anything to any group, try to make sure your message is appropriate to that group. Don't guess. Sample some postings.

If you're inclined to post the same message to multiple groups, consider whether the groups in question have many readers in common. In the case of the Macintosh question, there's a good chance that Mac enthusiasts will read several of the related groups. They are not going to want to run into your message six times. Some of them may even tell you so and perhaps not very nicely. And you would certainly be wasting a lot of bandwidth if you could get the answer after asking your question only once or twice.

When the information you're posting is relevant to readers of diverse groups, it's certainly OK to cross-post. In fact, it's a good idea. Suppose, for instance, that you live in New England (*ne* in the newsgroup hierarchy), and you're being transferred to the Philippines. You would love to take your beloved parrot Jasper with you, but he's a sensitive bird and wouldn't make the trip very well. So you decide to find a home for him, and USENET can help.

It's obvious you should post your parrot ad to *rec.pets.birds*. It also sounds like a good idea to try *ne.forsale*. (You don't want any money for him, but you'd like him to go to a local home if possible.) Should you also post to *rec.pets*, or would there be too much overlap in readership with *rec.pets.birds*? There would probably be some overlap, but there are no hard and fast rules to guide you in making calls like this. If you consider your audience (in this case, by reading the pet groups for a while), you'll find these particular people are fairly low-key and accepting. Odds are that no one's going to mind your posting to *rec.pets* as well. Maybe you'll even convince some guinea-pig parent to branch out.

So, sort out cross-posting issues as they come up. It's better for the system if cross-posting is done intelligently. But if you mess up (in someone's estimation), the worst thing they can do is flame you. And you'll live to cross-post another day.

— *Valerie Quercia*

Private Mail

It is generally considered bad taste to post a private message without the sender's permission. Sometimes the sender will imply permission (e.g., by replying to a question where you said you were going to summarize responses), or will explicitly note that you can pass the information along.

A specific case where posting private mail is frowned upon is this: when two parties are having a dispute via email, and one party decides to post to the Net, "See what this other guy is saying? Don't you agree with me that he is a moron?"

Spoilers

If you are discussing a recent movie or book, don't tell everybody the ending without giving them some kind of warning of what is coming, preferably on the "Subject:" line. People will not write and thank you for posting a message about the latest novel by their favorite mystery writer that starts off, "Who would have guessed it was the butler!?"

Homework: Don't Even THINK About It!

You will occasionally see a posting in one of the scientific or technical groups that goes something like this: "Here's something I've been thinking about lately. A right circular cone has a radius r and a height b. A right circular cylinder has a radius of the base of the cone as a diameter. Choose axes conveniently and write equations of the curve of intersection of the surfaces. Any ideas?"

Amazing as it seems, there are actually people who post questions like this, expecting someone to work out the answer and post it, so they can copy it down and turn it in as their own work. Much to their surprise, someone usually ends up forwarding it to someone in their academic department, who then forwards the message to the course instructor. That is, if the instructor isn't reading the newsgroup herself. There's an apocryphal story about a student whose instructor, under a pseudonym, answered all the students' homework problems. The instructor found this greatly amusing, but that didn't help the poor student's grade.

Seriously: if you're taking a course in, say, astronomy, it's pretty naive to assume that your professor or teaching assistant doesn't read *sci.astronomy* and related newsgroups. They certainly know what computers are, they certainly know what USENET is (after all, they've been around for a few years), and they're certainly interested in the subject, so you can bet that they'll be reading the relevant newsgroups. As I said: don't even *think* about it.

If you need to post a question that sounds suspiciously like a homework assignment, it's probably a good idea to state somewhere in your message that it's *not* a homework assignment.

Blatantly Commercial Messages

USENET is not free. People pay good money for the equipment and communication lines necessary for a connection to the Net, and they didn't do it in order to be bombarded by advertisements and money-making schemes all day long.* There are a few groups especially for commercial announcements and job postings. Take a look at the groups *misc.announce.newprod, misc.jobs.offered,* and *misc.jobs.resumes.* Advertising is also acceptable in the *biz* (business) newsgroups.

Here are a few pointers on what is generally considered to be in good taste.

- A line or two in your signature that mentions a product you sell, or your availability to work is usually OK, provided you keep it short and to the point. Two lines are OK, one line is better. Providing a pointer to a further source of information is probably the best. For example, "Send a message to *info@ora.com* for a catalog of O'Reilly Nutshell titles."

- Also acceptable is a brief note mentioning that you have posted a message in *misc.announce.newprod* or *misc.jobs.offered* that might be of interest to the readers of the newsgroup. Don't elaborate; just mention the other message.

- Posting anything to the Gnu hierarchy that even *remotely* hints at the exchange of money for software is a bad idea. One poster was flamed for posting a software request and simply mentioning that he was open to a solution that was commercially available.

Recently, a legal firm posted a blatant advertisement to every newsgroup in existence, not just newsgroups designated for advertisements, or even newsgroups related to legal topics. The USENET community was horrified; now it's not uncommon to see signatures that say "I don't patronize companies that advertise inappropriately on USENET." The event has now become part of USENET legend (the April 12, 1994 "Spamming"). But it's not one of the legends we like to remember. Activity of this sort is much more likely to bring about the "imminent death of USENET" than traffic volume.

A final word on chain letters, multilevel marketing plans, and the like. If these schemes really worked, everyone on the Net would already be rich. We're not, and they don't.

---

* That's why they subscribe to cable TV.

Where to Post

Knowing where to post is just as important as knowing when and what to post. Fortunately, this is easy to get right by following these guidelines:

In discussion groups

Source and binary newsgroups are for the posting of source and binary files—not discussions about source and binary files. Most of these groups have discussion groups, usually the name of the group with a ".d" appended. For example, discuss anything related to postings in *comp.sources* in *comp.sources.d*.

Note that some "text" groups share the same convention. These are groups that are designated for a particular kind of submission, like poetry. For example, *rec.humor* contains the group *rec.humor.d*. The first group is for the jokes themselves (and is moderated); the *.d* group is for discussions of jokes, news, questions, etc. Look to see if a *.d* group exists.

In advocacy groups

In the past year or so, a number of *.advocacy* groups have appeared (like *comp.os.ms-windows.advocacy*). The advocacy groups are intended for the discussions I mentioned earlier, like "Are PCs better than Macs?" Even in this case, though, it's better not to ask questions that lead to pointless discussions and to answer questions in ways that stimulate intelligent discussion.

In local groups

Try to discuss local issues in local groups. Not only do you cut down on network clutter, you are probably going to get better replies as well.

In correct groups

Finally, be careful to post in the correct groups. If you have a question on interfacing to a hardware device, post it to one of the groups in the *comp.sys.ibm.pc.hardware.** hierarchy. Don't post it to the C++ newsgroup just because you're writing your interface routine in C++.

Cancelling Articles

We've discussed when to post and not to post. Now, let's say that you ignored all our advice and would like to undo the mess you've created before it spreads any farther. A handy feature of USENET is the ability to cancel articles you no longer want posted to the Net. Some of the reasons you might want to do this include:

- You post a "for sale" message and sell the item.
- You post a request for help and get your answer.
- You mess up posting an encoded file and want to start from scratch.

- You reply to someone else's post for help but give the wrong answer. You realize the mistake seconds after posting.

- You realize you may be starting a flame war with your rash followup.

When you issue a cancel command (usually from within your newsreader), a control message is propagated to the Net in the same way a news article is. It will eventually arrive at every system your original message did. When the cancellation message is received, the original message will be deleted from the system. While this sounds like it should work, it's not very effective. In effect, the cancel message is chasing your posting all over the Net. Your original message will still appear on servers briefly, and people will still see the message, and the flame war you meant to avoid may start anyway. Cancelling only limits the damage. The moral of the story is clear: don't rely on the ability to cancel messages; it's better not to send the posting in the first place.

Multipart and Binary Postings

To wrap up this chapter, let's consider three special cases: very large files, groups of files, and binary files. These cases are all related, since converting binary files into text and creating an archive from many files usually produces one very large file which must be split into multiple parts before posting.

Multipart Text Files

This is the simplest of the three cases that we will consider. Most postings are just a screen or two long, and easily fit within the 64K byte limit of some posting software. Some postings (such as FAQ lists) can exceed that, so it is necessary to split the file up into pieces before posting. The easiest way to handle such a document is to maintain it in several separate files and post the files separately.

Sometimes, though, you can't maintain a file in separate pieces. If you have a large file you wish to split, you can use the *split* utility to do this by typing

```
% split filename prefix
```

where `filename` is the name of the file you wish to split, and `prefix` is the base name of the new file. For example, the command

```
% split myfile part.
```

would take the file *myfile* and split into the files *part.aa, part.bb*, etc., which you can then post individually. When posting, take care to provide an appropriate subject line that makes it clear that all parts belong to the same document and specifies the total number of parts and the number of each particular part. For example: "Baseball Card FAQ: Part 1 of 1" is appropriate for the first part of a large posting on baseball trading cards.

Shell Archives

The next special case to consider is the posting of shell archives, as discussed in Appendix D, *Where to Get News Software*. Shell archives are primarily used when posting a software distribution or any other collection of files. You could post each file as a separate message with instructions for saving the individual messages to files, but creating a shell archive is both more convenient and less error-prone (for both the poster and reader).

Let's create and post a sample distribution in two steps. First, use the *shar* program* to batch up the files in your directory and put them into some temporary files. We'll put the temporary files into the */temp* directory to keep them out of the way; remember to delete them when you're done.

```
% shar -f /tmp/shar.tmp *
***  Archive contains 7 files  ***
        Forming archive: /tmp/shar.tmp.7
        Forming archive: /tmp/shar.tmp.6
        Forming archive: /tmp/shar.tmp.5
        Forming archive: /tmp/shar.tmp.4
        Forming archive: /tmp/shar.tmp.3
        Forming archive: /tmp/shar.tmp.2
        Forming archive: /tmp/shar.tmp.1
```

Once you have created the shar files, you could simply start your favorite newsreader and post the files individually. Here's an easier way: use the *inews* program to insert the postings into the news stream from the command line. *inews* is a versatile program with several features. We can't cover them all here, but the manpage contains full details. Briefly, this script iterates over each of the seven temporary files, adding subject and newsgroup lines to each posting, and then posts it by piping the result to *inews*.

```
% sh
$ cd /tmp
$ ls shar.tmp.*
shar.tmp.1        shar.tmp.3        shar.tmp.5        shar.tmp.7
shar.tmp.2        shar.tmp.4        shar.tmp.6
$ for i in 1 2 3 4 5 6 7; do
> ( echo "Subject: myPkg [$i/7] package description"
> echo "Newsgroups: ora.test"
> echo
> cat shar.tmp.$i) | inews
> done
```

---

* Another version of this program is called *makekit*; you can use the two interchangeably.

```
$ exit
% rm /tmp/shar.temp.*
```

Note that we had to drop into the Bourne shell (*sh*) to execute the for command.

Finally, go into the newsgroup and check to see that your files have been posted correctly. Note that this lengthy incantation provides an appropriate subject for each part.

```
             ora.test (7T 7A OK 7H R)                 h=help

->  1  *   myPkg [1/7] package description      Mark A Harrison
    2  *   myPkg [2/7] package description      Mark A Harrison
    3  *   myPkg [3/7] package description      Mark A Harrison
    4  *   myPkg [4/7] package description      Mark A Harrison
    5  *   myPkg [5/7] package description      Mark A Harrison
    6  *   myPkg [6/7] package description      Mark A Harrison
    7  *   myPkg [7/7] package description      Mark A Harrison
```

Typing several lines of UNIX commands correctly is a pain. If you find yourself doing this regularly, consider writing a *shell script** to help.

Binary Files

USENET does not directly support the posting of binary files. Instead, binary files must be converted to a printable format, posted, and converted back to a binary file.

There are several ways to do this. The most obvious way is to uuencode a file as detailed in Appendix D, *Where to Get News Software*, split the resulting file, and post the individual sections as detailed above. If we were to post an image of a parrot, the process might look something like this:

```
% uuencode parrot.gif parrot.gif >parrot.gif.uue
% split parrot.gif.uue parrot.gif.uue.
% sh
$ for i in parrot.gif.uue.*; do
> ( echo "Subject: parrot.gif [$i] on the wing"
> echo "Newsgroups: ora.test"
> echo
> cat $i) | inews
> done
$ rm parrot.gif.uue.*
$ exit
%
```

---

* Shell scripts are beyond the scope of this book; they are covered in detail in the Nutshell handbook *Learning the Korn Shell*, and in *UNIX Power Tools*, both from O'Reilly & Associates.

This process is fine for occasional use and is more convenient than doing it by hand. Again, you could write a shell script to automate the process. An even better solution is to use a package such as *xmitBin*, written by Jim Howard. *xmitBin* has many useful features, but we'll cover just the basic steps, which does everything we did via *inews*. Specify the newsgroups with the *-d* flag, and the file to transmit via the *-f* flag. *xmitBin*'s default is to send the binary file to the address specified in the *-d* field; you can override that by specifying the *-post* option. Finally, we can add the description with the *-l* option.

```
% xmitBin -d ora.test -f parrot.gif -post -l "on the wing"
```

xmitBin places you in the editor in order to type in a description, and then gives you a last chance to change your minds.

```
>>>File description:<<<
        parrot.gif is a uuencoded file... This is a 256 color
picture of a parrot flying in a rain forest.

Post 'parrot.gif' to 'ora.test',
                    or change info? ([y], n, or c) -> y
```

xmitBin then uuencodes and splits the message, along with placing a shell wrapper around the files and calculating checksum and file size information. When the files are unpacked, the shell wrapper allows the reader to treat them as a shell archive or a set of uuencoded files, whichever is more convenient. A quick glance at the newsgroup shows the format of the posted articles.

```
                    ora.test  (4T 4A 0K 0H  R)                h=help

->   1  +    - parrot.gif (0/3) {on the wing} [sh]    Mark A Harrison
     2  +    - parrot.gif (1/3) {on the wing} [sh]    Mark A Harrison
     3  +    - parrot.gif (2/3) {on the wing} [sh]    Mark A Harrison
     4  +    - parrot.gif (3/3) {on the wing} [sh]    Mark A Harrison
```

Part 0 contains your description; by convention, the actual data in the message begins with Part 1. For decoding, these messages can be either uudecoded (reassemble the parts by hand, or let your newsreader do it for you) or executed as a series of shell scripts. Using *xmitBin* has may obvious advantages: it's easy and it automatically generates appropriate subjects for each message.

GETTING THE MOST OUT OF USENET

T here are many ways in which USENET can increase your personal and corporate productivity. This chapter tells you how to increase your productivity by using the resources mentioned on the USENET. If your boss starts wondering what he's getting from the time you and your companions are spending with news, show him this chapter!

FTP: Getting Files from Archives

While FTP is not really a part of the USENET, you'll see it mentioned frequently in USENET postings. FTP, or *File Transfer Protocol*, is the Internet's way of moving files from one remote computer to another.

Why is it such a big deal to be able to transfer files to other sites? For our purpose, it's because a large number of those sites have archives where many interesting files and programs are stored. Many postings on the Net describe some package or file, and refer the interested reader to an FTP site where the files can be obtained, rather than posting enormous files to the Net directly. Additionally, many of the USENET newsgroups are archived at these sites. If you want to get the most from USENET, you really need to know how to work with FTP.

NOTE

One of the best sources of information about what is available at FTP sites is the moderated newsgroup *comp.archives.*

The UNIX *ftp* program implements the FTP protocol; so, on a UNIX system, it's the program to use for transferring files. Mosaic, *Netscape*, and other programs also implement FTP; in addition, there are FTP implementations—possibly with different names—for just about every operating system around, including DOS, Windows, and Macintosh. In this chapter, we will stick to UNIX's *ftp* command.

Network Connectivity

To use FTP, you need more than the program itself. You also need a connection to the Internet. Depending on your site's network configuration, you will have:

- No access: your machine is not on a network that supports FTP.

- Access to your local machines only: you are using an Internet-style local area network, but are not connected to any sites other than your own.

- Access to sites other than your own: this is usually what people are referring to when they say they are "connected to the Internet," "have FTP access," or that they are an "Internet site."

Many commercial services that provide USENET access also provide FTP access. Some don't, and others provide it as part of a premium package.

The easiest way to find out which category you are in is to ask your system or network administrator. He may even be able to provide you with a document describing the various networking features on your system. If your administrator is not handy, here are a few tests you can try yourself.

- Try looking for the *ping* command. It is used to check some other system's status. It will most likely be in */usr/etc/ping*. If you find it, try *ping*ing your own system to see if the networking software has been installed and configured. You can specify your own system using the special identifier 127.0.0.1, which is always used to identify the current machine.

  ```
  % /usr/etc/ping 127.0.0.1
  127.0.0.1 is alive
  ```

- If this works, try *ping*ing a system on your network. It should tell you that the system is up. (It's a good idea to make sure that the system *is* up before you run these tests, of course.)

  ```
  % /usr/etc/ping allegra.jho.com
  allegra.jho.com is alive
  ```

If you get a message saying "unknown host", you may not be able to FTP. It's time to check with your administrator.

- If you can *ping* a local host, try *ping*ing a host out on the Internet. Here's an example using the UUNET FTP machine.

```
% /usr/etc/ping ftp.uu.net
ftp.uu.net is alive
```

- If you can't access the remote host by name, try using that host's IP number. (If the host name doesn't work but the IP number does, consider having a serious chat with your system administrator about your network configuration.) Here's another example using UUNET (*ftp.uu.net*), whose IP address is *192.48.96.9.*

```
% /usr/etc/ping 192.48.96.9
192.48.96.9 is alive
```

If either of the last two worked, you are on the Internet and can access files at other sites. If the last two tests didn't work, don't despair. Your site may have access only on selected machines, or your administrator may have other methods for obtaining files from other sites. Even if you are unable to FTP files directly from your site, you can still obtain files through other methods, such as the FTP mail servers described below.

Anonymous FTP

To transfer files between two systems, you normally have to have an account on both of them. You log into one normally and initiate an FTP session to the other machine. You can transfer any files on the other machine that you have permission to access normally.

Anonymous FTP was created so that administrators could let outside people access certain public files on their systems, without giving everyone who wanted the files a personal account. It's essentially a very limited guest account. To use anonymous FTP, start your *ftp* program, and point it at some interesting archive; in the example below, we'll use *ftp.uu.net*. When *ftp* asks you for your name, type **anonymous**.

```
% ftp ftp.uu.net
Connected to ftp.uu.net.
220 ftp.UU.NET FTP server Thu Apr 14 15:45:10 EDT 1994) ready.
Name (ftp.uu.net:mikel): anonymous
331 Guest login ok, send your complete e-mail address as password.
Password: type your email address
230-
230-        Welcome to the UUNET archive.
```

When you see the password prompt, enter your email address as the password. File transfers are usually logged, and most sites mention this in the welcome message. This is done so the site administrators can see how much the system is being utilized, and to let people who have placed something in the archive for public access see how many other people are interested in their work.

After Logging In

FTP has quite a few commands and options, but it is pretty easy to use the most common commands and features. Once you log in, the most useful commands are:

dir [wildcard]
> Shows the files in the current directory

cd dir
> Changes directory to *dir*

get filename
> Transfers the file *filename* to your system

mget wildcard
> Multiple *get*; similar to *get*, but accepts wildcards, so it can transfer several files with one command.

help [topic]
> Prints a help message

quit
> Exits FTP

binary
> Sets binary file mode; should be set for any non-textual files, such as compressed or archive files.

ascii
> Sets ASCII file mode; should be set for any non-compressed textual files.

Here's a sample FTP session. There is a posting in the newsgroup *comp.lang.tcl* announcing the availability of a set of tutorial slides for the TCL language. It sounds interesting, so let's download the file and take a look at it. According to the message, the file is named *tut.tar.Z*, and it's in the directory *ucb/tcl/* on the machine *ftp.cs.berkeley.edu*.

```
$ ftp ftp.cs.berkeley.edu
Connected to kohler.CS.Berkeley.EDU.
220 kohler FTP server (Version wu-2.4(4) Fri May 6 16:09:33 PDT 1994) ready.
Name (ftp.cs.berkeley.edu:mharriso): anonymous
331 Guest login ok, send your complete e-mail address as password.
Password: (we silently type our email address)
230-     Welcome to the UCB CS archive.
[...]
230 Guest login ok, access restrictions apply.
```

```
ftp> cd ucb/tcl
250-Please read the file README
250- it was last modified on Sun May 8 13:49:18 1994 - 59 days ago
250 CWD command successful.
ftp> dir
200 PORT command successful.
150 Opening ASCII mode data connection for /bin/ls.
total 42572
drwxr-sr-x  2 530        163     1024 Jun 25 21:10 .
drwxr-sr-x 30 ftp-arch  163     1024 Jun 24 15:29 ..
-rw-rw-r--  1 530        163     4752 May  8 13:49 README
[...]
-rw-rw-r--  1 530     163  1482599 Oct 21 1993 tk3.2.tar.Z
-rw-rw-r--  1 530     163  1158577 Oct 21 1993 tk3.3.tar.Z
-rw-rw-r--  1 530     163  1156588 Nov  1 1993 tk3.4.tar.Z
-rw-rw-r--  1 530     163  1165237 Nov 23 1993 tk3.6.tar.Z
-rw-rw-r--  1 530     163     3934 Dec 23 1993 tk3.6p1.patch
-rw-rw-r--  1 530     163   114778 Oct 21 1993 tkF10.ps
-rw-rw-r--  1 530     163   133639 Oct 21 1993 tkUsenix91.ps
-rw-rw-r--  1 530     163   271147 Dec 13 1993 tut.tar.Z
226 Transfer complete.
2446 bytes received in 0.3 seconds (7.9 Kbytes/s)
ftp> binary
200 Type set to I.
ftp> get tut.tar.Z
200 PORT command successful.
150 Opening BINARY mode data connection for tut.tar.Z (271147 bytes).
226 Transfer complete.
local: tut.tar.Z remote: tut.tar.Z
271147 bytes received in 16 seconds (16 Kbytes/s)
ftp> quit
221 Goodbye.
```

If you use FTP a lot, check out Mike Gleason's enhanced version called *ncftp*, which adds some nice features that make FTP easier to use. If it's not on your system, your system administrator can find it at most archive sites.

An Easy FTP Script

Here's a little shell script that's used a lot at my site. It provides a command-line interface to FTP and is handy to run while you're reading news. If you see an interesting file mentioned in a posting, run the *ftpget* command in the background from within your newsreader. When you've finished reading news, the file will be waiting for you.

```
#!/bin/sh
# ftpget -- get a file via ftp
# usage: ftpget host file [local-file-name]

ftp -n $1 <<EOF
user anonymous $USER@'hostname'
```

```
binary
cd $2
dir $3
get $3 $4
EOF
```

Here's how you could have used *ftpget* to get the file in the previous example. The script will echo the directory listing of the file as a confirmation that the file exists. If the file didn't exist, an error message would have printed.

```
$ ftpget ftp.cs.berkeley.edu ucb/tcl tut.tar.Z
-rw-rw-r-- 1 530  163    271147 Dec 13 1993 tut.tar.Z
```

Mail Servers

There are many sites that have email and USENET connections, but aren't on the Internet. One problem that people at these sites have is that they cannot obtain files from archive sites using anonymous FTP. Fortunately for these people, several public-minded Internet sites have set up FTP mail servers.

An FTP mail server is a system that accepts file requests via email, transfers the file via FTP, and then packages the file(s) into one or more mail messages, which are then returned to the requestor.

You interact with a mail server by sending it a mail message containing one or more requests for file transfer, directory listings, etc. When the server receives your mail message, it will obtain the files you requested from the specified host. After it has obtained the files or information you requested, it will package the files into one or more mail messages and return them to you via mail. When you receive the messages, save their contents to a file and unpack them.*

Procedures vary among sites, but one command that seems consistent among all servers is the request to receive a help message. To do this, send a mail message to the server with the one-line message

```
help
```

I advise requesting the help file before requesting files from any particular site.

Having said that, here are some representative mail-server commands. These are from the DECWRL *ftpmail* server.

---

* If you are planning on receiving files via mail with any kind of frequency, I *strongly* urge you to try an advanced mail package such as *MH* or *Z-Mail.* These mailers have facilities for automatically unpacking groups of files.

reply *mail-address*
> Send the files to *mail-address*. Use this if your mailer messes up your return address.

connect *[host [user [password [account]]]]*
> Specifies the FTP site to which you wish to connect. *host* defaults to *gate-keeper.dec.com*, *user* defaults to anonymous. Use your email address as the *password*. *account* is not usually needed for anonymous FTP.

ascii
> Specifies the transfer of printable text files

binary
> Specifies the transfer of binary files (including compressed or *tar* files); don't forget this.

chdir *directory*
> Changes to the specified directory. Only one *chdir* is allowed per session.

compress
> Compress files using the standard UNIX *compress* program. (Compressed files should then be uuencoded, so they can be sent through mail properly.)

uuencode
> Sends binary files using *uuencode* format. (Email only handles text files; it can't transfer binary data). On a UNIX system, decode the file using the command *uudecode*.

btoa
> Sends binary files using *btoa* format. Like *uuencode*, *btoa* is another way to send binary files through email, which is a text-only medium.

chunksize *size*
> Splits files into pieces of *size* bytes; the default is 64000.

ls *[wildcard]*
> Short directory listing

dir *[wildcard]*
> Long directory listing

index *item*
> Searches for *item* in the FTP server's index.

get *file*
> Retrieves *file* and mails it to you. There is a maximum of ten *get* commands per *ftpmail* session. If you ask for more, the server will ignore your entire request.

quit
> Finishes the request. This skips over your signature and any other text at the end of your mail message.

Here are a few examples:

- Connect to *gatekeeper.dec.com* and get a root directory listing:

```
connect
ls
quit
```

- Connect to *gatekeeper.dec.com* and get the *README.ftp* file:

```
connect
get README.ftp
quit
```

- Connect to *ftp.cs.berkeley.edu* and get the Tk tutorial (as we did in the previous section).

```
connect ftp.cs.berkeley.edu
binary
chdir ucb/tcl
get tut.tar.Z
quit
```

Sites

Here is a listing of a few of the most popular FTP mail servers, along with their geographic location. Try and use the ones closest to you. In particular, try and stay on the same continent; there's no use adding traffic to network links that are already more expensive and overburdened than usual. Many of these servers will refuse requests that aren't sufficiently local.

Table 8-1. Mail Servers

Site	Location
ftpmail@decwrl.dec.com	*USA*
ftpmail@cs.uow.edu.au	Australia
ftpmail@doc.ic.ac.uk	Great Britain
ftpmail@ftp.uni-stuttgart.de	Germany
ftpmail@grasp.insa-lyon.fr	France
ftpmail@ieunet.ie	Ireland
ftpmail@sunsite.unc.edu	USA
ftpmail@ftp.uu.net	USA

News from The Oval Office

The Clinton administration has taken their commitment to paving the electronic highway very seriously. You can visit the White House and access all kinds of government information resources via the World Wide Web. But even if you don't want to reach out to the President, he is reaching out to you.

The Clinton administration regularly posts news to several USENET newsgroups. They are not participating in the ongoing dialog—simply making information available. You can monitor these postings in the following groups:

- *alt.news-media*
- *alt.politics.clinton*
- *alt.politics.org.misc*
- *alt.politics.reform*
- *alt.politics.usa.misc*
- *talk.politics.misc*
- *misc.activism.progressive*

If you're more interested in the Clinton administration's postings than in the general discussion, you'll probably want to monitor one of the less trafficked groups. Try *alt.politics.reform* or *alt.politics.usa.misc*.

So, what sorts of documents is the White House posting? Press releases, speeches made by the President and Vice President, transcripts of press conferences, and even so-called "position papers," which are formal statements of the administration's intentions in different areas.

If you miss any of these postings, they are also available at the White House's World Wide Web site:

`http://www.whitehouse.gov/White_House/Publications/html/Publications.html`

The past several months of postings are also being archived at various publicly accessible sites. Here's some information about two of those sites and some notes about connecting and retrieving what you want:

1. *sunsite.unc.edu* (Internet address: *152.2.22.81*)

   Connect using FTP, Telnet, Gopher, or WAIS. If you use FTP, log in as anonymous. Beneath the *directory /pub/academic/political-science/white-house-papers* are directories for 1994 and 1995; beneath each of these are

—continued—

directories containing the papers released in each month of the year. If you *telnet* to the site, you can log in as "politics" to perform a WAIS search of the political databases. Online help explains some other options.

2. *maristb.marist.edu*

    Use anonymous FTP. Logs of White House papers are in the *clinton* directory. Each log ends in four numbers corresponding to the month and year. If you have a problem, send a message to Lee Sakkas who is located at *urls@vm.marist.edu.*

    — *Valerie Quercia*

Caveats

Mail servers are provided as a public service and are heavily used. It's important (and just plain good manners!) to use these servers with restraint, so that everyone can get their files and the host machines are not burdened beyond their endurance. Here are a few tips that will help you get maximum benefit from mail servers while causing the smallest burden for others.

- Don't grab huge packages. The best use for mail servers is to obtain small- to medium-sized packages that you can't get through other means. Don't try to obtain huge packages such as the X Window System distribution or *Emacs*.

  These packages will run to literally hundreds of mail messages. In addition to placing a big burden on the server, your own system mailbox may run out of disk space to receive the files. Additionally, if even one of the mail messages is corrupted, you won't be able to extract the other files sent to you.

- Try and get the software somewhere else. Check whether anyone at your site already has a copy. Ask your system administrator; many times they will have a disk or tape sitting around that has a large collection of FTP'able software or packages.

- Watch the source groups (*comp.sources.**) for the package or file you want. Many times packages or updates are posted here at the same time they are updated at FTP sites.

- If you get something from a mail server, send a quick note to other people at your site, letting them know of your recent acquisition. In addition to saving network bandwidth, you can also find others at your site who may share common interests. Posting this kind of information is an excellent use for a local newsgroup.

- If you have the choice of getting something from an FTP mail server or a specialized mail server, it's usually better to use the specialized mail server. Since specialized mail servers don't have to FTP the requested files, they use fewer network resources, and because they are more specialized, their queues are usually shorter and you'll get faster response time. In addition, by using a specialized mail server, you free up the FTP mail server for other requests.

Specialized Mail Servers

In addition to generalized FTP mail servers, there are specialized mail servers set up by individuals or organizations to distribute software or information. Table 8-2 lists several specialized mail servers that I have found to be useful.

Table 8-2. Some Specialized Mail Servers

Server	Description
ps-file-server@adobe.com	Adobe's PostScript file server. A sizable collection of utilities and documentation related to the PostScript printer language.
compilers-server@iecc.com	Archives of the articles posted to the *comp.compilers* newsgroup.
netlib@research.att.com	One of the older mail servers on the Net, this archive contains papers and software from researchers at Bell Labs.
mail-server@rtfm.mit.edu	This machine is an archive site for all the FAQ lists that are posted on the Net. In addition to providing anonymous FTP access, they run this mail server.
almanac@esusda.gov	The flagship of a group of servers offered by the U.S. Agricultural Extension. These servers aren't just for farm info; they provide all sorts of information generated by the U.S. government.

Frequently Asked Questions (FAQ) Lists

From the very beginning of the USENET, there have been certain questions that have been asked on a regular basis. At the start, most of these questions were UNIX-oriented, like "How do I delete a file whose name starts with a dash?" Gradually, these frequently asked questions became more general, like "How do I send email to a BITNET account?" As time went by, more and more new users were asking the same questions over and over; they probably never threatened to overwhelm the Net, but the old-timers got really tired of answering them!

In an attempt to help out these new users and reduce congestion, Jerry Schwarz (then with AT&T) compiled a "List of Frequently Asked Questions about UNIX," and started posting it at regular intervals. The acronym FAQ (pronounced "fack") entered the USENET vocabulary, and people started putting FAQ lists together for the newsgroups they were interested in. These range from simple two- or three-page summaries of particular groups, to postings of encyclopedic length and scope. (As an example, the C++ FAQ is over 25,000 words long and is posted in 20 parts!) At the time of writing, there are nearly 1,000 FAQ lists.

Just the FAQs, Ma'am

Almost all of the FAQ lists, as well as other "periodic informational postings," are cross-posted to the moderated group *news.answers*. Take a few minutes to check it out; there's a lot of incredibly good information there.

It's hard to overemphasize the usefulness of these lists. If you are interested in a particular newsgroup, don't hesitate to try and find that group's FAQ. Don't even *consider* posting a question (especially if you suspect it's a newbie-type question) before reading the FAQ. If the answer should happen to be in the FAQ, you will most likely get a curt reply like "Haven't you read the FAQ? Your question is #12."

Starting a FAQ List

If you are a regular participant in a newsgroup and see certain questions popping up on a regular basis, you might consider starting a FAQ list if one doesn't exist already. There's no official procedure to follow. Most of the FAQs that exist now were started when someone posted a message saying "I'm going to put a FAQ list together," and then listed a few starting questions and solicited input from other members in the group. One FAQ author puts it very well: "A FAQ is often prepared by someone who is not yet an expert, but who wants to take the effort to become one."

Finding the FAQs

Having problems finding a FAQ? Wondering if a particular FAQ exists? There are two great resources for checking this out. The first is the newsgroup *news.answers*. Anyone who posts a FAQ or other informational posting to any group on the Net is supposed to cross-post it to this newsgroup. This means that you can monitor this newsgroup and be pretty much assured that you will eventually see every information posting ever put out on the Net.

This is a lot of information, and it's probable that your site doesn't keep all of the postings in this group on line at all times. There is a site that does, however. You can use either anonymous FTP to access these archives at *rtfm.mit.edu*, or use their automated mail server. For more information on this mail server, send a message to *mail-server@rtfm.mit.edu* and include the line "help" in the subject line. You will receive a help message via return mail.

Using USENET at Work

There are a lot of bosses in this world who view the Net as a fringe benefit for their employees, and mostly harmless so long as people don't waste too much time reading it. This may, we have to admit, be a reasonable view sometimes; it's difficult to justify reading *rec.arts.star-trek* because it enhances your productivity at work. There are a few things that you can do, however, that will make the Net pay for itself in your company. Here are a few ideas that we have seen at various sites.

Local Newsgroups

Many sites set up a number of "local" newsgroups, which are distributed only within their company. Sometimes the groups begin with a prefix of *local*; sometimes they are prefixed by the company's name or the name of the corporate group that set up the newsgroup. Here are a few examples of some local groups that various sites have set up.

local.general
> Miscellaneous postings

local.announce
> Important announcements

local.questions
> Usually technical questions related to work. Sometimes questions relating to company policy or products.

local.forsale
> Items for sale or trade

local.frame
> For discussing the *FrameMaker* system. Some sites have a newsgroup for each of the "store-bought" packages they use.

local.admin
> System administration issues, downtime schedules

local.gripe
> General complaints about the state of the world

local.stock
> When can we retire?

local.project
> Many projects have their own newsgroups.

local.project.cvs[*]

A log of all file updates in the configuration-management system. (More on this in the next section.)

local.secretaries

For the secretaries in the company.[†] Discussions include office procedure, bartering for office supplies, and keeping track of who is doing what in the company.

Looking for Employees

If you have an opening in your group, post a description of your job offering to *misc.jobs.offered* or regional jobs group, such as *seattle.jobs.offered* or *ba.jobs*. You are guaranteed that you will be reaching people with enough technical savvy to read the Net, and saving one headhunter commission will pay for your Net usage for quite a while.

Logging Information to Newsgroups

One of the really interesting uses for network news is in logging administrative information from various programs. Some of the advantages to this include:

- Interested parties can view the information when they wish. You don't have to wait for someone to collate a report, or bother a busy administrator to generate or print miscellaneous project logs.

- No one is forced to view the information if they are not interested. This is a disadvantage of using mail to deliver reports, especially if the reports are long or are sent frequently.

- The information can be archived[‡] for later use.

As an example of this, we use the CVS package to manage the source code changes on our project. When a user commits a change to a source code module, CVS will ask for a log message and save that information in the file. Additionally, we have configured our system (with a few shell scripts) to post a message automatically to a particular newsgroup (for example, *local.project.cvs*) specifying the affected files and the log message entered by the person making the changes. This makes it easy for group members to scan a list of recently made changes and see if any will affect them.

---

[*] CVS stands for concurrent versioning system, and is used to maintain source code control over large numbers of files. If you are using SCCS or RCS but would like something that operates on entire directory trees, check it out.

[†] I feel obligated to say that some of the most enthusiastic USENET aficionados I know are secretaries.

[‡] See the section "Archiving Newsgroups" later in this chapter.

The best way to create a new local group is to ask your site's news administrator. There is a special "control" message for creating groups, but at most well-run sites, it's purely advisory; that is, it's delivered to the news administrator who then decides whether or not to put act on the message. You'll probably get better service if you ask your administrator in person, explaining what you need and why you need it.

Using Netscape to Read News

Not surprisingly, most newsreaders don't let you do much beyond reading and posting news. Some provide an interface to electronic mail so that you can respond directly to a news posting. But for the most part, newsreaders stand alone.

However, with the advent of the World Wide Web and other services geared towards integrating Internet resources, all this may change. Web browsers, for instance, are beginning to offer newsreading functions. Mosaic, perhaps the premier Web browser, has always provided a very simple newsreading function: you can read news, but you can't post.

Now *Netscape* is taking things a little further. A fast and efficient browser that's giving Mosaic a run for its money, *Netscape* offers posting capabilities and an email interface, in addition to basic newsreading. *Netscape* connects to your news server just like any other newsreader. It is also able to read your current news resource file (*.newsrc* on UNIX systems) to find out which groups you're subscribed to and how many unread articles you have in each. Since your news resource file is kept current, you can switch to another reader at any time, without losing your subscription information. The current article discusses the latest freeware version of *Netscape* (1.1 beta), which is available for Macintosh, Windows, and UNIX platforms at *ftp.mcom.com*. Commercial versions are also available from Netscape Communications Corporation (*sales@netscape.com*).

Since *Netscape* does a lot more than let you read news, how to do so is not obvious. In order to access news, you need to pull down the **Directory** menu from the toolbar along the top of the window; then select the **Go to Newsgroups** menu item. *Netscape* will display a screen entitled **Subscribed Newsgroups**, on which appears a list of the groups you generally read, as in Figure 8-1.

Each of the group names appears as a link. With a Web browser such as *Netscape*, this means that the name is highlighted and underlined, to signal that clicking on it will display the group in question in the *Netscape* window.

In addition to the list of subscribed newsgroups, the initial news screen also provides: a long button you can click on to **Unsubscribe** from selected groups, and a text window in which you can input new groups to add to your subscrip-

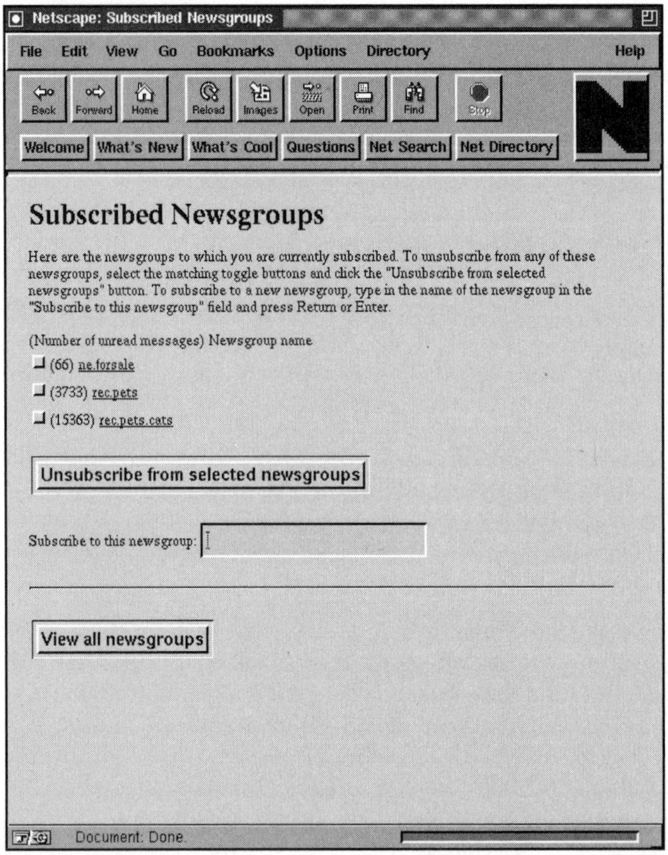

Figure 8-1. Initial Netscape *newsreading window lists groups with unread articles*

tion. The fine print beneath the page header gives more detail about these functions. If you are using a recent version of *Netscape* (1.1 beta or later), there will also be a button that allows you to **View all Newsgroups**, i.e., browse the newsgroup hierarchy. In a graphical browser such as *Netscape*, this hierarchy is naturally represented by icons with labels. In this case, folder icons are used to represent branches in the hierarchy (for example, *alt*) and page icons are used to represent the actual groups.

When you click on a newsgroup name from your subscription list, the *Netscape* window displays the list of unread articles from that group, as in Figure 8-2.

Netscape functions as a threaded newsreader, much like *tin*. To represent the threads within a particular newsgroup, *Netscape* displays the list of articles in an outline or tree format; the first article in each thread is in the leftmost column. Subsequent articles with the same subject line are identified only by their author

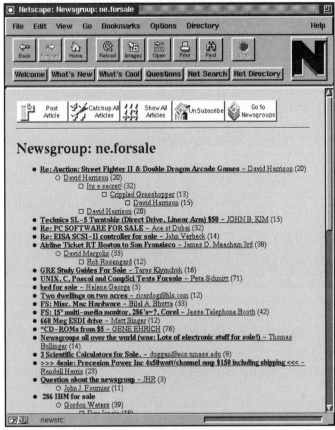

Figure 8-2. Listing the unread articles in ne.forsale *(New England for sale)*

and indented beneath the original message. Follow-up articles within a thread are also identified by author and indented below the article to which they refer.

Notice that five buttons appear above the newsgroup name, but below the *Netscape* menu bar: **Post Article, Catchup All Articles, Show All Articles, UnSubscribe,** and **Go to Newsgroups. Post Article** gives you a popup window in which you can enter a message to be posted. **Catchup** marks the articles in the current group as read and takes you back to the initial news screen. **Show All Articles** displays the list of all unread articles in the group (that's the stage we're at now). **Unsubscribe** edits your news resource file to remove the newsgroup currently displayed; it also bumps you to the preceding screen. **Go to Newsgroups** returns you to the previous level, the list of groups to which you are subscribed.

Each article appears as an underlined link; to read an article, simply click on it. When you select an article, it's displayed in a separate *Netscape* window, with its own selection of command buttons: **Catchup Thread** marks the articles in the current thread as read, and displays the next thread; **Post Followup** gives you a pop-up window in which to enter a follow-up article; **Reply to Sender** gives you yet another pop-up window, this one in which to send email to the poster of the message. On first glance, it might seem like there are two identical buttons both labeled **Go to Newsgroup**, but actually one ends with the singular and one the plural (Newsgroups). **Go to Newsgroup** takes you out of the message and back to the list of articles in the group. (Unfortunately, it does so in the same *Netscape* window, so you have two list windows at once. This seems likely to be changed in future releases.) The all-too-similar **Go to Newsgroups** button takes you back to the initial news screen.

To the left of these buttons are four buttons labeled only with arrows. The left and right arrows let you navigate between messages in the current thread. The up and down arrows move you backward or forward between threads.

The *Netscape* newsreader has some unique and interesting features largely by virtue of being part of a Web browser. Basically, news articles are made to function as much as possible like hypertext documents. What does this mean in practice? Well, if a uniform resource locator (URL)[*] appears in a posting, it is automatically converted into a link. So, say someone posts: "I've found the coolest Web page about styrofoam; go to *http://peanuts.com/cups/ricecakes.html.*" This URL appears as a link in the news article. If you click on it, *Netscape* will take you, via the World Wide Web, to the styrofoam page.

Similarly, if multiple newsgroup names are mentioned in the header of a message, these may be links to other groups. The **References** line in the header contains the article-identification numbers for each message in the current thread. (In *Netscape*, these IDs are displayed as whole numbers starting with 1.) These ID numbers are links to the associated messages.

The message in Figure 8-3 appeared in *rec.pets.* Within the header, notice the links back to the newsgroup and also to a single associated message (which is listed as number 1 under **References**). If the message had been cross-posted, there would be links to the other groups. Likewise, if there were more messages in the same thread, there would be additional links on the **References** line.

The text of the message (which tells you where to find online pictures of ferrets) includes two links: the URL to a World Wide Web site called "Ferret Central," where ferret enthusiasts can (among other things) view and download pictures of their favorite animal; and an *ftp* site from which binary files of ferret images can also be downloaded.

---

[*] A uniform resource locator (URL) is the address of a document on the World Wide Web. The address is contained in a link, which a client interprets in order to connect with the proper server.

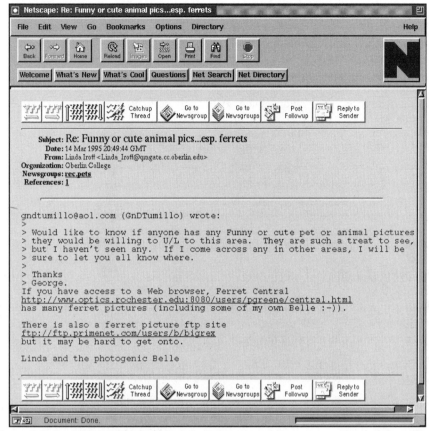

Figure 8-3. Ferreting out the links in a posting

Links within postings should please most newshounds, but *Netscape*'s newsreader does have some disadvantages (at least at this stage in its development). The most glaring one is that it has no kill-file capability. The current *Netscape* also falls short in decoding capabilities and in customization of outgoing messages. However, the program is relatively new, and undoubtedly these and other helpful features will be added.

One very probable addition will be the ability to decode and execute binary postings within *Netscape*. Rather than having to save an image file, decode it, and view it with an external program, you'll be able to read *alt.binary.pictures.puppies* and see the cute little picture of the Maltese in a Christmas sweater when you simply click on the article. Pretty fancy, huh? In the meantime, *Netscape* is at very least a fast and versatile newsreader with a lot of pluses. And if you're a Web surfer, you don't even have to come up for air.

Using USENET at School

Just about all of the uses in the previous section apply to using USENET in a school or university setting. In addition to the uses mentioned above, here are a couple of ideas for making USENET a valuable part of the classroom:

- Create a newsgroup for each class. It is a great forum to encourage students to interact (both with professors and with each other). Homework answers, examples, and supplemental materials can be posted there. It is much more efficient than sending a copy to the library and forcing every student to check out the class notebook and photocopying the material.

- Create a newsgroup for student clubs and associations. In addition to being a handy place to post announcements and other items of interest, it provides an extra avenue for members to interact and provides good exposure to people who might not otherwise have heard of the association.

Mailing Lists

In Chapter 1, we discussed how the first USENET newsgroups were started by creating gateways with ARPAnet mailing lists. Mailing lists are still very popular and relate to the USENET in several ways.

- Many mailing lists are gatewayed to USENET groups. This allows people to "subscribe" to newsgroups via email if they don't have USENET at their site.

- Mailing lists are good for "special-purpose" discussions or discussions among a small group of people. For example, the CVS-Maintainers list is used to communicate between the people who are actively maintaining and supporting the CVS package.

- Many newsgroups have been spawned from successful mailing lists. In fact, the overhead of operating a mailing list with many users is often the driving force behind creating a new newsgroup.

Most newsgroups have two addresses, one for the actual list, and one for administrative requests pertaining to the list (subscription requests, change of address notifications, etc.). To subscribe to a group, just send a note to the administrative address. Sometimes you will be requested to provide some specific information about yourself. For example, to subscribe to the list *camel-lovers@ora.com*, you'd send a message to *camel-lovers-request@ora.com*.

Mail-News Gateways

If there are several people at your site interested in subscribing to a particular mailing list, you might want to have your news administrator gateway the mailing list to a local newsgroup. All messages received are posted automatically to the group, and all messages you post are forwarded automatically to the mailing list. This is pretty handy if several people at your site are interested in subscribing to the list. One big advantage of this scheme is that your mailbox won't fill up with messages from the mailing list when you go on vacation.

A quick note regarding mailing lists: administrative issues such as subscribing and unsubscribing to the list are almost never sent to the list itself, but to an administrative mailing address. It is common for this address to be the mailing list name suffixed by *-request*.

Archiving Newsgroups

Unless you are incredibly wealthy and can afford the disk space to keep every message posted to the Net,* you will eventually have to expire articles and delete them from your system. This is OK in most cases, since most postings are short term in nature. There's no value in saving the contents of *misc.forsale*; within a few days, everything will be sold.

Other kinds of postings, however, are of a more permanent nature. These postings might include:

- Articles in a local group. Many companies will create newsgroups dedicated to supporting particular internal projects or processes. A full record of the newsgroup's activity, including problem reports and resolutions, can be a valuable tool in assessing the project and planning for future enhancements.

- FAQs and other informational messages that are periodically posted to various newsgroups

- Source code to packages posted in the *comp.sources* groups

- Selected articles in particular groups. For example, I save all the articles posted in the Perl newsgroup (*comp.lang.perl*) by Larry Wall and Randal Schwartz, the authors of *Programming Perl* (O'Reilly & Associates). We digest the most interesting and informative messages and send them to Perl users on our system. It's an excellent way to supplement their book.

There's no magic to archiving; just make sure that you (or your system administrator) know which groups are important to you, and that they're saved on some reliable backup medium (tape, floppy, etc.) so you have access to them in the future.

---

* As high-capacity storage devices such as CD-ROMs become more affordable. In fact, there are several subscription services that provide complete archives of USENET postings.

Creating a WAIS Index for Your Saved News Files

newsindex is a Perl script that creates a WAIS index for archived USENET news arti-cles. The index allows you to perform keyword searches on your news archive and quickly retrieve articles that contain those words. *newsindex* can be used to build indexes for both personal and system-wide news archives.

The *newsindex* script requires that Perl and the WAIS software package are installed on your system. A newer version of the WAIS software, such as freeWAIS 0.4 is recommended.

The script also presumes that the articles have UNIX-style mail headers. Since the *nn* newsreader normally changes headers when a posting is saved, you'll have to perform a simple customization of *nn* in order to use *newsindex*. See "Note to *nn* Users" later in this chapter. (The comments at the beginning of the script also mention this tip.)

The newsindex Script

Here's the text of the script. Take note of the initial comments; they summarize many of the points made in subsequent sections.

```perl
#!/usr/bin/perl

# This program is used to index archives of USENET news. It builds a WAIS
# index for all of the USENET articles stored under a given directory.
#
# The default is to index the articles found in "~/News" and store that
# index in "~/.index". These paths maybe changed though command line options
# and the defaults may be changed below.
#
# Once created, you may search this index with "swais -C index_directory",
# for example, if you used the defaults, use "swais -C ~/.index".
#
# Note to NN users: By default NN uses a non-standard format to save
# articles. "waisindex" does not understand this format and can not make
# usable indexes from these files. The following settings in your
# ".nn/init" file cause NN to save articles in UNIX mail format, which
# can then be indexed:
#
#     set mail-format on
#     unset embedded-header-escape

require 'getopts.pl';
# location of the "waisindex" program.
$waisindex = '/usr/local/bin/waisindex';
```

```
# $news_archive is the directory containing your news archive.
# This may be changed with the "-a" option.
$news_archive = "$ENV{'HOME'}/News";

# $index_name is the name of the index.
# This may be changed with the "-n" option.
$index_name = "News-Archive";

# The location of the WAIS index files. By default they are kept in
# subdirectory called ".index" in your home directory.
# This may be changed with the "-i" option.
$index_directory = "$ENV{'HOME'}/.index";

# By default we tell "waisindex" to be silent. The "-v" makes it verbose
$verbose = 0;

&Getopts("a:i:n:v")
   || die "Usage: newsindex [-a directory] [-d directory] [-n name]\en";

$news_archive = $opt_a if (defined($opt_a));
$index_directory = $opt_i if (defined($opt_i));
$index_name = $opt_n if (defined($opt_n));
$verbose = 10 if (defined($opt_v));

# cd to the news archive directory.
chdir "$news_archive"
   || die "Can't access ${news_archive}: $!.\en";

# Create the index directory if it doesn't exist.
if (!-e $index_directory) {
  mkdir($index_directory,0755)
     || die "Couldn't create $index_directory: $!.\en";
}

exec $waisindex, '-r', '-t', 'mail_or_rmail', '-l', $verbose, '-d',
   "$index_directory/$index_name", $news_archive;
```

Installing newsindex

newsindex can be installed in any directory in your path. The first line of the script gives the path for Perl as */usr/bin*. If Perl is found in another directory on your system, perhaps */usr/local/bin*, you need to change the first line of the script to match:

```
#!/usr/local/bin/perl
```

Likewise, you may need to edit the line that gives the path of the *waisindex* command. The default is */usr/local/bin*, and the line in the script defining it is:

```
$waisindex = '/usr/local/bin/waisindex';
```

On another system, I needed to change that to:

```
$waisindex = '/proj/src/freeWAIS-0.4/waisindex';
```

newsindex needs three additional pieces of information in order to build an index: the directory where the news articles are stored; the directory in which to store the index it builds; and the name of the index. The defaults: articles are stored in *~/News* (and any subdirectories thereof); the index lives in the directory *~/.index;* the index file is called *News-Archive.*

All of these can be changed with the command-line options described later in this article. If you want to change the defaults, edit the following lines in the *news-index* script.

```
$news_archive = "$ENV{'HOME'}/News"; $index_directory = "$ENV{'HOME'}/
.index"; $index_name = "News-Archive";
```

Using newsindex

Building or updating an index with *newsindex* is straightforward. If the defaults suit you, simply run the command:

```
% newsindex
```

If you want to index articles that are stored somewhere other than the default directory (*~/News*), you can override this with the *-a* option. If you want to store the index somewhere other that the default directory (*~/.index*), specify an alternative following the *-i* option. For example, to index the articles in the directory *USENET* and store that index in the directory *USENET-indexes*, you would use:

```
% newsindex -a USENET -i news-indexes
```

The first time you run *newsindex*, the index directory and index files will be automatically created. Whenever you run *newsindex* after that, the index will be updated.

Searching an Index

Once the index has been built, you can search it using the *swais* command:

```
% swais -C index_directory
```

If you used the defaults this would be:

```
% swais -C ~/.index
```

When you run *swais* on the index, you'll get a screen like this:

```
SWAIS                       Source Selection            Sources: 1
   #       Server                    Source              Cost
001:   [                 ]  News-Archive                 Free

Keywords:

<space> selects, w for keywords, arrows move, <return> searches, q quits, or ?
```

Press the Return key to move the text cursor to the **Keywords** prompt. Then enter the keyword(s) you want to search for, and hit Return again to initiate the database search. The following example shows the results of a search for the word "food":

```
SWAIS                       Search Results                Items:
9
   #    Score    Source                   Title                   Lines
001:   [1000] ( News-Archive)  Rebecca Bi Re:  Anything's Better Than Se    44
002:   [ 844] ( News-Archive)  rflan@omni Re: Conch Salad                   48
003:   [ 695] ( News-Archive)  pamram@bev Re: Nectarine and Berry Pie       60
004:   [ 613] ( News-Archive)  helen@isla Re: Correction: Strawberry che    56
005:   [ 538] ( News-Archive)  nanetteb@c Re: Doc Martin's Green Chili       71
006:   [ 472] ( News-Archive)  "Laurelin  Re: Conch Salad                   69
007:   [ 421] ( News-Archive)  waring@ima Re: Flour tortillas               80
008:   [ 337] ( News-Archive)  nanetteb@c Re: COLLECTION: Pierogies with   138
009:   [ 261] ( News-Archive)  rtsnlt@cor Re: King Cake Recipe             118
<space> selects, arrows move, w for keywords, s for sources, ? for help
```

You can then use your arrows keys to select an article and press the Return key to read it.

More About WAIS

Newer versions of WAIS offer some flexibility in keyword searching, and regardless of the version, you are not limited to a single keyword at a time. Any version of WAIS will accept a list of keywords in a single search and will match all articles that contain any one of the keywords matched. For example, if a food search is too broad, you might want to search for some specific foods, like "chili" and "beer":

```
Keywords: chili beer
```

This search will return articles that contain either or both of the words "chili" and "beer."

Newer versions let you fine tune multiple-word searches by using connectives like "or" and "and". For example, the request:

    Keywords: chili or beer

would also match articles that mention either keyword. To narrow the matching to articles that include both keywords, use "and" instead. For instance, if you would like a chili recipe that includes beer, search for:

    Keywords: chili and beer

If a version of WAIS recognizes "and," it should also accept "not" as an additional modifier. Thus, you can search for articles that do not have a particular word. If you don't like beer in your chili, you might search for:

    Keywords: chili and not beer

This command will match articles that contain "chili" but do not contain "beer."

Finally you can use parentheses to group keywords together for more complicated searches, as if you were writing a mathematical equation. If you want to find a chili recipe that has "beer" or "tomatoes" or both, the command:

    Keywords: chili and (beer or tomato)

will do the trick.

Note to nn Users

When the *nn* newsreader saves an article, it changes the article's headers in such a way that the WAIS indexing software can't find where one article ends and the next begins. (This limitation also affects other tools you might use with saved news articles.)

In order to get *nn* to save your articles in a more traditional format—one that WAIS and other tools can understand—add these settings to your *nn init* file:

    set mail-format on unset embedded-header-escape

Note, however, that this may create problems if you want to use *nn* to read your saved news archives.

Multiple and System-wide Indexes

According to *newsindex* defaults, a single index is created, even if your news archive takes up several directories in a tree. If you have more than one directory in which you store news, you can opt to build an index for each directory. Then you can do searches on a directory-specific basis. Since one directory generally corresponds to a single newsgroup, there is some sense to this.

If you want multiple indexes, you need to create each one with a *newsindex* command. Suppose you had two news-archive directories (called Work and Play) under your home directory. You need to tell *newsindex* the location of each directory (*-d*) and the name of the index you want created for it (*-n*). Each directory's index requires a separate command:

```
% newsindex -n Work-Archive -d ~/Work
% newsindex -n Fun-Archive -d ~/Fun
```

When you use *swais* to search your index you will have the option of searching either or both indexes:

```
SWAIS                     Source Selection           Sources: 1
    #        Server                   Source              Cost
001:   [              ]  Fun-Archive                     Free
002:   [              ]  Work-Archive                    Free

Keywords:                                    (

<space> selects, w for keywords, arrows move, <return> searches, q quits, or ?
```

Using the arrow keys, you can select and search either index by moving to its entry and hitting the Return key. To search multiple indexes at once, move to each of them sequentially and select by hitting the space bar; then type **w** to initiate the search through all selected indexes.

Creating New Groups

With hundreds of groups currently in the USENET hierarchy, and more being added every day, it's reasonable to ask how these groups were created.

As USENET moved from being a few connected sites to something larger, it became apparent that more groups were needed in order to handle the increasing traffic. Since the Net has no central control point, any site can issue the commands to create new groups. In order to keep the Net from collapsing into a chaotic mass of disassociated groups, a Net-wide discussion was held, and a consensus formed on the process for creating new groups.

The actual rules are reproduced in Appendix B, but they boil down to this:

- A formal, written proposal must be posted to *news.groups* and any groups likely to be affected by the proposed group. This is the "Call For Discussion," or CFD.

- After the designated discussion period, it may be obvious that there is no consensus for creating the new group. Reasons may include overlap with another group, lack of interest, or disagreements with the group as it was described in the proposal. If this is the case, no further action is taken, and the newsgroup will not be created.

- If there does seem to be interest in the new group, a "Call For Votes" (CFV) is posted to *news.groups* which details voting guidelines, cutoff dates, and the like. The person who issued the call for votes is usually responsible for tallying the votes cast and making sure the voting guidelines are followed. Voting is done by email. Usually two addresses are set up, one for "yes" votes and one for "no" votes. Individuals vote by sending a message to the address of their choice.

- After the time limit for voting has expired, the votes are tallied and the results issued. For the proposal to carry, there must have been at least 100 votes cast, and the number of "yes" votes must outnumber the number of "no" votes by at least 100. (A proposal has been made that, because of the ever-rising number of people on the Net, the number of "yes" votes should outnumber the number of "no" votes by at least a two-to-one margin.)

The Net has grown very successfully using this simple mechanism. As with any democratic process, though, people can get pretty emotional, and debate can be heated. Two famous examples of this can be summarized by asking the questions "Is *Star Trek* a branch of science fiction?" and "Is keeping an aquarium a recreational activity or a scientific one?" The consensus for the first question is that it is a kind of science fiction, but that it is unique enough in its own right to deserve a dedicated newsgroup. The utter lack of consensus on the second question can be deduced from the existence of both *rec.aquaria* and *sci.aquaria*. The fact that this episode also caused the group *alt.aquaria* to be formed gives some idea of the incredibly intense debate this seemingly innocent question caused.

This orderly process doesn't apply to the *alt* newsgroups, which are (by definition) a free-for-all. *alt* groups are created all the time; no votes are taken; and many groups are created only for shock value, or to show off a cute, obnoxious, or clever name. (If you don't have a clue as to what *alt.sports.tonya-harding.whack.whack.whack* might mean, you're a better person than I.)

No newsreader has a "create new group" command. Creating a group involves crafting a special kind of message and posting it. The format of the group-creation message is beyond the scope of this book. In the official (non-*alt*) groups, there is a recognized authority for issuing these messages, so if you create one on your own, it will be ignored.

Administration

This section contains a brief description of some of the issues involved in news administration. USENET administration is a topic large enough to deserve its own book,[*] but here are a few items that will get you started, and some pointers to interesting places to snoop around.

Administrators

Every USENET site requires some care and feeding to make sure that incoming news is really arriving, outgoing news is really going, new groups get created properly, and that the news articles don't overflow the disk. News administrators have the job of keeping everything running smoothly. Here are the three kinds of administrators.

The Good

One of the nice things about the Net is the fact that, from the user's perspective, it seems to run itself with absolutely no effort. Your local news administrator has probably put in quite a bit of work to see that this is the case. If you appreciate this, let your administrator know; sometimes they are on the receiving end of a lot of complaining, and a kind word now and then is greatly appreciated.[†]

The Bad

Sometimes, though, you may be at a really poorly administered site. Your connections are unreliable, your news feeds are erratic, and the whole thing is generally a mess. This can be caused by several factors. Your admin may be sincere in wanting to help, but is so swamped by everything else he is doing that he just doesn't have the time. He may want to help, but doesn't know how to get started (often the case when the person who set up news originally has moved on to other things).

In unfortunate cases, the administrator just plain doesn't care. He doesn't read news, and he doesn't think *you* should be reading news either. (It has been my experience that many times this is a defensive posture taken to cover up the fact that they don't even know *how* to read news, let alone administer it.)

The Volunteers

One cure for bad news administration is to volunteer to take on some of the administrative duties yourself. Most administrators will gladly accept offers of help, since it relieves them of some worries and frees up more of their time. In many cases, they just need someone who can double-check that things are working smoothly and let them know when there's a problem. This can include mundane but critical tasks such as checking system log files, disk-space usage,

---

[*] For example, *Managing UUCP and USENET* by O'Reilly & Associates.

[†] If you *really* want to see your admin fall on the floor, try sending a nice note to his or her boss.

and modem connections. You can gradually work your way up the ladder to becoming the chief USENET guru at your site.[*]

Some Commands and Files

As stated earlier, USENET administration is a pretty broad topic, and we couldn't hope to provide even a cursory overview of that topic in the limited space we have here. However, there are a few commands that come with the news software that are useful to know about, and that can give you insight into how the Net really operates. There are also a few configuration files that will help you understand your site's news situation. We mention most of these items because they are either commonly referred to on the Net, or because they are useful in their own right.[†]

A-news, B-news, C-news
> These are not individual programs, but rather the three main releases of the news-transport software. A-news was the original; B-news followed by several years and introduced a number of features. Most sites are currently running C-news, which has significant performance benefits over the earlier news versions. If your site is not using C-news or INN, get your administrator to upgrade to one or the other *immediately.*

INN
> Another news transport software system functionally equivalent to C-news. Common wisdom says that INN is better for large sites (i.e., sites with multiple incoming and outgoing news feeds).

NNTP
> The Network News Transport Protocol—used to transport articles over the Internet.

UUCP
> The UNIX-to-UNIX copy program—used to transport articles (and other things) between UNIX systems via modem

checknews
> Prints whether or not you have news to read; a handy thing to put in your login script.

addgroup
> Used to add a local group at your site. Groups added with this command will not be propagated to other sites.

delgroup
> Used to delete a local group created via *addgroup.*

---

[*] This is how I first became involved with news administration myself.

[†] For example, I mentioned in the section above that you can post revision control changes automatically to a local newsgroup. the *inews* program.

postnews

A simplified front end for posting articles to the Net. All its functionality is duplicated in most newsreaders, but it'd a handy program to use in building shell scripts, etc., that post messages to local groups.

inews

Creates an article and posts it on the Net. It stands for "insert news," and it is common to hear people refer to inserting an article into the news stream.

expire

The program that scans over the news directory and deletes (expires) old articles. The news administrator at each site can configure the expiration times for the various groups. If you find that articles are expiring in your favorite group, don't hesitate to ask your administrator to increase the expiration time.[*]

Where News Files Are Located

This varies from site to site, so double check with your administrator if you can't find them in the places mentioned in this section.

News articles

News articles are usually stored in the directories */usr/spool/news* or */var/spool/news* on your news server. Once you locate your news server and find this directory, the layout of the subdirectories below is pretty standard. Directories are created for each newsgroup, with each component of a group name being mapped to a subdirectory. So, for example, the newsgroup *comp.lang.tcl* is stored in the subdirectory *comp/lang/tcl* under your news spool directory. Therefore, the fully qualified name might be */usr/spool/news/comp/lang/tcl*.

Messages are stored, one per file, in the directory corresponding to the group the message was posted to. Filenames are numeric and correspond to the order in which the articles arrive at the site, so the filename of the first article received in a particular group is *1*, the second article is *2*, and so on. If you see an article *3752*, you can assume that your site has received 3,751 messages in this group prior to receiving this one. Because of expiration, only a few of those 3,751 messages will be on your system.

---

[*] In fact, it can be pretty interesting to check your system administrator's expiration parameters and see how long it takes *his* favorite groups to expire!

News configuration files

Configuration files are often stored in */usr/lib/news* or in */usr/local/lib/news*. Interesting files here include:

active
> Contains the list of newsgroups subscribed to at your site

history
> Contains an accounting of all message transfers, indexed by message ID, between your site and your neighbors. This is what keeps sites from receiving duplicate messages.

explist
> Controls the expiry of articles in the various newsgroups

newsgroups
> A listing of all current newsgroups. Most groups have a one-line description as well.

nntp.log
> The log of NNTP connections at your site. It can be interesting to browse through this file to see where your messages come from.

nn/
> This directory contains the various *nn* newsreader library files.

Over a local area network

If you can't find a spool directory and are on a LAN, the chances are pretty good that your site is storing articles on a central machine and using NNTP to transport the articles. This is very common at larger sites, where the potential disk savings can run literally into the gigabytes. To see if you are using NNTP, try running the command

```
% telnet hostname 119
```

where *hostname* is the name of a machine which might be the server. 119 is the TCP/IP communications port that is traditionally reserved for NNTP. It's probably best not to run this command unless you've had a little experience or are somewhat adventuresome. There's not a lot you can do to mess things up, but if you get stuck somewhere and need help to get out, you will have to explain exactly how it is you came to be in such a situation; try denying everything and start some rumors about "system crackers breaking into the computer." Whatever you do, don't tell them you read this here!

If you are able to connect, a banner message will be printed. A few interesting commands are:

list	Lists the available newsgroups
newgroup	Lists new groups since a particular time
newnews	Lists new articles since a particular time
group	Moves to a specified newsgroup
header	Sends the header of the current article
body	Sends the body of the current article
article	Sends both the body and header of the current article
stat	Prints some statistics
next	Moves to the next article
last	Moves to the last article
help	Prints a very brief help screen
quit	Leaves NNTP

In Case of Emergency, Break Glass or, When Bad Things Happen to Good Administrators

This section is for news administrators and their users. Does your site have an emergency policy? What will you do if your legal department calls you to let you know that someone is suing your company for something that someone is posting? What will you do if your mail spool fills up with thousands of angry messages aimed at one of your users? Here are some guidelines for handling (and preventing) this situation.

Before a problem occurs:

1. Make sure your site has a policy on objectionable postings and that your users know this policy. At the very least, this policy should be one of observing proper netiquette. Depending on your site it can also include guidelines on posting proprietary company data, source code, or issues of national security.

2. If you are at a corporation or other large institution, make sure your management chain and legal department are aware of the USENET. "What is this 'USENET' and why is someone suing us over it?" is not a good way to introduce someone to the Net.

If a problem occurs (such as receiving mail complaining about one of your users, or someone calling you threatening a lawsuit), take these actions:

1. Investigate the posting in question. Sometimes your user may be at fault; sometimes the person making the threat or complaint is a crackpot.

    If your user's postings are reasonable, do as little as possible—just enough to cool the complainant down or let him know that he is not going to get anywhere talking to you. Stirring up the pot with inflammatory words will not help the situation.

    If your user's posting does violate your site's policy, continue with these steps:

2. Have the user cancel the posting immediately. If you can't get in contact with your user and the posting is really bad, cancel it yourself.

3. Counsel the user about appropriate postings. Remind him of your site's guidelines.

4. If the user has violated netiquette, have her issue an apology to the groups she posted. If the user has offended a particular individual or group, have him issue apologies accordingly.

5. One stupid post can waste a lot of a news administrator's time. In cases where a user does something that invites an email letter-bomb attack* on your site, it can mess up incoming mail for everyone else at the site. Make sure that people know there was a problem, and that they can help ensure against future problems by observing your site's posting guidelines.

6. In case of repeat offenses from a particular user, consider restricting the offender's network access or removing his account. It is probably a bad idea to shut off news service for everyone based on an individual's foolish behavior.

For Users

1. Help your news administrator out by trying not to cause problems. Avoid flamage, think before you post, and observe good netiquette. Alienating your admins by causing them lots of extra work is never a good idea.

2. Don't depend on disclaimers attached to the bottom of your message. A good image for your site depends on good postings from your site. If you post

---

* Of course, an email letter-bomb attack cannot be nearly as dramatic or devastating as the real thing. Typically, an attack consists of a rapid-fire bombardment of thousands of senseless email messages to a particular address—enough potentially to cripple the site. This may be provoked by the (presumably unfortunate) act of someone at the site. But sometimes a mischief-making outsider will incite an email onslaught by posting a message that leads well-meaning people to believe that sending mail to this address would be a good thing. Just another form of hoax, I'm afraid. See "Hoaxes, Forgeries, and Other Such Matters" in Chapter 9.

from your workplace, ask yourself if you would feel comfortable printing your post on company letterhead and sending a copy to your boss.

3. If you see someone at another site committing a serious breach of netiquette, a simple note to that site's administrator (usually *postmaster@site*) is enough. Don't make life miserable for that administrator by contributing to an email letter-bomb campaign. If for no other reason, her or she might complain to your administrator and get a very sympathetic response.

When in doubt, just remember: the account you save might be your own.

FUN, FEAR, AND LOATHING IN USENET

I t doesn't take much experience reading news to realize that there's a whole culture of symbols, jargon, feuding, and folklore that have evolved (and continue to evolve) as part of USENET. In fact, without much stretch of the imagination, or the dictionary, we could easily consider USENET to be its own subculture:

> subculture: 1. A cultural subgroup differentiated by status, ethnic back-ground, residence, religion, or other factors that functionally unify the group and act collectively on each member...

The USENET subculture is clearly defined by "other factors" since it is remarkably diverse in most other ways. People of widely different backgrounds, locations, beliefs, and virtually any other quality that tends to define a subculture all float together in the USENET cauldron. That's not to say the system is completely demo-cratic and pervasive. Much of the world's population has a lot more serious problems to face than getting a newsfeed.

Still USENET participants combine to form an extremely large and in many ways unique subculture that is growing and evolving all the time. The current chapter surveys some of this culture, much of which should be familiar to anyone who's read news more than a few times. Like any culture, sub- or otherwise, you'll find the sweet and funny, the mad and outrageous, the just plain mad, and every flavor in between. Enjoy the fun, duck the punches and you'll have a fine time.

A Character's Worth a Thousand Words

In USENET, communication is 98% verbal. People offer you advice, information, insights. These communications may read like business letters, or people might lighten them up with jokes. Sometimes people will get excited about something, sometimes they'll even yell. And all of this takes place in print.

This is hardly a revelation. When you type a message, you generally type words. But USENET is not entirely limited to words either—at least not in the sense that we and the dictionary have traditionally thought of them.

If you try telling a friend a funny story in email, you'll quickly appreciate some of the limitations of communicating in type. The most obvious one is that you can't use any vocal inflection--to indicate that this part is suspenseful, or this is a surprise, somebody's mad, there are two voices here, this is a silly part, whatever. And you can't indicate any of this by raising an eyebrow, shrugging, smiling, or clapping a hand to your forehead either. In fact, all of the non-verbal clues we readily employ in other forms of communication are missing.

If all people did in USENET was straight reporting of information, this wouldn't be much of a handicap. Newspapers and magazines have lived happily with these limitations for centuries. But a lot of what goes on in USENET has to do with the mingling and clashing of personalities and opinions. And an ironic comment without the benefit of a laughing tone, or a wink, can easily be mistaken for belligerence, perhaps even a personal attack. The odds of misunderstandings like this occurring are increased tenfold by the fact that most of the contact in USENET is between people who have the slightest possible knowledge of each other.

So, in order to bring more life to USENET communications, and to avoid misunderstandings, a few conventions have evolved. Since we can't smile, or frown, or sneer at each other for that matter, a veritable library of pictographs, called *smileys*, have evolved to do it for us. Smileys employ regular old ASCII characters to create simple but highly communicative pictures.

An artist working solely with ASCII characters is not liable to end up in the Louvre, but people all over the Net have still managed to surpass the primitive smiley. ASCII representations of flowers, animals, cartoon characters, whatever, crop up all over USENET. Frequently, people use ASCII art to add color to their signature files (for more information on this type of file, see "Signature Files" later in this chapter). Here's a look at just a few of the smileys and ASCII art works you may encounter in USENET. Maybe the keyboard is a more flexible instrument than you thought.

Smileys

The smiley (also known by the unfortunate handle "emoticon") was devised to compensate for the lack of grins, winks, frowns, whistles, and other non-visual cues that are sadly absent from electronic communications. Smilies are used to indicate humor, laughter, anger, annoyance, and other emotions in a message. Here are some of the most common smileys:

:-) smile

:-(frown

;-) wink

:-| straight face

:-o astonishment

(Turn your head to the left, and you will see that they look like little faces.) Some people abbreviate the smiley to two characters, like :) or ;) . There are hundreds of elaborate variations on these, but only a few are in common use. According to *The New Hacker's Dictionary*,

> It appears that the emoticon was invented by one Scott Fahlman on the CMU bulletin board systems around 1980. He later wrote: "I wish I had saved the original post, or at least recorded the date for posterity, but I had no idea that I was starting something that would soon pollute all the world's communication channels."

For a large collection of Smileys that shows just how outrageous they can be, see David Sanderson's book *Smileys* (O'Reilly & Associates).

Prehistoric Smileys

Although there is no documented evidence that early peoples carved smileys into rocks, caves, and trees, early network users did express this same sentiment in a primitive form. Before the advent of the smiley pictograph :-) and its many variations, some Netters expressed their joy using the characters <G> to signify "grin."

When <G> proved rather limited in expressiveness, they expanded the emotional range by creating the symbol <VBG>, for "very big [or broad] grin." Later, as computer games and graphics became more sophisticated, the increasingly savvy users evolved the grin system to the smileys we know today. ;)

ASCII Art

Creating pictures with sequences of characters is a time-honored tradition that goes back to the earliest days of teletypewriters and hard-copy terminals. This tradition has been carried on by the USENET community, often showing up in people's signature files. Figure 9-1 shows a few examples.

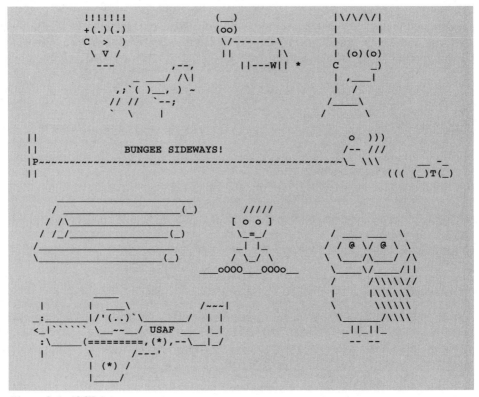

Figure 9-1. ASCII Art

The cow (top, center) is only the tip of a rather large iceberg; cow art is a genre in itself.

Signature Files

As you browse through articles on the Net, you will notice that many people end their messages with a block of text that includes things like names, address, phone numbers, philosophical observations, and the like. These have become know as "signatures" and are usually appended to the message automatically when the message is posted.

The main reason people need signature files is to compensate for mangled header fields in their message. In a perfect world, you would be able to look at the header of someone's message and immediately know their name, organization, and proper electronic address. In this imperfect world, however, this information is often missing or incorrect. Sometimes a person's site has not been properly configured; other times, an intermediate site has managed to mangle these items (this is especially true with return addresses, when the transport software helpfully tries to "correct" fields it believes to be incorrect or in the wrong format).

So, there are practical reasons to have a signature file and those are the reasons people need them. But they're not all of the reasons people have them. Signature files give otherwise faceless USENET participants a chance to show their personalities a little. Sure, some people give no more than the basic facts—a name and email address. Even if they go further, they may limit themselves to purely practical info: phone numbers, mailing addresses, alternate email addresses, even disclaimers ("These opinions are not necessarily those of my company"). But plenty of people make a point of including a bit more of themselves as well: quotes, ASCII art, political commentary, observations on life, etc.

The hard part about creating a snazzy signature is that traditionally it has been considered good taste to limit signatures to four lines or less. Long signatures waste time and disk space, and usually don't provide any more useful information than short ones. They also waste money—many people pay per minute for the time it takes to get their USENET news feed.

So you ask, "how long does it take to transfer a dozen-line signature?" Not long, I admit. But look at it this way. Many messages are short, so even if appropriate, the signature is often 20% of the message. (Headers are often 60%). That means, if it takes some site five hours of connection time to transfer its news feed, an hour of that time is spent transferring signatures—and that adds up to real money. Granted, three hours are spent transferring headers, but there's a difference: News doesn't work without headers; it gets along just fine without your 20-line signature. And there are efforts being made to cut down on useless headers. You can do your part in keeping the traffic down by keeping your signature brief. See "Signature Do's...and Don'ts" later in this chapter for illustrations of pithy yet creative signatures and signatures gone awry. Enjoy.

The Questionable Art of the Flame

As you read various groups on the Net, you will notice that people who are normally polite, well-adjusted individuals will occasionally become raging maniacs posting angry, vicious messages about various topics. Usually, there are several participants, having a heated debate about some topic that came up in a newsgroup. They are participating in a flame war, the electronic equivalent of a bar-room brawl. Sometimes these exchanges are short, limited to a single message (a "flame"); other times they go on for weeks and involve dozens of participants.

Signature Do's...

Do:

- Supply your name and email address.

- Give your *.signature* a little panache if you want.

- Keep it short and to the point.

These *.sigs* would fit the bill:

```
                                ,--,
Nicole M. Gipson         _ ___/ /\:      O'Reilly & Associates, Inc.
Production Editor      ,;( )__, )        90 Sherman Street
nicole@ora.com         // //   '--;      Cambridge, MA 02140
                       \    |


Forrest Gump                           forrest@bubba.gump.com
"Life is like a box of chocolates . . ."


\\\\\\\\\\\\\\\\\\\\\\\\\\\\\\\\\\\\\\\\\\\\\\\\\\\\\\\\\\\\\\\\\\\\
Wile E. Coyote, Genius                  coyote@acme.com
              "That's all folks . . ."
//////////////////////////////////////////////////////////////


    /\ /\
   ^o o^      Cat Ballou
   ->T<-      cat@hoosegow.gov
     ~        Sioux City, Wyoming  -"Where They Hang 'Em High"
___oOo___oOo___


angus@scottish.com --> Angus MacTavish, The Scottish Shoppe
"If it isn't Scottish, it's crrrrrap!"


$$$$$$$$$$$$$$$$$$$$$$$$$$$$$$$$$$$$$$$$$$$$$$$$$$$$$$$$$$$$$$$$$$$$$
H. Ross Poirot                         poirot@orient.express.com
Billionaire Sleuth   Call me when you do somethin' stupid, aw right?
$$$$$$$$$$$$$$$$$$$$$$$$$$$$$$$$$$$$$$$$$$$$$$$$$$$$$$$$$$$$$$$$$$$$$
```

—continued—

...And Don'ts

Don't:

- Get carried away with graphics.

- Use more than four or five lines total.

- Say anything you'll be sorry for later.

Of course, if you want a more elaborate *.signature* to use on a limited basis (i.e., when no one is going to mind paying for the transfer), go nuts!

Here are some *.sig*s from hell:

```
*************************************************************************
Ted Baxter, Anchorman, WJM TV News, Minneapolis, Minnesota
Founder, President, and Dean of Ted Baxter's Famous Broadcasters School
School song: "We have no teams and we have no rules,
                    but we have heart at
          Ted Baxter's Famous Broadcasters School..."
Tuition: $395.  Make tuition checks payable to Ted Baxter
Mailing address: Ted Baxter, Ted Baxter's Famous Broadcasters School,
          P.O. Box 8668, Minneapolis, Minnesota


Good evening, Mr. and Mrs. Internet.  It all started in a 10,000 watt
radio station in Fresno, California...
*************************************************************************
+++++++++++++++++++++++++++++++++++++++++++++++++++++++++++++++++++++++++
E A Poe                                         poe@wayside.tavern.com
Scary Lit Cheap                                    Will Write For Food
                    The Raven
     Once upon a midnight dreary, while I pondered, weak and weary,
     Over many a quaint and curious volume of forgotten lore---
     While I nodded, nearly napping, suddenly there came a tapping,
     As of some one gently rapping, rapping at my chamber door---
     "'Tis some visiter," I muttered, "tapping at my chamber door---
          Only this and nothing more."

     Ah, distinctly I remember it was in the bleak December;
     And each separate dying ember wrought its ghost upon the floor.
     Eagerly I wished the morrow;---vainly I had sought to borrow
     From my books surcease of sorrow---sorrow for the lost Lenore---
     For the rare and radiant maiden whom the angels name Lenore---
          Nameless here for evermore...

To find out what happens to the narrator and the raven, tune in for
the next installment of my .signature file.

Additional samples available upon request.
+++++++++++++++++++++++++++++++++++++++++++++++++++++++++++++++++++++++++
```

— *Valerie Quercia*

Flames and flame wars are not the most admirable events in USENET culture. In many cases, the original point of discussion is lost; it becomes a case of having to win an argument at all costs, or a personality clash between posters. Usually, there are no clear winners, in the sense that one person admits "yes, you were right, I understand your point now." Exhaustion sets in, and the participants sulkily retreat to their own corners.

There is an long-standing USENET tradition that once one party compares the other to Nazis, the topic has bottomed out and no more worthwhile information will be forthcoming. At this time, all parties are expected to stop posting and save their bile for another day.

I am indebted to Wayne Sewell of Tachyon Consulting (*wayne@tachyon.com*) for the following summary he posted of a flame war carried out over a message cross-posted to *comp.org.decus*, *comp.os.vms*, *comp.sys.dec*, and *comp.unix.advocacy*[*] with the title "Is VMS Dying?" There were hundreds of follow ups, and the discussion raged for weeks. It finally came to this:

```
When unixoids who were technical joined in, the resulting flame war was
just like this one: i-can-do-this-with-dcl, but-I-can-do-this-with-the-
shell, which-shell, you-do-it-this-way-with-vms, you-do-it-this-way-with-
unix, which-unix, you-are-a-clueless-jackass, carl-that-isnt-nice-i-will-
tell-your-mommy, vms-cant-do-this, yes-it-can-heres-how, but-this-unix-way-
is-better, but-that-only-works-on-sunos, vms-is-proprietary-and-evil,
sunos-is-proprietary-too, thats-okay-because-its-unix-and-open, dcl-is-too-
wordy, shell-syntax-is-incomprehensible...
These flame wars wouldn't be so bad if they served a purpose other than
raising blood pressure. How many people have switched from VMS to Unix or
from Unix to VMS because of something they read in a flame war?
```

Flame wars may have a purpose. If you enjoy collecting spectacular insults, a flame war is the right place to look. Just don't try them out on your friends.

Cascades

Cascades are among the more unusual forms of communications on the Net. They frequently pop up near the end of flame wars, indicating that this particular topic has been totally mined out. It starts when one person follows up a message with some kind of meaningless reply, usually one that rhymes with something in the

---

[*] This is an excellent way to start a flame war and irritate a large number of people. If you feel compelled to ask questions like "is language *x* better than language *y*," don't post it to both groups. Better yet, don't post questions like this, which are both pointless and unanswerable.

And a Good Time Was Virtually Had By All

What has 179 heads, a dozen cases of champagne, truckloads of lobster and Spam, a cruise ship, a vintage railroad car, more celebrities than the Oscars, a line of blenders constantly mixing margaritas, a murder mystery, and enough diamonds to pay off the national debt? A *net.party*, of course!

In some newsgroups, flame wars are the primary means of communication, and friendliness is considered to be a faux pas. Other newsgroups are warm havens where friendships can be formed between people who may never meet, but who nonetheless enjoy each other's company. Like any large group of friends, these Net friends occasionally decide to get together and get down—and so a *net.party* is born.

The advantages to *net parties* are many: They require almost no planning; you can offer up the most extravagant menu at no cost to anyone; you can have Bruce Springsteen and the E Street Band provide the live entertainment; there are no consequences to be paid for overindulging; and you can present yourself to your friends in whatever manner you'd like to be seen. Consider this entrance to a recent Christmas party in *rec.arts.tv.soaps*:

```
The floor-length green satin was the *right* choice. How she
wished she had stayed with Razz, Tangy and Applet to shop, though!!
The jewelry was okay, but *it had beenworn before*! She hoped no
one would notice. One, two, three, four steps, and turn...The
satin swished softly as she paced. It would be perfect, she thought,
for the waltz with Tom.

Razz stood on the Q[uartermain] front porch and smoothed the velvet of
her cranberry-colored gown..Razz could only commend the Doctor for his
wonderful menu suggestions. The Roast Duck and crisp Chardonnay he had
recommended were a perfect addition to the dinner..Reginald answered,
took her wrap, and asked her if she wanted a tour. Of course, she did!
The house was decorated to perfection. Pine garlands were festooned
around the main bannister. She could see the enormous tree in the
living room. It was decorated in gold and silver. No doubt all real,
thought Razz, knowing the Qs.
```

At first glance, *net.parties* are a truly bizarre phenomenon. Come to think of it, they're bizarre even after you've gotten used to and participated in them. But they're also a lot of fun and provide the opportunity for creativity and a little vicarious living. Since the guest list is as virtual as the menu, I've been able to dance with Sean Connery, sing show tunes with Patrick Stewart, and exchange ribald stories over a bean dip with Myrna Loy.

—continued—

> And if that's not exciting enough for you, as the parties wear on, they often start to resemble...how should I put this...more adult entertainment. Some of this could certainly be considered offensive. The thing to remember as you blush and avert your eyes to the next posting is that the participants are friends who feel comfortable flirting and being silly over the Net. If a stranger were to jump into one of the bawdier threads, he or she would probably be ignored.
>
> Some people hate *net.parties*, feeling that they've got nothing to do with the subject of the newsgroup, and that they waste bandwidth. They're probably right, to a point. But the same could be said for real parties—they take up time and resources and serve no useful purpose, except to make people happy.
>
> — *Clairemarie Fisher O'Leary*

original message. Without further comment, here are two examples. Many more can be found in the group *alt.cascade*, where these things can run to pages.

```
>>>>This is a test message. Please ignore.
>>>Misses a pest message. Peas big more.
>>Kisses for best massage. Frieze dig bore.
>Fishes are best dressaged. Sleaze fig war.
```

This thread started as a discussion of the merits of various operating systems.

```
>>>>This statement is true.
>>>This statement is false.
>>This statement is of indeterminable truth value.
>This statement is irrelevant.
Prepare to be assimilated.
```

A net.jargon Guide

If you've read news for a while, you've undoubtedly run into smileys and ASCII art, and most likely you've also encountered acronyms and shorthand for some common expressions. Everyone knows FYI means "for your information," and FYI shows up in the real world all the time. But USENET has been a breeding ground for lots of FYI-like acronyms, some of them as generic and harmless, and others, well, not entirely polite. Acronyms come in particularly handy when you have a lot to say in a short spurt—like in a flame. The example below contains a flame that employs just about every USENET acronym you'd ever want to see. ;-)

```
Dear Witless Nerd,
FYI, I tried to use your FOAF's program code the other day, and IMHO you
should both RTFM and UTSL. TANSTAAFL, even if you've both been sponging
one for a long time. I have submitted an RFC to the relevant newsgroups.
(BTW, WRT your competence, I understand why you are filled with FUD.) For
```

now, stop spamming us with code that looks like it came from the Rosetta Stone.
And furthermore, your slur against my IYFEG shows you don't know AFT about netiquette. I am going to visit you RSN.
But right now I'm going down to the Foo Bar to have a drink. I would recommend that you find a bar yourself, but you are liable to run into MOTOS, and I wouldn't wish you on them. Heck, I wouldn't wish you on MOTSS. Wipe that smiley off your face.

P.S. Kibo sucks eggs.

If you've lost something in the translation, here's the key:

AFT

"A fine* thing!"

bar

Along with "foo," one of the standard place-holder words. "Suppose you have two files, foo and bar..."

BTW

"By the way..."

CIS

CompuServe Information Service, many times spelled as CI$, to commemorate the cost of the service

FOAF

"Friend of a friend." This term originated when discussing urban legends, and is used as a disclaimer when discussing something the writer cannot personally verify. "I heard from a FOAF that..." The newsgroup *alt.folklore.urban* discusses many stories like this.

foo

Along with "bar," one of the standard place-holder words. The origin of these words is the military acronym FUBAR, which stands for "fouled[†] up beyond all recognition."

FUD

"Fear, uncertainty, and doubt." A marketing strategy practiced by large computing companies.

FYI

"For your information"

IMO, IMHO

"In my opinion" and "in my humble opinion." This phrase prefaces a remark the author feels might be controversial or debatable, to acknowledge that this

---

* Again, several adjectives can be used here.
† Choice of adjectives varies among individuals.

is a personal opinion. The phrase IMNSHO, "in my not-so-humble opinion," is also used, usually in a humorous context.

IYFEG

"Insert your favorite ethnic group." Used in telling jokes in which the ethnic group doesn't really matter. Many such jokes are also told like this: "So an *ethnic-1* says to an *ethnic-2...*"

KIBO

"Knowledge in, BS out." A very popular USENET phenomenon. Also the name of a pseudo religion (see *alt.religion.kibology*).

MOTSS

"Member of the same sex." Also, MOTOS (member of the opposite sex) and MOTAS (member of the appropriate sex).

netiquette

Short for "network etiquette"

RFC

"Request for comment." One of the series of documents that define the Internet protocol standards. These are specified by number, so, for example, RFC 822 discusses the format of electronic mail messages. RFC 1036 discusses the format of USENET articles.

RSN

"Real soon now." This phrase, coined by the writer and computer columnist Jerry Pournelle, is used to indicate skepticism, usually with regards to product delivery dates. "The new version is supposed to be available RSN..."

RTFM

"Read the fine* manual!" This is the standard response to people who breach netiquette by asking questions that can be looked up in a readily available source. This is also used when asking a question to indicate that you have tried looking up the answer yourself but were unsuccessful.

spamming

Flooding the Net with junk articles, often advertising. The name comes from a *Monty Python* skit in which everyone sings, "spam, spam, spam, spam..."

TANSTAAFL

"There ain't no such thing as a free lunch." This phrase was originally coined by the science-fiction writer Robert Heinlein.

TIA

"Thanks in advance." This phrase is often seen in requests for information.

---

* Again, several adjectives can be used here.

Alchemy, FidoDidoism, and Kibology

What are these strange, specious-sounding sciences, and what do they mean to USENET enthusiasts? Let's take a little quiz. Match the clues in Column A with the names in Column B.

Column A	Column B
1. A medieval discipline that aimed to transform the base metals (e.g., lead) into gold; this so-called science has been featured in *Beowulf, The Once and Future King*, and *Bill and Ted's Excellent Adventure*.	A. FidoDidoism
2. The study (made up by me) of a comic-strip-character-sans-strip, in the tradition of Kilroy.	B. Alchemy
3. A USENET pseudo religion, named for its originator, James "Kibo" Parry, who seems to have created it, among other reasons, because he could.	C. Kibology

And the answers are, of course, 1. B (Alchemy), 2. A (FidoDidoism), and 3. C (Kibology). Why should these disciplines interest USENET participants? Actually, I see no reason why they should. As a matter of fact, any mention of the first two would surprise me (especially the second one since I just made it up).

Kibology (or kibo), on the other hand, has cropped up in the names of several alt newsgroups, including *alt.religion.kibology* and *alt.exploding.kibo*. What do people in these groups talk about?

It's hard to say. Some define "kibo" as an acronym for "knowledge in, bull out," which seems to be a goal of the system, though "goal" may be a bit too definitive. From an outsider's perspective, kibology might seem like James "Kibo" Parry's Mencken-esque attempt to have hundreds of people dutifully parrot his name. But insiders assure me that kibology is a meaningful and fun phenomenon. One satisfied participant explains it this way:

```
The Kibology that can be described is not the true Kibology.

Kibology is one of those undefinable things that you can only really
understand through experience.  There's a lot of practical joking,
trolls (which are usually cases of blatant misinformation posted with
the intent of exposing people who are so blinded by their own self-
importance that they shoot their mouths off without thinking), and
just general good-natured mayhem.  And of course, there's net.god
Kibo, who wields the almighty grep engine and a mischievous sense of
```

—continued—

> humor far greater than any mere mortal being. But any serious attempt
> to describe it to people who haven't experienced it will just unfairly
> portray the phenomenon as a bunch of net.weenies acting like little
> brats.
>
> -Peter F. Dubuque, Enemy of Reason

There you have it. Kibology has to be lived. If you're interested, look for it in an *alt* newsgroup near you.

— Valerie Quercia

TLA

"Three-letter acronym." There are several variations on this, such as YAT (yet another TLA). When a friend started working at IBM, he was told "We have lots of TLAs here at IBM."

UTSL

"Use the source, Luke!" Adapted from the *Star Wars* motion picture. This is a common phrase in groups discussing complicated or poorly documented software packages.

WRT

"With regards to"

Encoded Messages

Another odd form of communication is the encoded message. This pops up in signatures occasionally, and every once in a while in the body of a message. To decode a message, save it to a file and run it through the *uudecode* program (see Chapter 10 for details). A typical message might look like:

```
begin 644 asdf.uue
E22!C86XG="!B96QI979E('EO=2=R96%D:6YG('1H:7,A,A"O_]

end
```

and would decode to:

```
I can't believe you're reading this!
```

Hoaxes, Forgeries, and Other Such Matters

This section lists a few of the better known forgeries and hoaxes that have made the rounds on the Net. Many of them are just electronic versions of well-known

Incidental Takeovers and USENET Terrorism

That's a scary sounding title, isn't it? Well, one of these phenomena is a little scary. The other is just silly. But you're liable to run into both in your USENET travels, so…

If you participate in any alt groups, you may notice that some of these have a definite and obvious mission. Take, for instance, alt.internet.services, where you can find out about all kinds of resources available on the Internet, or alt.native, in which participants discuss Native American culture and issues.

But since almost anyone can create an alt group at any time, there are some nonsense groups no one ever posts to. There are also groups with no clearly defined focus. The originator of a vaguely defined group may have a definite purpose in mind. But if he or she doesn't convey that focus adequately, it's easy for readers to shift to another track. When enough readers think Subject B is really Subject A, well then, in effect, the group becomes about Subject B. I've opted for calling this phenomenon an "incidental takeover" because no one means for it to happen. Hardly anyone even notices when it does, except maybe the people who set out to have a group about Subject A. (For a case in which the originators actually set out to take back the group, see "The Amazing Tale of net.suicide" later in this chapter.)

But not everything you encounter in USENET will be so amusing, or even innocuous. I hate to use the word terrorism in combination with USENET. Even at the height of a flame war, USENET news is still only a lot of words. At least I hope it is.

Because the truth is that some people abuse their USENET access by deliberately tormenting other participants and generally inciting trouble. And I am not just talking about razzing people or giving them a rough time. Newsgroup terrorism commonly involves posting sick and deeply disturbing messages—generally to a newsgroup frequented by people very likely to be upset by them.

I do not intend to encourage or gratify anybody who uses cruelty like some people use a remote control, so I will not quote their postings, even indirectly. But here's the spirit of what goes on, from the perpetrator's perspective. You're reading news and you gather from someone's postings that they suffer from extreme claustrophobia. What a hoot. Your idea of a good time is telling this person a story about how you like to shut your child up in a refrigerator. What a scream. The claustrophobic person suffers, and most everyone else who reads this posting is also horrified. They don't know whether you have a kid or not, but, boy, are they worried about it. Look at them scramble trying to figure out if you're for real. Is this a great time, or what?

—continued—

Perhaps even scarier than the individuals who entertain themselves in this way is the fact that several of them have joined together to form their own little espionage newsgroup, *alt.syntax.tactical*, dedicated, believe it or not, to "invading" and wreaking havoc in other groups. According to their FAQ, one of their key strategies involves setting up their own people as credible and rational participants in the group to be attacked—and then letting them loose. Newsgroup sieges also commonly originate from within the readership of *alt.flame* and *alt.evil*, both very aptly named groups.

I guess it's one of the prices we pay for free speech, but I will never cease to be amazed and appalled at this phenomenon. Luckily, it's only news.

— Valerie Quercia

urban legends, but a few of them are unique to USENET. Spreading rumors is nothing to take lightly, so if you see anyone posting any of the items mentioned here, do your part to help stamp it out!

Send a Card to Craig?

Occasionally, there have been postings encouraging people to send cards to a young boy trying to get into the *Guinness Book of World Records*. Unfortunately, these messages are years out of date, as the following posting explains.

```
From: spaf@cs.purdue.edu (Gene Spafford)
Newsgroups: news.announce.important
Subject: DO NOT SEND ANY {GET WELL, POST, BUSINESS} CARDS TO CRAIG SHERGOLD!
Date: 17 Feb 92 19:43:21 GMT
Organization: SERC, Department of Computer Sciences, Purdue Univ.

..Many years ago, Craig Shergold had a brain tumor, believed inoperable. He
sought to set the Guinness record for get-well cards. The call was well-
publicized, and he did indeed set the record (consult a recent edition of
the book—he has received in excess of 16 million cards to date; he
officially set the record as of 17 Nov 1989).

As part of this whole story, his plight caught the attention of John
Kluge, the US billionaire, who paid for Craig to come to the US and
receive specialized treatment. As a result, Craig has recovered completely
from his tumor. He is also no longer seven, but well into his teens (you
can see how out-of-date the request for cards is from this—it's like
circulating a letter encouraging people to vote for Carter for President)...

The Shergold family has publicly appealed many times that people cease to
mail them cards and letters, and that no more appeals be made on their
behalf. One easily accessible way to verify this is with the article on
page 24 of the 19 July 1990 NY Times. People Magazine wrote an article
```

about it on June 1, 1991, page 63. Even Ann Landers has carried an item on this [6/23/91], but people still keep trying to send cards...

This appeal for Craig, as well as many urban legends, regularly appears on electronic bulletin boards around the world, and in many organizational newsletters and bulletins. It is both heartening and unfortunate that there are so many well-meaning people who continue to propagate these stories. It is too bad that so many people are unwilling to verify their information before passing such things along, especially when a simple phone call will suffice to do so. In this case, opening a recent copy of a book carried by nearly every library and bookstore would illuminate the situation.

Spaf is Spoofed!

Professor Eugene Spafford, better known on the Net as "Spaf," has been a prominent force on the Net since its earliest days. He has taken it upon himself to see that several useful documents concerning the Net (like the message concerning Craig Shergold quoted above) are regularly posted to the newsgroups *news.announce.important* and *news.answers*. Given this high visibility, it was inevitable that he would be the victim of an April Fool's forgery. The ironic thing is that the forgery was so well done, that, even with the obvious clues given in message itself, so many people were duped.

As you read the message, pay careful attention to the advice given and be sure to check the message's own headers against that advice.

```
Date: Thu, 1 Apr 93 09:07:38 -0600
Message-Id: <4-1-1993@medusa.cs.purdue.edu>
From: spaf@cs.purdue.EDU
Subject: Re: Warning: April Fools Time again (forged messages on the
loose!)
Newsgroups: news.announce.important,news.admin.misc
```

Warning: April 1 is rapidly approaching, and with it comes a USENET tradition. On April Fools day comes a series of forged, tongue-in-cheek messages, either from non-existent sites or using the name of a Well Known USENET person. In general, these messages are harmless and meant as a joke, and people who respond to these messages without thinking, either by flaming or otherwise responding, generally end up looking rather silly when the forgery is exposed.

So, for the few weeks, if you see a message that seems completely out of line or is otherwise unusual, think twice before posting a followup or responding to it; it's very likely a forgery.

There are a few ways of checking to see if a message is a forgery. These aren't foolproof, but since most forgery posters want people to figure it out, they will allow you to track down the vast majority of forgeries:

-- Russian computers. For historic reasons most forged messages have as part of their Path: a non-existent (we think!) russian computer, either kremvax or moscvax. Other possibilities are nsacyber or wobegon. Please note, however, that walldrug is a real site and isn't a forgery. Really.

-- Posted dates. Almost invariably, the date of the posting is forged to be April 1.

-- Funky Message-ID. Subtle hints are often lodged into the Message-Id, as that field is more or less an unparsed text string and can contain random information. Common values include pi, the phone number of the red phone in the white house, and the name of the forger's parrot.

-- Subtle mispellings. Look for subtle misspellings of the host names in the Path: field when a message is forged in the name of a Big Name USENET person. This is done so that the person being forged actually gets a chance to see the message and wonder when he actually posted it.

Forged messages, of course, are not to be condoned. But they happen, and it's important for people on the Net not to overreact. They happen at this time every year, and the forger generally gets their kicks from watching the novice users take the posting seriously and try to flame their tails off. If we can keep a level head and not react to these postings, they'll taper off rather quickly and we can return to the normal state of affairs: chaos.

Thanks for your support.
Gene Spafford, Chairman, USENET Control Freaks, Inc.

President Announces Tax Rate Hike on Modems

It's true in nearly any venue, but in USENET especially: you can't believe everything you hear. About once a year, someone on USENET restarts the rumor that the FCC is about to institute a "modem tax."[*] Whenever this rumor is recirculated, it causes a minor stir. Newbies of all sorts get upset, write disgruntled letters to the FCC, and so on, until they find out that it's a hoax. The FCC isn't amused, but you wouldn't expect them to be. For the record, they don't have, and never had, plans to tax modems.

The modem tax hoax is very old news, and at this point, rather stale. It's never even been all that amusing. Still it is one of an increasing number of USENET legends. Like legends and folktales of all kinds, no matter how often they crop up, there's someone green enough to believe them. And who can really blame them? USENET hoaxes can be fairly elaborate and convincing.

---

[*] This story was most recently resurrected on 5 February 1995.

In November 1994, I saw a "next-generation" USENET legend in the form of a posting cautioning people that the FCC was about to introduce license exams for Internet users. Here's an excerpt:

```
FCC to regulate the Internet

WASHINGTON, DC - The White House confirmed today that the FCC would assume
responsibility for regulating the so called "Information Super Highway."
Today, this consists of an autonomous network of computers known
collectively as the Internet. Usually reliable sources revealed that the
government has become increasingly apprehensive about the Internet's
uncontrollable growth and the potential for damage to the national
security..."Irresponsible individuals can easily transmit messages
worldwide. Clearly, there is a need for government regulation."

In response to these concerns, the FCC is rumored to be preparing
restrictive regulations to ensure "responsible use" of the Internet...
Although details are sketchy at this time, regulations are likely to take
the form of a license examination for Internet users...

Based on the FCC's history, the test will likely consist of three parts:
theory, jurisprudence, and practice...
The practice portion of the examination is likely to be the most
controversial. Reportedly, all candidates must pass a typing skills test
and achieve no less than 40 words per minute to obtain a temporary novice
license... Novices will be restricted to operating networked computers
with speeds less than 5 MHz or operation of SLIP or dial-up connections of
no greater than 2400 baud...
```

The typing speed versus system/modem speed restrictions seem obviously ridiculous. However, the description of the test contains some far more arcane humor; the test closely resembles that required for a ham radio operator's license. The ham here is of a different type, of course.

But something about the power of the printed--or in this case, the typed--word lends to information the weight of truth. In other words, plenty of people bought this rowboat of bilge, hook, line, and sinker. The flames abounded. How dare they do that to us? Isn't this a free country? Move over Big Brother, Uncle Sam wants to log in!

Given the government's growing concern over various forms of electronic crime (system cracking, software pirating, etc.), some attempt to regulate networking seems likely. But a typing test? I don't think so. Still, given this climate, we should expect to run into the modem tax hoax, the Info-road driver's test hoax, and others in the same vein, over and over again. In order to minimize their impact, and maybe even get a laugh out of it, stay calm and try to sort out the truth from the fiction.

A Lawsuit April Fools!

Here is a message that was posted to the newsgroup *comp.lang.tcl*, which discusses the tool command language, Tcl, and its X toolkit, Tk.

```
Subject: Lawsuit against Tcl/Tk
From: ouster@sprite.Berkeley.EDU (John Ousterhout)
Newsgroups: comp.lang.tcl
Subject: Lawsuit against Tcl/Tk
Date: 1 Apr 1993 22:35:50 GMT
Organization: U.C. Berkeley Sprite Project
Lines: 17
Distribution: world
Message-ID: <1pfqo6$ja9@agate.berkeley.edu>

I'm afraid that I have some very bad news. Last Friday the Open Software
Foundation filed a suit in District Court in Boston against the University
of California, charging the Tk toolkit with a series of intellectual
property infringements relative to its Motif products. They have demanded
immediate withdrawal of all Tk C code from distribution, along with all
Tcl scripts that use Tk features, plus royalties and damages for all use
of the code and scripts to date.
To make matters worse, the University feels that it cannot fight two suits
like this at the same time. They've decided to focus on the USL lawsuit,
so they have asked me to withdraw the Tk distribution and to try to work
out a deal with OSF on my own.

Needless to say, I'm pretty stunned by all this and don't know exactly
what to do about it, except to say "April fools!" Hee hee hee. Apologies
to anyone from OSF who might happen to read this message, or who might
receive nasty mail from other people who didn't read the whole message.
```

Tcl and Tk are now a well-established part of the computing scene, but at the time it caused quite a shock to readers of the newsgroup and it took a while for things to recover and get back to normal.

The Great Cookie Caper

This is an urban legend that has been floating around the Net for years. It is even included in the GNU Emacs distribution.

It seems that a lady received a telephone call from a large organization which made cookies (sometimes attributed to Mrs. Fields, sometimes to Neiman Marcus) and was asked if she would be interested in purchasing a cookie recipe for "two ninety-five." Thinking this was two dollars and ninety-five cents, she agreed, charged this to her credit card, and was sent the "secret" recipe. Much to her surprise, when she received her credit card statement, she had been billed two hundred and ninety-five *dollars*. In order to take revenge on the large corporation that had taken advantage of her in such a ruthless manner, she started to distribute the secret recipe as widely as she could.

If you are interested in trying the recipe, it is shown in Figure 9-2.

Both Mrs. Fields and Neiman Marcus deny billing unwary customers for their recipe. In fact, both deny that this is their recipe. They're probably right; the hoax apparently originated in the 1940s and involved some completely different store. So the story predates Mrs. Fields, USENET, and even computers (though possibly not Neiman Marcus). In any case, the recipe is pretty good. It's up to you to decide whether or not it resembles any commercial product.

The $295 Cookie

Cream together:
2 cups butter
2 cups sugar
2 cups brown sugar

Add:
4 eggs
2 tsp vanilla

Mix together in separate bowl:
4 cups flour
5 cups oatmeal*
1 tsp salt
2 tsp baking powder
2 tsp baking soda

Mix all of the above and add:
24 oz. bag of chocolate chips and
1 finely grated 8 oz Hershey bar (plain)
3 cups chopped nuts (any kind)

Place golf ball sized balls about two inches apart on a greased cookie sheet and bake at 350 degrees for 8 - 10 minutes. DO NOT OVERBAKE. Makes 112 cookies.

* *(Put small amounts of oatmeal in blender until it turns to powder. Measure out 5 cups of oatmeal and only "powderize" that, NOT 5 cups of "powderized" oatmeal.)*

Figure 9-2. The infamous USENET *cookie recipe*

The Amazing Tale of net.suicide

USENET started out as a very small, quiet community, where almost everyone knew almost everyone else; it was growing rapidly, but it was still relatively controlled. Things changed forever in September 1981, when large numbers of students were added, creating the USENET we know today: endless dumb questions, endless idiots posing as savants, and (of course) endless victims for practical jokes. Does this sound familiar? Every few months, some new organization gets a gateway to USENET, and there's a new crowd.

The short history of *net.suicide* shows how little (or how much) has changed. On December 8, 1981, the newsgroup *net.suicide* was created with the following message:

```
From: research!rob
Newsgroups: net.suicide
Title: net.suicide

I am interested in talking to other people on the network interested in
suicide. I belonged to a club in graduate school, but we couldn't keep
membership up.
```

The group was a forum for bad jokes, particularly about suicide (either personal or computational). A few confused people came along who actually thought that the group was a place to discuss suicide, people who have considered suicide, and the like. And a few very confused people used it as a place to discuss the pros and cons of riding motorcycles without helmets. Another phenomenon that hasn't stopped: the hijacking of one group for a completely unrelated purpose by people who didn't understand the group in the first place.

We usually assume that most newsgroup posters are "real people," more-or-less. At the start, this was true of *net.suicide*. However, after a few months, a "character" called C. C. (Chuck) Festoon appeared. Festoon was a pompous bureaucrat/philosopher who was prone to confuse Sigmund Freud with Brian Kernighan, and deserves a story in his own right. About a month later, Rob Pike decided to up the ante by creating a character, called Bimmler, who would stage a coup and purge undesirable elements:

```
From: rabbit!bimmler
Newsgroups: net.suicide
Title: Coup d'Etat

There has been a coup. This netnews group has been taken over. While you
slept, thousands of ruthless information soldiers assaulted the network
and captured the previous, now powerless and forgotten, autocrats. I am
now in power. This newsgroup is strong, for I am in control and I am
strong. No more will this newsgroup be tainted by whining sops seeking a
brief flicker of fame by feigning wisdom of sacred rituals. The submitters
of such subversive articles shall be dealt with justly and efficiently.

I do not enjoy violence, but I have ways of maintaining control.

net.suicide is dead! Long live net.suicide!
```

The rules under which Bimmler operated were that he was vicious; his messages didn't refer to suicide (or any other topic) in any intelligible fashion; his attacks were primarily ad-hominem and even ad-nominem (i.e., attacks on someone's name)

Response was immediate. Support quickly came from Festoon, whose author (Ron Hardin) had helped in Bimmler's creation. Here are Festoon's comments on Bimmler's coup:

> I, for one, support Mr. Bimmler and await that dark day when self demolition regains its rightful position at the apex of our culture. Until then, Mr. Bimmler's firm, yet benevolent, hand will guide us. Stay the course!
>
> Let those who think otherwise make a statement with their life (as Mr. Bimmler has often done). Perhaps 6 months in the Karen Carpenter Diet Program will shed not only pounds but also illusions.

Of course, Bimmler's coup did nothing to discourage the people who really thought that *net.suicide* was a place to talk about suicide, more or less narrowly defined. And they responded in protest: how could this uncaring person divert the group from what was its "obvious" intent? Bimmler responded with attacks that make most modern-era flame wars look tame; his vitriol was particularly directed against those who espoused "caring" in any form:

> ...You must know much about hell, living with yourself; I am aware of some of that hell, myself. During your "travels down the road" you have attacked us with a form of gastric chemical warfare illegal on five continents. Next time clean up after yourself...

One of the more significant voices was Lady Arwen, who is amusing mostly because she never seemed to catch on, unless Lady Arwen was a character herself, whose role included complete naivete about the Bimmler hoax. Lady Arwen got really confused when Bimmler forged "fan mail" from Jack of Shadows, who was one of her friends. Here's her response:

> I KNOW Jack of Shadows, he's one of my best friends, and he has been bitching about rabbit!bimmler for WEEKS!!! He'd NEVER send a letter like that to save his LIFE, especially since one of bimmler's first pseudo-acts was to censor his original account, iz328, off the Net!!
>
> I don't mean to say that *I* dislike/like or otherwise whatever bimmler, just that I *know* how JoS feels and it sure ain't admiration!!

The semi-retraction in the last paragraph leads to some interesting questions: is the Lady really a secret admirer? Is she so incessantly polite that she doesn't have the stomach to attack Bimmler personally? Is she afraid for her life? Or, as it has been suggested, is she just another character in the game, whose role is to remain eternally clueless?

At Bimmler's high point, there were over ten submitters regularly appearing in Netnews. All but one were known to be characters; the creators of these characters exchanged email and phone calls to plan and coordinate their submissions. Some theorized that the whole affair was nothing more than a conspiracy to drive the unfortunate Lady Arwen mad. Keeping up became too much work, so Rob finally shut the whole thing down by having Bimmler send a "suicide note": a final control message that deleted the newsgroup.

Mark V. Shaney: The Next Generation

The problem with Bimmler was that writing messages by hand required too much work. The obvious alternative, then, was to write a program! Rob Pike and Bruce Ellis created a program, based on an idea from Don Mitchell, that computed a probability matrix based on some selected input, and then generated random text based on that input.* The result was a USENET character named Mark V. Shaney.

For input, Rob and Bruce selected messages from the previous day's postings to the *net.singles* newsgroup. Unlike other random text generators, Shaney's output really looked like it ought to make sense; because Shaney was controlled by a probability table generated by analyzing the previous day's postings, his output tended to look like crazed replies to those same postings. Here are a few extracts:

> The longer one "waits" to experience sex, the more important ones virginity becomes and the more artificially important it can be in relation to the posting on the dead cat and eating of same, which I absolutely refuse to repost.

> Often when we say "I love you" what we really mean is: "You're pretty close to the defense of advertising agencies", but it's no big deal.

> Lately I've had sex; I wonder if it will be tonight? I can teleport. Any volunteers? (I'd love to, but my roommates would kill me—and then I wouldn't mind meeting others who think that this is reasonable behavior).

As with Bimmler, there were those who never caught on; a lot of people thought that he was a genuine person who belonged in a drug rehabilitation center; there were even some who genuinely wanted to meet him and calm his obviously tormented mind.

The obvious conclusion to draw from this is that USENET was, and remains, a forum where even artificial stupidity can masquerade as intelligence. As Rob said, "On the Internet, no one knows you're a program." Are there any other conclusions worth drawing? Probably not, but the next time you see a vicious debate on the merit of John Cage's musical works, or the morality of artificially inseminating tuna, ask yourself "Are these guys for real?" Unfortunately, they probably are. But, as Rob has shown, maybe there's room for hope.

---

* If you want the details, it used third-order Markov chains, in which the next word is chosen based on the two previous words; punctuation marks were considered part of the preceding word, which made the output much more reasonable; and the humans were allowed to select and reorder sentences, but not to alter the sentences themselves.

Many thanks to Rob Pike, who revealed this history in a talk at USENIX (Summer, 1994) entitled "On the Internet, No One Knows You're a Program."

Related Newsgroups

If you have enjoyed this section, there are two newsgroups that you might like to check out. *alt.forgeries* is a group especially designed for the posting of forged messages, and provides a harmless outlet for experimentation. (It's a serious breach of netiquette to post forgeries anywhere else, however!) Another group, *alt.folklore.urban*, specializes in "urban folklore" and "friend of a friend" (FOAF) stories.

## CHAPTER TEN

SOFTWARE, PICTURES, AND OTHER GOODIES

What's Out There?

As we've seen so far, the USENET has a wide array of newsgroups discussing every topic under the sun. This chapter deals with the Net's "non-discussion" items such as software and pictures.

The majority of the non-discussion groups are for the posting of computer software. This seems appropriate, since the USENET is, after all, a computer network. Software is posted in both source and binary forms. Source code is usually distributed as *shar* files, while program binary files (executable programs, etc.) are usually distributed in the form of "uuencoded" archive files. These formats are described in the last section of this chapter.

Binary files are much more common in hardware-specific groups such as *comp.binaries.ibm.pc.* and *comp.binaries.mac.* Programs for UNIX are usually distributed in source form, since it is not practical to pre-build the software for the large number of computers that run UNIX.

Non-source files come in a variety of flavors. These include:

Documents
You already know about text files. Documents are often available in PostScript format. PostScript is a language for talking to laser printers. The files tend to be large and may include graphics. PostScript files usually have names that end in *.ps*.

Pictures
A number of groups are designed for posting pictures of one kind or another. A FAQ list in *alt.binaries.pictures.d* will tell you about different file formats and the viewers available. In short, the two most important formats are JPEG (*.jpg*) and GIF (*.gif*). Both support full-color images. GIF files are certainly

larger. All picture files are large, though, with sizes ranging between 35K bytes and 500K bytes.

If you're interested in knowing more about picture formats, see the *Encyclopedia of Graphic File Formats* from O'Reilly & Associates. If you're not, you still need to be aware of one thing. JPEG and GIF images are *not* ASCII art. If you try to display one with your favorite word processor, it won't work. The quick-and-dirty way to get a viewer is to get a good World Wide Web browser like *Netscape*, which has a decent viewer for both formats built-in. (For more information on *Netscape*, see Chapter 8.) However, there are better viewers available; for UNIX, the best is a shareware program called *xv*.

Sounds

A few groups exist for posting audio files. You can get information about audio formats and appropriate newsgroups from the FAQs in *alt.binaries.sounds.d*. As with pictures, you need some kind of player to listen to them; as many different audio formats are used, you may also need some software for converting one kind to another. The FAQ list will tell you about all this. And of course, you may need some special hardware, though most newer computers have audio hardware built in.

The most commonly used sound file types are *.wav* (Microsoft) and *.au* (Sun). A software package called Lsox converts sound files from one format to another. Sound files are relatively large; the *.wav* and *.au* formats require 8,000 bytes per second of audio output for moderate quality.

Video

The multimedia groups often contain video postings, occasionally with accompanying sound files. Again, there are many formats. The most interesting is the MPEG format (*.mpg*), which will probably be the motion picture industry's standard for digitized video. MPEG files are very large—over one megabyte per minute, though the actual file size varies depending on the content.

Copyrights and Licensing

There is a reasonable amount of confusion about how netware is copyrighted. There are dozens of different varieties, but most of them are variations on a few basic schemes.

Public domain

Software that is in the public domain may be used freely by anybody for any purpose. Copyrightable material (including things such as software, music, and written material) fall into the public domain under two conditions: when a copyright expires,[*] and when material is placed explicitly in the public

---

[*] According to a post on *misc.legal* (the extent of my legal knowledge), copyrights expire 50 years after the author's death, so this is probably not very applicable for software.

domain. Very little software on the Net is in the public domain, but instead falls into the next category.

Copyrighted, but freely available

This category covers a much larger portion of things posted on the Net. The copyright is retained by the author, but you are allowed to use the software freely. Sometimes, various restrictions are made, such as not being able to resell the software for profit or use the software in a commercial setting. Software released for public use by institutions such as universities and corporations usually includes two requirements: you cannot hold the institution responsible for any problems you encounter, and you may not use the institution's name in any advertising.

Shareware

A lot of the software posted in the binaries groups falls into the category of shareware. Shareware is commercial software, and the author retains the copyright. You are allowed to use the software on a trial basis for a short time, but you are expected to pay for the software if you use it regularly. Usually, payment of the registration fee includes benefits such as a printed manual, support, or an enhanced version of the program.

Copylefted

Probably the most controversial (and certainly the most discussed) copyright scheme is the *GNU General Public License,* or *GPL,* originally devised by the originators of GNU *Emacs* and promoted by the Free Software Foundation. Software that has been placed under the GPL is usually referred to as being copylefted. Briefly stated, if a program is copylefted, you can receive the source code and use the program with no restrictions. You may also modify the program to fit your needs, but any changes must also be copylefted (so that other people can benefit from your modifications). You may redistribute the software, but you must include the source, and you may not limit the recipient's right to further redistribution.

The full text of the GPL is distributed with any copylefted software distribution. You can also view it in Emacs by typing **Ctrl-h Ctrl-c**. Discussions regarding the GPL and the GNU project are usually held in *gnu.misc.discuss.*

Where to Look

Just about every group has some kind of goodie posted to it, even if it's only a FAQ list. Several hierarchies are solely intended for the distribution of source and binary files. The following tables (culled from the newsgroup lists in Appendixes E and F) describe some of these groups.

Table 10-1 lists the newsgroups that specialize in source postings for various computers. As you can imagine, the amount of traffic in each group differs greatly. Most of the software posted in these groups is freely available or copylefted.

Table 10-1. Source Groups

Group	Description
comp.sources.amiga	Source code-only postings for the Amiga
comp.sources.apple2	Source code and discussion for the Apple2
comp.sources.atari.st	Source code-only postings for the Atari ST
comp.sources.games	Postings of recreational software
comp.sources.hp48	Programs for the HP48 and HP28 calculators
comp.sources.mac	Software for the Apple Macintosh
comp.sources.misc	Posting of software
comp.sources.postscript	Source code for programs written in PostScript
comp.sources.reviewed	Source code evaluated by peer review
comp.sources.sun	Software for Sun workstations
comp.sources.unix	Postings of complete, UNIX-oriented sources
comp.sources.x	Software for the X Window System
alt.sources	Alternative source code, unmoderated. Caveat emptor.
alt.sources.amiga	Source code for the Amiga
alt.sources.mac	Source code for Apple Macintosh

The software binaries groups are for posts of precompiled applications for various machines. Usually, the applications are archived together with online documentation, configuration files, etc., and then posted as a series of uuencoded files. A lot of the postings in this category are shareware.

Table 10-2. Software Binaries Groups

Group	Description
comp.binaries.amiga	Encoded public domain programs in binary
comp.binaries.apple2	Binary-only postings for the Apple II
comp.binaries.atari.st	Binary-only postings for the Atari ST
comp.binaries.cbm	For the transfer of 8-bit Commodore binaries
comp.binaries.ibm.pc	Binary-only postings for IBM PC/MS-DOS
comp.binaries.mac	Encoded Macintosh programs in binary
comp.binaries.ms-windows	Binary programs for Microsoft Windows
comp.binaries.newton	Apple Newton binaries, sources, books, etc.
comp.binaries.os2	Binaries for use under the OS/2 ABI

The non-software binaries groups span a wide range of topics, although most of them relate to pictures of one form or another. They can take up quite a lot of disk space, so they are usually expired quickly. Many sites do not subscribe to these groups at all.

Table 10-3. Non-Software Binaries Groups

Group	Description
alt.binaries.clip-art	Distribution of DOS, Mac, and UNIX clipart
alt.binaries.misc	Random large files without a more appropriate group
alt.binaries.multimedia	Sound, text, and graphics data rolled in one
alt.binaries.pictures	Additional volume in the form of huge image files
alt.binaries.pictures.anime	Images from Japanese animation
alt.binaries.pictures.ascii	Pictures composed of ASCII characters
alt.binaries.pictures.cartoons	Images from animated cartoons
alt.binaries.pictures.fine-art.digitized	Art from conventional media
alt.binaries.pictures.fine-art.graphics	Art created on computers
alt.binaries.pictures.fractals	Cheaper just to send the program parameters!
alt.binaries.pictures.furry	Originally funny animal art
alt.binaries.pictures.misc	Have we saturated the network yet?
alt.binaries.sounds.misc	Digitized audio adventures
alt.binaries.sounds.mods	MODs and related sound formats
alt.binaries.sounds.movies	Sounds from copyrighted movies
alt.binaries.sounds.music	Music samples in MOD/669 format
alt.binaries.sounds.tv	Sounds from copyrighted television shows

comp.archives: *What Else Is Out There?*

The newsgroup *comp.archives* is another resource if you are interested in seeing what else is on the Net. It is a moderated newsgroup used to cross-reference announcements made on other groups. A program automatically scans all incoming posts at the moderator's site and flags any articles that pertain to announcements of new software or other information. It also adds some information, such as the original newsgroup name, to the headers. The moderator double-checks the posting to make sure that the program didn't make an incorrect guess

JPEG Image Viewers

If you're working in a UNIX environment, *xv* is the hands-down winner among competing graphic file viewers. In addition to JPEG files, *xv* lets you display, modify, and save a large variety of graphic file types, including GIF, PBM, Post-Script, and TIFF. Not surprisingly, *xv* is the most popular helper application used by World Wide Web browsers to display linked graphics. The shareware price is $25. The current version (as of this printing) is 3.10a; it can be found at the site ftp.cis.upenn.edu, in the pub/*xv* directory.

If you want to look at JPEG images in a DOS or Windows environment, the choices are far more confusing. In the DOS world, QPEG may be the fastest non-commercial JPEG viewer, but you sacrifice a bit in image quality for the speed (particularly on displays that handle 256 colors or fewer). QPEG comes in very handy for viewing several images sequentially, however; it has a small preview window that lets you quickly browse a large number of images. It can also display GIF, TGA, BMP, and PCX images.

QPEG requires a 386-or-better CPU and VGA-or-better display card. It is shareware ($20). The current version is 1.5e, which is available from *ftp.tu-clausthal.de:/pub/msdos/graphics/qpeg15e.zip*. It is also available from the so-called Simtel archives, the largest collection of PC-related programs on the Internet. The principle site for these archives is *oak.oakland.edu*; regardless of the Simtel archive site, archived files can always be found in the */Simtel* directory. The QPEG viewer is */SimTel/msdos/graphics/qpeg15e.zip*. For Simtel mirror sites, follow the newsgroup comp.archives.msdos.announce.

For a DOS freeware alternative, try DVPEG, which can display JPEG GIF, Targa, and PPM files. DVPEG has a less-than-elegant interface, but it is a perfectly functional viewer that works on 286, 386, or 486 machines. On high-color displays, it is almost as fast a QPEG. It's slower on 8-bit displays, but provides better image quality at this level than QPEG. The current version of DVPEG is 3.0l (that's 3.0 and a lowercase l, not the number 3.01); it's available at *sunee.uwaterloo.ca:/pub/jpeg/viewers/dvpeg30l.zip*.

QPEG and DVPEG work under Windows, but only in full-screen mode (i.e., not in a window); this is a serious limitation. For Windows users, LView Pro is both a functional and economical choice. It provides viewing, editing, and conversion capabilities for JPEG, GIF, BMP, and other graphic file formats. It can display JPEG images in either fast/low-quality or slow/high-quality modes. Version 1.A is available as *win3/graphics/lviewp1a.zip* at any Simtel site. It requires at least a 386 CPU. The shareware payment ($30) is required only for business usage or to obtain versions optimized for Win32s/NT, 486, or Pentium CPUs.

—continued—

WinJPEG (shareware, $25) displays and converts JPEG, GIF, Targa, TIFF, PCX, and BMP files. It provides some highly useful functions including screen capture, color-balance adjustment, and even a slideshow capability. The current version is 2.65, available from Simtel sites, file *win3/graphics/winjp265.zip*. (This is a 286-compatible version; if you register, you'll get the 386-and-up version, which is roughly twice as fast.)

The shareware ACDSee program ($15) may be the simplest choice for Windows users. It's a very fast JPEG and GIF viewer, with few options. The current version is 1.2, which is available from *ftp.cica.indiana.edu* in the directory */pub/pc/ win3/desktop/acdc12.zip*.

— *Valerie Quercia*

---

about the intent of the article, and posts it. The example below shows a sample screen:

```
comp.archives (134T 133A 0K 0H R)                    h=help

   21  +    [comp.robotics] 68HC11F1 schematics available etc.
   22  +    [comp.dcom.sys.cisco] NeTraMet 2.1 now available
   23  +    [comp.sys.amiga.announce] FastLife available for FTP
   24  +    [comp.sys.amiga.announce] CLIExchange 1.2 available for FTP
   25  +    [comp.text.tex] European [Dutch] Ispell 3.1.00 mirror + dictionary
   26  +    [comp.lang.prolog] bibtex entries for Journals and LP Conferences:
   27  +    [comp.lang.misc] Python 1.0.0 is out!
   28  +    [alt.cyberpunk] Guide to SF on the Internet
   29  +    [comp.sys.ibm.pc.games.misc] GAME WIZARD
   30  +    [rec.aviation.products] Weather facsimile program for Macintosh no
-> 31  +    [comp.lang.tcl] [ANNOUNCE] Picasso3.6 available
   32  +    [comp.infosystems.www] Revised UK server map
   33  +    [comp.sys.amiga.programmer] Annoucing ExtData 1.00
   34  +    [comp.lang.tcl] ANNOUNCE:  Widget tour 2.0
   35  +    [rec.radio.amateur.digital.misc] New NET/Mac (hamradio TCP/IP) for
   36  +    [comp.unix.osf.osf1] SunOS to DEC OSF/1 Porting Guide
   37  +    [comp.dcom.lans.ethernet] Guide to Ethernet available
   38  +    Anonymous FTP: Frequently Asked Questions (FAQ) List
   39  +    Anonymous FTP: Sitelist Part 1 of 11      [01/11]
   40  +    Anonymous FTP: Sitelist Part 2 of 11      [02/11]
```

When people ask me what groups they should read, I always recommend this group as a good starting point. In addition to showing the variety of available resources, it's an interesting overview of a lot of newsgroups. If you see something interesting cross-referenced in *comp.archives*, it's a good bet that you'll enjoy reading the group the article was originally posted to.

File Formats

The remainder of this chapter discusses the various ways that files can be archived, compressed, and transmitted. We'll start with some techniques for dealing with text (ASCII) files and groups of files. Then we'll cover binary files.

One of the drawbacks of USENET is that it limits transmission to character-based (ASCII) data only. Trying to post a binary file not only doesn't work, but ensures that the poster will receive numerous (usually very vocal) complaints. To solve this problem, several ways of posting binary files have been devised. All the solutions for posting binary files are based on the *uuencode/uudecode* utilities that come with almost every UNIX system; Appendix D tells you where to find DOS/Windows versions. The MKS Toolkit is a commercial package that provides DOS and Windows versions of most of the UNIX utilities mentioned in this chapter. If you're willing to pay the money, it's a worthwhile investment.

"Cut Here" Files

The simplest way to transmit an ASCII file is to include it in a posting. This is effective for small (several lines) coding samples or corrections to a previous post. Usually these are placed between lines of hyphens, with instructions to "cut here" or some similar phrase. Often, a pair of ASCII scissors (8<) are included. As files become larger, however, this method becomes less desirable. The possibility of corruptions being introduced becomes greater, while the possibility of noticing them becomes smaller. Additionally, some systems do unfriendly things like translating tabs to spaces, and occasionally truncate long lines. Use this method for short files. Better methods for longer or multiple files are covered later.

Here is a small C program that creates a self-reproducing program. It has been floating around on the Net for some time.[*] Join the lines together (so the program will be one long line) before compiling.

```
---------------------8<--cut here----8<---------------------
*a[]={"*a[]={","};s(){putchar(34);}main(b){printf(*a);s();--b
?putchar(','),s(),printf(a[1]),s():(main(b),puts(a[1]));}"};
s(){putchar(34);}main(b){printf(*a);s();--b?putchar(','),s(),
printf(a[1]),s():(main(b),puts(a[1]));}
---------------------8<--cut here----8<---------------------
```

---

[*] Special thanks are due to *snow@dcs.warwick.ac.uk*, who sent me a copy after I accidentally deleted mine. As an example of the efficiency of the Net, I posted the request around 6:00 p.m., and had the reply when I resumed work at around 10:00 the same evening.

shar files

This is one of the oldest and most popular methods of transmitting files. It consists of creating a UNIX shell script that will create the appropriate files and directories. Additional error checks such as file size are also done. A multipart *shar* file will indicate how many parts have been un*shar*'d, which parts are remaining, etc.

Figuring out what you have

The easiest way to tell if you have a *shar* file is by looking at the subject; it should say [sh] or something to that effect. Unfortunately, not everyone does this, so you should also know what the file looks like. Here is the result of creating a *shar* file with the command.[*]

```
% makekit sample-file
```

This is the original file:

```
This is a small two-line file that has been shar'ed.
The name of this file is sample_file.
```

This is the *shar* file:

```
#!/bin/sh
# This is a shell archive. Remove anything before this line, then unpack
# it by saving it into a file and typing "sh file". To overwrite existing
# files, type "sh file -c". You can also feed this as standard input via
# unshar, or by typing "sh <file", e.g.. If this archive is complete, you
# will see the following message at the end:
#        "End of shell archive."
# Contents:  sample_file
# Wrapped by harrison@vivaldi on Tue May 19 16:51:31 1992
PATH=/bin:/usr/bin:/usr/ucb ; export PATH
if test -f 'sample_file' -a "${1}" != "-c" ; then
  echo shar: Will not clobber existing file \"'sample_file'\"
else
echo shar: Extracting \"'sample_file'\" \(91 characters\)
sed "s/^X//" >'sample_file' <<'END_OF_FILE'
XThis is a small two-line file that has been shar'ed.
XThe name of this file is sample_file.
END_OF_FILE
if test 91 -ne 'wc -c <'sample_file''; then
    echo shar: \"'sample_file'\" unpacked with wrong size!
fi
# end of 'sample_file'
```

---

[*] *makekit* and *unshar* were both written by Rich Salz, for many years the moderator of the newsgroup *comp.unix.sources.*

```
fi
echo shar: End of shell archive.
exit 0
```

Decoding

Since the *shar* file is a UNIX shell script, you can simply save the message, edit it to remove the message headers, and execute it with the command

    % **sh** *filename*

or, if you wish to overwrite existing files in the directory,

    % **sh** *filename* **-c**

This has a few drawbacks, however. First, you have to edit the file. This is not much of a problem for one or two files, but can be tedious for a larger number.

The other problem can be more serious. Since the *shar* file is just a shell script, an unethical person could add some lines containing commands to quietly do some devious activity.[*] These might include deleting, modifying, or changing permissions to a file, or sending sensitive information out of the system using *mail.*

For both of these reasons, it is a good idea to use the *unshar* program. It is a shell script interpreter that strips the headers from the files and interprets the rest of the script. Only safe actions are executed.

There is one interesting variant of the "shell archive": shell archives of uuencoded binaries. These can be handled either way (as *shar* files or as uuencoded files); the latter is probably safer.

Of course, if you're not a UNIX user, you won't have the shell and other utilities available for unpacking *shar* files. There are various free solutions, but the best is probably to buy the MKS Toolkit; it contains everything you need in one package.

Creating

Several programs exist to create *shar* files. The most commonly used program is *makekit,* which we used to create the previous example. If files are too large to put into one *shar* file,[†] *makekit* automatically packs them into appropriately sized *shar* files.

---

[*] This is called a "Trojan horse," named after the gift the Greeks left to the city of Troy.

[†] You generally don't want to make a mail message or USENET posting larger than 60K, as some machines on the Net won't handle larger files. I've mailed (*not* posted) files as large as several megabytes with no ill effects. Of course, the recipient and I were familiar with the routing and made sure all the machines involved could handle it.

ROT13 Articles

This doesn't really have anything to do with posting software, but it is a specially formatted message. Occasionally, someone will post an article that is potentially offensive or perhaps gives away the answer to a puzzle or reveals the ending of a movie. It is customary for posters of such articles to encrypt such articles so that people who don't wish to view the material won't accidentally see it. These are called *rotated* or *ROT13* articles.

The encryption method is a Caesar cipher, where every character is replaced by the one 13 positions to the left. For example, "a" is replaced by "m", "b" by "n", and so forth. When "z" is reached, counting is resumed at "a."

To view a rotated article, use your newsreader or the UNIX character rotation program, *tr*. Depending on the version of UNIX you are running, one of these commands should work:

```
% tr A-Za-z N-ZA-Mn-za-m <your-file
% tr "[a-m][n-z][A-M][N-Z]" "[n-z][a-m][N-Z][A-M]" <your-file
```

If you're not a UNIX user, you'll have to concoct your own command. The *ROT13* encoding is so simple that this should be easy.

Patch Files

Software posted to the Net is being constantly revised and updated. In order to reduce network traffic, these updates are usually released in the form of *patches**[*] generated by the command:[†]

```
% diff -c oldfile newfile >patchfile
```

When you receive these patches, they can be easily integrated into your copy of the source code.

Figuring out what you have

The subject line should identify the message as a *patch* file. You can also recognize a *patch* file by looking at it (see the example below), but that isn't very useful. Just knowing that a file is a "patch" won't help you. You also need to know very precisely what it patches.

---

[*] The original version of *patch* was written by Larry Wall, of *perl* fame.

[†] The *diff* command lists the differences between files. The *−c* option generates a *context diff*, where several lines surrounding the changed lines are displayed, showing the context.

Decoding and applying a patch

First, scan the *patch* files for any notes regarding the patches. For example, they might give some special instructions about *patch* options to use, or a note on which directories need to be patched. Save the *patch* files to the original source directory. For each *patch* file, issue the command

```
% patch <patchfile
```

patch will print a running commentary on the patches, and integrate the patches into the files. The original files are kept in files with an extension of *.orig*.

Creating a patch

Here is the original file:

```
if (incoming_icbm = TRUE)
    retaliate();
```

And this is a corrected version, fixing a bug reported by an end user:

```
if (incoming_icbm == TRUE)
    retaliate();
```

Running the command

```
% diff -c file.v1 file.v2
```

produces the following context *diff*, which can be posted as is, with a descriptive subject and some commentary added at the beginning.

```
*** file.v1   Thu Jul  2 10:33:09 1994
--- file.v2   Thu Jul  2 10:33:22 1994
***************
*** 1,2 ****
! if (incoming_icbm = TRUE)
      retaliate();
--- 1,2 ----
! if (incoming_icbm == TRUE)
      retaliate();
```

Uuencoded Files

The program *uuencode*[*] converts a binary file into a form that uses ASCII characters. This makes it possible to include it in a news posting or mail message.

---

[*] *uuencode* was originally written for the UUCP (UNIX-to-UNIX copy) suite of programs and is standard on most UNIX systems. Versions of *uuencode* and *uudecode* are available for DOS, Windows, and Macintosh systems.

It is necessary to uuencode files that have non-printable characters in them, for example *tar* or picture files. It is common for uuencoded files to have a *.uue* in their name.

Figuring out what you have

Here is a uuencoded version of the file *sample* used previously.

```
begin 644 sample
M5VAE;B!I;B!T<F]U8FQE(&]R(&EN(&1O=6)T+ I2=6X@:6X@8VER8VQE<RP@2<V-R96%M(&&%N9"!S:&]U="$$*
end
```

The "begin" line is a giveaway that this is a uuencoded file. If a file looks like a uuencoded file or claims to be one, but doesn't have a "begin" line, it's broken.

Decoding a uuencoded file

Use the *uudecode* program. The file access permission and destination filename are on the "begin" line. You can change these as you like with a text editor.

> % **uudecode** *encoded-file*

If *encoded-file* is not specified, the coded information is read from the standard input.

I mentioned earlier that uuencoded files are sometimes packaged as a variation of a *shar* file. Such files can be unpacked either way.

Creating a uuencoded file

Use the command:

> % **uuencode** *filename [input-file]*

where *filename* is the name that is placed in the begin line. If *input-file* is not specified, the standard input is encoded.

Compressed (.Z) Files

compress is a standard UNIX utility that reduces the size of a file and appends a *.Z* file extension. The utilities *uncompress* and *zcat* are used to restore the file. Compression can easily make a binary file 40% smaller or a larger text file 60% smaller. Then again, compressed files must by uuencoded, and uuencoding makes a file about 30% larger; overall, compression is a "win," but not as much as you might think. Picture and sound files are rarely compressed; the picture encodings have compression built-in already.

There is also a version of *compress* that runs on MS-DOS. Due to DOS's memory limitations, the program can handle only 13-bit file compression. Since the UNIX version defaults to 16-bit file compression, MS-DOS *compress* will not be able to uncompress these files.

Figuring out what you have

Compressed files are always binary, so they must be uuencoded before being posted. Start by uudecoding the posting you have received. After uudecoding, compressed files usually have an extension of *.Z*. The *file* command will also identify compressed files.

Decoding a compressed file

To uncompress a file, use one of these commands:

```
% uncompress filename
% compress -d filename
```

If you have the *zcat* command, you can uncompress the file on the fly for use as part of a pipeline:

```
% zcat filename | other command...
```

Creating a compressed file

To compress a file, use one of these commands:

```
% compress files...
% compress -b13 files...
```

Use the second command if you want files that can be uncompressed on an MS-DOS system; as noted above, DOS cannot handle 16-bit compression. In either case, make sure to uuencode the *.Z* file before posting it to USENET.

GNU Zip (.gz) Files

gzip is a widely used file-compression utility that is distributed as part of the GNU project. It is functionally similar to *compress*, but has several advantages over that utility. It is faster and makes smaller files, and an MS-DOS version exists that needs no special treatment.

Figuring out what you have

Like compressed files, gzipped files are always binary and must be uuencoded before they are posted to USENET. Therefore, when you receive a posting that has been compressed, you must uudecode it first. After decoding, compressed files usually have an extension of *.gz*. Very old versions of *gzip* used an extension of *.z*.

Decoding a GNU Zip file

To "unzip" a file, use one of the commands:

```
% gzip -d filename
% gunzip filename
```

You can unzip the file on the fly for use as part of a pipeline:

```
% gzip -cd filename | other command...
```

Creating a GNU Zip file

To "zip" a file, use the command:

```
% gzip files...
```

Be sure to uuencode the file before posting it to USENET.

tar (Tape Archive) Files

tar is a general purpose archive program. It comes standard with UNIX, and clones are available for many other operating systems. The "t" originally stood for tape, but *tar* also writes to standard files, allowing it to be used for many other things.

Since *tar* files contain binary characters, they need to be uuencoded before being placed on the Net. They are usually compressed or zipped as well, so it is fairly common to see files with extensions of *.tar.Z*, *.tar.gz*, or *.tgz*. If you don't see proper identification in the file's subject line or the start of the message body, check the *uuencode* "begin" line; that will tell you the file's name when it is decoded.

Decoding a tar file

First, make sure that the file has been uudecoded. Then look at what you have; it may be a "plain" *tar* file, or a compressed (gzipped) *tar* file. If the file is compressed or gzipped, you can do three things:*

- You can uncompress it by typing one of the following commands:

```
% uncompress file
% compress -d file
```

---

* With *gzip* files, replace "compress" and "uncompress" with "gzip" and "gunzip," respectively.

- If your system has the *zcat* command, you can uncompress the file on the fly and pipe the results to *tar*. If you do this, you need to give *tar* the flag *f* − (put a space between the "f" and the hyphen), which means that *tar* will read from the standard input. See below for more details.

  ```
  % zcat file.tar.Z | tar vxf -
  ```

- If you have the GNU version of *tar*, it has built-in support for both compressed and gzipped files. You can add the *z* flag to your *tar* command to handle the decompression of the archive.

  ```
  % tar xzvf archive.tar.Z
  ```

Assuming that you have a plain old *tar* file, how do you handle it? *tar* has a number of commands and options. The commands we are concerned with are:

t   Print a table of contents

x   Extract files from a *tar* file

c   Create a *tar* file from the named files

The options we are concerned with are:

v   Verbose; give lots of information about what's in the archive

f file
    Take input from *file*. A filename consisting of a hyphen (-) means to read from the standard input.

Given the file *archive.tar*, you would get a list of what's in it with the command:

```
% tar tvf archive.tar
```

And you would extract (unpack) the files from the archive with:

```
% tar vxf archive.tar
```

In both cases, I've specified the *v* (verbose) option; it isn't really necessary, but it never hurts.

CAUTION

Some *tar* files include a directory name as part of each file's pathname. Be sure to double-check where your files will be placed when they are extracted. It is a real mess to extract files into the wrong directory!

Creating a tar file

tar files are created with the *c* command; to create a *tar* archive from all the C source and header files in your current directory, use the command:

```
% tar cvf filesarchive.tar *.[ch]
```

What if you're a DOS or Windows user? There are free version of *tar* for the PC, but I've had trouble getting them to work correctly. The best solution is probably the MKS Toolkit.

arc Files

arc archive files have been in common use on MS-DOS machines since 1985, when the *arc* program was introduced as shareware by System Enhancement Associates. Another version was introduced the next year by PKWARE. *pkarc* and *pkxarc* are generally believed to operate a little faster. There is also a version that runs on UNIX.

Creating arc files

arc files are not generally used to archive files on UNIX, but are generally created on the PC, uploaded to the UNIX machine with a communications program such as Kermit, and then uuencoded and distributed.

CAUTION

Be sure to upload or download the file in binary mode.

zip Files

The *zip* file format and the programs *pkzip* and *pkunzip* were released in 1989 by PKWARE. Like *arc* files, *zip* files are generally used on MS-DOS systems, and uploaded and downloaded to UNIX machines when posted to the Net.

CAUTION

Be sure to upload or download the file in binary mode.

Multipart Archives

Many uuencoded postings or shell archives are *multipart archives* in which one file is split into many smaller parts. By convention, the subject lines should look something like this:

```
myprogram for DOS [0 of 2]
myprogram for DOS [1 of 2]
myprogram for DOS [2 of 2]
```

Part 0, if it exists, should be a more thorough description of what the program is and how to unpack it. This convention isn't always obeyed, though.

When faced with a multipart posting, you can either:

- Let the newsreader decode it for you; we've given examples in Chapters 3 and 4.
- Save each part separately, put them together by hand (deleting headers), and uudecode (or unshar) the posting.

Obviously, I recommend the former; it's much less work.

File Combinations

It's common to see several of the operations I've discussed applied to a file; for example, a set of binary files may be *tar*'d, gzipped, uuencoded, and split! The best way to decipher these files is to look at the name; for example, let's say that you uudecode some article and are left with the unlikely name *sample.tar.gz*. This file should be unzipped with *gzip* (*.gz*), then extracted with *tar x* (*.tar*)—that is, take care of extensions from right to left.

In groups that cater to DOS users, you may see extensions like *.tgz* (e.g., *sample.tgz*). This gets around the DOS limitation on filename extensions, which may be only three characters long. Like the previous example, a *.tgz* file should be unzipped (with *gunzip*) and then extracted with *tar*.

## CHAPTER ELEVEN

USING MAIL

What Is Electronic Mail?
Mail Addressing
Using UNIX Mail
Other Mail Packages
Electronic Mail and Privacy

E lectronic mail (email) is an important adjunct to network news. Many discussions started in a newsgroup will be continued in private conversations via email, saving network bandwidth and maintaining a higher degree of privacy

These days, the chances are pretty good that you already use an email package on a regular basis. In case you don't, this chapter provides a brief overview of electronic mail and how to use it. We'll cover the basic commands using the standard mail programs that come with most UNIX systems, and point you to a few other mail packages that have more functionality and a better user interface.

What Is Electronic Mail?

Electronic mail systems allow messages to be sent between individual users. Mail sent to you is saved in your system mailbox. After you read the message, you can:

- Save the message for future reference
- Reply to the message, possibly including excerpts from the original message
- Forward the message to other interested parties

If you have never used electronic mail, you will be amazed at how rapidly you will become dependent upon it. It provides a full transcript of conversations, and it can be answered at your convenience. There's no such thing as "email tag"!

Electronic mail is fairly similar to news. Email messages look a lot like news articles, and have many of the same headers. Sociologically, there's a lot of similarity too: in both mediums, there's a tendency for arguments to get out of hand and degenerate into flaming. And there's an even stronger dislike of anything remotely resembling junk mail or advertising in personal mail. Every day, your postal mailbox is probably full of trash; many of us are worried that, within a few years, electronic mail will be similar.

Mail Addressing

If you have used electronic mail to communicate with other people at your site, you are already familiar with using people's login IDs as their email address. The major difference when sending a message to someone at another site is that, in addition to specifying their login name, you will need to specify their location as well.

There are a variety of methods for specifying remote mail addresses.[*] The two most common methods, domain-style addressing and UUCP bang-path addressing, should handle the majority of the people on the Net.

Domain-Style Addressing

By far the most commonly used style of addressing is the style popularized by the Internet, often referred to as *domain-style addressing*. The general format of this style is *user-name@site-name*. *user-name* is usually the person's login name; *site-name* is the name of the machine where the person receives mail.

Domain names are similar to newsgroup names in that they are hierarchical specifications for a particular machine's location on the Net. The term "domain addressing" is used because the network is divided into a number of domains, which are further divided into subdomains, and so forth until each machine has a unique domain name that identifies it. Some of the top-level domains used in the United States are *.com* (commercial sites), *.edu* (educational sites), and *.gov* (government sites).

Outside of the United States, addressing is predominantly geographical; that is, your top-level domain is based on where you are located (or where your company's headquarters is located). Presently, there exists a top-level domain for every country. For example, Canada's top-level domain is *.ca*, while Japan's is *.jp*.[†] The top-level geographical domain for the United States is *.us*; it is used (largely by personal systems, which don't really qualify as "educational" or "commercial"), but you won't see it too often.

Usually, the second part[‡] of the domain name is the name of the organization (as in *ibm.com* or *mit.edu*), and then division, regional, or any other names needed. For many small- or medium-sized organizations, a short domain name such as *ora.com* (O'Reilly & Associates) is sufficient. Large organizations can have large (and sometimes hard to remember) names. Two reviewers of this book have the

---

[*] See *!%@:: A Directory of Electronic Mail Addressing and Networks*, by Donnalyn Frey and Rick Adams (O'Reilly & Associates).

[†] See Appendix C.

[‡] Which really means "second to last," since the most general part of the domain name is at the end.

domain address of *cnad.dl.nec.com* (Corporate Network Administration Division, Dallas region, NEC USA, Inc., in the commercial domain—whew!)

Figure 11-1 gives a simple illustration of some domain names. Note the hierarchical (tree-like) structure of the domains. Another interesting observation is the fact that domain names are built from right to left (i.e., from specific to general), unlike USENET newsgroup names which are built from left to right (general to specific).

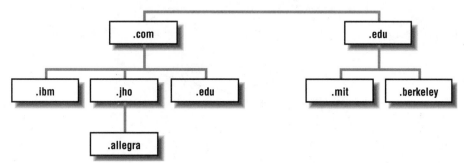

Figure 11-1. An example of domain name addressing

This type of addressing was originally limited to machines that were connected to the Internet, but currently there are methods to allow domain addressing to span across other networks. In particular, it's now possible for sites with a UUCP connection to register a domain name and receive mail addressed in this fashion rather than with the UUCP *bang-path* discussed in the next section. It's a lot more convenient and less likely to change. If you don't have this type of addressing, ask your system administrator to check into getting it.[*]

UUCP Bang-path Addressing

As you might guess from the name, this style of addressing was originated by the UNIX UUCP suite of communications programs. Rather than relying on any particular network topology or naming scheme, UUCP uses the simple method of listing each machine in the path that from the sender to the recipient, separated by exclamation marks (often referred to as "bangs"). For a concrete example of this, look at the UUCP network shown in Figure 11-2. There are four machines on the network, connected by dial-up telephone lines. The machine named *jho* is connected to both *digi* and *wiz*, as is the machine *raven*. Steve, who is logged on at *jho*, wishes to send a message to Doug, who is logged on at *raven*. He could address his message to either *digi!raven!doug* or *wiz!raven!doug*, and the

---

[*] In case your administrator isn't familiar with this, it's called an *MX record*, and he can find out more about it in the newsgroup *comp.mail.admin*.

message would be delivered via one of the intermediary machines. Likewise, Doug could send mail to Steve by reversing the path: either *wiz!jho!steve* or *digi!jho!steve*. Which route is preferable might depend on several factors: the speed of the communication links, the stability of a particular machine, and long distance charges all come into play.

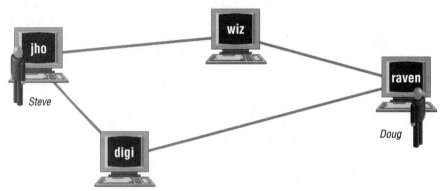

Figure 11-2. A sample UUCP network

Since UUCP-style addressing requires that the sender specify the complete path to the recipient, this causes problems for USENET messages that are sent to all machines on the network. This is usually handled by specifying a partial path to your location from one or more large, well-known sites. If someone wishes to reply to you, chances are they will be able to figure out the addressing as far as that site, and fill in the remainder of the path from the information you provided. This is often specified as *....!big-machine!your-machine!your-name*, with an ellipsis showing the part of the path the sender needs to provide.

For example, a friend's machine *jho* is connected to the machine *uunet*, which is one of the larger sites on the Net. If we wanted to send a message to a user at that site, we would send a message to *....!uunet!jho!user-name*. If that user knew that his machine was connected to *uunet* via the machine *relay*, he could address the message as *relay!uunet!jho!user-name*.

As you can see, this type of addressing can be a little confusing, and sites that have registered domain names save their users a lot of trouble. There is some help, however. There is a program called *uupath* which can take a lot of the guesswork out of determining the path to a particular site. You simply type the command *uupath site-name** and it will display an optimal mail path to that site.

---

* This is not a standard program that comes with the system. It is usually installed by the mail administrator when he is setting up mail initially. If you can't find it on your system, check with your administrator.

Interestingly enough, this program is made possible by the USENET, where the data and UUCP mapping files are distributed in the newsgroup *comp.mail.maps.*

CAUTION

If you are using the C shell, remember that the C shell uses the bang (!) character for command history. If you use bang-path addressing in the C shell, you must remember to precede each bang with a backslash: *machine\!name.* If you don't do this, you will get an error message "Event not found."

Using UNIX Mail

This section discusses the basics of reading and sending mail using the standard UNIX mail package. This is made somewhat difficult by the fact that there are actually *several* standard mail packages, depending on what variant of UNIX you happen to be running.* The original version of mail, sometimes referred to as */bin/ mail* or simply *binmail,* had few features and could not transmit mail messages from one machine to another. Some time later, the *Mail* package was written for Berkeley UNIX. In addition to supporting mail transfers over a network, it has many enhancements and features, including the ability to manage multiple mail files. The *mailx* package was likewise added to AT&T UNIX. SVR4 UNIX comes with an enhanced *mail* package that also supports many of these features.

The chief disadvantage of all these versions of mail is that they lack full-screen or graphical user interfaces. Fortunately, there are several very good freely available packages that make up for this shortcoming and provide other enhancements as well (see below).

Given that there are many much nicer mail packages, why should you worry about UNIX *mail* at all? Well, that's a good question. If a better tool is available, you should use it. However, UNIX *mail* is as close to ubiquitous as a software package can be. If you buy an account on some public-access UNIX system, or talk a local college into giving you an account, you can be sure that *mail* will be available. *pine, elm,* and *zmail* may be nicer, but you can't assume you'll have access to them.

---

* Like many other UNIX features!

Sending Mail

Sending mail is pretty straightforward. In its most basic form, you specify the recipients on the command line, enter the subject, and type the text, ending the message with a **CTRL-D** (or however you've defined your end-of-text key).

```
% mail joe@somewhere.com mary@somewhere.else.com
Subject: meet for lunch?
Joe, Mary,
How about lunch on Tuesday?  I've got a project
proposal to show you.
^D
```

Depending on which version of mail you are using, there are quite a few options you can specify. You can consult your system documentation for details, but most of the mail systems will print a help message if you type a line consisting of ~h. The ~ (tilde) must be the first character on the line.

Reading Mail

To read mail, run the *mail* command with no parameters.

```
% mail
```

If you don't have any mail, you will receive a message informing you of that fact:

```
No mail for harrison
```

If you do have mail, a summary of your mail will be printed, and you will be able to enter commands to save, read, and reply to your mail.

```
% mail
Mail version SMI 4.0 Thu Jul 23 13:52:20 PDT 1992  Type ? for help.
"/usr/spool/mail/harrison": 4 messages 4 new
>N  1 john                 Mon May  3 11:49    6/115   lunch?
 N  2 mikel@ora.com        Tue May  4 14:38   17/354   The new chapter
 N  3 rrao@dsccc.com       Tue May  4 17:09   11/313   New switch load
 N  4 murthy@asl.dl.nec.c  Tue May  4 09:26   23/417   cd rom reader
&
```

Once again, you can consult your system documentation for details on the version of mail that came with your system, but there are a few commands common to the different versions.

h   Print a help message

return
     Page through the current message

number
     Typing the number of a particular message will view that message

r   Reply to the current message

s *filename*
    Save the current message in *filename*

z   View the next screenful of messages

Z   View the previous screenful of messages

Other Mail Packages

In addition to the standard mail software that comes with various versions of UNIX, there are a number of mail packages available with extra features and a better user interface. Most workstation vendors provide some kind of enhanced mail package, and there are a number of excellent packages that may be purchased from various software vendors.

In addition to these packages, there are several freely available[*] packages that provide many useful features and enhancements over the standard mail software. If you don't have any enhanced mail software packages installed at your site, I strongly recommend that you try out one of the packages listed below.[†]

elm—Electronic Mail

elm is a powerful, easy-to-use mail system. The system is more than just a single program; it includes programs like *frm* to list a table of contents of your mail, *printmail* to quickly paginate mail files (to allow clean printouts), and *autoreply*, a systemwide daemon that can auto-answer mail for people while they're on vacation without having multiple copies spawned on the system. Newer versions also include support for MIME (multimedia extensions to electronic mail).

The most significant difference between *elm* and other mail systems is that *elm* is only screen-oriented. But users will soon find that *elm* is also easier to use and intelligent about sending mail and so on.

elm is particularly good for novices. Its main disadvantage (in some people's view) is that it is less user configurable than some other mailers (for example, *mush*); though if you're a new user, you probably don't want a lot of configuration options to worry about. It is commonly found on public-access UNIX systems.

---

[*] This term is a catch-all for programs that you can use without paying real money. It includes both public-domain (uncopyrighted) software and free copyrighted software.

[†] I am greatly indebted to Chris Lewis for this information. He is the keeper of the "UNIX Email Software" FAQ, which is posted regularly on *comp.mail.misc* and *news.answers*.

pine—Easy and Powerful

pine is a mailer developed by the University of Washington Office of Computing and Communications. It runs on many UNIX platforms and was designed with the novice user in mind. According to its documentation, *pine*'s guiding principles are: careful limitation of features, one-character mnemonic commands, always-present command menus, immediate user feedback, and high tolerance for user mistakes. It's supposed to be learned by exploration rather than by reading manuals.

A standalone version of Pico, *pine*'s message composition editor, is also included. It is a simple text editor with text justification and a spelling checker.

Some of *pine*'s more useful features include an address book that supports aliases and distribution lists, a folder management screen for filing and keeping track of messages, a full-screen message composer, and context-sensitive help for each screen. It also supports MIME.

pine was originally based on *elm*, but it has evolved a great deal. *pine* is an acronym for "Pine Is No-longer Elm." It's probably the most popular mailer for new users and, for this reason, is available on many public-access UNIX sites.

mush and Z-Mail

mush (Mail User's Shell) is a shell for mail users. It has its own environment in which you can configure not only the user interface, but the actual internal mechanisms. *mush* has a shell-like scripting language, command-line aliases, file completion, if-else statements, command piping, and so on. Because you can build your own commands, you can create your own library of email features.

mush has two terminal-based interfaces: the standard character-based interface (similar to the standard UNIX mail packages) and a screen-oriented mode similar to that of the text editors *vi* and *Emacs*. You can set up key bindings that execute one or more *mush* commands, personalized commands, or even UNIX commands. You can even emulate keyboard input with keyboard macros and mappings.

The next generation of *mush* is a commercial product called *Z-Mail* from NCD. All aspects of *mush* are retained, yet it has grown to be far more powerful. It runs on workstations with a fancy graphical interface and also supports multimedia, user functions, and a suite of new features, including a powerful scripting language.

mush and *Z-Mail* are discussed in the newsgroup *comp.mail.mush*. Because *Z-Mail* is a commercial product, and public-access UNIX sites tend to be low-budget operations, you probably won't find it on too many public-access UNIX sites. If it's available, it's worth trying.

MH—Mail Handler

MH is a mailer that has been around quite a while. It's not very easy to use, but it may be the most powerful mailer out there. However, I'm not sure whether it ought to be called the "Cadillac" of email systems, or the "erector set."

The big difference between *MH* and most other mail packages is that you can use *MH* from a UNIX shell prompt. In *MH*, each command is a separate program, and the shell is used as an interpreter. So, all the power of UNIX shells (pipes, redirection, history, aliases, and so on) works with *MH*—you don't have to learn a new interface. This can be a big advantage in building software packages that need to interface with the mail system. My own administrator uses a package built on top of *MH* to log and respond to user requests. It's very nice, as users can view and monitor items in the administration queue. This is really where *MH* comes into its own: if you want to build tools that respond to mail automatically, or if you want something that can sort your mail, consider *MH*. The disadvantage is that it's more like a toolkit than a tool.

There are *MH* interfaces for the X Window System called *xmh* and *exmh*, as well as an interface to *Emacs* called *mh-e*. The newsgroup *comp.mail.mh* is dedicated to discussing *MH*. The Nutshell Handbook *MH and xmh* (O'Reilly & Associates) is a complete discussion of these mailers.

Rmail—Read Mail for GNU Emacs

Rmail is a popular package for reading mail within *Emacs*. Reading the messages in an *Rmail* file is done in a special major mode, Rmail mode, which redefines most letters to run commands for managing mail. *Rmail* can do the standard things such as displaying, deleting, filing, or replying to messages.

If you are the kind of person who enjoys doing everything from within *Emacs*, this is the mailer for you.

Electronic Mail and Privacy

A word about "private" email: Don't be fooled into thinking such a thing exists. Once you enter your message, anyone with root access at your site is capable of reading it. Once it leaves your site, even larger numbers of people are capable of capturing and reading your mail. Opinions differ as to exactly what is legal or ethical with regards to what administrators, employers, or others are allowed to do with private electronic correspondence, but I strongly recommend that you *never* send confidential information such as credit card numbers or closely held secrets via electronic mail.[*]

Likewise, you should be aware of how easily messages can be forged. If you receive a message that you suspect may not be authentic (it may be oddly formatted, especially the headers, or seem out of character for the person sending it), double-check with the sender to make sure the message was from them. It doesn't hurt to include a copy of the message for their reference.

Finally, a few words of caution regarding your own messages are in order. If you are going to send a confidential message to Mary complaining about how much you dislike working with Bob, *don't* accidentally send it to Bob instead of Mary. At a previous job, a pair of co-op students created a great deal of entertainment for the entire company by not noticing that some of their romantic messages were being copied to the rest of the development staff. Likewise, if you don't trust someone to keep a secret, don't send them email. It's one thing for people to hear rumors about a particular topic, and another (much worse) for them to see it in print. Remember that the Iran-Contra scandal was investigated in part by inspecting system backup tapes containing email files.

On a related note, if you're using your company's computers to read your email, you should be aware that your company may have a policy stating that email is company property (as are all files that exist on their computers), and may be read by company management at any time. The ethics and ownership of email are under debate—just one more reason not to consider email "private." No matter where you stand on this debate, make sure you find out about any policies that govern the computers on which you send and receive mail. (There are services that provide a certain degree of anonymity for email and USENET news participants, however. See the following article, "If USENET Isn't Anonymous Enough for You.")

---

[*] There are several packages that provide encryption and validation for electronic mail. If your site routinely sends confidential data across public networks, it's probably good to ask your mail administrator to look into them. Look at the *alt.security* newsgroups (particularly *alt.security.pgp*, which discusses one widely used encryption package) for more information.

If USENET Isn't Anonymous Enough for You

When you consider the number of flames sent out on a regular basis, it seems that many people feel somewhat sheltered by the relative anonymity of USENET—for better and worse. Certainly, few people will be able to put a face to your login name, unless you participate in a newsgroup peopled by professional colleagues, students from the same school, etc.

But there may be occasions when you want more complete anonymity. Perhaps you have an embarrassing problem about which you really need advice. Or you want to discuss something that's going on at your office, and you'd rather your co-workers didn't find out. Well, there is at least one service that will help you post news anonymously. You can also send and receive electronic mail under this anonymous guise. How? Well, if you send email to *help@anon.penet.fi*, you'll get pages of information and instructions. Sorting through this help file reveals that you need to register with the anonymous server and also get a password before you can send messages anonymously. First, send an empty email message to:

```
anon@anon.penet.fi
```

The server will automatically assign you an alias beginning with the letters "an" and ending with four digits. This code will be mailed to you:

```
From daemon@anon.penet.fi Tue Mar 7 11:44:45 1995
Date: Tue, 7 Mar 95 18:16:57 +0200
From: daemon@anon.penet.fi (System Daemon)
Message-Id: <9503071616.AA00483@anon.penet.fi>
To: cheshire@ora.com
Subject: Anonymous code name allocated.

You have sent a message using the anonymous contact service.
You have been allocated the code name an207908.
You can be reached anonymously using the address
an207908@anon.penet.fi.

If you want to use a nickname, please send a message to
nick@anon.penet.fi, with a Subject: field containing your nickname.

For instructions, send a message to help@anon.penet.fi.
```

As the message from the anonymous server indicates, people can return email to you using your assigned anonymous address.

But before you can send an anonymous message, you need to register a password with the server. Why? Well, it's actually possible for a savvy user

—continued—

to find out something about you, despite the anonymous server's defenses. The presence of passwords makes snooping more difficult.

To register your password, send email to *password@anon.penet.fi*. Your message must contain nothing but the password you want to use. For instance:

```
To: password@anon.penet.fi
ABCDEFGGGG8846590K
```

Now that you have a code name and password (isn't this fun?), you can send anonymous email messages or news postings. In order to do so, you must send your messages to *anon@anon.penet.fi*, and adhere to the following syntax. First, you have to specify the recipients as the first line of the message body:

```
To: anon@anon.penet.fi
Subject:
X-Anon-To: alt.planet.krypton,alt.geniuses.evil
```

Notice that newsgroup names are valid recipients. If you want to send an anonymous message to an individual, supply his or her email address. We've left the subject field blank, but if you give one, it will be conveyed with the message. If you would like to send your message to multiple recipients, separate the names by commas, without whitespace, as in our example. In practice, combining newsgroup names and email addresses in the same message does not seem to work, however.

Second, you have to include your password. Put it on its own line, following the X-Anon-To: line. Preface the password with the words **X-Anon-Password**, as in the following:

```
To: anon@anon.penet.fi
Subject:
X-Anon-To: superman@krypton.org,lexluther@world.takeover.com
X-Anon-Password: ABCDEFGGGG8846590K
```

Then enter your intended message and send. The server will convey your message to the recipients you specified, giving your anonymous email address as the return address. The server will also send you an email acknowledgement of a successful transmission or an error message if something goes wrong.

The initial greeting from the anonymous server leaves out a detail you should know: If someone sends you mail using your anonymous address, his or her identity will also be masked. In other words, the anonymity works in both directions. So if you post news anonymously and people follow up via email, you're not going to know who they are either. Fair is fair.

—continued—

But there are appropriate and even non-embarrassing times to use an anonymous mail/news server. If you do decide to use this one, and you want to post news, you will be limited to groups that are received at the site where the anonymous service lives. All groups distributed "worldwide" are available, but many local groups may not be. If you want to post any test messages, please send them to *alt.test* or *misc.test*.

Another thing the greeting from the anonymous server doesn't tell you, but that the help message, not to mention a little common sense, suggests: some people want to remain anonymous for less innocuous reasons than the ones mentioned at the beginning of this article. The help message gives an example of posting news anonymously to *alt.sex.bestiality*.

Well, I can see why someone might not want to jump right up to own such a proclivity. But I can also be turned off from using a service that is commonly employed for such purposes. An anonymous server can also assist in the unsavory business of USENET terrorism. See Chapter 9 for a discussion of that bizarre phenomenon.

However, in the help message, the gentleman who provides this service makes clear that one of the reasons he's doing it is to assist people who require anonymity for very good reasons. Specifically, he mentions people posting news to *alt.sexual.abuse.recovery*.

But he is also aware that people can use such a service for less noble purposes. He even goes so far as to state:

```
Please don't do anything stupid that would force me to close down the
service. As I am running my own company, there is very little
political pressure anyone can put on me, but if somebody starts using
the system for criminal activities, the authorities might be able to
order me to shut down the service.
```

I don't know if anyone has used this service to pursue "criminal activities." But I'm pretty sure it's used for other purposes I probably wouldn't condone. And I would be lying if I said it doesn't bother me. But I like free speech, and toleration is part of the deal. And the fact that the service is helping people who need it, well, that makes it a little easier to take.

For more information about the service, send email to *help@anon.penet.fi*.

— *Valerie Quercia*

GEOGRAPHIC DISTRIBUTIONS

G eographic distributions limit the area over which a news posting is distributed. For example, a posting with a distribution of *ba* is only propagated to the San Francisco Bay area.

There are a few things to be aware of:

- Distributions are *not* newsgroup hierarchies, though there are many local hierarchies (like *ba.**) that correspond to these distributions.

- Distributions do *not* work particularly well; it's better to post to a local newsgroup than to rely on a distribution to limit circulation. But do not use this as an excuse for ignoring distributions when posting to a world-wide group.

- You may *only* post to a distribution if you are already within that distribution. If you're a Texan, you can't post articles with a distribution of *ba*. However, you can post to the *ba* newsgroup; and your site may even receive the *ba* newsgroup hierarchy.

In addition to the distributions shown here, there are many organizational distributions for companies, universities, and networking groups. Ask your system administrator what distributions are appropriate for you to use.

Again, if there's a local newsgroup, it's better to use that than the corresponding distribution. Newsgroups are always propagated correctly; distributions frequently aren't.

5col
  Pioneer Valley/Massachusetts/USA

aa
  Ann Arbor/MI/USA

ab
  Alberta/CAN

akron
  Akron/OH/USA

amiga
  Amiga Programmers/Germany

atl
  Atlanta/GA/USA

atl
  Atlantic Provinces/NS, New Brunswick, Prince Edward Island, Newfoundland/CAN

aus
  Australia

austin
  Austin/TX/USA

az
  Arizona/USA

ba
  San Francisco Bay Area/CA/USA

bc
  British Columbia/CAN

belwue
Baden-Wuerttemberg/Germany/Europe

bergen
Bergen County/NJ/USA

bnet
Belgium*

ca
California/USA

can
Canada

capdist
Capital District/Albany, Schenectady,
Troy/NY/USA

ch
Switzerland

chi
Chicago/IL/USA

chico
Chico/CA/USA

chile
Chile

cle
Cleveland/OH/USA

cmh
Columbus/OH/USA

co
Colorado/USA

cov
Coventry/Midlands/UK

dc
Washington, D.C./USA

det
Detroit/MI/USA

dfw
Dallas-Ft. Worth/TX/USA

dsm
Des Moines/IA/USA

ed
Edinborough/SCOT/UK

edm
Edmonton/AB/CAN

es
Spain/EUNET

5col
Pioneer Valley/Massachusetts/USA

fj
Japan

fl
Florida/USA

ga
Georgia/USA

hfx
Halifax/NS/CAN

hk
Hong Kong

houston
Houston/TX/USA

hsv
Huntsville/Alabama/USA

ia
Iowa/USA

ie
Ireland

il
Illinois/USA

il
Israel

in
Indiana/USA

iowacity
Iowa City/IA/USA

ka
Karlsruhe/BELWUE/Germany/Europe

kc
Kansas City/Kansas City metro/USA

kingston
Kingston/ONT/CAN

ks
Kansas/USA

kw
Kitchener-Waterloo/ONT/CAN

ky
Kentucky/USA

la
Los Angeles County/CA/USA

lon
The London area/England/UK

lou
Louisiana/USA

md
Maryland/USA

mhk
Manhattan/KS/USA

mi
Michigan/USA

miami
Miami/FL/USA

midlands
Midlands/UK

milw
Milwaukee/WI/USA

mlb
Melbourne/BREVARD/FL/USA

mn
Minnesota/USA

mo
Missouri/USA

mtl
Montreal/QC/CAN

na
North America/Mexico, CAN,USA

nc
North Carolina/USA

ne
New England/Connecticut,
Massachusetts, Maine, New Hampshire,
Rhode Island, Vermont/USA

neworleans
New Orleans/LOU/USA

nj
New Jersey/USA

nlnet
Netherlands

no
Norway

ns
Nova Scotia/CAN

ny
New York/USA

nyc
New York City/NY/USA

nz
New Zealand

oau
Orlando/FL/USA

oc
Orange County/CA/USA

oh
Ohio/USA

ok
Oklahoma/USA

ont
Ontario/CAN

or
Oregon/USA

ott
Ottawa/ONT/CAN

pa
Pennsylvania/USA

pdx
Portland/OR/USA

pgh
Pittsburgh/PA/USA

phl
Philadelphia/PA/USA

pnw
Pacific North West/Idaho, OR, WA/USA

qc
Quebec/CAN

relcom
Relcom/Russia/SU

rg
Rio Grande Valley/New Mexico/USA

rv
Rogue Valley/OR/USA

sac
Sacramento/CA/USA

sarasota
Sarasota/FL/USA

sba
Santa Barbara/CA/USA

sbay
South San Francisco Bay area/Santa
Clara and Santa Cruz Counties-CA/USA

scot
Scotland/UK

scruz
Santa Cruz County/CA/US

sdnet
San Diego County/CA/USA

sea
Seattle/WA/USA

seattle
Seattle/WA/USA

sfnet
Finland

stgt
  Stuttgart/Baden-Wuerttemberg/Germany/
  Europe

stl
  St. Louis/MO/USA

su
  Soviet Union

tba
  Tampa Bay area/FL/USA

tdw
  Tidewater/VA/USA

tn
  Tennessee/USA

tor
  Toronto/ONT/CAN

triangle
  Research Triangle Park area/NC/USA

tx
  Texas/USA

uk
  United Kingdom

usa
  United States of America

utah
  Utah/USA

va
  Virginia/USA

vic
  Victoria/BC/CAN

wa
  Washington/USA

wgtn
  Wellington/NZ

wi
  Wisconsin/USA

wny
  Western NY (Rochester, Buffalo)/NY/
  USA

za
  South Africa

USENET ARTICLES

This appendix contains articles that are posted on a regular basis to *news.announce.newusers*. The Net would be a much more enjoyable place if every person new to USENET were to read and follow the advice of these articles. I have reproduced these articles exactly as you would see them on the Net: words, style, spelling, and all.

The Original Announcement

USENET - A General Access UNIX Network

Stephen Daniel, James Ellis, and Tom Truscott

Duke University

A group of UNIX systems at Duke University and the University of North Carolina, Chapel Hill, have established a uucp-based computer communication network. Admission to the net is open to all UNIX licensees. In addition to providing the "uu" services available in the Seventh Edition of UNIX (remote mail, file transfer, job execution), it provides a network news service. A prospective system must have a call-in facility, call-out facility, or some other means of communication with another UNIX net system. The system must have, or be able to legitimately obtain, uucp and related software.

Systems which do not call-out to the net must be polled occasionally. We will poll any system that so requests, and will bill the polled system for phone costs. Phone costs are typically $10-$20/month. There are no connection fees or other charges for using the network. Requests for an application[*] should be sent to

---

[*] Remember that this article appeared 15 or 20 years ago. Do NOT try to contact Jim Ellis, Duke University, or call the phone number given. Fortunately, there are now hundreds (probably thousands) of organizations that can give you a USENET connection, including any company that sells Internet access.

James Ellis
Department of Computer Science
Duke University
Durham, NC 27706
Telephone: (919) 684-3048

SERVICES

A goal of USENET has been to give every UNIX system the opportunity to join and benefit from a computer network (a poor man's ARPANET, if you will). New systems will probably find that the rapid access newsletter is the initially most significant service. Via news (available on the Delaware conference distribution tape), any system can submit an article which will in due course propagate to all other interested systems. Most articles concern bug fixes, requests for help, and general information.

The mail command provides a convenient means for responding to intriguing articles. In general, small groups of users with common interests use mail to communicate. If the group size grows sufficiently, they can start a new "newsgroup" (this will be discussed later).

It is hoped that USENIX will take an active (indeed central) role in the network. There is the problem of members not on the net, so hardware newsletters should remain the standard communication method. However, use of the net for preparation of newsletters seems like a good idea.

NEWS

News is designed to meet the information interchange needs of large communities of computer users. Through the mechanism of "newsgroups", news minimizes file space usage and network traffic while allowing multiple, overlapping interest groups to coexist and dynamically evolve. Conceptually, a newsgroup is a name for a category of news articles. Users on a given system may individually subscribe and submit articles to arbitrary sets of newsgroups. When a user runs news, articles matching that user's interests are presented. Various options may be specified to permit the reading of old news or news from other newsgroups.

Remote systems can also subscribe to newsgroups on an individual basis. For each such system, a subscription list and a transmission protocol are maintained. Whenever an article should be sent to a remote system, the transmission protocol for that system is executed with a formatted version of the article as input. This program performs the necessary magic to send an article to the news program on the remote system. This might, for example, be done by remote execution of news, or the article could be encapsulated and mailed to the remote system, where another program would recover it and pass it on to the local news program.

The individual system subscription lists also allow the creation of subnetworks. For example, the systems near Duke all subscribe to the newsgroup "triangle" which is used for colloquium announcements and other items of local interest.

Duke's news is used primarily for articles of strictly local interest; however, the ones off the net tend to be more interesting. For example, there have been over a dozen bug reports, about half of which have suggested fixes. Two different bugs were found in the kernel's swapping code: one may cause the swap area to be trashed, the other may cause a user to lose his floating point registers. (A fix was given in each case.) There have also been several articles of more general interest, such as how to get a draft copy of the IEEE assembly language standard.

QUESTIONS ANSWERED

1. Isn't this expensive?

Not at all. Night time phone costs are about $0.50/3 minutes, in which time uucp can transfer about 3000 bytes of data (300 baud).* Daily polling then costs $15/Month, which is half what Duke pays just for an office phone.

2. Can Duke really handle all the phone calls?

Sure. We have two call-out lines: at five minutes/call, we can handle 24 calls/hour. Other systems also perform the call-out function.

3. What about abuse of the network?

In general, it will be straightforward to detect when abuse has occurred and who did it. The uucp system, like UNIX, is not designed to prevent abuses of overconsumption. Experience will show what uses of the net are in fact abuses, and what should be done about them.

Certain abuses of the net can be serious indeed. As with ordinary abuses, they can be thought about, looked for, and even programmed against, but only experience will show what matters. Uucp provides some measure of protection. It runs as an ordinary user, and has strict access controls. It is safe to say that it poses no greater threat than that inherent in a call-in line.

4. Who would be responsible when something bad happens?

Not us! And we do not intend that any innocent bystander be held liable either. We are looking into this matter. Suggestions are solicited.

5. Okay, so a few systems have the net started. What next?

---

* Remember, this was written in 1980.

What Is USENET?

Original-from: chip@tct.com (Chip Salzenberg)
Comment: edited until 5/93 by spaf@cs.purdue.edu (Gene Spafford)
Last-change: 5 July 1994 by netannounce@deshaw.com (Mark Moraes)

The first thing to understand about Usenet is that it is widely misunderstood. Every day on Usenet, the "blind men and the elephant" phenomenon is evident, in spades. In my opinion, more flame wars arise because of a lack of understanding of the nature of Usenet than from any other source. And consider that such flame wars arise, of necessity, among people who are on Usenet. Imagine, then, how poorly understood Usenet must be by those outside!

Any essay on the nature of Usenet cannot ignore the erroneous impressions held by many Usenet users. Therefore, this article will treat falsehoods first. Keep reading for truth. (Beauty, alas, is not relevant to Usenet.)

WHAT USENET IS NOT

1. Usenet is not an organization.

No person or group has authority over Usenet as a whole. No one controls who gets a news feed, which articles are propagated where, who can post articles, or anything else. There is no "Usenet Incorporated," nor is there a "Usenet User's Group." You're on your own.

Granted, there are various activities organized by means of Usenet newsgroups. The newsgroup creation process is one such activity. But it would be a mistake to equate Usenet with the organized activities it makes possible. If they were to stop tomorrow, Usenet would go on without them.

2. Usenet is not a democracy.

Since there is no person or group in charge of Usenet as a whole -- i.e. there is no Usenet "government" -- it follows that Usenet cannot be a democracy, autocracy, or any other kind of "-acy." (But see "The Camel's Nose?" below.)

3. Usenet is not fair.

After all, who shall decide what's fair? For that matter, if someone is behaving unfairly, who's going to stop him? Neither you nor I, that's certain.

4. Usenet is not a right.

Some people misunderstand their local right of "freedom of speech" to mean that they have a legal right to use others' computers to say what they wish in whatever way they wish, and the owners of said computers have no right to stop them. Those people are wrong. Freedom of speech also means freedom not to speak. If I choose not to use my computer to aid your speech, that is my right. Freedom of the press belongs to those who own one.

5. Usenet is not a public utility.

Some Usenet sites are publicly funded or subsidized. Most of them, by plain count, are not. There is no government monopoly on Usenet, and little or no government control.

6. Usenet is not an academic network.

It is no surprise that many Usenet sites are universities, research labs or other academic institutions. Usenet originated with a link between two universities, and the exchange of ideas and information is what such institutions are all about. But the passage of years has changed Usenet's character. Today, by plain count, most Usenet sites are commercial entities.

7. Usenet is not an advertising medium.

Because of Usenet's roots in academia, and because Usenet depends so heavily on cooperation (sometimes among competitors), custom dictates that advertising be kept to a minimum. It is tolerated if it is infrequent, informative, and low-hype. The "comp.newprod" newsgroup is NOT an exception to this rule: product announcements are screened by a moderator in an attempt to keep the hype-to-information ratio in check.

If you must engage in flackery for your company, use the "biz" hierarchy, which is explicitly "advertising-allowed", and which (like all of Usenet) is carried only by those sites that want it.

8. Usenet is not the Internet.

The Internet is a wide-ranging network, parts of which are subsidized by various governments. It carries many kinds of traffic, of which Usenet is only one. And the Internet is only one of the various networks carrying Usenet traffic.

9. Usenet is not a UUCP network.

UUCP is a protocol (actually a "protocol suite," but that's a technical quibble) for sending data over point-to-point connections, typically using dialup modems. Sites use UUCP to carry many kinds of traffic, of which Usenet is only one. And UUCP is only one of the various transports carrying Usenet traffic.

10. Usenet is not a United States network.

It is true that Usenet originated in the United States, and the fastest growth in Usenet sites has been there. Nowadays, however, Usenet extends worldwide. The heaviest concentrations of Usenet sites outside the U.S. seem to be in Canada, Europe, Australia and Japan.

Keep Usenet's worldwide nature in mind when you post articles. Even those who can read your language may have a culture wildly different from yours. When your words are read, they might not mean what you think they mean.

11. Usenet is not a UNIX network.

Don't assume that everyone is using "rn" on a UNIX machine. Among the systems used to read and post to Usenet are Vaxen running VMS, IBM mainframes, Amigas, and MS-DOS PCs.

12. Usenet is not an ASCII network.

The A in ASCII stands for "American". Sites in other countries often use character sets better suited to their language(s) of choice; such are typically, though not always, supersets of ASCII. Even in the United States, ASCII is not universally used: IBM mainframes use (shudder) EBCDIC. Ignore non-ASCII sites if you like, but they exist.

13. Usenet is not software.

There are dozens of software packages used at various sites to transport and read Usenet articles. So no one program or package can be called "the Usenet software." Software designed to support Usenet traffic can be (and is) used for other kinds of communication, usually without risk of mixing the two. Such private communication networks are typically kept distinct from Usenet by the invention of newsgroup names different from the universally-recognized ones.

Well, enough negativity.

WHAT USENET IS

Usenet is the set of people who exchange articles tagged with one or more universally-recognized labels, called "newsgroups" (or "groups" for short).

(Note that the term "newsgroup" is correct, while "area," "base," "board," "bboard," "conference," "round table," "SIG," etc. are incorrect. If you want to be understood, be accurate.)

DIVERSITY

If the above definition of Usenet sounds vague, that's because it is.

It is almost impossible to generalize over all Usenet sites in any non-trivial way. Usenet encompasses government agencies, large universities, high schools, businesses of all sizes, home computers of all descriptions, etc, etc. (In response to the above paragraphs, it has been written that there is nothing vague about a network that carries megabytes of traffic per day. I agree. But at the fringes of Usenet, traffic is not so heavy. In the shadowy world of news-mail gateways and mailing lists, the line between Usenet and not-Usenet becomes very hard to draw.)

CONTROL

Every administrator controls his own site. No one has any real control over any site but his own.

The administrator gets her power from the owner of the system she administers. As long as her job performance pleases the owner, she can do whatever she pleases, up to and including cutting off Usenet entirely. Them's the breaks.

Sites are not entirely without influence on their neighbors, however. There is a vague notion of "upstream" and "downstream" related to the direction of high-volume news flow. To the extent that "upstream" sites decide what traffic they will carry for their "downstream" neighbors, those "upstream" sites have some influence on their neighbors' participation in Usenet. But such influence is usually easy to circumvent; and heavy-handed manipulation typically results in a backlash of resentment.

PERIODIC POSTINGS

To help hold Usenet together, various articles (including this one) are periodically posted in newsgroups in the "news" hierarchy. These articles are provided as a public service by various volunteers. They are few but valuable. Learn them well.

Among the periodic postings are lists of active newsgroups, both "standard" (for lack of a better term) and "alternative." These lists, maintained by David Lawrence, reflect his personal view of Usenet, and as such are not "official" in any sense of the word. However, if you're looking for a description of subjects discussed on Usenet, or if you're starting up a new Usenet site, David's lists are an eminently reasonable place to start.

PROPAGATION

In the old days, when UUCP over long-distance dialup lines was the dominant means of article transmission, a few well-connected sites had real influence in

determining which newsgroups would be carried where. Those sites called themselves "the backbone."

But things have changed. Nowadays, even the smallest Internet site has connectivity the likes of which the backbone admin of yesteryear could only dream. In
addition, in the U.S., the advent of cheaper long-distance calls and high-speed
modems has made long-distance Usenet feeds thinkable for smaller companies.

There is only one pre-eminent site for UUCP transport of Usenet in the U.S.,
namely UUNET. But UUNET isn't a player in the propagation wars, because it
never refuses any traffic. UUNET charges by the minute, after all; and besides, to
refuse based on content might jeopardize its legal status as an enhanced service
provider.

All of the above applies to the U.S. In Europe, different cost structures favored
the creation of strictly controlled hierarchical organizations with central registries.
This is all very unlike the traditional mode of U.S. sites (pick a name, get the software, get a feed, you're on). Europe's "benign monopolies," long uncontested,
now face competition from looser organizations patterned after the U.S. model.

NEWSGROUP CREATION

The document that describes the current procedure for creating a new newsgroup
is entitled "How To Create A New Newsgroup." Its common name, however, is
"the guidelines."

If you follow the guidelines, it is probable that your group will be created and
will be widely propagated.

HOWEVER: Because of the nature of Usenet, there is no way for any user to
enforce the results of a newsgroup vote (or any other decision, for that matter).
Therefore, for your new newsgroup to be propagated widely, you must not only
follow the letter of the guidelines; you must also follow its spirit. And you must
not allow even a whiff of shady dealings or dirty tricks to mar the vote. In other
words, don't tick off system administrators; they will get their revenge.

So, you may ask: How is a new user supposed to know anything about the
"spirit" of the guidelines? Obviously, he can't. This fact leads inexorably to the
following recommendation:

>> If you are a new user, don't try to create a new newsgroup. <<

If you have a good newsgroup idea, then read the "news.groups" newsgroup for
a while (six months, at least) to find out how things work. If you're too impatient
to wait six months, then you really need to learn; read "news.groups" for a year
instead. If you just can't wait, find a Usenet old hand to run the vote for you.
Readers may think this advice unnecessarily strict. Ignore it at your peril. It is

embarrassing to speak before learning. It is foolish to jump into a society you don't understand with your mouth open. And it is futile to try to force your will on people who can tune you out with the press of a key.

THE CAMEL'S NOSE?

As was observed above in "What Usenet Is Not," Usenet as a whole is not a democracy. However, there is exactly one feature of Usenet that has a form of democracy: newsgroup creation. A new newsgroup is unlikely to be widely propagated unless its sponsor follows the newsgroup creation guidelines; and the current guidelines require a new newsgroup to pass an open vote.

There are those who consider the newsgroup creation process to be a remarkably powerful form of democracy, since without any coercion, its decisions are almost always carried out. In their view, the democratic aspect of newsgroup creation is the precursor to an organized and democratic Usenet Of The Future.

On the other hand, some consider the democratic aspect of the newsgroup creation process a sham and a fraud, since there is no power of enforcement behind its decisions, and since there appears little likelihood that any such power of enforcement will ever be given it. For them, the appearance of democracy is only a tool used to keep proponents of flawed newsgroup proposals from complaining about their losses.

So, is Usenet on its way to full democracy? Or will property rights and mistrust of central authority win the day? Beats me.

IF YOU ARE UNHAPPY...

Property rights being what they are, there is no higher authority on Usenet than the people who own the machines on which Usenet traffic is carried. If the owner of the machine you use says, "We will not carry alt.sex on this machine," and you are not happy with that order, you have no Usenet recourse. What can we outsiders do, after all?

That doesn't mean you are without options. Depending on the nature of your site, you may have some internal political recourse. Or you might find external pressure helpful. Or, with a minimal investment, you can get a feed of your own from somewhere else. Computers capable of taking Usenet feeds are down in the $500 range now, UNIX-capable boxes are going for under $2000 and there are several freely-redistributable UNIX-like operating systems (NetBSD, FreeBSD, 386BSD and Linux from ftp sites all around the world, complete with source code and all the software needed to run a Usenet site) and at least two commercial UNIX or UNIX-like systems in the $100 price range.

No matter what, though, appealing to "Usenet" won't help. Even if those who read such an appeal are sympathetic to your cause, they will almost certainly have even less influence at your site than you do.

By the same token, if you don't like what some user at another site is doing, only the administrator and owner of that site have any authority to do anything about it. Persuade them that the user in question is a problem for them, and they might do something -- if they feel like it, that is.

If the user in question is the administrator or owner of the site from which she posts, forget it; you can't win. If you can, arrange for your newsreading software to ignore articles from her; and chalk one up to experience.

WORDS TO LIVE BY #1:

USENET AS SOCIETY. Those who have never tried electronic communication may not be aware of what a "social skill" really is. One social skill that must be learned, is that other people have points of view that are not only different, but *threatening*, to your own. In turn, your opinions may be threatening to others. There is nothing wrong with this. Your beliefs need not be hidden behind a facade, as happens with face-to-face conversation. Not everybody in the world is a bosom buddy, but you can still have a meaningful conversation with them. The person who cannot do this lacks in social skills.

-- Nick Szabo

WORDS TO LIVE BY #2:

USENET AS ANARCHY. Anarchy means having to put up with things that really piss you off.

-- Unknown

What Is USENET? A Second Opinion

Original-author: emv@msen.com (Edward Vielmetti)
Last-change: 17 Jul 94 by emv@msen.com (Edward Vielmetti)

The periodiocally posted "What is Usenet?" posting goes:
>
>Archive-name: what-is-usenet/part1
>Original-from: chip@tct.com (Chip Salzenberg)
>
>The first thing to understand about Usenet is that it is widely
>misunderstood. Every day on Usenet, the "blind men and the elephant"
>phenomenon is evident, in spades. In my opinion, more flame wars
>arise because of a lack of understanding of the nature of Usenet than

>from any other source. And consider that such flame wars arise, of
>necessity, among people who are on Usenet. Imagine, then, how poorly
>understood Usenet must be by those outside!

Imagine, indeed, how poorly understood Usenet must be by those who have the determined will to explain what it is by what it is not? "Usenet is not a bicycle. Usenet is not a fish." Any posting like this that doesn't get revised every few months quickly becomes a quaint historical document, which at best yields a prescriptivist grammar for how the net "should be" and at worst tries to shape how the Usenet "really is". The first thing to understand about Usenet is that it is big. Really big. Netnews (and netnews-like things) have percolated into many more places than are even known about by people who track such things. There is no grand unified list of everything that's out there, no way to know beforehand who is going to read what you post, and no history books to guide you that would let you know even a small piece of any of the in jokes that pop up in most newsgroups. Distrust any grand sweeping statements about "Usenet", because you can always find a counterexample. (Distrust this message, too :-).

>Any essay on the nature of Usenet cannot ignore the erroneous
>impressions held by many Usenet users. Therefore, this article will
>treat falsehoods first. Keep reading for truth. (Beauty, alas, is
>not relevant to Usenet.)

Any essay on the nature of Usenet that doesn't change every so often to reflect its ever changing nature is erroneous. Usenet is not a matter of "truth", "beauty", "falsehood", "right", or "wrong", except insofar as it is a conduit for people to talk about these and many other things.

>WHAT USENET IS NOT
> 1. Usenet is not an organization.

Usenet is organized. There are a number of people who contribute to its continued organization -- people who post lists of things, people who collect "frequently asked questions" postings, people who give out or sell newsfeeds, people who keep archives of groups, people who put those archives into web servers, people who turn those archives into printed books, talk shows, and game shows. This organization is accompanied by a certain amount of disorganization

. . .

In the short run, the person or group who runs the system that you read news from and the sites which that system exchanges news with control who gets a feed, which articles are propogated to what places and how quickly, and who can post articles. In the long run, there are a number of alternatives for Usenet access, including companies which can sell you feeds for a fee, and user groups which provide feeds for their members; while you are on your own right now as you type this in, over the long haul there are many choices you have on how to deal with the net.

> 2. Usenet is not a democracy.

Usenet has some very "democratic" sorts of traditions. Traffic is ultimately generated by readers, and people who read news ultimately control what will and will not be discussed on the net. While the details of any individual person's news reading system may limit or constrain what is easy or convenient for them to do right now, in the long haul the decisions on what is or is not happening rests with the people.

On the other hand, there have been (and always will be) people who have been on the net longer than you or I have been, and who have a strong sense of tradition and the way things are normally done. There are certain things which are simply "not done". Any sort of decision that involves counting the number of people yes or no on a particular vote has to cope with the entrenched interests who aren't about to change their habits, their posting software, or the formatting of their headers just to satisfy a new idea.

> 3. Usenet is not fair.

Usenet is fair, cocktail party, town meeting, notes of a secret cabal, chatter in the hallway at a conference, friday night fish fry, post-coital gossip, conversations overhead on an airplane, and a bunch of other things.

> 4. Usenet is not a right.

Usenet is a right, a left, a jab, and a sharp uppercut to the jaw. The postman hits! You have new mail.

> 5. Usenet is not a public utility.

Usenet is carried in large part over circuits provided by public utilities, including the public switched phone network and lines leased from public carriers. In some countries the national networking authority has some amount of monopoly power over the provision of these services, and thus the flow of information is controlled in some manner by the whims and desires (and pricing structure) of the public utility.

Most Usenet sites are operated by organizations which are not public utilities, not in the ordinary sense. You rarely get your newsfeed from National Telecom, it's more likely to be National U. or Private Networking Inc.

> 6. Usenet is not an academic network.

Usenet is a network with many parts to it. Some parts are academic, some parts aren't. Usenet is clearly not a commercial network like Sprintnet or Tymenet, and it's not an academic network like BITNET. But parts of BITNET are parts of Usenet, though some of the traffic on usenet violates the BITNET acceptable use guidelines, even though the people who are actually on BITNET sites reading these groups don't necessarily mind that they are violating the guidelines.

Whew. Usenet is a lot of networks, and none of them. You name another network, and it's not Usenet.

> 7. Usenet is not an advertising medium.

A man walks into a crowded theater and shouts, "ANYBODY WANT TO BUY A CAR?" The crowd stands up and shouts back, "WRONG THEATER!"

Ever since the first dinette set for sale in New Jersey was advertised around the world, people have been using Usenet for personal and for corporate gain. If you're careful about it and don't make people mad, Usenet can be an effective means of letting the world know about things which you find valuable. But take care...

- Marketing hype will be flamed immediately. If you need to post a press release, edit it first.

- Speak nice of your competitors. If your product is better than theirs, don't say theirs is "brain damaged", "broken", or "worthless". After all someone else might have the same opinion of your product.

- Dance around the issue. Post relevant information (like price, availability and features) but make sure you don't send everything out. If someone wants the hard sell let them request it from you by e-mail.

- Don't be an idiot. If you sell toasters for a living, don't spout off in net.bread-crumbs about an international conspiracy to poison pigeons orchestrated by the secret Usenet Cabal; toaster-buyers will get word of your reputation for idiocy and avoid your toasters even if they are the best in the market.

- Disclaimers are worthless. If you post from foobar.com, and put a note on the bottom "not the opinions of foobar inc.,", you may satisfy the lawyers but your corporate reputation still will be affected. To maintain a separate net.identity, post from a different site.

> 8. Usenet is not the Internet.

It would be very difficult to sustain the level of traffic that's flowing on Usenet today if it weren't for people sending news feeds over dedicated circuits with TCP/IP on the Internet. That's not to say that if a sudden disease wiped out all RS/6000s and Cisco routers that form the NSFnet backbone, CIX hub, and MAE East interconnect, that some people wouldn't be inconvenienced or cut off from the net entirely. (Based on the reliability of the MAE East, perhaps the "sudden disease" has already hit?) There's a certain symbiosis between netnews and Internet connections; the cost of maintaining a full newsfeed with NNTP is so much less than doing the same thing with dialup UUCP that sites which depend enough on the information flowing through news are some of the most eager to get on the Internet. The Usenet is not the Internet. Certain governments have laws which prevent other countries from getting onto the Internet, but that doesn't stop netnews from flowing in and out. Chances are pretty good that a site which has a usenet feed you can send mail to from the Internet, but even that's not guaranteed in some odd cases (news feeds sent on CD-ROM, for instance).

> 9. Usenet is not a UUCP network.

UUCP carried the first netnews traffic, and a considerable number of sites get their newsfeed using UUCP. But it's also fed using NNTP, mag tapes, CD-ROMs, and printed out on paper to be tacked up on bulletin boards and pasted on refrigerators.

>10. Usenet is not a United States network.

A 1991 analysis of the top 1000 Usenet sites showed about 58% US sites, 15% unknown, 8% Germany, 6% Canada, 2-3% each the UK, Japan, and Australia, and the rest mostly scattered around Europe. Things have not doubt changed since then, but I don't have that data close at hand. The state of California is the center of the net, with about 14% of the mapped top sites there. The Washington, DC area is also the center of the net, with several large providers headquartered there. You can read netnews on all seven continents, including Antarctica.

If you're looking for a somewhat less US-centered view of the world, try reading regional newsgroups from various different states or groups from various far-away places (which depending on where you are at could be Japanese, German, Canadian, or Australian). There are a lot of people out there who are different from you.

>11. Usenet is not a UNIX network.

Well...ok, if you don't have a UNIX machine, you can read news. In fact, there are substantial sets of newsgroups (bit.*) which are transported and gatewayed primarily through IBM VM systems, and a set of newsgroups (vmsnet.*) which has major traffic through DEC VMS systems. Reasonable news relay software runs on Macs (uAccess), Amiga (a C news port), MS-DOS (Waffle), and no doubt quite a few more. I'm was typing on a DOS machine when I first wrote this sentence, and it's been edited on Macs and X terminals since then. There is a certain culture about the net that has grown up on Unix machines, which occasioly runs into fierce clashes with the culture that has grown up on IBM machines (LIST-SERV), Commodore 64's (B1FF 1S A K00L D00D), MS-DOS Fidonet systems, commercial chat systems (America Online), and "family oriented" systems (Prodigy).

If you are not running on a Unix machine or if you don't have one handy there are things about the net which are going to be puzzling or maddening, much as if you are reading a BITNET list and you don't have a CMS system handy.

>12. Usenet is not an ASCII network.

There are reasonably standard ways to type Japanese, Russian, Swedish, Finnish, Icelandic, and Vietnamese that use the ASCII character set to encode your national character set. The fundamental assumption of most netnews software is that you're dealing with something that looks a lot like US ASCII, but if you're willing to work within those bounds and be clever it's quite possible to use ASCII to discuss things in any language.

>13. Usenet is not software.

Usenet software has gotten much better over time to cope with the ever increasing aggregate flow of netnews and (in some cases) the extreme volume that newsgroups generate. If you were reading news now with the same news software that was running 10 years ago, you'd never be able to keep up. Your system would choke and die and spend all of its time either processing incoming news or expiring old news. Without software and constant improvements to same, Usenet would not be here. There is no "standard" Usenet software, but there are standards for what Usenet articles look like, and what sites are expected to do with them. It's possible to write a fairly simple minded news system directly from the standards documents and be reasonably sure that it will work with other systems, though thorough testing is necessary if it's going to be used in the real world. You should not assume that all systems have been tested before they have been deployed.

>WHAT USENET IS

Usenet is in part about people. There are people who are "on the net", who read rec.humor.funny every so often, who know the same jokes you do, who tell you stories about funny or stupid things they've seen. Usenet is the set of people who know what Usenet is. Usenet is a bunch of bits, lots of bits, millions of bits each day full of nonsense, argument, reasonable technical discussion, scholarly analysis, and naughty pictures.

Usenet (or netnews) is about newsgroups (or groups). Not bboards, not LIST-SERV, not areas, not conferences, not mailing lists, they're groups. If someone calls them something else they're not looking at things from a Usenet perspective. That's not to say that they're "incorrect" -- who is to say what is the right way of viewing the world? -- just that it's not the Net Way. In particular, if they read Usenet news all mixed in with their important every day mail (like reminders of who to go to lunch with Thursday) they're not seeing netnews the way most people see netnews. Some newsgroups are also (or "really") Fidonet echoes (alt.bbs.allsysop), BITNET LISTSERV groups (bit.listserv.pacs-l), or even both at once! (misc.handicap). So be prepared for some violent culture clashes if someone refers to you favorite net.hangout as a "board".

Newsgroups have names. These names are both very arbitrary and very meaningful. People will fight for months or years about what to name a newsgroup. If a newsgroup doesn't have a name (even a dumb one like misc.misc) it's not a newsgroup. In particular newsgroup names have dots in them, and people abbreviate them by taking the first letters of the names (so alt.folklore.urban is afu, and soc.culture.china is scc).

>DIVERSITY

There is nothing vague about Usenet. (Vague, vague, it's filling up millions of dollars worth of disk drives and you want to call it vague? Sheesh!) It may be hard to pin down what is and isn't part of usenet at the fringes, but netnews has tended to grow amoeba-like to encompass more or less anything in its path, so you can be pretty sure that if it isn't Usenet now it will be once it's been in contact with Usenet for long enough. There are a lot of systems that are part of Usenet. Chances are that you don't have any clue where all your articles will end up going or what news reading software will be used to look at them. Any message of any appreciable size or with any substantial personal opinion in it is probably in violation of some network use policy or local ordinance in some state or municipality.

>CONTROL

Some people are control freaks. They want to present their opinion of how things are, who runs what, what is OK and not OK to do, which things are "good" and which are "bad". You will run across them every so often. They serve a useful purpose; there's a lot of chaos inherent in a largely self-governing system, and people with a strong sense of purpose and order can make things a lot easier. Just don't believe everything they say. In particular, don't believe them when they say "don't believe everything they say", because if they post the same answers month after month some other people are bound to believe them.

If you run a news system you can be a petty tyrant. You can decide what groups to carry, who to kick off your system, how to expire old news so that you keep 60 days worth of misc.petunias but expire rec.pets.fish almost immediately. In the long run you will probably be happiest if you make these decisions relatively even-handedly since that's the posture least likely to get people to notice that you actually do have control.

Your right to exercise control over netnews usually ends at your neighbor's spool directory. Pleading, cajoling, appealing to good nature, or paying your news feed will generally yield a better response than flames on the net.

>PERIODIC POSTINGS

One of the ways to exert control over the workings of the net is to take the time to put together a relatively accurate set of answers to some frequently asked questions and post it every month. If you do this right, the article will be stored for months on sites around the world, and you'll be able to tell people "idiot, don't ask this question until you've read the FAQ, especially answer #42". The periodic postings include several lists of newsgroups, along with comments as to what the contents of the groups are supposed to be. Anyone who has the time and energy can put together a list like this, and if they post it for several months running they will get some measure of net.recognition for themselves as being the "official" keeper of the "official" list. But don't delude yourself into thinking that anything on the net is official in any real way; the lists serve to perpetuate common myths about who's talking about what where, but that's no guarantee that things will actually work out that way.

>PROPAGATION

In the old days, when it cost real money to make long distance phone calls to send netnews around the world, some people were able to get their management to look the other way when they racked up multi-thousand dollar phone bills. These people were called the "backbone cabal", and they had a disproportionate influence on news traffic because, after all, they were managing to get someone else to pay for it.

Nowadays, communications costs are (for many sites) buried in with a general "internet service". If you want to have a disproportionate influence on news traffic, you need to be able to beg, borrow, buy or steal access to great big disk drives (so that you can keep a full feed) and lots of memory (so that you can feed a lot of sites at once).

There is a vigorous, competetive cash market for news feeds; you can get a news-feed from a local provider via modem or via Internet in all 50 states of the USA, more than 50 countries, and via satellite in most of North America. The notion that any one system is a "pre-eminent site" is outdated; communications costs have gotten low enough, and traffic high enough, that if any one node were to get wiped out completely it would still be possible for everyone to be back on the net within weeks.

>NEWSGROUP CREATION

You're better off starting up a mailing list.

If you *must* start a newsgroup, you're best off starting a mailing list anyway - even an informal one - to plan the newsgroup. Get a half dozen people to all agree on the basic goals, topics of conversation, etc. Figure that you have about two months to agree that there's something worth talking about, get a hundred other people to see your way, and run the vote. There are time-honored rituals for newsgroup creation, designed mostly to minimize the amount of work that news administrators (the people who have managed to corral a bunch of disk space to store news) have to do; in particular, this involves minimizing the number of mail messages they have to read every day. The process involves handing off responsibility to a group of people well-steeped in ritual (the Usenet Volunteer Votetakers) who can run through the process for you.

>THE CAMEL'S NOSE?

I'm not sure what camels have to do with anything. The only real camel that has anything to do with Usenet is Larry Wall and Randall Schwartz's "Programming perl", aka the "Camel Book", published by O'Reilley. Larry wrote "rn", one of the second generation of news readers that let you ignore some news that you didn't want to read. The process of getting rid of unread news got to be a complex enough decision process that he wrote a programming language (perl) to help him write a newsreader to replace "rn".

He never finished the new newsreader, though that's not at all surprising. "perl" is a pretty useful language, though. If you can understand "perl" you'll have a much greater appreciation for the ability of news admins to get rid of things they don't want to see.

There are easily $12M worth of computers that I can point to that are responsible for the transportation of netnews around the world, plus another $12M per year in communications bills spent to keep news flowing. Much has been made of the risk that miscreants will do something horrendous that will mean The Death Of The Net As We Know It. It seems unlikely, however, that this collective enterprise will be endangered by any one user's actions, no matter how bold they might be about trying to propogate their message against the collective will of the rest of the net trying to keep them in check.

>IF YOU ARE UNHAPPY...

If you are unhappy, what are you doing reading netnews? Take a break. Stretch. Walk outside in the sunshine or the snow. Relax your brain, watch some TV for a while, listen to the radio. If you need to communicate with someone else, give them a phone call, or see them in person. It's good to not spend too much time all in the same place with a fixed focus - rest your eyes everyone once in a while by looking around at something else. Don't worry about missing anything, it'll all get re-posted if it's any good.

>WORDS TO LIVE BY #1:

Hours can slip by, people can come and go, and you'll be locked in Cyberspace. Remember to do your work!

-- Brendan Kehoe

>WORDS TO LIVE BY #2:

Part of the apprenticeship for a network guru was knowing enough other poeple and attending enough conferences to find out where things were hidden. This worked just fine when the Internet was a small network. -- Ed Krol

>WORDS TO LIVE BY #3:

The second newsreader philosophy believes that you want to read only 10 percent of the articles in any given group.... This philosophy is far more realistic. -- Adam Engst

Answers to Frequently Asked Questions About USENET

This is a FAQ posting that every newcomer should read. We have deleted a few of the questions that are exclusively related to UNIX, obsolete, or just repeat things that have been said elsewhere in this book.* To see the full version, read *news.answers.questions.*

From: netannounce@deshaw.com (Mark Moraes)
Original-author: jerry@eagle.UUCP (Jerry Schwarz)
Comment: enhanced & edited until 5/93 by spaf@cs.purdue.edu (Gene Spafford)
Last-change: 15 July 1994 by netannounce@deshaw.com (Mark Moraes)

This document discusses some questions and topics that occur repeatedly on USENET. They frequently are submitted by new users, and result in many followups, sometimes swamping groups for weeks. The purpose of this note is to head off these annoying events by answering some questions and warning about the inevitable consequence of asking others. If you don't like these answers, let the poster of thie article know.

Note that some newsgroups have their own special "Frequent Questions & Answers" posting. You should read a group for a while before posting any questions, because the answers may already be present. Comp.unix.questions and comp.unix.internals are examples -- Steve Hayman regularly posts an article that answers common questions, including some of the ones asked here.

This list is often referred to as FAQ -- the Frequently Asked Questions. If you are a new user of the Usenet and don't find an answer to your questions here, you can try asking in the news.newusers.questions group. You might also read through other FAQ lists, cross-posted to the news.answers group.

. . .

---

* Though we have retained some items that make an important general point—like question 11.

Questions and Answers

1. What does UNIX stand for?[*]

It is not an acronym, but is a pun on "Multics". Multics is a large operating system that was being developed shortly before UNIX was created. Brian Kernighan is credited with the name.

. . .

3. Is a machine at "foo" on the net?

These questions belong in news.config (if anywhere), but in fact your best bet is usually to phone somebody at "foo" to find out. If you don't know anybody at "foo" you can always try calling and asking for the "comp center." Also, see the newsgroup comp.mail.maps where maps of USENET and the uucp network are posted regularly. If you have access to telnet, connect to ds.internic.net and try the "whois" command. (See also the answer to question #7, below.)

. . .

7. misc.misc or misc.wanted: Is John Doe out there anywhere?

I suspect that these items are people looking for Freshman room- mates that they haven't seen in ten years. If you have some idea where the person is, you are usually better off calling the organization. For example, if you call any Bell Labs location and request John Doe's number they can give it to you even if he works at a different location. If you must try the net, use newsgroup soc.net-people *NOT* misc.misc or misc.wanted. Also, you can try the "whois" command (see item #3). There is a periodic posting in the news.newusers.questions and news.answers newsgroups that gives information on other ways to locate people.

8. sci.math: Proofs that 1=0.

Almost everyone has seen one or more of these in high school. They are almost always based on either division by 0, confusing the positive and negative square roots of a number, or performing some ill-defined operation.

9. rec.games.*: Where can I get the source for empire or rogue?

You can't get the source of rogue. The authors of the game, as is their right, have chosen not to make the sources available. However, several rogue-like games have been posted to the comp.sources.games group and they are available in the

---

[*] Well, we can't really delete Question 1, can we?

archives. You can obtain the source to a version of empire if you provide a tape and SASE *plus* a photocopy of your UNIX source license. To obtain further info, contact mcnc!rti-sel!polyof!john. You can also call John at +1 516 454-5191 (9am-9pm EST only).

Sites with Internet access can ftp several versions of empire from site ftp.ms.uky.edu in the directory pub/games/empire. Also, please note that the wizards' passwords in games like these are usually system-dependent and it does no good to ask the net-at-large what they are.[*]

. . .

11. comp.unix.internals: There is a bug in the way UNIX handles protection for programs that run suid, or any other report of bugs with standard software.

There are indeed problems with the treatment of protection in setuid programs. When this is brought up, suggestions for changes range from implementing a full capability list arrangement to new kernel calls for allowing more control over when the effective id is used and when the real id is used to control accesses. Sooner or later you can expect this to be improved. For now you just have to live with it.

Always discuss suspected bugs or problems with your site software experts before you post to the net. It is likely that the bugs have already been reported. They might also be local changes and not something you need to describe to the whole Usenet.

12. Volatile topics, e.g., soc.women: What do you think about abortion?

Although abortion might appear to be an appropriate topic for soc.women, more heat than light is generated when it is brought up. All abortion-related discussion should take place in the newsgroup talk.abortion. If your site administrators have chosen not to receive this group, you should respect this and not post articles about abortion at all.

This principle applies to other topics: religious upbringing of children should be restricted to talk.religion.misc and kept out of misc.kids. Similarly, rape discussions should be kept to talk.rape and not in soc.singles, alt.sex and/or soc.women, Zionism discussions should be kept to talk.politics.mideast and not in soc.culture.jewish; likewise, evangelical and proseletyzing discussions of Jesus or of religions other than Judaism should go to newsgroups for the appropriate religion or to talk.religion.misc or alt.messianic. Any attempts to proselytize any

---

[*] Check the current version of the FAQ before calling or emailing the people here. This set of information can change very quickly.

religious view belongs in talk.religion.misc, if they belong on the net at all. Discussions on the merits of Affirmative Action and racial quotas belong in a talk.politics subgroup or alt.discrimination, not in soc.culture.african.american. Discussions about evolution vs. creationism should be confined to the talk.origins group. USENET newsgroups are named for mostly historical reasons, and are not intended to be fully general discussion groups for everything about the named topic. Please accept this and post articles in their appropriate forums.

. . .

14. soc.singles and elsewhere: What does HASA stand for?

The acronym HASA originated with the Heathen and Atheistic SCUM Alliance; the Hedonistic Asti-Spumante Alliance, Heroes Against Spaghetti Altering, the Society for Creative Atheism (SCATHE), SASA, SALSA, PASTA, and many others too numerous to mention all followed. HASA started in (what is now) talk.religion.misc and also turns up in soc.singles, talk.bizarre, et al. because members post there too.

15. sci.space.shuttle: Shouldn't this group be merged with sci.space?

No. sci.space.shuttle is for timely news bulletins. sci.space is for discussions.

16. How do I use the "Distribution" feature?

When your posting software (e.g., Pnews or postnews) prompts you for a distribution, it's asking how widely distributed you want your article. The set of possible replies is different, depending on where you are, but at Bell Labs in Murray Hill, New Jersey, possibilities include (for example):

local	local to this machine
mh	Bell Labs, Murray Hill Branch
nj	all sites in New Jersey
btl	All Bell Labs machines
att	All AT&T machines
usa	Everywhere in the USA
na	Everywhere in North America
world	Everywhere on USENET in the world

Many of the posting programs will provide a list of distributions, if your site admin has kept the files up-to-date.

If you hit return, you'll get the default, which is usually "world.". This default is often not appropriate -- PLEASE take a moment to think about how far away people are likely to be interested in what you have to say. Used car ads, housing wanted ads, and things for sale other than specialized equipment like computers certainly shouldn't be distributed to Europe and Korea, or even to the next state.

It is generally not possible to post an article to a distribution that your own machine does not receive. For instance, if you live in Indiana, you can't post an article for distribution only in New Jersey or Germany unless your site happens to exchange those particular distributions with another site. Try mailing the article to someone in the appropriate area and asking them to post it for you.

If you cannot determine what distributions are valid for your site, ask someone locally rather than posting a query to the whole network!*

17. Why do some people put funny lines ("bug killers") at the beginning of their articles?

Some earlier versions (mid-80s) of news had a bug which would drop the first 512 or 1024 bytes of text of certain articles. The bug was triggered whenever the article started with whitespace (a blank or a tab). A fix many people adopted was to begin their articles with a line containing a character other than white space. This gradually evolved into the habit of including amusing first lines.

The original bug has since been fixed in newer version of news, and sites running older versions of news have applied a patch to prevent articles from losing text. The "bug-killer" lines are therefore probably no longer needed, but they linger on.

18. What is the address or phone number of the "foo" company?

Try the white and yellow pages of your phone directory, first; a sales representative will surely know, and if you're a potential customer they will be who you're looking for. Phone books for other cities are usually available in libraries of any size. Whoever buys or recommends things for your company will probably have some buyer's guides or national company directories. Call or visit the reference desk of your library; they have several company and organization directories and many will answer questions like this over the phone. Remember if you only know the city where the company is, you can telephone to find out their full address or a dealer. Calls to 1-800-555-1212 will reveal if the company has an "800" number you can call for information. The network is NOT a free resource, although it may look like that to some people. It is far better to spend a few minutes of your own time researching an answer rather than broadcast your laziness and/or ineptitude to the net.

. . .

---

* Don't count on distributions to be effective. Most areas have some regional newsgroups; that's a better way to handle the problem.

20. How do I get from BITNET to UUCP, Internet to BITNET, JANET etc.?

There are so many networks and mail systems in use now, it would take a book to describe all of them and how to send mail between them. Luckily, there are a couple of excellent books that do exactly that, and in a helpful, easy-to-use manner:

"!%@:: A Directory of Electronic Mail Addressing & Networks" by Donnalyn Frey and Rick Adams, O'Reilly & Associates, Inc, 2nd edition 1990.

"The Matrix: Computer Networks and Conferencing Systems Worldwide" by John Quarterman, Digital Press, 1990.

Another excellent book to have on your bookshelf (to keep those two company) is "The User's Directory of Computer Networks" edited by Tracy LaQuey, Digital Press, 1990.

. . .

23. What is "food for the NSA line-eater"?

This refers to the alleged scanning of all USENET traffic by the National Security Agency (and possibly other intelligence organizations) for interesting keywords. The "food" is believed to contain some of those keywords in the fond hope of overloading NSA's poor computers. Other posters have taken up this practice, either as an ambiguous form of political statement, or as an attempt at humor. The bottom line is that excessive signatures in any form are discouraged, the joke has worn stale amongst long-time net readers, and there are specific newsgroups for the discussion of politics.

24. Does anyone know the {pinouts, schematics, switch settings, what does jumper J3 do} for widget X?

These postings are almost always inappropriate unless the manufacturer has gone out of business or no longer supports the device. If neither of these is the case, you're likely to get a better and faster response by simply telephoning the manufacturer.

. . .

26. What is UUNET?

UUNET is a for-profit communications service designed to provide access to USENET news, mail, and various source archives at low cost by obtaining volume discounts. Charges are calculated to recover costs.

For more information send your US mail address to info@uunet.uu.net (uunet!info).

27. Isn't the posting mechanism broken? When I post an article to both a moderated group and unmoderated groups, it gets mailed to the moderator and not posted to the unmoderated groups.

This is a question that is debated every few months. The answer is "No, it was designed to work that way." The software is designed so that the moderator can crosspost the article so it appears in the regular groups as well as the moderated group, if appropriate. If the article were to be posted immediately to the unmoderated groups, the moderated group name would have to be deleted from the header and you would lose the crossposting.

Whether or not this is correct behavior is a matter of opinion. If you want your article to go out immediately to the unmoderated groups, post it twice -- once to the unmoderated groups and once to the moderated groups.

. . .

29. Would someone repost {large software distribution}?

This question should never be posted unless you are reporting a widespread problem in article propagation. Lamentably, there ARE occasional glitches in article transport. Large source or binary postings, by their sheer size, are an inviting target.

If the problem is isolated, it is much better to take it upon yourself to obtain the bad portions of the program than to ask thousands of sites to spend thousands of dollars to needlessly move several hundred kilobytes of code. There are archive sites around the net that make most source/binary newsgroups available via anonymous FTP and UUCP. If you get desperate, you can always mail the author a blank disk or magnetic tape with provisions for return postage.

30. How do I contact the moderator of an Internet mailing list rather than post to the entire list?

To do this you should know that there are, by convention, two mailing addresses for every mailing list (except where noted by the List of Lists):

list-request@host   (e.g. xpert-request@x.org)

list@host   (e.g. xpert@x.org)

When you have something for everyone on the mailing list to read, mail to the list@host address. HOWEVER, if you have an administrative request to make (e.g. "please add me to this list", "please remove me from this list", "where are the archives?", "what is this mailer error I got from sending to this list?"), it should be directed to the list-request@host address, which goes only to the mailing list administrator. It is considered to be in bad taste to send administrative requests to the entire mailing list in question, and if (as is often the case) the administrator does not read the mailing list (i.e. he just takes care of the admin tasks for the list), he will not see your request if you don't send it to the right address.

. . .

32. Are there any restrictions on posting e-mail someone sends to me?

At a minimum, it is only polite for you to contact the author of the letter and secure her or his permission to post it to the net.

On a more serious note, it can be argued that posting someone's e-mail to the net without their permission is a violation of copyright law. Under that law, even though a letter was addressed to you, it does not grant you the right to publish the contents, as that is the work of the author and the author retains copyright (even if no explicit copyright mark appears). Basically, your letters are your intellectual property. If someone publishes your letters they are violating your copyright. This principle is well-founded in "paper media," and while untested in electronic forums such as Usenet, the same would probably apply if tested in court.

33. What's an FQDN?

A fully-qualified domain name. That is, a hostname containing full, dotted qualification of its name up to the root of the Internet domain naming system tree. Example: uiucuxc is the single-word hostname (suitable for, e.g., UUCP transport purposes) of the machine whose FQDN is uxc.cso.uiuc.edu.

. . .

36. What is the last year of the 20th century A.D.?

The A.D. (Latin, Anno Domini, In the Year of Our Lord) system was devised before "origin 0 counting" was invented. The year during which Jesus was (incorrectly) assumed to have been born was numbered 1. (The preceding year was 1 B.C.) So the 1st century was 1 to 100, the 2nd was 101 to 200, the 20th is 1901 to 2000. This is standard terminology no matter how much some of you may dislike it. However, "a" century is any span of 100 years; so if you want to celebrate the end of "the century", meaning the 1900's, on December 31, 1999, nobody will stop you. It just isn't the end of the "20th century A.D.".

. . .

39. Is there a public access Unix system near me? How can I get access to system for news and mail?

Phil Eschallier posts a list of open access Unix sites (he calls them "Nixpub" sites) on a regular basis to the following newsgroups: comp.misc and alt.bbs. Check his posting for information on sites you can contact.

Furthermore, a list of open access sites that are not necessarily Unix sites is posted regularly in alt.bbs.lists; see the postings entitled "NetPub listing" for more information.

40. In rec.pets: My pet has suddenly developed the following symptoms .... Is it serious? In sci.med: I have these symptoms .... Is it serious?

Could be. The only way to tell for sure is to see an expert. The network reaches a vast audience with considerable talent, but that can never replace the expert observation and diagnosis of a trained professional. Do yourself or your pet a big favor -- if there is a problem, go see an appropriate practitioner. If there is a serious problem, it is important that it is dealt with promptly.

41. I have this great idea to make money. Alternatively, wouldn't an electronic chain letter be a nifty idea?

In a few words: don't even think about it. Trying to use the net to make vast sums of money or send chain letters is a very bad idea. First of all, it is an inappropriate use of resources, and tends to use up vast amounts of net bandwidth. Second, such usage of the net tends to produce extremely negative reactions by people on the net, adding even more to the volume -- most of it directed to you. Users, particularly system admins, do not like that kind of activity, and they will flood your mailbox with notices to that effect.

And last, and perhaps most important, some of this activity is against the law in many places. In the US, you can (and will) be reported by hacked-off system administrators for suspicion of wire fraud or mail fraud. In one incident, at *least* a half dozen people reported the poster to Postal Service inspectors; I'm not sure what the outcome was, but it probably was not a nice experience.

Bottom line: don't try clever schemes to sell things, solicit donations, or run any kind of pyramid or Ponzi scheme. Also, don't start or support electronic chain letters.

42. Where can I get archives of Usenet postings?

Most Usenet newsgroups are not archived in any organized fashion, though it's likely that if you look hard enough someone will have kept much or most of the traffic (either on disk or on some tape gathering dust somewhere). The volume on Usenet is simply too high to keep everything on rotating magnetic media forever, however. The signal-to-noise ratio is too low in many groups to make them good candidates for archiving.

One person's signal is another person's noise; if you're lucky, you'll find someone who has been keeping the good parts of a particular newsgroup in their own personal stash to save up for later. How to get access to a group that *is* archived depends on what kind of group it is:

- The "sources" and "binaries" groups are generally archived at multiple sites; for more information about getting access to them, see the posting entitled "How to find sources" in comp.sources.wanted.

- Some non-source newsgroups can be found by asking "archie" about the group name. See the comp.sources.wanted posting mentioned above for information about how to use "archie."

- In other groups, if the group has a Frequently Asked Questions posting or another periodic posting about the group, check that posting to see if it mentions where the group is archived. If not, then you'll have to post a message in the newsgroup and ask if it is archived anywhere.

43. Is it possible to post messages to the Usenet via electronic mail?

There are a few sites on the Usenet that offer a full-scale mail to news gateway, so that you can post via E-mail to any newsgroup available on that site. One of them is decwrl.dec.com. To use its gateway, you mail the message you wish to post to newsgroup.name.usenet@decwrl.dec.com. For example, to post to news.newusers.questions, you would send your message to news.newusers.questions.usenet@decwrl.dec.com. This gateway is an unsupported service, as are most other such gateways.

Mail-to-news gateways of this sort tend to be overloaded. Therefore, please do not use this gateway or any other similar gateway if you have other posting access to the Usenet.

44. Is it possible to read Usenet newsgroups via electronic mail?

Most Usenet newsgroups do not correspond to any mailing list, so the conventional answer to this question is "no" for most groups. However, there are some newsgroups that are gatewayed to mailing lists. For a list of them, see the "List of Active Newsgroups" or the "Mailing Lists Available in Usenet" postings in news.lists. If you know a Usenet site admin who is willing to act as a personal gateway for you, you might be able to get him/her to set up his/her system to forward messages from individual newsgroups to you via E-mail. However, most admins don't like to do this because it adds to the outgoing traffic from their site, so don't post messages to the net saying, "Hey, is there someone willing to gateway newsgroups to me?"

45. How do I get the news software to include a signature with my postings?

This is a question that is best answered by examining the documentation for the software you're using, as the answer varies depending on the software.

However, if you're reading news on a Unix machine, then you can probably get a signature to appear on your outgoing messages by creating a file called ".signature" in your home directory. Two important things to remember are:

1. Many article-posting programs will restrict the length of the signature. For example, the "inews" program will often only include the first four lines. This is not something you should be trying to find a way to defeat; it is there for a reason. If your signature is too long, according to the software, then shorten it. Even if the software does not complain, keep your .signature under four lines as a courtesy to others.

2. Under some news configurations, your .signature file must be world-readable, and your home directory world-executable, for your signature to be included correctly in your articles. If your .signature does not get included, try running these commands:

```
% chmod a+x $HOME
% chmod a+r ~/.signature
```

. . .

47. What is a "flame"?

A "flame" usually refers to any message or article that contains strong criticism, usually irrational or highly emotional. Avoid "flames", and if you do get "flamed", relax, calm down and decide if it's really worth "counter-flaming". Usually, it isn't worth it -- a complete waste of bandwidth and time; it also gets you perceived as a "flamer" by the large silent majority of Usenet readers, who will probably start ignoring your articles.

48. What is a mail-server/list-server?

Mail servers are a family of programs that answer email automatically. These programs are also called list servers (or listserv, from the original BITNET LISTSERV list management program) when the automatically maintain mailing lists, or info-servers or netlibs if they permit automatic software retrieval). Most mail servers will tell you all about themselves if you send them a message with no Subject: and the one-line body help (without the indentation, of course!)

How to Create a New USENET Newsgroup

Original-author: woods@ncar.ucar.edu (Greg Woods)
Comment: enhanced & edited until 5/93 by spaf@cs.purdue.edu (Gene Spafford)
From: tale@uunet.uu.net (David C Lawrence)

GUIDELINES FOR USENET GROUP CREATION

REQUIREMENTS FOR GROUP CREATION:

These are guidelines that have been generally agreed upon across USENET as appropriate for following in the creating of new newsgroups in the "standard" USENET newsgroup hierarchy. They are NOT intended as guidelines for setting USENET policy other than group creations, and they are not intended to apply to "alternative" or local news hierarchies. The part of the namespace affected is comp, news, sci, misc, soc, talk, rec, which are the most widely-distributed areas of the USENET hierarchy.

Any group creation request which follows these guidelines to a successful result should be honored, and any request which fails to follow these procedures or to obtain a successful result from doing so should be dropped, except under extraordinary circumstances. The reason these are called guidelines and not absolute rules is that it is not possible to predict in advance what "extraordinary circumstances" are or how they might arise.

It should be pointed out here that, as always, the decision whether or not to create a newsgroup on a given machine rests with the administrator of that machine. These guidelines are intended merely as an aid in making those decisions.

The Discussion

1) A request for discussion on creation of a new newsgroup should be posted to news.announce.newgroups, and also to any other groups or mailing lists at all related to the proposed topic if desired. The group is moderated, and the Followup-to: header will be set so that the actual discussion takes place only in news.groups. Users on sites which have difficulty posting to moderated groups may mail submissions intended for news.announce.newgroups to newgroups-@uunet.uu.net.

The article should be cross-posted among the newsgroups, including news.announce.newgroups, rather than posted as separate articles. Note that standard behaviour for posting software is to not present the articles in any groups when cross-posted to a moderated group; the moderator will handle that for you.

2) The name and charter of the proposed group and whether it will be moderated or unmoderated (and if the former, who the moderator(s) will be) should be determined during the discussion period. If there is no general agreement on these

points among the proponents of a new group at the end of 30 days of discussion, the discussion should be taken offline (into mail instead of news.groups) and the proponents should iron out the details among themselves. Once that is done, a new, more specific proposal may be made, going back to step 1) above.

3) Group advocates seeking help in choosing a name to suit the proposed charter, or looking for any other guidance in the creation procedure, can send a message to group-advice@uunet.uu.net; a few seasoned news administrators are available through this address. The Vote The Usenet Volunteer Votetakers (UVV) are a group of neutral third-party vote-takers who currently handle vote gathering and counting for all newsgroup proposals. Ron Dippold <rdippold@qual-comm.com> co-ordinates this group. Contact him to arrange the handling of the vote. The mechanics of vote will be handled in accord with the paragraphs below.

1) AFTER the discussion period, if it has been determined that a new group is really desired, a name and charter are agreed upon, and it has been determined whether the group will be moderated and if so who will moderate it, a call for votes may be posted to news.announce.newgroups and any other groups or mailing lists that the original request for discussion might have been posted to. There should be minimal delay between the end of the discussion period and the issuing of a call for votes.

The call for votes should include clear instructions for how to cast a vote. It must be as clearly explained and as easy to do to cast a vote for creation as against it, and vice versa. It is explicitly permitted to set up two separate addresses to mail yes and no votes to provided that they are on the same machine, to set up an address different than that the article was posted from to mail votes to, or to just accept replies to the call for votes article, as long as it is clearly and explicitly stated in the call for votes article how to cast a vote. If two addresses are used for a vote, the reply address must process and accept both yes and no votes OR reject them both.

2) The voting period should last for at least 21 days and no more than 31 days, no matter what the preliminary results of the vote are. The exact date that the voting period will end should be stated in the call for votes. Only votes that arrive on the vote-taker's machine prior to this date will be counted.

3) A couple of repeats of the call for votes may be posted during the vote, provided that they contain similar clear, unbiased instructions for casting a vote as the original, and provided that it is really a repeat of the call for votes on the SAME proposal (see #5 below). Partial vote results should NOT be included; only a statement of the specific new group proposal, that a vote is in progress on it, and how to cast a vote. It is permitted to post a "mass acknowledgement" in which all the names of those from whom votes have been received are posted, as long

as no indication is made of which way anybody voted until the voting period is officially over.

4) ONLY votes MAILED to the vote-taker will count. Votes posted to the net for any reason (including inability to get mail to the vote-taker) and proxy votes (such as having a mailing list maintainer claim a vote for each member of the list) will not be counted.

5) Votes may not be transferred to other, similar proposals. A vote shall count only for the EXACT proposal that it is a response to. In particular, a vote for or against a newsgroup under one name shall NOT be counted as a vote for or against a newsgroup with a different name or charter, a different moderated/ unmoderated status or (if moderated) a different moderator or set of moderators.

6) Votes MUST be explicit; they should be of the form "I vote for the group foo.bar as proposed" or "I vote against the group foo.bar as proposed". The wording doesn't have to be exact, it just needs to be unambiguous. In particular, statements of the form "I would vote for this group if..." should be considered comments only and not counted as votes.

7) A vote should be run only for a single group proposal. Attempts to create multiple groups should be handled by running multiple parallel votes rather than one vote to create all of the groups.

The Result

1) At the completion of the voting period, the vote taker must post the vote tally and the E-mail addresses and (if available) names of the voters received to news.announce.newgroups and any other groups or mailing lists to which the original call for votes was posted. The tally should include a statement of which way each voter voted so that the results can be verified.

2) AFTER the vote result is posted, there will be a 5 day waiting period, beginning when the voting results actually appear in news.announce.newgroups, during which the net will have a chance to correct any errors in the voter list or the voting procedure.

3) AFTER the waiting period, and if there were no serious objections that might invalidate the vote, and if 100 more valid YES/create votes are received than NO/ don't create AND at least 2/3 of the total number of valid votes received are in favor of creation, a newgroup control message may be sent out. If the 100 vote margin or 2/3 percentage is not met, the group should not be created.

4) The newgroup message will be sent by the news.announce.newgroups moder- ator at the end of the waiting period of a successful vote. If the new group is moderated, the vote-taker should send a message during the waiting period to

David C. Lawrence <tale@uunet.uu.net> with both the moderator's contact address and the group's submission address.

5) A proposal which has failed under point (3) above should not again be brought up for discussion until at least six months have passed from the close of the vote. This limitation does not apply to proposals which never went to vote.

WILDCARDS AND REGULAR EXPRESSIONS

Wildcards and regular expressions are used for text-pattern matching almost everywhere in news software. Exact details vary according to the program you are using, so check the documentation to see if there are any advanced features that might be helpful to you. Having said that, most packages implement a pretty common set of basic features, which we'll cover here.

Wildcards

Wildcards are simpler than regular expressions, and are most commonly used by the shell for filename expansion. There are two special constructs used in wildcards:

* An asterisk matches any number of characters.

? A question mark matches exactly one character.

This table shows some examples of how they are used.

Wildcard	Matches
news	The single word *news*
news*	Any word that begins with *news*, such as *newsgroup* or *newsreader*
news*er	Any word that begins with *news* and ends with *er*, such as *newspaper* or *newsreader*, but not *newsgroup*
new?	Any four-letter word that begins with *new*, such as *news* or *newt*.

Regular Expressions

Regular expressions have a reputation for being difficult to learn and confusing to read. This doesn't have to be so—if you break down the regular expression pattern by pattern, you will soon get used to scanning them. There are more elements to a regular expression than to wildcards. These are:

x	Any single character or string of characters matches itself.
.	A period matches any single character.
[*xyz*]	Character sets are indicated by square brackets. This construct matches one character that is in the set.
[*x-y*]	A hyphen can be used to indicate a range of characters.
[*^xyz*]	If a caret is the first character in a character set, the sense of the match is reversed. Any single character *not* in the set specified matches.
*	An asterisk matches zero or more of the previous pattern.
+	A plus sign matches one or more of the previous pattern.
|	A vertical bar indicates a multiple choice selection; i.e., *a* | *b* matches either *a* or *b*.
^	When placed at the beginning of a regular expression, a caret anchors the search to the beginning of a line.
$	When placed at the end of a regular expression, a dollar sign anchors the search to the end of a line.
( )	Items can be grouped by parentheses.

This table shows some examples:

Regular Expression	Matches
new	The single word *news*
new.	Any four letter word that begins with *new*, such as *news* or *newt*
news.*	Any word that begins with *news*
[0123456789]	Any single numeric digit
[0-9]	An easier way to specify a single digit
[0-9]+	A multidigit number. The square brackets match any single digit, and the plus sign matches one or more of the previous pattern, so the entire pattern can be read "one or more digits."

Regular Expression	Matches
[0-9]*	An optional multidigit number. The square brackets match any single digit, and the asterisk matches zero or more of the previous pattern, so the entire pattern can be read "zero or more digits."
^news	The word *news* at the beginning of a line
news$	The word *news* at the end of a line
^news$	A line consisting only of the word *news*. The *n* must be the first character of the line, and the *s* must be the last character.
news(reader|group)	The word *news* followed immediately by either reader or group. The only two words that will match this expression are, of course, *newsreader* and *newsgroup*.

WHERE TO GET NEWS SOFTWARE

Newsreaders
Email Software
Compression and Archival Software

T his appendix lists some of the places where you can obtain the various software packages mentioned in the book. For details on using FTP to get these files, see Chapter 8, *Getting the Most Out of USENET.*

Some of the items in this list are individual files, and are marked by "File:". The other items, marked "Directory:", are made up of a number of files in the directory specified. You will need to get all of the files in the directory in order to build. In many cases, there will be a *README* file that contains further directions on what to get and how to build the software.

To distribute the networking load, we've given alternative sites for each package. Please get the package from the site "nearest you."

Newsreaders

nn

Host *ftp.uu.net*
    File: *networking/news/readers/nn/nn.tar.Z*

Host *romulus.ucs.uoknor.edu*
    File: */networking/news/readers/nn/nn.tar.Z*

Host *ftp.cs.umn.edu*
    File: */.archive1/usenet/comp.sources.unix/volume19/nn/nn.tar.gz*

Host *ee.utah.edu*
    Directory: */nn/*

tin

Host *ftp.Germany.EU.net*
    Dir: */pub/news/tin*

Host *src.doc.ic.ac.uk*
    Dir: */computing/usenet/software/readers/tin*

Host *ftp.uwp.edu*
    Dir: */pub/tin*

Host *yoyo.cc.monash.edu.au*
    Dir: */pub/tin*

Emacs

Host *ftp.uu.net*
    Directory: *systems/gnu/emacs/*

Host *midway.uchicago.edu*
    Directory: */pub/gnu/emacs/*

Trumpet

Host *dorm.rutgers.edu*
    Directory: */pub/msdos/trumpet/*

Host *ftp.cs.yale.edu*
    Directory: */WWW/pub/MS-Windows/tattam/trumpet/*

Host *ftp.cyberspace.com*
    Directory: */pub/ppp/Windows/trumpet/*

Host *gumby.dsd.trw.com*
    Directory: */pub/news/newsreaders/ibm-pc/trumpet/*

Email Software

elm

Host *ftp.uu.net*
    Directory: *networking/mail/elm/*

Host *dsinc.dsi.com*
    Directory: */pub/elm/*

Host *ftp.cs.umn.edu*
    Directory: */.archive1/usenet/comp.sources.unix/volume6/elm/*

Host *slopoke.mlb.semi.harris.com*
    Directory: */pub/semi/elm/*

mh

Host *ftp.cc.utexas.edu*
    Directory: */source/mail/mh-6.8/*

Host *ftp.cc.utexas.edu*
    Directory: */source/mail/mh-6.8.3/*

Host *ftp.isi.edu*
    Directory: */pub/vmh/mh-6.8/*

mush

Host *ftp.uu.net*
    Directory: *vendor/z-code/mush/cse.ogi.edu/pub/mush/*

Host *usc.edu*
    Directory: */archive/usenet/sources/comp.sources.misc/volume32/mush/*

pine

Host *ftp.cyberspace.com*
    Directory: */pub/unix/linux/slackware/contents/pine/*

Host *osceola.cs.ucf.edu*
    Directory: */pub/gopher/Local-Software/Mail_Utilities/pine/*

rmail

Host *ftp.cc.utexas.edu*
    Directory: */source/mail/sendmail-8.6.8/rmail/*

Host *romulus.ucs.uoknor.edu*
    Directory: */src/mail/sendmail.8.6.8/rmail/*

Host *shiva.com*
    File: */src/MAIL/sendmail-5.64/rmail/rmail*

Compression and Archival Software

gzip

Host *ftp.uu.net*
    File: */gzip.tar*

Host *ftp.wang.com*
    Directory: */wjs/gnu/gzip/*

gzip (MS-DOS version)

Host: *ftp.msc.cornell.edu*
    File: */pub/dos/bin/gzip.exe*

Host *ftp.cs.yale.edu*
    File: */WWW/pub/gzip.exe*

Host *ftp.germany.eu.net*
    File: */pub/os/Linux/Local.EUnet/Packages/slackware/GZIP.EXE*

patch

Host *ftp.uu.net*
    File: *pub/archiving/patch.tar.Z*

shar

Host *ftp.uu.net*
    File: *systems/unix/bsd-sources/usr.bin/shar/shar.sh.Z*

Host *hpcsos.col.hp.com*
    Directory: */mirrors/.hpib1/NetBSD/NetBSD-current/src/shar/*

Host *ftp.iastate.edu*
    Directory: */pub/netbsd/NetBSD-current/src/src/shar/*

Host *math.sunysb.edu*
    Directory: */programs/shar/*

uuencode

Host *ftp.uu.net*
    File: *systems/unix/bsd-sources/usr.bin/uuencode/uuencode.c.Z*

Host *romulus.ucs.uoknor.edu*
    Directory: */src/freeunix/uuencode/*

Host *ftp.wang.com*
>   Directory: */pub/uuencode/*

Host *ames.arc.nasa.gov*
>   Directory: */pub/UNIX/uucp/uuencode/*

uudecode

Host *ftp.uu.net*
>   File: *systems/unix/bsd-sources/usr.bin/uudecode/uudecode.c.Z*

uuencode/uudecode (MS-DOS version)

Host: *ftp.cica.indiana.edu*
>   File: */pub/pc/win3/util/uucode20.zip*

xmitBin

Host: *ftp.sterling.com*
>   Directory: */usenet/alt.sources/volume94/Jan*
>   Files: *940130.01 940130.02 940130.03 940130.04*

MKS Toolkit

The MKS (Mortice Kern Systems) Toolkit isn't free but is a reliable source for various helpful UNIX utilities that can run under DOS. You can email them for more information.
>   Email: *sales@mks.com*
>   Compuserve: *73260,1043*

NEWSGROUPS

T his is a listing of the official *newsgroup* hierarchy at the time of printing. An up-to-date copy of this list is posted to *news.lists* on a periodic basis. The original version was written by Gene Spafford; the list is now maintained by David Lawrence. We've trimmed the list in several places; if you see something like *comp.unix.**, it's up to you to investigate what specific groups are available. The descriptions are part of the official newsgroup list.

comp

Topics of interest to both computer professionals and hobbyists, including topics in computer science, software source, and information on hardware and software systems.

comp.admin.policy
Discussions of site-administration policies

comp.ai
Artificial-intelligence discussions

comp.ai.alife
Research about artificial life

comp.ai.fuzzy
Fuzzy-set theory, aka fuzzy logic

comp.ai.genetic
Genetic algorithms in computing

comp.ai.jair.announce
Announcements and abstracts of the *Journal of AI Research*†

comp.ai.jair.papers
Papers published by the *Journal of AI Research*†

comp.ai.nat-lang
Natural-language processing by computers

comp.ai.neural-nets
All aspects of neural networks

comp.ai.nlang-know-rep
Natural Language and Knowledge Representation†

comp.ai.philosophy
Philosophical aspects of artificial intelligence

comp.ai.shells
Artificial intelligence applied to shells

comp.answers
Repository for periodic USENET articles†

comp.apps.spreadsheets
Spreadsheets on various platforms

comp.arch
Computer architecture

comp.arch.arithmetic
Implementing arithmetic on computers/digital systems

comp.arch.bus.vmebus
Hardware and software for VMEbus systems

comp.arch.fpga
Field programmable gate array-based computing systems

comp.arch.storage
Storage system issues, both hardware and software

---

† - Moderated

comp.archives
Descriptions of public-access archives†

comp.archives.admin
Issues relating to computer-archive administration

comp.archives.msdos.announce
Announcements about MS-DOS archives†

comp.archives.msdos.d
Discussion of materials available in MS-DOS archives

comp.bbs.misc
All aspects of computer bulletin-board systems

comp.bbs.tbbs
The Bread Board System bulletin-board software

comp.bbs.waffle
The Waffle BBS and USENET system on all platforms

comp.benchmarks
Discussion of benchmarking techniques and results

comp.binaries.acorn
Binary-only postings for Acorn machines†

comp.binaries.amiga
Encoded publicly available programs in binary†

comp.binaries.apple2
Binary-only postings for the Apple II computer

comp.binaries.atari.st
Binary-only postings for the Atari ST†

comp.binaries.cbm
For the transfer of 8-bit Commodore binaries†

comp.binaries.geos
Binaries for the GEOS OS†

comp.binaries.ibm.pc
Binary-only postings for IBM PC/MS-DOS†

comp.binaries.ibm.pc.d
Discussions about IBM/PC binary postings

comp.binaries.ibm.pc.wanted
Requests for IBM PC and compatible programs

comp.binaries.mac
Encoded Macintosh programs in binary†

comp.binaries.ms-windows
Binary programs for Microsoft Windows†

comp.binaries.newton
Apple Newton binaries, sources, books, etc.†

comp.binaries.os2
Binaries for use under the OS/2 ABI†

comp.bugs.2bsd
Reports of UNIX version 2BSD-related bugs

comp.bugs.4bsd
Reports of UNIX version 4BSD-related bugs

comp.bugs.4bsd.ucb-fixes
Bug reports/fixes for BSD UNIX†

comp.bugs.misc
General UNIX bug reports and fixes (including V7, UUCP)

comp.bugs.sys5
Reports of USG (System III, V, etc.) bugs

comp.cad.cadence
Users of Cadence Design Systems products

comp.cad.compass
Compass Design Automation EDA tools

comp.cad.pro-engineer
Parametric Technology's Pro/Engineer design package

comp.cad.synthesis
Research and production in the field of logic synthesis

comp.client-server
Topics relating to client/server technology

comp.cog-eng
Cognitive engineering

comp.compilers
Compiler construction, theory, etc.†

comp.compilers.tools.pccts
Construction of compilers and tools with PCCTS

comp.compression
Data-compression algorithms and theory

comp.compression.research
Discussions about data-compression research†

comp.constraints
Constraint processing and related topics

comp.databases
Database and data-management issues and theory

comp.databases.informix
Informix database-management-software discussions

comp.databases.ingres
Issues relating to INGRES products

comp.databases.ms-access
MS-Windows' relational database system, Access

comp.databases.object
Object-oriented paradigms in database systems

comp.databases.oracle
Oracle Corp.'s SQL database products

comp.databases.paradox
Borland's database for DOS and MS Windows

comp.databases.pick
Pick-like, post-relational, database systems

comp.databases.rdb
The relational database engine RDB from DEC

comp.databases.sybase
Implementations of the SQL server

comp.databases.theory
Discussing advances in database technology

comp.databases.xbase.fox
Fox Software's xBase system and compatibles

comp.databases.xbase.misc
Discussion of xBase (dBASE-like) products

comp.dcom.cabling
Cabling selection, installation, and use

comp.dcom.cell-relay
Discussion of cell relay-based products

comp.dcom.fax
FAX hardware, software, and protocols

comp.dcom.isdn
The Integrated Services Digital Network (ISDN)

comp.dcom.lans.ethernet
Discussions of the Ethernet/IEEE 8023 protocols

comp.dcom.lans.fddi
Discussions of the FDDI protocol suite

comp.dcom.lans.misc
Local area network hardware and software

comp.dcom.lans.token-ring
Installing and using token-ring networks

comp.dcom.modems
Data communications hardware and software

comp.dcom.servers
Selecting and operating data-communications servers

comp.dcom.sys.cisco
Info on Cisco routers and bridges

comp.dcom.sys.wellfleet
Wellfleet's bridge and router systems hardware and software

comp.dcom.telecom
Telecommunications digest[†]

comp.dcom.telecom.tech
Discussion of technical aspects of telephony

comp.doc
Archived publicly available documentation[†]

comp.doc.techreports
Lists of technical reports[†]

comp.dsp
Digital signal processing using computers

comp.edu
Computer science education

comp.edu.languages.natural
Computer-assisted languages instruction issues

comp.emacs
Emacs editors of different flavors

comp.emulators.announce
Emulator news, FAQs, announcements[†]

comp.emulators.apple2
Emulators of Apple II systems

comp.emulators.cbm
Emulators of C-64, C-128, PET, and VIC-20 systems

comp.emulators.misc
Emulators of miscellaneous computer systems

comp.emulators.ms-windows.wine
A free MS-Windows emulator under X

comp.fonts
Typefonts: design, conversion, use, etc.

comp.graphics
Computer graphics, art, animation, image processing

comp.graphics.algorithms
Algorithms used in producing computer graphics

comp.graphics.animation
Technical aspects of computer animation

comp.graphics.avs
The Application Visualization System

comp.graphics.data-explorer
IBM's Visualization Data Explorer, aka DX

comp.graphics.explorer
The Explorer Modular Visualisation Environment (MVE)

comp.graphics.gnuplot
The GNUPLOT interactive function plotter

comp.graphics.opengl
The OpenGL 3D application programming interface

comp.graphics.raytracing
Ray tracing software, tools and methods

comp.graphics.research
Highly technical computer graphics discussion[†]

comp.graphics.visualization
Info on scientific visualization

comp.groupware
Software and hardware for shared interactive environments

comp.groupware.lotus-notes.misc
Lotus Notes related discussions

comp.home.automation
Home automation devices, setup, sources, etc.

comp.home.misc
Media, technology and information in domestic spaces[†]

comp.human-factors
Issues related to human-computer interaction (HCI)

comp.infosystems
Discussion of information systems

comp.infosystems.announce
Announcements of Internet information services[†]

comp.infosystems.gis
All aspects of geographic information systems

comp.infosystems.gopher
Discussion of the Gopher information service

comp.infosystems.interpedia
The Internet encyclopedia

comp.infosystems.kiosks
Information kiosks[†]

comp.infosystems.wais
The Z3950-based WAIS full-text search system

comp.infosystems.www
The World Wide Web information system

comp.infosystems.www.misc
Miscellaneous WWW discussion

comp.infosystems.www.providers
WWW provider issues (info providers)

comp.infosystems.www.users
WWW user issues (Mosaic, Lynx, etc.)

comp.internet.library
Discussing electronic libraries[†]

comp.ivideodisc
Interactive videodiscs: uses, potential, etc.

comp.lang.ada
Discussion about Ada

comp.lang.apl
Discussion about APL

comp.lang.basic.misc
Other dialects and aspects of BASIC

comp.lang.basic.visual
Microsoft Visual BASIC and App BASIC; Windows and DOS

comp.lang.c
Discussion about C

comp.lang.c++
The object-oriented C++ language

comp.lang.clos
Common LISP Object System discussions

comp.lang.dylan
Discussion of the Dylan language

comp.lang.eiffel
The object-oriented Eiffel language

comp.lang.forth
Discussion about Forth

comp.lang.fortran
Discussion about FORTRAN

comp.lang.functional
Discussion about functional languages

comp.lang.hermes
The Hermes language for distributed applications

comp.lang.idl-pvwave
IDL and PV-Wave language discussions

comp.lang.lisp
Discussion about LISP

comp.lang.lisp.mcl
Discussing Apple's Macintosh Common LISP

comp.lang.logo
The LOGO teaching/learning language

comp.lang.misc
Different computer languages not specifically listed

comp.lang.ml
ML languages including Standard ML, CAML, Lazy ML, etc.[†]

comp.lang.modula2
Discussion about Modula-2

comp.lang.modula3
Discussion about Modula-3

comp.lang.mumps
The MUMPS language and technology

comp.lang.oberon
The Oberon language and system

comp.lang.objective-c
The Objective-C language and environment

comp.lang.pascal
Discussion about Pascal

comp.lang.perl
Discussion of Larry Wall's Perl system

comp.lang.pop
Pop11 and the Plug user group

comp.lang.postscript
The PostScript page-description language

comp.lang.prograph
Prograph, a visual object-oriented dataflow language

comp.lang.prolog
Discussion about PROLOG

comp.lang.python
The Python computer language

comp.lang.sather
The object-oriented computer language Sather

comp.lang.scheme
The Scheme programming language

comp.lang.sigplan
Info and announcements from ACM SIGPLAN[†]

comp.lang.smalltalk
Discussion about SmallTalk 80

comp.lang.tcl
The Tcl programming language and related tools

comp.lang.verilog
Discussing Verilog and PLI

comp.lang.vhdl
VHSIC hardware-description language, IEEE 1076/87

comp.laser-printers
Laser printers, hardware and software[†]

comp.lsi
Large scale integrated circuits

comp.lsi.testing
Testing of electronic circuits

comp.mail.elm
Discussion and fixes for the *elm* mail system

comp.mail.headers
Gatewayed from the Internet header-people list

comp.mail.maps
Various maps, including UUCP maps[†]

comp.mail.mh
The UCI version of the Rand message-handling system

comp.mail.mime
Multipurpose Internet mail extensions of RFC 1341

comp.mail.misc
General discussions about computer mail

comp.mail.mush
The Mail User's Shell (MUSH)

comp.mail.pine
The *pine* mail user agent

comp.mail.sendmail
Configuring and using the BSD *sendmail* agent

comp.mail.smail
Administering and using the smail email transport system

comp.mail.uucp
Mail in the UUCP network environment

comp.misc
General topics about computers not covered elsewhere

comp.multimedia
Interactive multimedia technologies of all kinds

comp.newprod
Announcements of new products of interest[†]

comp.object
Object-oriented programming and languages

comp.object.logic
Integrating object-oriented and logic programming

comp.org.acm
Topics about the Association for Computing Machinery

comp.org.cpsr.announce
Computer Professionals for Social Responsibility[†]

comp.org.cpsr.talk
Issues of computing and social responsibility

comp.org.decus
Digital Equipment Computer Users' Society newsgroup

comp.org.eff.news
News from the Electronic Frontier Foundation[†]

comp.org.eff.talk
Discussion of EFF goals, strategies, etc.

comp.org.fidonet
FIDONews digest, official news of the FIDONet Association[†]

comp.org.ieee
Issues and announcements about the IEEE and its members

comp.org.issnnet
The International Student Society for Neural Networks

comp.org.lisp-users
Association of LISP users discussions

comp.org.sug
Talk about/for the the Sun Users Group

comp.org.usenix
USENIX Association events and announcements

comp.org.usenix.roomshare
Finding lodging during USENIX conferences

comp.os.386bsd.announce
Announcements relating to the 386bsd OS[†]

comp.os.386bsd.apps
Applications that run under 386bsd

comp.os.386bsd.bugs
Bugs and fixes for the 386bsd OS and its clients

comp.os.386bsd.development
Working on 386bsd internals

comp.os.386bsd.misc
General aspects of 386bsd not covered by other groups

comp.os.386bsd.questions
General questions about 386bsd

comp.os.chorus
CHORUS microkernel issues, research, and developments

comp.os.coherent
Discussion and support of the Coherent OS

comp.os.cpm
Discussion about the CP/M OS

comp.os.geos
The GEOS OS by GeoWorks for PC clones

comp.os.linux.admin
Installing and administering Linux systems

comp.os.linux.announce
Announcements important to the Linux community[†]

comp.os.linux.development
Ongoing work on the Linux OSs

comp.os.linux.help
Questions and advice about Linux

comp.os.linux.misc
Linux-specific topics not covered by other groups

comp.os.lynx
Discussion of LynxOS and Lynx real-time systems

comp.os.mach
The MACH OS from CMU and other places

comp.os.minix
Discussion of Tanenbaum's MINIX system

comp.os.misc
General OS-oriented discussion not carried elsewhere

comp.os.ms-windows.advocacy
Speculation and debate about Microsoft Windows

comp.os.ms-windows.announce
Announcements relating to MS-Windows[†]

comp.os.ms-windows.*
Groups on specific aspects of MS-Windows (including applications, networking, and NT)

comp.os.ms-windows.programmers*
Groups on specific aspects of MS-Windows programming

comp.os.msdos*
Various aspects of MS-DOS

comp.os.os2.advocacy
Supporting and flaming OS/2

comp.os.os2.announce
Notable news related to OS/2[†]

comp.os.os2*
Various aspects of the OS/2 OS

comp.os.os9
Discussions about the OS/9 OS

comp.os.parix
Forum for users of the parallel OS PARIX

comp.os.qnx
Using and developing under the QNX OS

comp.os.research
Operating systems and related areas[†]

comp.os.vms
DEC's VAX line of computers and VMS

comp.os.vxworks
The VxWorks real-time OS

comp.os.xinu
The XINU OS from Purdue (D Comer)

comp.parallel
Massively parallel hardware/software[†]

comp.parallel.mpi
Message Passing Interface (MPI)

comp.parallel.pvm
The PVM system of multicomputer parallelization

comp.patents
Discussing patents of computer technology[†]

comp.periphs
Peripheral devices

comp.periphs.scsi
Discussion of SCSI-based peripheral devices

comp.programming
Programming issues that transcend languages and OSs

comp.programming.literate
Literate programs and programming tools

comp.protocols.appletalk
AppleBus hardware and software

comp.protocols.dicom
Digital imaging and communications in medicine

comp.protocols.ibm
Networking with IBM mainframes

comp.protocols.iso
The ISO protocol stack

comp.protocols.kerberos
The Kerberos authentication server

comp.protocols.kermit
Info about the Kermit package[†]

comp.protocols.misc
Various forms and types of protocol

comp.protocols.nfs
Discussion about the Network File System protocol

comp.protocols.ppp
Discussion of the Internet Point to Point Protocol

comp.protocols.tcp-ip
TCP/IP network protocols

comp.protocols.tcp-ip.ibmpc
TCP/IP for IBM(-like) personal computers

comp.publish.cdrom.hardware
Hardware used in publishing with CD-ROM

comp.publish.cdrom.multimedia
Software for multimedia authoring and publishing

comp.publish.cdrom.software
Software used in publishing with CD-ROM

comp.publish.prepress
Electronic prepress

comp.realtime
Issues related to real-time computing

comp.research.japan
The nature of research in Japan[†]

comp.risks
Risks to the public from computers[†]

comp.robotics
All aspects of robots and their applications

comp.security.misc
Security issues of computers and networks

comp.security.unix
Discussion of UNIX security

comp.simulation
Simulation methods, problems, uses[†]

comp.society
The impact of technology on society[†]

comp.society.cu-digest
The *Computer Underground Digest*[†]

comp.society.development
Computer technology in developing countries

comp.society.folklore
Computer folklore and culture, past and present[†]

comp.society.futures
Events in technology affecting future computing

comp.society.privacy
Effects of technology on privacy[†]

comp.soft-sys.khoros
The Khoros X11 visualization system

comp.soft-sys.matlab
The MathWorks calculation and visualization package

comp.soft-sys.powerbuilder
Application development tools from PowerSoft

comp.soft-sys.ptolemy
The Ptolemy simulation/code generation environment

comp.soft-sys.sas
The SAS statistics package

comp.soft-sys.shazam
The SHAZAM econometrics computer program

comp.soft-sys.spss
The SPSS statistics package

comp.soft-sys.wavefront
Wavefront software products, problems

comp.software-eng
Software engineering and related topics

comp.software.config-mgmt
Configuration management, tools, and procedures

comp.software.international
Finding, using, and writing non-English software

comp.software.licensing
Software licensing technology

comp.software.testing
All aspects of testing computer systems

comp.sources.3b1
Source code-only posts for the AT&T 3b1[†]

comp.sources.acorn
Source code-only posts for the Acorn[†]

comp.sources.amiga
Source code-only posts for the Amiga[†]

comp.sources.apple2
Source code, discussion for the Apple II[†]

comp.sources.atari.st
Source code-only posts for the Atari ST[†]

comp.sources.bugs
Bug reports, fixes, discussion for posted sources

comp.sources.d
Discussion of source postings

comp.sources.games
Postings of recreational software[†]

comp.sources.games.bugs
Bug reports, fixes for posted game software

comp.sources.hp48
Programs for the HP48 and HP28 calculators[†]

comp.sources.mac
Software for the Apple Macintosh[†]

comp.sources.misc
Posting of software[†]

comp.sources.postscript
Source code for programs written in PostScript[†]

comp.sources.reviewed
Source code evaluated by peer review[†]

comp.sources.sun
Software for Sun workstations[†]

comp.sources.testers
Finding people to test software

comp.sources.unix
Postings of complete, UNIX-oriented sources[†]

comp.sources.wanted
Requests for software and fixes

comp.sources.x
Software for the X Windows System[†]

comp.specification
Languages and methodologies for formal specification

comp.specification.z
Discussion about the formal specification notation Z

comp.speech
Research and applications in speech science and technology

comp.std.c
Discussion about C language standards

comp.std.c++
Discussion about C++ language, library, standards

comp.std.internat
Discussion about international standards

comp.std.lisp
User group (ALU) supported standards[†]

comp.std.misc
Discussion about various standards

comp.std.mumps
Discussion for the X111 committee on MUMPS[†]

comp.std.unix
Discussion for the P1003 committee on UNIX[†]

comp.std.wireless
Examining standards for wireless network technology[†]

comp.sw.components
Software components and related technology

comp.sys.3b1
Discussion and support of AT&T 7300/ 3B1/UNIXPC

comp.sys.acorn
Discussion on Acorn and ARM-based computers

comp.sys.acorn.advocacy
Why Acorn computers and programs are better

comp.sys.acorn.announce
Announcements for Acorn and ARM users[†]

comp.sys.amiga*
Various aspects of the Amiga computer and OS

comp.sys.apollo
Apollo computer systems

comp.sys.apple2
Discussion about Apple II micros

comp.sys.apple2.comm
Apple II data communications

comp.sys.apple2.gno
The AppleIIgs GNO multitasking environment

comp.sys.apple2.marketplace
Buying, selling, and trading Apple II equipment

comp.sys.apple2.programmer
Programming on the Apple II

comp.sys.apple2.usergroups
All about Apple II user groups

comp.sys.atari.8bit
Discussion about 8-bit Atari micros

comp.sys.atari.advocacy
Attacking and defending Atari computers

comp.sys.atari.announce
Atari-related hard and software announcements[†]

comp.sys.atari.st
Discussion about 16-bit Atari micros

comp.sys.atari.st.tech
Technical discussions of Atari ST hardware and software

comp.sys.att
Discussions about AT&T microcomputers

comp.sys.cbm
Discussion about Commodore micros

comp.sys.concurrent
The Concurrent/Masscomp line of computers[†]

comp.sys.convex
Convex computer systems hardware and software

comp.sys.dec
Discussions about DEC computer systems

comp.sys.dec.micro
DEC microcomputers (Rainbow, Professional 350/380)

comp.sys.encore
Encore's MultiMax computers

comp.sys.harris
Harris computer systems, especially real-time systems

comp.sys.hp.apps
Discussion of software and apps on Hewlett-Packard platforms

comp.sys.hp.hardware
Discussion of HP system hardware

comp.sys.hp.hpux
Issues pertaining to HP-UX and 9000 series computers

comp.sys.hp.misc
Issues not covered in any other *comp.sys.hp** group

comp.sys.hp.mpe
Issues pertaining to MPE and 3000 series computers

comp.sys.hp48
HP's HP48 and HP28 calculators

comp.sys.ibm.pc.demos
Demonstration programs that showcase programmer skill

comp.sys.ibm.pc.digest
The IBM PC, PC-XT, and PC-AT[†]

*comp.sys.ibm.pc**
Various aspects of the IBM PC and its clones

comp.sys.ibm.ps2.hardware
Microchannel hardware, any vendor

comp.sys.intel
Discussions about Intel systems and parts

comp.sys.isis
The ISIS distributed system from Cornell

comp.sys.laptops
Laptop (portable) computers

comp.sys.m6809
Discussion about 6809s

comp.sys.m68k
Discussion about 68ks

comp.sys.m68k.pc
Discussion about 68k-based PCs[†]

comp.sys.m88k
Discussion about 88k-based computers

comp.sys.mac.advocacy
The Macintosh computer family compared to others

comp.sys.mac.announce
Important notices for Macintosh users[†]

*comp.sys.mac**
Various aspects of the Macintosh computer and OS

comp.sys.mentor
Mentor Graphics products and the Silicon Compiler System

comp.sys.mips
Systems based on MIPS chips

comp.sys.misc
Discussion about computers of all kinds

comp.sys.ncr
Discussion about NCR computers

comp.sys.newton.announce
Newton information posts[†]

comp.sys.newton.misc
Miscellaneous discussion about Newton systems

comp.sys.newton.programmer
Discussion of Newton software development

comp.sys.next.advocacy
The NeXT religion

comp.sys.next.announce
Announcements related to the NeXT computer system[†]

comp.sys.next*
Various aspects of the NeXT computer and OS

comp.sys.novell
Discussion of Novell Netware products

comp.sys.nsc.32k
National Semiconductor 32000 series chips

comp.sys.palmtops
Super-powered calculators in the palm of your hand

comp.sys.pen
Interacting with computers through pen gestures

comp.sys.powerpc
General PowerPC discussion

comp.sys.prime
Prime Computer products

comp.sys.proteon
Proteon gateway products

comp.sys.psion
Discussion about PSION Personal Computers and Organizers

comp.sys.pyramid
Pyramid 90x computers

comp.sys.ridge
Ridge 32 computers and ROS

comp.sys.sequent
Sequent systems (Balance and Symmetry)

comp.sys.sgi.admin
System administration on Silicon Graphics' Iris

comp.sys.sgi.announce
Announcements for the SGI community[†]

comp.sys.sgi.apps
Applications that run on the Iris

comp.sys.sgi.audio
Audio on SGI systems

comp.sys.sgi.bugs
Bugs found in the Irix OS

comp.sys.sgi.graphics
Graphics packages and issues on SGI machines

comp.sys.sgi.hardware
Base systems and peripherals for Iris computers

comp.sys.sgi.misc
General discussion about SGI machines

comp.sys.sinclair
Sinclair computers, e.g., the ZX81, Spectrum and QL

comp.sys.stratus
Stratus products, including System/88, CPS-32, VOS and FTX

comp.sys.sun.admin
Sun system administration issues and questions

comp.sys.sun.announce
Sun announcements, Sunergy mailings[†]

comp.sys.sun.apps
Software applications for Sun systems

comp.sys.sun.hardware
Sun Microsystems hardware

comp.sys.sun.misc
Miscellaneous discussions about Sun products

comp.sys.sun.wanted
People looking for Sun products and support

comp.sys.tahoe
CCI 6/32, Harris HCX/7, and Sperry 7000 computers

comp.sys.tandy
Discussion about Tandy computers, new and old

comp.sys.ti
Discussion about Texas Instruments

comp.sys.transputer
The Transputer computer and OCCAM language

comp.sys.unisys
Sperry, Burroughs, Convergent, and Unisys systems

comp.sys.xerox
Xerox 1100 workstations and protocols

comp.sys.zenith.z100
The Zenith Z-100 (Heath H-100) family of computers

comp.terminals
All sorts of terminals

comp.text
Text-processing issues and methods

comp.text.desktop
Technology and techniques of desktop publishing

comp.text.frame
Desktop publishing with FrameMaker

comp.text.interleaf
Applications and use of Interleaf software

comp.text.sgml
ISO 8879 SGML, structured documents, markup languages

comp.text.tex
Discussion about the TeX and LaTeX systems and macros

comp.theory.info-retrieval
Information retrieval topics[†]

comp.unix.admin
Administering a UNIX-based system

comp.unix.advocacy
Arguments for and against UNIX and UNIX versions

comp.unix.aix
IBM's version of UNIX

comp.unix.amiga
Minix, SYSV4 on an Amiga

comp.unix.aux
The version of UNIX for Apple Macintosh II computers

comp.unix.bsd
Discussion of Berkeley Software Distribution UNIX

comp.unix.dos-under-unix
MS-DOS running under UNIX by whatever means

comp.unix.internals
Discussions on hacking UNIX internals

comp.unix.large
UNIX on mainframes and in large networks

comp.unix.misc
Various topics that don't fit other groups

comp.unix.osf.misc
Various aspects of Open Software Foundation products

comp.unix.osf.osf1
The Open Software Foundation's OSF/1

comp.unix.pc-clone.16bit
UNIX on 286 architectures

comp.unix.pc-clone.32bit
UNIX on 386 and 486 architectures

comp.unix.programmer
Q&A for UNIX programming

comp.unix.questions
UNIX neophytes group

comp.unix.shell
Using and programming the UNIX shell

comp.unix.sys3
System III UNIX discussions

comp.unix.sys5.misc
Versions of System V that predate Release 3

comp.unix.sys5.r3
Discussing System V Release 3

comp.unix.sys5.r4
Discussing System V Release 4

comp.unix.ultrix
Discussing DEC's Ultrix

comp.unix.unixware
Discussing Novell's UnixWare products

comp.unix.user-friendly
Discussing UNIX user-friendliness

comp.unix.wizards
For true UNIX wizards[†]

comp.unix.xenix.misc
General discussions regarding XENIX (except SCO)

comp.unix.xenix.sco
XENIX versions from the Santa Cruz Operation

comp.virus
Computer viruses and security†

comp.windows.garnet
The Garnet user interface development environment

comp.windows.interviews
The InterViews object-oriented windowing system

comp.windows.misc
Various issues about windowing systems

comp.windows.news
Sun Microsystems' NeWS window system

comp.windows.open-look
Discussion about the Open Look GUI

comp.windows.suit
The SUIT user-interface toolkit

comp.windows.x
Discussion about the X Window System

comp.windows.x.announce
X Consortium announcements†

comp.windows.x.apps
Getting and using, not programming, applications for X

comp.windows.x.i386unix
The XFree86 window system and others

comp.windows.x.intrinsics
Discussion of the X Toolkit

comp.windows.x.pex
The PHIGS extension of the X Window System

misc

misc consists of groups that address themes not easily classified under other headings or which incorporate themes from multiple categories.

misc.activism.progressive
Information for progressive activists†

misc.answers
Repository for periodic USENET articles†

misc.books.technical
Discussion of books on technical topics

misc.consumers
Consumer interests: product reviews, etc.

misc.consumers.house
Discussion about owning and maintaining a house

misc.creativity
Promoting the use of creativity in all human endeavors

misc.education
Discussion of the educational system

misc.education.adult
Adult education and adult literacy practice/research

misc.education.home-school.christian
Christian home schooling

misc.education.home-school.misc
Almost anything about home schooling

misc.education.language.english
Teaching English to speakers of other languages

misc.education.medical
Issues related to medical education

misc.education.multimedia
Multimedia for education†

misc.education.science
Issues related to science education

misc.emerg-services
Forum for paramedics and other first responders

misc.entrepreneurs
Discussions on operating a business

misc.fitness
Physical fitness, exercise, bodybuilding, etc.

misc.forsale
Short, tasteful postings about items for sale

misc.forsale.computers.d
Discussion of *misc.for.sale.computers*

misc.forsale.computers.mac
Macintosh-related computer items

misc.forsale.computers.other
Selling miscellaneous computer stuff

misc.forsale.computers.pc-clone
IBM PC-related computer items

misc.forsale.computers.workstation
Workstation-related computer items

misc.handicap
Items of interest for/about the
handicapped[†]

misc.headlines
Current items of interest

misc.health.alternative
Alternative, complementary, holistic
health care

misc.health.diabetes
Discussion of diabetes management in
day-to-day life

misc.int-property
Discussion of intellectual property rights

misc.invest
Investments and the handling of money

misc.invest.canada
Investing in Canadian financial markets

misc.invest.funds
Sharing info about bond, stock, real-
estate funds

misc.invest.real-estate
Property investments

misc.invest.stocks
Forum for sharing information about
stocks and options

misc.invest.technical
Analyzing market trends with technical
methods

misc.jobs.contract
Discussions about contract labor

misc.jobs.misc
Discussion about employment,
workplaces, careers

misc.jobs.offered
Announcements of positions available

misc.jobs.offered.entry
Job listings only for entry-level positions

misc.jobs.resumes
Postings of resumes and "situation
wanted" articles

misc.kids
Children, their behavior and activities

misc.kids.computer
The use of computers by children

misc.kids.vacation
Discussion on all forms of family-
oriented vacationing

misc.legal
Legalities and the ethics of law

misc.legal.computing
Discussing the legal climate of the
computing world

misc.legal.moderated
All aspects of law[†]

misc.misc
Various discussions not fitting in any
other group

misc.news.east-europe.rferl
Radio Free Europe/Radio Liberty Daily
Report[†]

misc.news.southasia
News from Bangladesh, India, Nepal,
etc.[†]

misc.rural
Devoted to issues concerning rural living

misc.taxes
Tax laws and advice

misc.test
For testing of network software; very
boring

misc.test.moderated
Testing of posting to moderated groups[†]

misc.transport.urban-transit
Metropolitan public transportation
systems

misc.wanted
Requests for things that are needed (*not*
software)

misc.writing
Discussion of writing in all of its forms

news

The *news* hierarchy consists of groups concerned with the news network and software

news.admin.misc
General topics of network news administration

news.admin.policy
Policy issues of USENET

news.admin.technical
Technical aspects of maintaining network news[†]

news.announce.conferences
Calls for papers and conference announcements[†]

news.announce.important
General announcements of interest to all[†]

news.announce.newgroups
Calls for newgroups and announcements of same[†]

news.announce.newusers
Explanatory postings for new users[†]

news.answers
Repository for periodic USENET articles[†]

news.config
Postings of system down times and interruptions

news.future
The future technology of network news systems

news.groups
Discussions and lists of newsgroups

news.groups.questions
Where can I find talk about topic X?

news.groups.reviews
What is going on in group or mailing list named X?[†]

news.lists
News-related statistics and lists[†]

news.lists.ps-maps
Maps relating to USENET traffic flows[†]

news.misc
Discussions of USENET itself

news.newsites
Postings of new site announcements

news.newusers.questions
Q&A for users new to the USENET

news.software.anu-news
VMS B-news software from Australian National University

news.software.b
Discussion about B-news-compatible software

news.software.nn
Discussion about the *nn* newsreader package

news.software.notes
Notesfile software from the University of Illinois

news.software.readers
Discussion of software used to read network news

rec

Groups oriented to the arts, hobbies and recreational activities. Many have corresponding groups in the *alt* hierarchy.

rec.answers
Repository for periodic USENET articles[†]

rec.antiques
Discussing antiques and vintage items

rec.aquaria
Keeping fish and aquaria as a hobby

rec.arts.animation
Discussion of various kinds of animation

rec.arts.anime
Japanese animation discussion

rec.arts.anime.info
Announcements about Japanese animation[†]

rec.arts.anime.marketplace
Things for sale in the Japanese animation world

rec.arts.anime.stories
All about Japanese comic fanzines[†]

rec.arts.ascii
ASCII art, info on archives, art, artists[†]

rec.arts.bodyart
Tattoos and body-decoration discussions

rec.arts.bonsai
Dwarfish trees and shrubbery

rec.arts.books
Books of all genres, and the publishing industry

rec.arts.books.marketplace
Buying and selling of books

rec.arts.books.tolkien
The works of JRR Tolkien

rec.arts.cinema
Discussion of the art of cinema[†]

rec.arts.comics.creative
Encouraging good superhero-style writing

rec.arts.comics.info
Reviews, convention information, and other comics news[†]

rec.arts.comics.marketplace
The exchange of comics and comic related items

rec.arts.comics.misc
Comic books, graphic novels, sequential art

rec.arts.comics.strips
Discussion of short-form comics

rec.arts.comics.xbooks
The Mutant Universe of Marvel comics

rec.arts.dance
Any aspects of dance not covered in another newsgroup

rec.arts.disney
Discussion of any Disney-related subjects

rec.arts.drwho
Discussion about Dr. Who

rec.arts.erotica
Erotic fiction and verse[†]

rec.arts.fine
Fine arts and artists

rec.arts.int-fiction
Discussions about interactive fiction

rec.arts.manga
All aspects of the Japanese storytelling art form

rec.arts.marching.drumcorps
Drum and bugle corps

rec.arts.marching.misc
Marching-related performance activities

rec.arts.misc
Discussions about the arts not in other groups

rec.arts.movies
Discussions of movies and movie making

rec.arts.movies.production
Filmmaking, amateur and professional

rec.arts.movies.reviews
Reviews of movies[†]

rec.arts.poems
For the posting of poems

rec.arts.prose
Short works of prose fiction and followup discussion

rec.arts.sf.announce
Major announcements of the science-fiction world[†]

rec.arts.sf.fandom
Discussions of SF fan activities

rec.arts.sf.marketplace
Personal forsale notices of SF materials

rec.arts.sf.misc
SF lovers' newsgroup

rec.arts.sf.movies
Discussing SF motion pictures

rec.arts.sf.reviews
Reviews of SF/fantasy/horror works[†]

rec.arts.sf.science
Real and speculative aspects of SF science

rec.arts.sf.starwars
Discussion of the *Star Wars* universe

rec.arts.sf.tv
Discussing general television SF

rec.arts.sf.tv.babylon5
Babylon 5 creators meet *Babylon 5* fans

rec.arts.sf.tv.quantum-leap
Quantum Leap TV, comics, cons, etc.

rec.arts.sf.written
Discussion of written SF and fantasy

rec.arts.sf.written.robert-jordan
Books by author Robert Jordan

rec.arts.startrek.current
New Star Trek shows, movies and books

rec.arts.startrek.fandom
Star Trek conventions and memorabilia

rec.arts.startrek.info
Info about the universe of Star Trek[†]

rec.arts.startrek.misc
General discussions of Star Trek

rec.arts.startrek.reviews
Reviews of Star Trek books, episodes, films, etc.[†]

rec.arts.startrek.tech
Star Trek's depiction of future technologies

rec.arts.theatre
Discussion of all aspects of stage work and theatre

rec.arts.theatre.misc
Miscellaneous topics and issues in theatre

rec.arts.theatre.musicals
Musical theatre around the world

rec.arts.theatre.plays
Dramaturgy and discussion of plays

rec.arts.theatre.stagecraft
Issues in stagecraft and production

rec.arts.tv
The boob tube, its history, and past and current shows

rec.arts.tv.mst3k
For fans of *Mystery Science Theater 3000*

rec.arts.tv.soaps
Postings about soap operas

rec.arts.tv.uk
Discussions of telly shows from the U.K.

rec.arts.wobegon
A Prairie Home Companion radio show discussion

rec.audio
High-fidelity audio (various groups including "marketplace")

rec.autos*
Discussing all aspects of automobiles in various groups

rec.aviation.announce
Events of interest to the aviation community[†]

rec.aviation.answers
Frequently asked questions about aviation[†]

rec.aviation*
Various groups discussing all aspects of flying

rec.backcountry
Activities in the Great Outdoors

rec.bicycles.marketplace
Buying, selling, reviewing items for cycling

rec.bicycles.misc
General discussion of bicycling

rec.bicycles.racing
Bicycle-racing techniques, rules, results

rec.bicycles.rides
Discussions of tours and training or commuting routes

rec.bicycles.soc
Societal issues of bicycling

rec.bicycles.tech
Cycling product design, construction, maintenance, etc.

rec.birds
Hobbyists interested in bird watching

rec.boats
Hobbyists interested in boating

rec.boats.paddle
Talk about any boats with oars, paddles, etc.

rec.climbing
Climbing techniques, competition announcements, etc.

rec.collecting
Discussion among collectors of many things

rec.collecting.cards
Collecting all sorts of sport and non-sport cards

rec.collecting.stamps
Discussion of all things related to philately

rec.crafts.brewing
The art of making beers and meads

rec.crafts.jewelry
All aspects of jewelry making and
lapidary work

rec.crafts.metalworking
All aspects of working with metal

rec.crafts.misc
Handiwork arts not covered elsewhere

rec.crafts.quilting
All about quilts and other quilted items

rec.crafts.textiles
Sewing, weaving, knitting, and other
fiber arts

rec.crafts.winemaking
The tasteful art of making wine

rec.equestrian
Discussion of things equestrian

rec.folk-dancing
Folk dances, dancers, and dancing

rec.food.cooking
Food, cooking, cookbooks, and recipes

rec.food.drink
Wines and spirits

rec.food.drink.beer
All things beer

rec.food.drink.coffee
The making and drinking of coffee

rec.food.historic
The history of food-making arts

rec.food.recipes
Recipes for interesting food and drink[†]

rec.food.restaurants
Discussion of dining out

rec.food.sourdough
Making and baking with sourdough

rec.food.veg
Vegetarians

rec.food.veg.cooking
Vegetarian recipes, cooking, nutrition[†]

rec.gambling
Articles on games of chance and betting

*rec.games**
Many groups about various games,
including chess, Go, board games, etc.

rec.gardens
Gardening, methods and results

rec.gardens.orchids
Growing, hybridizing, and general care
of orchids

rec.gardens.roses
Gardening information related to roses

rec.guns
Discussions about firearms[†]

rec.heraldry
Discussion of coats of arms

rec.humor
Jokes and the like. May be somewhat
offensive

rec.humor.d
Discussions on the content of *rec.humor*
articles

rec.humor.funny
Jokes that are funny (in the moderator's
opinion)[†]

rec.humor.oracle
Sagacious advice from the USENET
Oracle[†]

rec.humor.oracle.d
Comments about the USENET Oracle's
comments

rec.hunting
Discussions about hunting[†]

rec.juggling
Juggling techniques, equipment, and
events

rec.kites
Talk about kites and kiting

rec.mag
Magazine summaries, tables of contents,
etc.

rec.martial-arts
Discussion of the various martial art
forms

rec.misc
General topics about recreational/
participant sports

rec.models.railroad
Model railroads of all scales

rec.models.rc
Radio-controlled models for hobbyists

rec.models.rockets
Model rockets for hobbyists

rec.models.scale
Construction of models

rec.motorcycles
Motorcycles and related products and laws

rec.motorcycles.dirt
Riding motorcycles and ATVs off-road

rec.motorcycles.harley
All aspects of Harley-Davidson motorcycles

rec.motorcycles.racing
Discussion of all aspects of racing motorcycles

rec.music*
Many groups on music, including classical, folk, and many performers and bands

rec.music.makers*
Several groups for performers

rec.nude
Hobbyists interested in naturist/nudist activities

rec.org.mensa
Talking with members of the high IQ society Mensa

rec.org.sca
Society for Creative Anachronism

rec.outdoors.fishing
All aspects of sport, commercial fishing

rec.outdoors.fishing.fly
Fly fishing in general

rec.outdoors.fishing.saltwater
Saltwater fishing, methods, gear, Q&A

rec.parks.theme
Entertainment theme parks

rec.pets
Pets, pet care, and household animals in general

rec.pets.birds
The culture and care of indoor birds

rec.pets.cats
Discussion about domestic cats

rec.pets.dogs
Subjects relating to dogs as pets

rec.pets.herp
Reptiles, amphibians, and other exotic vivarium pets

rec.photo
Hobbyists interested in photography

rec.photo.advanced
Advanced topics (equipment and technique)

rec.photo.darkroom
Developing, printing and other darkroom issues

rec.photo.help
Beginners questions about photography (and answers)

rec.photo.marketplace
Trading of personal photographic equipment

rec.photo.misc
General issues related to photography

rec.puzzles
Puzzles, problems, and quizzes

rec.puzzles.crosswords
Making and playing gridded word puzzles

rec.pyrotechnics
Fireworks, rocketry, safety, and other topics

rec.radio.amateur.antenna
Antennas: theory, techniques and construction

rec.radio.amateur.digital.misc
Packet radio and other digital radio modes

rec.radio.amateur.equipment
All about production amateur radio hardware

rec.radio.amateur.homebrew
Amateur radio construction and experimentation

rec.radio.amateur.misc
Amateur radio practices, contests, events, rules, etc.

rec.radio.amateur.policy
Radio use and regulation policy

rec.radio.amateur.space
Amateur radio transmissions through space

rec.radio.broadcasting
Discussion of global domestic broadcast radio[†]

rec.radio.cb
Citizen-band radio

rec.radio.info
Informational postings related to radio[†]

rec.radio.noncomm
Topics relating to noncommercial radio

rec.radio.scanner
Utility broadcasting traffic above 30 MHz

rec.radio.shortwave
Shortwave radio enthusiasts

rec.radio.swap
Offers to trade and swap radio equipment

rec.railroad
For fans of real trains, ferroequinologists

rec.roller-coaster
Roller coasters and other amusement park rides

rec.running
Running for enjoyment, sport, exercise, etc.

rec.scouting
Scouting youth organizations worldwide

rec.scuba
Hobbyists interested in SCUBA diving

rec.skate
Ice skating and roller skating

rec.skiing.alpine
Downhill skiing technique, equipment, etc.

rec.skiing.announce
FAQ, competition results, automated snow reports[†]

rec.skiing.nordic
Cross-country skiing technique, equipment, etc.

rec.skiing.snowboard
Snowboarding technique, equipment, etc.

rec.skydiving
Hobbyists interested in skydiving

rec.sport.baseball
Discussion about baseball

rec.sport.baseball.analysis
Analysis and discussion of baseball[†]

rec.sport.baseball.college
Baseball on the collegiate level

rec.sport.baseball.data
Raw baseball data (stats, birthdays, schedules)

rec.sport.baseball.fantasy
Rotisserie (fantasy) baseball play

rec.sport.basketball.college
Hoops on the collegiate level

rec.sport.basketball.misc
Discussion about basketball

rec.sport.basketball.pro
Talk of professional basketball

rec.sport.basketball.women
Women's basketball at all levels

rec.sport.boxing
Boxing in all its pugilistic facets and forms

rec.sport.cricket
Discussion about the sport of cricket

rec.sport.cricket.info
News, scores, and info related to cricket[†]

rec.sport.disc
Discussion of flying-disc-based sports

rec.sport.fencing
All aspects of swordplay

rec.sport.football.australian
Discussion of Australian (rules) Football

rec.sport.football.canadian
All about Canadian rules football

rec.sport.football.college
U.S.-style college football

rec.sport.football.fantasy
Rotisserie (fantasy) football play

rec.sport.football.misc
Discussion about American-style football

rec.sport.football.pro
U.S.-style professional football

rec.sport.golf
Discussion about all aspects of golfing

rec.sport.hockey
Discussion about ice hockey

rec.sport.hockey.field
Discussion of the sport of field hockey

rec.sport.misc
Spectator sports

rec.sport.olympics
All aspects of the Olympic Games

rec.sport.paintball
Discussing all aspects of the survival game paintball

rec.sport.pro-wrestling
Discussion about professional wrestling

rec.sport.rowing
Crew for competition or fitness

rec.sport.rugby
Discussion about the game of rugby

rec.sport.soccer
Discussion about soccer (Association Football)

rec.sport.swimming
Training for and competing in swimming events

rec.sport.table-tennis
Things related to table tennis (aka Ping Pong)

rec.sport.tennis
Things related to the sport of tennis

rec.sport.triathlon
Discussing all aspects of multi-event sports

rec.sport.volleyball
Discussion about volleyball

rec.sport.water-polo
Discussion of water polo

rec.sport.waterski
Waterskiing and other boat-towed activities

rec.toys.lego
Discussion of Lego, Duplo (and compatible) toys

rec.toys.misc
Discussion of toys that lack a specific newsgroup

rec.travel
Traveling all over the world

rec.travel.air
Airline travel around the world

rec.travel.asia
Travel in Asia

rec.travel.cruises
Travel by cruise ship

rec.travel.europe
Travel in Europe

rec.travel.marketplace
Tickets and accomodations wanted and for sale

rec.travel.misc
Everything and anything about travel

rec.travel.usa-canada
Travel in the United States and Canada

rec.video
Video and video components

rec.video.cable-tv
Technical and regulatory issues of cable television

rec.video.desktop
Amateur, computer-based video editing and production

rec.video.production
Making professional quality video productions

rec.video.releases
Pre-recorded video releases on laserdisk and videotape

rec.video.satellite
Getting shows via satellite

rec.windsurfing
Riding the waves as a hobby

rec.woodworking
Hobbyists interested in woodworking

sci

Discussions marked by special and usually practical knowledge, relating to research in or application of the established sciences.

sci.aeronautics
The science of aeronautics and related technology[†]

sci.aeronautics.airliners
Airliner technology[†]

sci.aeronautics.simulation
Aerospace simulation technology[†]

sci.agriculture
Farming, agriculture, and related topics

sci.agriculture.beekeeping
Beekeeping, bee culture, and hive products

sci.answers
Repository for periodic USENET articles†

sci.anthropology
All aspects of studying humankind

sci.anthropology.paleo
Evolution of man and other primates

sci.aquaria
Scientifically-oriented postings about aquaria

sci.archaeology
Studying antiquities of the world

sci.archaeology.mesoamerican
The field of mesoamerican archaeology

sci.astro
Astronomy discussions and information

sci.astro.fits
Issues related to the Flexible Image Transport System

sci.astro.hubble
Processing Hubble Space Telescope data†

sci.astro.planetarium
Discussion of planetariums

sci.astro.research
Forum in astronomy/astrophysics research†

sci.bio
Biology and related sciences

sci.bio.ecology
Ecological research

sci.bio.ethology
Animal behavior and behavioral ecology

sci.bio.evolution
Discussions of evolutionary biology†

sci.bio.herp
Biology of amphibians and reptiles

sci.chem
Chemistry and related sciences

sci.chem.electrochem
The field of electrochemistry

sci.chem.labware
Chemical laboratory equipment

sci.chem.organomet
Organometallic chemistry

sci.classics
Studying classical history, languages, art, and more

sci.cognitive
Perception, memory, judgement, and reasoning

sci.comp-aided
The use of computers as tools in scientific research

sci.cryonics
Theory and practice of biostasis, suspended animation

sci.crypt
Different methods of data en/decryption

sci.data.formats
Modelling, storage, and retrieval of scientific data

sci.econ
The science of economics

sci.econ.research
Research in all fields of economics†

sci.edu
The science of education

sci.electronics
Circuits, theory, electrons, and discussions

sci.electronics.cad
Schematic drafting, printed circuit layout, simulation

sci.electronics.repair
Fixing electronic equipment

sci.energy
Discussions about energy, science, and technology

sci.energy.hydrogen
All about hydrogen as an alternative fuel

sci.engr
Technical discussions about engineering tasks

sci.engr.advanced-tv
HDTV/DATV standards, formats, equipment, practices

sci.engr.biomed
Discussing the field of biomedical engineering

sci.engr.chem
All aspects of chemical engineering

sci.engr.civil
Topics related to civil engineering

sci.engr.control
The engineering of control systems

sci.engr.lighting
Light, vision, and color in architecture, media, etc.

sci.engr.manufacturing
Manufacturing technology

sci.engr.mech
The field of mechanical engineering

sci.engr.semiconductors
Semiconductor devices, processes, materials, physics

sci.environment
Discussions about the environment and ecology

sci.fractals
Objects of non-integral dimension and other chaos

sci.geo.eos
NASA's Earth Observation System (EOS)

sci.geo.fluids
Discussion of geophysical fluid dynamics

sci.geo.geology
Discussion of solid earth sciences

sci.geo.hydrology
Surface and groundwater hydrology

sci.geo.meteorology
Discussion of meteorology and related topics

sci.geo.satellite-nav
Satellite navigation systems, especially GPS

sci.image.processing
Scientific image processing and analysis

sci.lang
Natural languages, communication, etc.

sci.lang.japan
The Japanese language, both spoken and written

sci.life-extension
Slowing, stopping or reversing the ageing process

sci.logic
Logic—math, philosophy, and computational aspects

sci.materials
All aspects of materials engineering

sci.math
Mathematical discussions and pursuits

sci.math.research
Discussion of current mathematical research[†]

sci.math.symbolic
Symbolic algebra discussion

sci.mech.fluids
All aspects of fluid mechanics

sci.med
Medicine and its related products and regulations

sci.med.aids
AIDS: treatment, pathology/biology of HIV, prevention[†]

sci.med.dentistry
Dentally related topics; all about teeth

sci.med.nursing
Nursing questions and discussion

sci.med.nutrition
Physiological impacts of diet

sci.med.occupational
Preventing, detecting, and treating occupational injuries

sci.med.pharmacy
The teaching and practice of pharmacy

sci.med.physics
Issues of physics in medical testing/care

sci.med.psychobiology
Dialog and news in psychiatry and psychobiology

sci.med.radiology
All aspects of radiology

sci.med.telemedicine
Hospital/physician networks. No diagnosis questions

sci.military
Discussion about science and the military[†]

sci.misc
Short-lived discussions on subjects in the sciences

sci.nanotech
Self-reproducing molecular-scale machines[†]

sci.nonlinear
Chaotic systems and other nonlinear scientific study

sci.op-research
Research, teaching, and application of operations research

sci.optics
Discussion relating to the science of optics

sci.philosophy.tech
Technical philosophy: math, science, logic, etc.

sci.physics
Physical laws, properties, etc.

sci.physics.accelerators
Particle accelerators and the physics of beams

sci.physics.computational.fluid-dynamics
Computational fluid dynamics

sci.physics.electromag
Electromagnetic theory and applications

sci.physics.fusion
Info on fusion, esp. "cold" fusion

sci.physics.particle
Particle physics discussions

sci.physics.plasma
Plasma Science and Technology community exchange[†]

sci.physics.research
Current physics research[†]

sci.polymers
All aspects of polymer science

sci.psychology
Topics related to psychology

sci.psychology.digest
PSYCOLOQUY: Refereed Psychology Journal and Newsletter[†]

sci.psychology.research
Research issues in psychology[†]

sci.research
Research methods, funding, ethics, and whatever

sci.research.careers
Issues relevant to careers in scientific research

sci.research.postdoc
Anything about postdoctoral studies, including offers

sci.skeptic
Skeptics discussing pseudo-science

sci.space.news
Announcements of space-related news items[†]

sci.space.policy
Discussions about space policy

sci.space.science
Space and planetary science and related technical work[†]

sci.space.shuttle
The space shuttle and the STS program

sci.space.tech
Technical and general issues related to space flight[†]

sci.stat.consult
Statistical consulting

sci.stat.edu
Statistics education

sci.stat.math
Statistics from a strictly mathematical viewpoint

sci.systems
The theory and application of systems science

sci.techniques.mag-resonance
Magnetic resonance imaging and spectroscopy

sci.techniques.microscopy
The field of microscopy

sci.techniques.spectroscopy
Spectrum analysis

sci.techniques.xtallography
The field of crystallography

sci.virtual-worlds
Virtual reality: technology and culture[†]

sci.virtual-worlds.apps
Current and future uses of virtual-worlds technology[†]

SOC

Groups that address social issues and socializing

soc.answers
Repository for periodic USENET articles†

soc.bi
Discussions of bisexuality

soc.college
College, college activities, campus life, etc.

soc.college.grad
General issues related to graduate schools

soc.college.gradinfo
Information about graduate schools

soc.college.org.aiesec
The International Association of Business and Commerce Students

soc.college.teaching-asst
Issues affecting collegiate teaching assistants

soc.couples
Discussions for couples (*cf.soc.singles*)

soc.couples.intercultural
Intercultural and interracial relationships

soc.culture.afghanistan
Discussion of the Afghan society

soc.culture.african
Discussions about Africa and things African

soc.culture.african.american
Discussions about Afro-American issues

soc.culture.arabic
Technological and cultural issues, *not* politics

soc.culture.argentina
All about life in Argentina

soc.culture.asean
Countries of the Association of Southeastern Asian Nations

soc.culture.asian.american
Issues and discussion about Asian-Americans

soc.culture.australian
Australian culture and society

soc.culture.austria
Austria and its people

soc.culture.baltics
People of the Baltic states

soc.culture.bangladesh
Issues and discussion about Bangladesh

soc.culture.belgium
Belgian society, culture(s) and people

soc.culture.berber
The Berber language, history, and culture

soc.culture.bosna-herzgvna
The independent states of Bosnia and Herzegovina

soc.culture.brazil
Talking about the people and country of Brazil

soc.culture.british
Issues about Britain and those of British descent

soc.culture.bulgaria
Discussing Bulgarian society

soc.culture.burma
Politics, culture, news, discussion about Burma

soc.culture.canada
Discussions of Canada and its people

soc.culture.caribbean
Life in the Caribbean

soc.culture.celtic
Irish, Scottish, Breton, Cornish, Manx, and Welsh

soc.culture.chile
All about Chile and its people

soc.culture.china
About China and Chinese culture

soc.culture.colombia
Colombian talk, social, politics, science

soc.culture.croatia
The lives of people of Croatia

soc.culture.cuba
Cuban culture, society, and politics

soc.culture.czecho-slovak
Bohemian, Slovak, Moravian, and Silesian life

soc.culture.europe
Discussing all aspects of all-European society

soc.culture.filipino
Group about the Filipino culture

soc.culture.french
French culture, history, and related discussions

soc.culture.german
Discussions about German culture and history

soc.culture.greek
Group about Greeks

soc.culture.hongkong
Discussions pertaining to Hong Kong

soc.culture.hongkong.entertainment
Entertainment in Hong Kong

soc.culture.indian
Group for discussion about India and things Indian

soc.culture.indian.info
Info group for *soc.culture.indian*, etc.†

soc.culture.indian.telugu
The culture of the Telugu people of India

soc.culture.indonesia
All about the Indonesian nation

soc.culture.iranian
Discussions about Iran and things Iranian/Persian

soc.culture.israel
Israel and Israelis

soc.culture.italian
The Italian people and their culture

soc.culture.japan
Everything Japanese, except the Japanese language

soc.culture.jewish
Jewish culture and religion (*cf.talk.politics.mideast*)

soc.culture.jewish.holocaust
The Shoah†

soc.culture.korean
Discussions about Korea and things Korean

soc.culture.laos
Cultural and social aspects of Laos

soc.culture.latin-america
Topics about Latin-America

soc.culture.lebanon
Discussion about things Lebanese

soc.culture.maghreb
North African society and culture

soc.culture.magyar
The Hungarian people and their culture

soc.culture.malaysia
All about Malaysian society

soc.culture.mexican
Discussion of Mexico's society

soc.culture.mexican.american
Mexican-American/Chicano culture and issues

soc.culture.misc
Group for discussion about other cultures

soc.culture.mongolian
Everything related to Mongols and Mongolia

soc.culture.native
Aboriginal people around the world

soc.culture.nepal
Discussion of people and things in and from Nepal

soc.culture.netherlands
People from the Netherlands and Belgium

soc.culture.new-zealand
Discussion of topics related to New Zealand

soc.culture.nordic
Discussion about culture up north

soc.culture.pakistan
Topics of discussion about Pakistan

soc.culture.palestine
Palestinian people, culture and politics

soc.culture.peru
All about the people of Peru

soc.culture.polish
Polish culture, past, and politics

soc.culture.portuguese
Discussion of the people of Portugal

soc.culture.puerto-rico
Puerto Rican culture, society, and politics

soc.culture.romanian
Discussion of Romanian and Moldavian people

soc.culture.scientists
Cultural issues about scientists and scientific projects

soc.culture.singapore
The past, present, and future of Singapore

soc.culture.slovenia
Slovenia and Slovenian people

soc.culture.somalia
Somalian affairs, society, and culture

soc.culture.soviet
Topics relating to Russian or Soviet culture

soc.culture.spain
Spain and the Spanish

soc.culture.sri-lanka
Things and people from Sri Lanka

soc.culture.swiss
Swiss culture

soc.culture.taiwan
Discussion about things Taiwanese

soc.culture.tamil
Tamil language, history, and culture

soc.culture.thai
Thai people and their culture

soc.culture.turkish
Discussion about things Turkish

soc.culture.ukrainian
The lives and times of the Ukrainian people

soc.culture.uruguay
Discussions of Uruguay for those at home and abroad

soc.culture.usa
The culture of the United States of America

soc.culture.venezuela
Discussion of topics related to Venezuela

soc.culture.vietnamese
Issues and discussions of Vietnamese culture

soc.culture.yugoslavia
Discussions of Yugoslavia and its people

soc.feminism
Discussion of feminism and feminist issues[†]

soc.history
Discussions of things historical

soc.history.moderated
All aspects of history[†]

soc.history.war.misc
History and events of wars in general

soc.history.war.world-war-ii
History and events of World War II[†]

soc.libraries.talk
Discussing all aspects of libraries

soc.men
Issues related to men, their problems and relationships

soc.misc
Socially oriented topics not in other groups

soc.motss
Issues pertaining to homosexuality

soc.net-people
Announcements, requests, etc., about people on the net

soc.org.nonprofit
Nonprofit organizations

soc.org.service-clubs.misc
General info on all service topics

soc.penpals
In search of *net.friendships*

soc.politics
Political problems, systems, solutions[†]

soc.politics.arms-d
Arms discussion digest[†]

soc.religion.bahai
Discussion of the Baha'i faith[†]

soc.religion.christian
Christianity and related topics[†]

soc.religion.christian.bible-study
Examining the Holy Bible[†]

soc.religion.christian.youth-work
Christians working with young people[†]

soc.religion.eastern
Discussions of Eastern religions†

soc.religion.gnosis
Gnosis, marifat, jnana and direct sacred experience†

soc.religion.islam
Discussions of the Islamic faith†

soc.religion.quaker
The Religious Society of Friends

soc.religion.shamanism
Discussion of the full range of shamanic experience†

soc.rights.human
Human rights and activism (e.g., Amnesty International)

soc.roots
Discussing genealogy and genealogical matters

soc.singles
Newsgroup for single people, their activities, etc.

soc.support.transgendered
Transgendered and intersexed persons

soc.veterans
Social issues relating to military veterans

soc.women
Issues related to women, their problems and relationships

talk

Groups that are largely debate-oriented and tend to feature long discussions without resolution and without appreciable amounts of useful information.

talk.abortion
All sorts of discussions and arguments on abortion

talk.answers
Repository for periodic USENET articles†

talk.bizarre
The unusual, bizarre, curious, and often stupid

talk.environment
Discussion about the state of the environment and what to do

talk.origins
Evolution versus creationism (sometimes hot!)

talk.philosophy.misc
Philosophical musings on all topics

talk.politics.animals
The use and/or abuse of animals

talk.politics.china
Discussion of political issues related to China

talk.politics.crypto
The relation between cryptography and government

talk.politics.drugs
The politics of drug issues

talk.politics.guns
The politics of firearm ownership and (mis)use

talk.politics.medicine
The politics and ethics involved with health care

talk.politics.mideast
Discussion and debate over Middle Eastern events

talk.politics.misc
Political discussions and ravings of all kinds

talk.politics.soviet
Discussion of Soviet politics, domestic and foreign

talk.politics.theory
Theory of politics and political systems

talk.politics.tibet
The politics of Tibet and the Tibetan people

talk.rape
Discussions on stopping rape; not to be crossposted

talk.religion.misc
Religious, ethical, and moral implications

talk.religion.newage
Esoteric and minority religions and philosophies

talk.rumors
For the posting of rumors

ClariNet

The *ClariNet* hierarchy consists of newsgroups gatewayed from commercial news services and other official sources. A feed of the ClariNet groups requires payment of a fee and execution of a license. More information may be obtained by sending mail to *info@clarinet.com.*

GNU

gnUSENET (gnUSENET is Not USENET) is a set of newsgroups that are gated bidirectionally with the Internet mailing lists of the GNU Project of the Free Software Foundation. GNU (GNU's Not UNIX) will be a complete operating system, including application programs, with freely redistributable source code. Please use *only gnu.misc. discuss* for discussion of topics considered contrary to GNU aims and political philosophy (e.g., porting of GNU code to Apple machines, usefulness of intellectual property laws, etc.).

gnu.announce
  Status and announcements from the Project[†]

gnu.bash.bug
  Bourne Again SHell bug reports and suggested fixes[†]

gnu.chess
  Announcements about the GNU Chess program

gnu.emacs.announce
  Announcements about GNU *Emacs*[†]

gnu.emacs.bug
  GNU *Emacs* bug reports and suggested fixes[†]

gnu.emacs.gnews
  News reading under GNU *Emacs* using Weemba's Gnews

gnu.emacs.gnus
  News reading under GNU using *gnus* (in English)

gnu.emacs.help
  User queries and answers

gnu.emacs.sources
  Only (please!) C and LISP source code for GNU *Emacs*

gnu.emacs.vm.bug
  Bug reports on the *Emacs* VM mail package

gnu.emacs.vm.info
  Information about the *Emacs* VM mail package

gnu.emacs.vms
  VMS port of GNU *Emacs*

gnu.epoch.misc
  The Epoch X11 extensions to *Emacs*

gnu.g++.announce
  Announcements about the GNU C++ compiler[†]

gnu.g++.bug
  g++ bug reports and suggested fixes[†]

gnu.g++.help
  GNU C++ compiler (G++) user queries and answers

gnu.g++.lib.bug
  g++ library bug reports/suggested fixes[†]

gnu.gcc.announce
  Announcements about the GNU C compiler[†]

gnu.gcc.bug
  GNU C compiler bug reports andsuggested fixes[†]

gnu.gcc.help
  GNU C compiler (*gcc*) user queries and answers

gnu.gdb.bug
  gcc/g++ deBugger bugs and suggested fixes[†]

gnu.ghostscript.bug
GNU Ghostscript interpreter bugs[†]

gnu.gnusenet.config
GNU's Not USENET administration and configuration

gnu.gnusenet.test
GNU's Not USENET alternative hierarchy testing

gnu.groff.bug
Bugs in the GNU *roff* programs[†]

gnu.misc.discuss
Serious discussion about GNU and freed software

gnu.smalltalk.bug
Bugs in GNU SmallTalk[†]

gnu.utils.bug
GNU utilities bugs (e.g., *make, gawk ls*)[†]

HEPnet

HEPnet is a collection of networks connecting high-energy and nuclear-physics research sites. The HEPnet news hierarchy was created to facilitate discussions in the HEP and NP communitites and is maintained by National HEPnet Management. All groups are bidirectionally gatewayed to mailing lists and automatically archived. All questions, requests for feeds, and group deletions/additions should be sent to *netnews@hep.net* (Internet), *netnews @hepnet* (BITNET), or *hepnet:netnews* (HEP-ES DECnet).

hepnet.admin
Discussions among HEPnet netnews administrators

hepnet.announce
Announcements of general interest

hepnet.conferences
Discussions of conferences and workshops

hepnet.freehep
Discussions about the freeHEP archives

hepnet.general
Discussions of general interest

hepnet.hepix
Discussions on the use of UNIX

hepnet.heplib
Discussions about HEPLIB

hepnet.jobs
Job announcements and discussions

hepnet.lang.c++
Discussions of the use of C++

hepnet.test
Test postings

hepnet.videoconf
Discussions on the use of videoconferencing

IEEE

The *IEEE* newsgroups discuss the activities of the Institute of Electrical and Electronics Engineers.

ieee.announce
General announcements for IEEE community

ieee.config
Postings about managing IEEE groups

ieee.general
General discussion

ieee.pcnfs
Discussion and tips on PC-NFS

ieee.rab.announce
Announcements about the Regional Activities Board

ieee.rab.general
General discussion about the Regional Activities Board

ieee.region1
Region 1 announcements

ieee.tab.announce
Announcements about the Technical Activities Board

ieee.tab.general
General discussion about the Technical Activities Board

ieee.tcos
  The Technical Committee on Operating
  Systems[†]

ieee.usab.announce
  Announcements about the USAB

ieee.usab.general
  General discussion about the USAB

Inet/DDN

Another alternative hierarchy is the *Inet/DDN* distribution. This consists of many newsgroups bearing names similar to traditional USENET groups and corresponding to Internet discussion lists.

These groups are circulated using the NNTP transport mechanism amongst sites on the Internet in an attempt to reduce the number of copies of these groups flowing through the mail (some sites get these groups via UUCP and other transport mechanisms, but the volume can be substantial and load may be significant without a high-speed. Further details may be obtained by writing to Erik Fair *fair@apple.com*.

info

The *info* hierarchy is a collection of mailing lists gatewayed into news at the University of Illinois. The lists are selected based on local interests but have proven popular at a number of sites. Groups are removed when they become available via more mainstream hierarchies. Sites are encouraged to mark *'ed groups as "n" in their active file. These groups are generally concerned with getting real work done, and readers dislike extraneous postings. Postings can still be made by emailing to the listed contact address.

K12

K12Net is a collection of conferences devoted to K-12 educational curriculum, language exchanges with native speakers, and classroom-to-classroom projects designed by teachers. The conferences are privately distributed among FIDONet-compatible electronic bulletin board systems in Africa, Asia, Australia, Europe, and North America, as well as available from *uunet.uu.net* as USENET newsgroups in the hierarchy k12.*

Classroom-to-classroom projects are featured in the K12 channels that are periodically reassigned based on usage and appropriate project length. They comprise the *k12.sys* hierarchy.

Forums for casual conversation among students are divided by grade level in the *k12.chat* hierarchy; there is also an area for teachers to exchange general ideas about using telecommunications in education.

k12.chat.elementary
  Casual conversation for elementary
  students, grades K-5

k12.chat.junior
Casual conversation for students in grades 6-8

k12.chat.senior
Casual conversation for high school students

k12.chat.teacher
Casual conversation for teachers of grades K-12

k12.ed.art
Arts and crafts curricula in K-12 education

k12.ed.business
Business education curricula in grades K-12

k12.ed.comp.literacy
Teaching computer literacy in grades K-12

k12.ed.health-pe
Health and Physical Education curricula in grades K-12

k12.ed.life-skills
Home Economics, career education, and school counseling

k12.ed.math
Mathematics curriculum in K-12 education

k12.ed.music
Music and performing-arts curriculum in K-12 education

k12.ed.science
Science curriculum in K-12 education

k12.ed.soc-studies
Social studies and history curriculum in K-12 education

k12.ed.special
Educating students with handicaps and/or special needs

k12.ed.tag
K-12 education for gifted and talented students

k12.ed.tech
Industrial arts and vocational education in grades K-12

k12.lang.art
The art of teaching language skills in grades K-12

k12.lang.deutsch-eng
Bilingual German/English practice with native speakers

k12.lang.esp-eng
Bilingual Spanish/English practice with native speakers

k12.lang.francais
French practice with native speakers

k12.lang.russian
Bilingual Russian/English practice with native speakers

k12.library
Implementing information technologies in school libraries

k12.sys*
Current projects

relcom

relcom is the hierarchy of Russian-language news-groups distributed mostly on the territory of the former Soviet Union (non-CIS countries included). These groups are available in Europe and Northern America. Due to the 8-bit encoding (KOI-8) of Cyrillic letters, minor software modifications may be required.

relcom.ads
Non-commercial ads[†]

relcom.archives
Messages about new items on archive sites

relcom.archives.d
Discussions on file servers, archives

relcom.arts.epic
Literary arts of epical kind (more than 10K bytes)

relcom.arts.qwerty
Literary arts of small forms (less than 10K bytes)

relcom.banktech
Discussions on banking technologies

relcom.bbs
BBS news

relcom.bbs.list
Lists of Russian-language BBSs†

relcom.commerce.audio-video
Audio and video equipment

relcom.commerce.chemical
Chemical production

relcom.commerce.computers
Computer hardware

relcom.commerce.construction
Construction materials and equipment

relcom.commerce.consume
Cosmetics, parfumes, dresses, shoes

relcom.commerce.energy
Gas, coal, oil, fuel, generators, etc.

relcom.commerce.estate
Real estate

relcom.commerce.food
Food and drinks (including alcoholic)

relcom.commerce.food.drinks
Spirits and soft drinks

relcom.commerce.food.sweet
Sweets and sugar

relcom.commerce.household
All for the house: furniture, freezers, ovens, etc.

relcom.commerce.infoserv
Information services

relcom.commerce.jobs
Jobs offered/wanted

relcom.commerce.machinery
Machinery, plant equipment

relcom.commerce.medicine
Medical services, equipment, drugs

relcom.commerce.metals
Metals and metal products

relcom.commerce.money
Credits, deposits, currency

relcom.commerce.orgtech
Office equipment

relcom.commerce.other
Miscellanea

relcom.commerce.publishing
Books, publishing services

relcom.commerce.software
Software

relcom.commerce.software.demo
Demo versions of commercial software

relcom.commerce.stocks
Stocks and bonds

relcom.commerce.talk
Discussions about commercial groups

relcom.commerce.tobacco
Cigarettes and tobacco

relcom.commerce.tour
Tourism, leisure, entertainment opportunities

relcom.commerce.transport
Vehicles and spare parts

relcom.comp.animation
Discussions on computer-animation programs†

relcom.comp.binaries
Binary codes of computer programs†

relcom.comp.crosstools
Crosstools for embedded systems, single-chip computers

relcom.comp.dbms.clipper
Clarion database-management system

relcom.comp.dbms.foxpro
FoxPro database-development system

relcom.comp.dbms.vista
db_Vista discussions

relcom.comp.demo
Demo versions of various software†

relcom.comp.demo.d
Discussions of demonstration programs

relcom.comp.gis
Geographical information systems

relcom.comp.lang.forth
Forth programming language, systems

relcom.comp.lang.pascal
Using of Pascal programming language

relcom.comp.law
Political and legal aspects of computers

relcom.comp.os.os2
FIDOnet area, OS/2 operational system

relcom.comp.os.vms
VMS operational system

relcom.comp.os.windows
FIDOnet area, MS-Windows operational system

relcom.comp.os.windows.prog
FIDOnet area, programming under MS-Windows

relcom.comp.security
Computer security discussions

relcom.comp.sources.d
Discussions on sources

relcom.comp.sources.misc
Software sources[†]

relcom.consumers
Consumer information on products and services. No ads.

relcom.currency
Money matters in the ex-USSR

relcom.education
Education discussions

relcom.exnet
Discussions on ExNet electronic exchange

relcom.exnet.quote
ExNet quotes

relcom.expo
Exhibitions and fairs announcements and reviews[†]

relcom.fido.flirt
FIDOnet, just talking of love

relcom.fido.ru.hacker
FIDOnet, hackers and crackers (legal!)

relcom.fido.ru.modem
Internetwork discussion on modems

relcom.fido.ru.networks
Internetwork discussion of global nets

relcom.fido.ru.strack
FIDOnet, digitized sound

relcom.fido.ru.unix
Internetwork challenge to OS UNIX

relcom.fido.su.books
FIDOnet, for book readers and lovers

relcom.fido.su.c-c++
FIDOnet, C and C++ language

relcom.fido.su.dbms
FIDOnet, database management systems

relcom.fido.su.general
FIDOnet, about everything and nothing

relcom.fido.su.hardw
FIDOnet, computer hardware

relcom.fido.su.magic
FIDOnet, magic, and occult sciences

relcom.fido.su.softw
FIDOnet, software in general

relcom.fido.su.tolkien
FIDOnet, creations of JRR Tolkien

relcom.fido.su.virus
FIDOnet, viruses, and vaccines

relcom.games
Games

relcom.humor
Ha-ha-ha jokes, you know them, funny

relcom.infomarket.quote
Ex-USSR exchanges's quotes /ASMP/[†]

relcom.infomarket.talk
Discussion on market development/ASMP/[†]

relcom.internic.net-happenings
InterNIC net-happenings mail-list

relcom.jusinf
Information on laws by "Justicinform"[†]

relcom.kids
About kids

relcom.lan
Internetwork discussion on LANs

relcom.maps
Relcom maps

relcom.msdos
MS-DOS software

relcom.music
Music lovers

relcom.netnews
Announcements and articles important for all netters

relcom.netnews.big
General BIG articles

relcom.newusers
Q&A of new Relcom users

relcom.penpals
To find friends, colleagues, etc.

relcom.politics
Political discussions

relcom.postmasters
For RELCOM postmasters, official[†]

relcom.postmasters.d
Discussion of postmaster's troubles and bright ideas

relcom.relarn.general
Scientific academical subnet RELARN: general issues[t]

relcom.renews
Net magazine *RENEWS*[t]

relcom.sci.libraries
Discussion of libraries and related info[t]

relcom.spbnews
Political and economic news digest by SPB news agency[t]

relcom.talk
Unfettered talk

relcom.tcpip
TCP/IP protocols and their implementation

relcom.terms
Discussion of terms and terminology

relcom.test
"Wow, does it really work?"

relcom.wtc
Commercial proposals of World Trade Centers

relcom.x
X Windows discussion

U3B

These are groups that deal with AT&T 3B {2,5,15,20,4000} computers, everything except for the UNIX PC/3B1

VMSnet

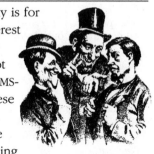

This hierarchy is for topics of interest to VAX/VMS users (but not necessarily VMS-specific). These groups are a project of the VMSnet working group of the VAX SIG of the U.S. Chapter of DECUS (the Digital Equipment Computer User's Society). They are carried by most major USENET news sites, and almost half of all netnews sites. To find a feed, contact the system managers of news sites near you, and/or post to a local or regional newsgroup and ask if anyone in the area is carrying the VMSnet newsgroups.

vmsnet.alpha
Discussion about Alpha AXP architecture, systems, porting, etc.

vmsnet.announce
General announcements of interest to all[t]

vmsnet.announce.newusers
Orientation info for new users[t]

vmsnet.databases.rdb
DEC's Rdb relational DBMS and related topics

vmsnet.decus.journal
The *DECUServe Journal*[t]

vmsnet.decus.lugs
Discussion of DECUS Local User Groups and related issues

vmsnet.employment
Jobs sought/offered, workplace- and employment-related issues[t]

vmsnet.epsilon-cd
DEC's free, unsupported OpenVMS AXP CD

vmsnet.groups
Administration of the VMSnet newsgroups

vmsnet.infosystems.gopher
Gopher software for VMS, gatewayed to VMSGopher-L

vmsnet.infosystems.misc
Miscellaneous infosystem software for VMS (e.g., WAIS, WWW, etc.)

vmsnet.internals
VMS internals, MACRO-32, Bliss, etc., gatewayed to MACRO-32 list

vmsnet.mail.misc
Other electronic mail software

vmsnet.mail.mx
MX email system, gatewayed to MX mailing list

vmsnet.mail.pmdf
PMDF email system, gatewayed to *ipmdf* mailing list.

vmsnet.misc
General VMS topics not covered elsewhere

vmsnet.networks.desktop.misc
Other desktop integration software

vmsnet.networks.desktop.pathworks
DEC Pathworks desktop integration software

vmsnet.networks.management.decmcc
DECmcc and related software

vmsnet.networks.management.misc
Other network-management solutions

vmsnet.networks.misc
General networking topics not covered elsewhere

vmsnet.networks.tcp-ip.cmu-tek
CMU-TEK TCP/IP package, gatewayed to *cmu-openvms-ip@drycas.club.ccc.mu.edu*

vmsnet.networks.tcp-ip.misc
Other TCP/IP solutions for VMS

vmsnet.networks.tcp-ip.multinet
TGV's Multinet TCP/IP, gatewayed to *info-multinet*

vmsnet.networks.tcp-ip.tcpware
Discussion of Process Software's TCPWARE TCP/IP software

vmsnet.networks.tcp-ip.ucx
DEC's VMS/Ultrix Connection (or TCP/IP services for VMS) product

vmsnet.networks.tcp-ip.wintcp
The Wollongong Group's WIN-TCP TCP/IP software

vmsnet.pdp-11
PDP-11 hardware and software, gatewayed to *info-pdp11*

vmsnet.sources
Source code postings *only*†

vmsnet.sources.d
Discussion about or requests for sources

vmsnet.sources.games
Recreational software postings

vmsnet.sysmgt
VMS system management

vmsnet.test
Test messages

vmsnet.tpu
TPU language and applications, gatewayed to *info-tpu*

vmsnet.uucp
DECUS UUCP software, gatewayed to VMSnet mailing list

vmsnet.vms-posix
Discussion about VMS POSIX

ALTERNATIVE NEWSGROUPS

alt

This is a listing of the *alt* hierarchy at the time of printing. An up-to-date copy of this list is posted to *news.lists* on a periodic basis. The original list was written by Gene Spafford, and it is currently maintained by David Lawrence. In several places, this list has been trimmed to preserve space. We figure that if you see *alt.tv.**, you'll take it upon yourself to figure out whether or not your favorite show has its own group. The descriptions are part of the semi-official list and are often acerbic, so don't blame us. It's completely unclear what many of these newsgroups are about, even if you participate in them.

alt.1d
  One-dimensional imaging, and the thinking behind it
alt.2600
  The magazine or the game system

alt.2600.hope.tech
  Technology concerns for Hackers on Planet Earth 1994
alt.3d
  Three-dimensional imaging
alt.abortion.inequity
  Paternal obligations of failing to abort unwanted child
alt.abuse.recovery
  Helping victims of abuse to recover
alt.abuse.transcendence
  Non-standard ways to deal with all forms of abuse
alt.activism
  Activities for activists
alt.activism.d
  A place to discuss issues in *alt.activism*
alt.activism.death-penalty
  For people opposed to capital punishment
alt.adjective.noun.verb.verb.verb
  The penultimate *alt* group
alt.adoption
  For those involved with or contemplating adoption
alt.agriculture.misc
  Like *sci.agriculture*, only different
alt.alcohol
  Don't drink and drive on the Info... no, I can't say it

† - Moderated

alt.aldus.freehand
The other hand is busy

alt.aldus.pagemaker
Don't use expensive user support, come here instead

alt.alien.vampire.flonk.flonk.flonk
Something about simoN

alt.alien.visitors
Space Aliens on Earth! Abduction! Gov't Coverup!

alt.amateur-comp
Discussion and input for *Amateur Computerist Newsletter*

alt.amazon-women.admirers
Worshiping women you have to look up to

alt.anagrams
Playing with words

alt.angst
Anxiety in the modern world

alt.animals.dolphins
Flipper, Darwin, and all their friends

alt.animation.warner-bros
Discussions about Warner Brothers cartoons

alt.answers
As if anyone on alt has the answers†

alt.aol-sucks
Why some people hate AOL and its users

alt.aol.rejects
Another forum for gripes about America Online

alt.appalachian
Appalachian region awareness, events, and culture

alt.aquaria
The aquarium and related as a hobby

alt.aquaria.killies
Killifish, members of family cyprinodontidae

alt.archery
Robin Hood had the right idea

alt.architecture
Building design/construction and related topics

alt.architecture.alternative
Non-traditional building designs

alt.architecture.int-design
Interior design of man-made spaces

alt.artcom
Artistic community, arts and communication

alt.arts.ballet
All aspects of ballet and modern dance as performing art

alt.ascii-art
Pictures composed of ASCII characters

alt.ascii-art.animation
Movies composed of ASCII characters

alt.asian-movies
Movies from Hong Kong, Taiwan, and the Chinese mainland

alt.astrology
Twinkle, twinkle, little planet

alt.atari-jaguar.discussion
As opposed to simply *alt.atari.jaguar*

alt.atari.2600
The Atari 2600 game system, not *2600 Magazine*

alt.atheism
Godless heathens

alt.atheism.moderated
Focused Godless heathens†

alt.atheism.satire
Atheism-related humor and satire

alt.authorware
About Authorware, produced by Authorware. So subtle.

alt.autos.antique
Discussion of all facets of older automobiles

alt.autos.camaro.firebird
A couple of American sports cars

alt.autos.rod-n-custom
Vehicles with modified engines and/or appearance

alt.backrubs
Lower to the rightaaaah!

alt.banjo
Someone's in the kitchen with Dinah

alt.barney.dinosaur.die.die.die
"There's enough hatred of Barney for everyone!"

alt.basement.graveyard
Another side of the do-it-yourself movement

alt.bbs
Computer BBS systems and software

alt.bbs.ads
Ads for various computer BBSs

alt.bbs.allsysop
SysOp concerns of ALL networks and technologies

alt.bbs.first-class
The First Class Mac GUI BBS

alt.bbs.gigo-gateway
Garbage in, garbage out—*alt** in a nutshell

alt.bbs.internet
BBSs that are hooked up to the Internet

alt.bbs.lists
Postings of regional BBS listings

alt.bbs.majorbbs
The MajorBBS by Galacticomm, Inc.

alt.bbs.metal
The Metal Telecommunications Environment

alt.bbs.pcboard
Technical support for the PCBoard BBS

alt.bbs.pcbuucp
The commerical PCBoard gateway, PCB-UUCP

alt.bbs.renegade
The James Dean of BBSs

alt.bbs.unixbbs
UnixBBS, from Nervous XTC

alt.bbs.watergate
The WaterGate mail processor

alt.bbs.wildcat
WILDCAT! BBS from Mustang Software, Inc.

alt.beadworld
We must appease the Bead Gods

alt.beer
Good for what ales ya

alt.best.of.internet
It was a time of sorrow, it was a time of joy

alt.bigfoot
Dr Scholl's gone native

alt.binaries.clip-art
Distribution of DOS, Mac, and UNIX clip art

alt.binaries.doom
Binaries for or of the DOOM PC game

alt.binaries.misc
Random large files without a more appropriate group

alt.binaries.multimedia
Sound, text, and graphics data rolled in one

alt.binaries.pictures.*
Digitized pictures, in many topic oriented groups, incluking cartoons, animals, fine art, and erotica

alt.binaries.pictures.utilities
Posting of pictures-related utilities

alt.binaries.sounds.*
Digitized audio of various sorts in various formats

alt.binaries.sounds.utilities
Sound utilities

alt.birthright
Birthright Party propaganda

alt.bitch.pork
Flames in a particular vein

alt.bitterness
No matter what it's for, you know how it'll turn out

alt.bonehead.tom-servo
Paying homage to the Mad Newgrouper

alt.bonsai
Little trees and battle screams

alt.books.anne-rice
The Vampire Thermostat

alt.books.deryni
Katherine Kurtz's books, especially the Deryni series

alt.books.isaac-asimov
Fans of the late SF/science author Isaac Asimov

alt.books.m-lackey
Author Mercedes Lackey and her books

alt.books.reviews
"If you want to know how it turns out, read it!"

alt.books.stephen-king
The works of horror writer Stephen King

alt.books.technical
Discussion of technical books

alt.boomerang
The angular throwing club, not the Eddie Murphy flick

alt.brother-jed
The born-again minister touring U.S. campuses

alt.buddha.short.fat.guy
Religion. And not religion. Both. Neither.

alt.business.import-export
Business aspects of international trade

alt.business.misc
All aspects of commerce

alt.business.multi-level
Multilevel (network) marketing businesses

alt.cad
Computer-aided design

alt.cad.autocad
CAD as practiced by customers of Autodesk

alt.california
The state and the state of mind

alt.callahans
Callahan's bar for puns and fellowship

alt.captain.sarcastic
For the captain's minions

alt.cars.Ford-Probe
"PROBE ME"–actual Viriginia woman's license plate

alt.cascade
Art or litter you decide

alt.caving
Spelunk

alt.cd-rom
Discussions of optical-storage media

alt.cd-rom.reviews
Reviews of various published things available on CD-ROM

alt.celebrities
Famous people and their sycophants

alt.cellular-phone-tech
Brilliant telephony mind blows netnews naming

alt.censorship
Discussion about restricting speech/press

alt.cereal
Breakfast cereals and their (m)ilk

alt.cesium
College Educated Students in Universal Mainland

alt.child-support
Raising children in a split family

alt.chinchilla
The nature of chinchilla farming in America today

alt.chinese.computing
Discussion group for Chinese computing

alt.chinese.text
Postings in Chinese; Chinese language software

alt.chinese.text.big5
Posting in Chinese[BIG 5]

alt.christnet
Gathering place for Christian ministers and users

alt.christnet.bible
Bible discussion and research

alt.christnet.evangelical
Some aspect of evangelism

alt.christnet.hypocrisy
"Vengeance is mine!" sayeth jfurr

alt.christnet.philosophy
Philosophical implications of Christianity

alt.christnet.second-coming.real-soon-now
It could happen

alt.christnet.theology
The distinctives of God of Christian theology

alt.clearing.technology
Traumatic Incident Reduction and Clearing

alt.clothing.lingerie
The special secrets under wraps

alt.clothing.sneakers
Sports, casual, collection, or just one pair

alt.co-ops
Discussion about co-operatives

alt.cobol
Relationship between programming and stone axes

alt.coffee
Another group worshipping caffeine

alt.collecting.autographs
WOW! You got Pete Rose's? What about Kibo's?

alt.college.college-bowl
Discussions of the College Bowl competition

alt.college.food
Dining halls, cafeterias, mystery meat, and more

alt.college.fraternities
College and university fraternities

alt.college.sororities
College and university sororities

alt.college.tunnels
Tunnelling beneath the campuses

alt.college.us
Is that "us" as in "U.S." or do you just mean y'all?

alt.comedy.british
Discussion of British comedy in a variety of media

alt.comedy.british.blackadder
The Black Adder programme

alt.comedy.firesgn-thtre
Firesign Theatre in all its flaming glory

alt.comedy.slapstick.3-stooges
Hey, Mo!

alt.comedy.standup
Discussion of stand-up comedy and comedians

alt.comics.alternative
You could try a book without pictures, for example

alt.comics.batman
Marketing mania

alt.comics.elfquest
W & R Pini's ElfQuest series

alt.comics.lnb
Interactive net.madness in the superhero genre

alt.comics.superman
No one knows it is also *alt.clarkkent*

alt.comp.acad-freedom.news
Academic freedom issues related to computers[†]

alt.comp.acad-freedom.talk
Academic freedom issues related to computers

alt.comp.compression
Like *comp.compression*, only different

alt.comp.databases.xbase.clipper
The Clipper database language

alt.comp.fsp
A file transport protocol

alt.comp.hardware.homebuilt
Designing devious devices in the den

alt.computer.consultants
The business of consulting about computers

alt.config
Alternative subnet discussions and connectivity

alt.consciousness
Discussions on the study of the human consciousness

alt.consciousness.mysticism
The quest for ultimate reality

alt.consciousness.near-death-exp
Discussion of the near-death experience

alt.conspiracy
Be paranoid—they're out to get you

alt.conspiracy.jfk
The Kennedy assassination

alt.consumers.free-stuff
Free offers and how to take advantage of them

alt.cosuard
Sysops against rate discrimination

alt.coupons
/koo pahns/, not /kew pahns/ Try it

alt.cows.moo.moo.moo
Like cows would cluck or something

alt.creative-cook
Like *rec.food.cooking*, only different

alt.creative-cooking
Like *rec.food.cooking*, only different

alt.cuddle
What cows do with their food; should be alt.cows.cuddle

alt.cult-movies
Movies with a cult following

alt.cult-movies.evil-deads
The Evil Dead movie series

alt.cult-movies.rocky-horror
Virgin! Virgin! Virgin! Virgin!

alt.culture.alaska
Is this where the ice weasels come from?

alt.culture.austrian
You'll find more Austrians in *soc.culture.austria*

alt.culture.hawaii
Ua Mau Ke Ea O Ka 'Aina I Ka Pono

alt.culture.indonesia
Indonesian culture, news, etc

alt.culture.internet
The culture(s) of the Internet

alt.culture.karnataka
Culture and language of the Indian state of Karnataka

alt.culture.kerala
People of Keralite origin and the Malayalam language

alt.culture.ny-upstate
New York State, above Westchester

alt.culture.oregon
Discussion about the state of Oregon

alt.culture.tuva
Topics related to the Republic of Tuva, South Siberia

alt.culture.us.1970s
At least pick a good decade to be stuck in the past

alt.culture.us.asian-indian
Asian Indians in the U.S. and Canada

alt.culture.us.southwest
Basking in the sun of the U.S.'s lower left

alt.culture.usenet
A self-referential oxymoron

alt.culture.zippies
Zippie Culture

*alt.current-events.**
Topics oriented for discussing, well, whatever's current

alt.cyberpunk
High-tech low-life

alt.cyberpunk.chatsubo
Literary virtual reality in a cyberpunk hangout

alt.cyberpunk.chatsubo.d
Meta-discussion about Chatsubo stories

alt.cyberpunk.movement
A little laxative might help

alt.cyberpunk.tech
Cyberspace and cyberpunk technology

alt.cyberspace
Cyberspace and how it should work

alt.dads-rights
Rights of fathers[†]

alt.dcom.telecom
Discussion of telecommunications technology

alt.dear.whitehouse
When Hints from Heloise aren't enough

alt.decathena
Digital's DECathena product[†]

alt.desert-storm
Continuing proof that *alt* groups never die

alt.destroy.the.earth
Please leave the light on when you leave

alt.dev.null
The ultimate in moderated newsgroups[†]

alt.devilbunnies
Probably better left undescribed

alt.discordia
All hail Eris, etc

alt.discrimination
Quotas, affirmative action, bigotry, persecution

alt.divination
Divination techniques (e.g., I Ching, Tarot, runes)

alt.dragons-inn
Breathing fire tends to make one very thirsty

alt.dreams
What do they mean?

alt.dreams.lucid
What do they *really* mean?

alt.drinks.kool-aid
Beverage break on the Information
Superhighway

alt.drugs
Recreational pharmaceuticals and related
flames

alt.drugs.caffeine
All about the world's most-used
stimulant drug

alt.drugs.chemistry
Discussion of drug chemistry and
synthesis

alt.drugs.culture
Entertainment while under the influence

alt.drugs.pot
Cannabis conversations

alt.drumcorps
Like *rec.arts.marching.drumcorps*, only
different

alt.drunken.bastards
Peeing in the potted plants

alt.duck.quack.quack.quack
It looks like a duck, but it's an *alt* group

alt.dumpster
Oscar has always wanted a roomier
place

alt.education.disabled
Education for people with physical/
mental disabilities

alt.education.distance
Learning from teachers who are far away

alt.education.email-project
The Email project for teaching English

alt.education.research
Studying about studying

alt.elvis.king
Fat and dead, too. Pretty useless king

alt.emusic
Ethnic, exotic, electronic, elaborate, etc,
music

alt.energy.renewable
Fueling ourselves without depleting
everything

alt.engr.explosives
BOOM

alt.evil
Tales from the dark side

alt.exotic-music
Exotic music discussions

alt.fairs.renaissance
Discussions of Renaissance Faires and
Festivals

alt.fan.actors
Discussion of actors and actresses

alt.fan.*
Many groups for fans of many authors,
actors, and musicians

alt.fandom.cons
Announcements of conventions (SciFi
and others)

alt.fashion
All facets of the fashion industry
discussed

alt.fax
Like *comp.dcom.fax*, only different

alt.feminism
Like *soc.feminism*, only different

alt.feminism.individualism
Discussions about feminism and
individualism

alt.fishing
Like *rec.outdoors.fishing*, only different

alt.flame
Alternative, literate, pithy, succinct
screaming

alt.flame.roommate
Putting the pig on a spit

alt.flame.spelling
USENET's favourite fallacious argoomint

alt.folklore.college
Collegiate humor

alt.folklore.computers
Stories and anecdotes about computers
(some true!)

alt.folklore.ghost-stories
Boo!

alt.folklore.herbs
Discussion of aspects
of herbs and
their uses

alt.folklore.info
Current urban legends and other folklore[†]

alt.folklore.military
Military-oriented urban legends and folklore

alt.folklore.science
The folklore of science, not the science of folklore

alt.folklore.suburban
Serious discussion of urban legends[†]

alt.folklore.urban
Urban legends, ala Jan Harold Brunvand

alt.food.cocacola
An American Classic. Buy our nostalgic art.

alt.food.coffee
Black gold of another sort. Colombian tea

alt.food.fat-free
Quest for thinness

alt.food.ice-cream
I scream, you scream, we all scream for ice cream

alt.food.mcdonalds
Carl Sagan's favorite burger place

alt.food.sushi
The ancient art of preparing raw fish

alt.food.waffle-house
Not just for breakfast anymore

alt.food.wine
All about wine, for oeneophiles

alt.fractal-design.painter
Fractal Design's "Natural Media" painting

alt.fraternity.sorority
Discussions of fraternity/sorority life and issues

alt.freaks
Rick James, we love you!

alt.freemasonry
Someone will build my basement for free? Cool

alt.galactic-guide
Hitch Hiker's Guide to the Known Galaxy Project

alt.gambling
Like recgambling, only different

alt.games.*
Many groups for discussing various games, mostly computer or video games

alt.gathering.rainbow
For discussing the annual Rainbow Gathering

alt.geek
To fulfill an observed need

alt.genealogy
Like *soc.roots*, only different

alt.good.morning
Would you like coffee with that?

alt.good.news
A place for some news that's good news

alt.gopher
Discussion of the Gopher information service

alt.gothic
The gothic movement: things mournful and dark

alt.gourmand
Recipes and cooking info[†]

alt.grad-student.tenured
Professional students

alt.graffiti
The writing is on the wall

alt.graphics.pixutils
Discussion of pixmap utilities

alt.great-lakes
Discussions of the Great Lakes and adjacent places

alt.guitar
You axed for it, you got it

alt.guitar.bass
Bass guitars

alt.guitar.tab
Discussions about guitar tablature music

alt.hackers
Descriptions of projects currently under development[†]

alt.health.cfids-action
Chronic Fatigue Snydrome Action Group[†]

alt.hemp
It's about knot-tying with rope Knot!

alt.hindu
The Hindu religion[†]

alt.history.living
A forum for discussing the hobby of living history

alt.history.what-if
What would the net have been like without this group?

alt.home.repair
Bob Vila would love this group

alt.homosexual
Same as *alt.sex.homosexual*

alt.horror
The horror genre

alt.horror.cthulhu
Campus Crusade for Cthulhu, Ctulhu, Ctulu, and the rest

alt.horror.shub-internet
The process with a thousand young

alt.horror.werewolves
They were wolves, now they're something to be wary of

alt.hotrod
High speed automobiles[†]

alt.humor.best-of-usenet
What the moderator thinks is funniest[†]

alt.humor.best-of-usenet.d
Discussion of *alt.humor.best-of-usenet* posts

alt.humor.puns
Not here

alt.hypertext
Discussion of hypertext: uses, transport, etc.

alt.hypnosis
When you awaken, you will forget about this newsgroup

alt.illuminati
See *alt.cabal.fnord*

alt.image.medical
Medical image exchange discussions

alt.impeach.clinton
Some think he performs as though he is impeared

alt.india.progressive
Progressive politics in the Indian sub-continent[†]

alt.individualism
Philosophies where individual rights are paramount

alt.industrial
The Industrial Computing Society claimed this name

alt.infertility
Discussion of infertility causes and treatments

alt.internet.access.wanted
"Oh OK, how about just an MX ecord for now?"

alt.internet.media-coverage
To discuss the coverage of the Internet by the media

alt.internet.services
Not available in the UUCP world, even via email

alt.internet.talk-radio
Carl Malamud's Internet Talk Radio program

alt.irc
Internet Relay Chat material

alt.irc.announce
Announcements about Internet Relay Chat (IRC)[†]

alt.irc.hottub
Discussion of the IRC channel #hottub

alt.irc.jeopardy
For discussion of the IRC channel #jeopardy

alt.irc.questions
How-to questions for IRC (International Relay Chat)

alt.is.doomed
If it's a sewer, let's treat it like one![†]

alt.japanese.text
Postings in Japanese; Japanese language software

alt.journalism
Shop talk by journalists and journalism students

alt.journalism.criticism
I write, therefore I'm biased

alt.journalism.gonzo
Hunter S. Thomspon's approach to reporting

alt.kalbo
Bald guys of the world, unite!

alt.ketchup
Whak* Whak* shake Whak* Damn, all over my tie

alt.kids-talk
A place for the pre-college set on the net

alt.kill.the.whales
And fulfill the prophecy of Star Trek IV!

alt.lang.asm
Assembly languages of various flavors

alt.lang.basic
The Language That Would Not Die

alt.lang.ca-realizer
Discussion of the GUI programming environment

alt.language.urdu.poetry
Poetry in the Indic Urdu language

alt.law-enforcement
No, ossifer, there's nothing illegal going on in alt

alt.lefthanders
How gauche

alt.lemmings
Rodents with a death wish

alt.locksmithing
You locked your keys in *where*?

alt.lucid-emacs.bug
Bug reports about Lucid Emacs

alt.lucid-emacs.help
QandA and general discussion of Lucid Emacs

alt.lycra
The WunderFabrik

alt.mag.playboy
Four decades of appreciation or degradation. Your pick.

alt.magic
For discussion about stage magic

alt.magick
For discussion about supernatural arts

alt.magick.chaos
Do not meddle in the affairs of wizards

alt.magick.ethics
Discussion of the ethics/morals of magickal work

alt.magick.order
Discussion of magickopolitical hierarchy

alt.magick.sex
Pursuing spirituality through sexuality and vice versa

alt.magick.tyagi
Magick as revealed by Mordred Nagasiva

alt.make.money.fast
And piss off thousands of people even faster

alt.manga
Like *rec.arts.manga*, only different

alt.math.iams
Internet Amateur Mathematics Society[†]

alt.mcdonalds
Can I get fries with that?

alt.med.allergy
Helping people with allergies

alt.med.cfs
Chronic fatigue syndrome information

alt.med.fibromyalgia
Fibromyalgia Fibrositis List

alt.meditation
General discussion of meditation

alt.meditation.quanyin
The Quan Yin method of meditation

alt.meditation.transcendental
Contemplation of states beyond the teeth

alt.mensa.steiner.whiner.whiner.whiner
Steiner makes some friends

alt.messianic
Messianic traditions

alt.military.cadet
Preparing for the coming apocalypse

alt.mindcontrol
Are you sure those thoughts are really your own?

alt.misanthropy
People who hate people

alt.missing-kids
Locating missing children

alt.motd
The messages of the day

alt.motherjones
Mother Jones magazine

alt.motorcycles.harley
Like *rec.motorcycles.harley*, only different

alt.movies.monster
Godzilla! The Wolfman! The Thing!
Aiiieee!!

alt.msdos.programmer
For the serious MS-DOS programmer
(no forsale ads)

alt.mud
Like *rec.games.mud*, only different

alt.music.*
Groups for discussing (musical) groups

alt.my.head.hurts
So don't do that

alt.mythology
Zeus rules

alt.mythology.mythic-animals
Creatures of myth, fantasy, and
imagination

alt.native
People indigenous to an area before
modern colonization

alt.necromicon
Big time death wish

alt.newbie
The altnet housewarming committee

alt.newbies
Housewarming for a group

alt.newgroup.for.fun.fun.fun
Yes, we delight in your games

alt.news-media
Don't believe the hype

alt.news.macedonia
News concerning Macedonia in the
Balkan Region

alt.noise
Ow, quit it

alt.non.sequitur
Richard Nixon

alt.nuke.the.USA
Last one out is a radioactive egg

alt.online-service
Large commercial online services and
the Internet

alt.online-service.america-online
Or should that be "America Offline?"

alt.online-service.compuserve
Discussions and questions about
Compuserve

alt.online-service.delphi
Run! It's the Delphoids!

alt.online-service.freenet
Public FreeNet systems

alt.online-service.genie
Discussions and questions about GEnie

alt.online-service.prodigy
The Sears Prodigy system

alt.org.earth-first
Discussion of the Earth First! society

alt.org.toastmasters
Public speaking and Toastmasters
International

alt.os.multics
30 years old and going strong

alt.out-of-body
Out of Body Experiences

alt.pagan
Discussions about paganism and religion

alt.paranet.abduct
"They replaced Jim-Bob with a look-
alike!"

alt.paranet.metaphysics
Philosphical ontology, cosmology, and
cosmetology

alt.paranet.paranormal
"If it exists, how can supernatural be
beyond natural?"

alt.paranet.psi
"How much pressure can you generate
with your brain?"

alt.paranet.science
"Maybe if we dissect the psychic "

alt.paranet.skeptic
"I don't believe they turned you into a
newt"

alt.paranet.ufo
"Heck, I guess naming it "UFO"
identifies it"

alt.paranormal
Phenomena not scientifically explicable

alt.paranormal.channeling
Spiritual mediumship,
channeling, and
channelers

alt.parents-teens
Parent-teenager relationships

alt.party
Parties, celebration, and general debauchery

alt.pave.the.earth
Damn the environmentalists, full speed ahead!

alt.peace-corps
The works of the Peace Corps

alt.peeves
Discussion of peeves and related

alt.periphs.pcmcia
Credit card sized plug in peripherals (PCMCIA, JEDIA)

alt.personals.*
Do you really want to meet someone this way?

alt.pets.rabbits
Coneys abound See also *alt.fan.john-palmer*

alt.philosophy.jarf
The Jarf philosphy/metaphysics/ religion/ culture

alt.philosophy.objectivism
A product of the Ayn Rand corporation

alt.philosophy.zen
Meditating on how the *alt** namespace works

alt.pinecone
The heart of camp arts and crafts

alt.planning.urban
Urban development

alt.politics.british
Politics and a real Queen, too

alt.politics.clinton
Discussing Slick Willie and Co

alt.politics.correct
A Neil Bush fan club

alt.politics.datahighway
Electronic interstate infrastructure

alt.politics.ec
The European economic community

alt.politics.economics
War = Poverty, and other discussions

alt.politics.elections
All about the process of electing leaders

alt.politics.europe.misc
The general political situation in Europe

alt.politics.greens
Green party politics and activities worldwide

alt.politics.homosexuality
As the name implies

alt.politics.libertarian
The libertarian ideology

alt.politics.org.batf
Politics of the U.S. firearms (etc) regulation agency

alt.politics.org.cia
The United States Centrial Intelligence Agency

alt.politics.org.misc
Political organizations

alt.politics.org.nsa
The ultrasecret security arm of the US government

alt.politics.perot
Discussion of the non-candidate

alt.politics.radical-left
Who remains after the radicals left?

alt.politics.reform
Political reform

alt.politics.sex
Not a good idea to mix them, sez Marilyn and Profumo

alt.politics.socialism.trotsky
Trotskyite socialism discussions

alt.politics.usa.constitution
U.S. Constitutional politics

alt.politics.usa.misc
Miscellaneous U.S. politics

alt.politics.usa.republican
Discussions of the U.S. Republican Party

alt.polyamory
For those who maintain multiple love relationships

alt.postmodern
Postmodernism, semiotics, deconstruction, and the like

alt.president.clinton
Will the CIA undermine his efforts?

alt.prisons
Can I get an *alt** feed in the slammer?

alt.privacy
Privacy issues in cyberspace

alt.privacy.clipper
The U.S. administration's Clipper encryption plan

alt.prophecies.nostradamus
Mystic verse

alt.prose
Postings of original writings, fictional and otherwise

alt.psychoactives
Better living through chemistry

alt.psychology.help
An alt.support group away from home

alt.psychology.personality
Personality taxonomy, such as Myers-Briggs

alt.psychotic.roommates
Single white female seeks roommate

alt.pub-ban.homolka
About the publication ban on the Karla Homolka trial

alt.pub.coffeehouse.amethyst
Realistic place to meet and chat with friends

alt.pub.dragons-inn
Fantasy virtual reality pub similar to *alt.callahans*

alt.pud
"Discussion of the TFiLE PuD!@#@#!@$!" Whatever

alt.punk
Burning them keeps insects away

alt.punk.straight-edge
Shaving eyebrows for fun and profit

alt.quotations
Quotations, quips, sig lines, witticisms, et al

alt.radio.networks.npr
US National Public Radio: shows, stories, hosts, etc

alt.radio.pirate
Hide the gear, here comes the magic station-wagons

alt.radio.scanner
Like *rec.radio.scanner*, only different

alt.radio.uk
Radio in the United Kingdom

alt.rap
For fans of rap music

alt.rap-gdead
Fans of The Grateful Dead and Rap

alt.rave
Techno-culture: music, dancing, drugs, dancing, etc

alt.rec.camping
Like *rec.back.country*, only different

alt.recovery
For people in recovery programs (e.g., AA, ACA, GA)

alt.recovery.addiction.sexual
Recovering sex addicts

alt.recovery.catholicism
Getting over a Roman Catholic upbringing

alt.recovery.codependency
Mutually destructive relationships

alt.recovery.religion
The twelve steps from the Ten Commandments

alt.religion.all-worlds
Grokking the Church of All Worlds from Heinlein's book

alt.religion.amiga
Rumours of Commodore's death are greatly exaggerated

alt.religion.buddhism.tibetan
The teachings of Buddha as studied in Tibet

alt.religion.christian
Unmoderated forum for discussing Christianity

alt.religion.computers
Tiresome technical tirades

alt.religion.eckankar
Eckankar, the religion of the Light and Sound of God

alt.religion.emacs
Emacs. Umacs. We all macs.

alt.religion.gnostic
History and philosophies of the Gnostic sects

alt.religion.islam
Discussion of Islamic Faith and
SocReligionIslam

alt.religion.kibology
He's Fred, Jim

alt.religion.monica
Discussion about net-venus Monica and
her works

alt.religion.mormon
Mormon religion

alt.religion.scientology
L Ron Hubbard's Church of Scientology

alt.religion.sexuality
The politics of sexuality and religion

alt.religion.zoroastrianism
Zoraster's/Zarathustra's religion,
mazdaism

alt.revenge
Two wrongs trying to make a right

alt.revisionism
"It CAN'T be that way 'cause here's the
FACTS"

alt.revolution.counter
Discussions of counter-revolutionary
issues

alt.rhode_island
A little state with apparently worldwide
interest

alt.rock-n-roll*
More groups about groups

alt.romance
Discussion about the romantic side of
love

alt.romance.chat
Talk about no sex

alt.romance.unhappy
alt.angst on the run

alt.rush-limbaugh
Fans of the conservative activist radio
announcer

alt.rv
Rotten varmints or recreational vehicles,
you decide

alt.satanism
Not such a bad dude once you get to
know him

alt.satellite.tv.europe
All about European satellite TV

alt.save.the.earth
Environmentalist causes

alt.sb.programmer
Programming the Sound Blaster PC
sound card

alt.school.homework-help
Looking for assistance with schoolwork

alt.sci.physics.new-theories
Scientific theories you won't find in
journals

alt.sci.planetary
Studies in planetary science

alt.sci.sociology
People are really interesting when you
watch them

alt.sci.tech.indonesian
Science and technology in Indonesia

alt.scooter
Motor scooters, like Vespas, Lambrettas,
etc

alt.security
Security issues on computer systems

alt.security.index
Pointers to good stuff in *alt.security*[†]

alt.security.pgp
The Pretty Good Privacy package

alt.sega.genesis
Another addiction

alt.self-improve
Self-improvement in less than 14
characters

alt.sewing
A group that is not as it seams

alt.sex.*
Postings of a prurient nature

alt.sexual.abuse.recovery
Helping others deal with traumatic
experiences

alt.shared-reality.startrek.klingon
Klingons: Blood, Honor, and Tribbles

alt.shenanigans
Practical jokes, pranks, randomness, etc

alt.showbiz.gossip
A misguided attempt to centralize gossip

alt.shut.the.hell.up.geek
Group for USENET motto

alt.silly.group.names.d
Eponymy

alt.skate
Like *rec.skate*, only different

alt.skate-board
Discussion of all aspects of skateboarding

alt.skinheads
The skinhead culture/anti-culture

alt.sl9
Crashing into Jupiter

alt.slack
Posting relating to the Church of the Subgenius

alt.smokers
Puffing on tobacco

alt.smokers.cigars
From stogies to cubans

alt.smokers.pipes
Briars, meerschaums, and calabashes

alt.snail-mail
Mail sent on paper. Some people still do that.

alt.snowmobiles
For bikers who don't like two wheels in snow and ice

alt.society.anarchy
Societies without rulers

alt.society.ati
The *Activist Times Digest*†

alt.society.civil-liberties
Same as *alt.society.civil-liberty*

alt.society.civil-liberty
Same as *alt.society.civil-liberties*

alt.society.conservatism
Social, cultural, and political conservatism

alt.society.futures
Musing on where we're all headed

alt.society.generation-x
Lifestyles of those born 1960-early-1970s

alt.society.neutopia
A place to further the cause of peace and love

alt.society.paradigms
Social and cultural patterns

alt.society.underwear
What's the big deal, anyway?

alt.soft-sys.corel.draw
The CorelDraw graphics package

alt.soulmates
Richard Bach and his Herculean odds

alt.sources
Alternative source code, unmoderated. Caveat emptor.

alt.sources.amiga
Source code for the Amiga

alt.sources.d
Discussion of posted sources

alt.sources.index
Pointers to source code in *alt.sources**†

alt.sources.mac
Source code for Apple Macintosh computers

alt.sources.wanted
Requests for source code

alt.spam
What is that stuff that doth jiggle in the breeze?

alt.sport.bowling
In the gutter again

alt.sport.darts
Look what you've done to the wall!

alt.sport.foosball
Table soccer and dizzy little men

alt.sport.jet-ski
Discussion of personal watercraft

alt.sport.lasertag
Indoor splatball with infrared lasers

alt.sport.paintball
Splat, you're it

alt.sport.pool
Knock your balls into your pockets for fun

alt.sport.racquetball
All aspects of indoor racquetball and related sports

alt.sport.squash
With the proper technique, vegetables can go very fast

alt.sports.baseball.*
A group for most every team

alt.sports.basketball.*

alt.sports.football.*

alt.sports.hockey.nhl.*

alt.sports.hockey.nhl.*

alt.sports.college.ivy-league
Ivy League athletics

alt.sports.football.pro.wash-redskins
Washington Redskins football talk

alt.sports.hockey.rhi
Some hockey league, maybe

alt.sports.oj-simpson
His time has passed, but some still want to discuss it

alt.stagecraft
Technical theatre issues

alt.starfleet.rpg
Starfleet role-playing stories

alt.startrek.creative
Stories and parodies related to Star Trek

alt.startrek.klingon
AcK! What is that thing on your head?!

alt.stop.spamming
Trying to prevent net abuse

alt.stupidity
Discussion about stupid newsgroups

alt.suicide.holiday
Talk of why suicides increase at holidays

alt.super.nes
Like *rec.games.video.nintendo*, only different

alt.supermodels
Discussing famous and beautiful models

alt.supermodels.cindy-crawford
House of Style's overexposed host

alt.support
Dealing with emotional situations and experiences

alt.support.abuse-partners
People with people who were abused

alt.support.anxiety-panic
Support for people who have panic attacks

alt.support.arthritis
Helping people with stiff joints

alt.support.asthma
Dealing with labored breathing

alt.support.attn-deficit
Attention Deficit Disorder

alt.support.big-folks
Sizeism can be as awful as sexism or racism

alt.support.cancer
Emotional aid for people with cancer

alt.support.cerebral-palsy
Cerebral Palsy support

alt.support.crohns-colitis
Support for sufferers of ulcerative colitis

alt.support.depression
Depression and mood disorders

alt.support.diet
Seeking enlightenment through weight loss

alt.support.divorce
Discussion of marital breakups

alt.support.eating-disord
People over the edge about weight loss

alt.support.epilepsy
Epilepsy support

alt.support.loneliness
It's not easy being green

alt.support.mult-sclerosis
Living with multiple sclerosis

alt.support.non-smokers
Discussing issues relating to second-hand smoke

alt.support.obesity
Support/resources to treat obesity[†]

alt.support.shyness
Um, er, <blush>, well, maybe I will post, after all

alt.support.stop-smoking
Getting over the nicotine addiction

alt.support.stuttering
Support for people who stutter

alt.support.tall
Issues of interest to tall people

alt.support.tinnitus
Coping with ringing ears and other head noises

alt.surfing
Riding the ocean waves

alt.surrealism
Surrealist ideologies and their influences

alt.sustainable.agriculture
Such as the Mekong Delta before Agent Orange

alt.swedish.chef.bork.bork.bork
The beginning of the end

alt.sys.amiga.demos
Code and talk to show off the Amiga

alt.sys.amiga.uucp
AmigaUUCP

alt.sys.intergraph
Support for Intergraph machines

alt.sys.pc-clone.gateway2000
A PC clone vendor

alt.sys.pc-clone.zeos
Zeos computer systems

alt.sys.perq
PERQ graphics workstations

alt.sys.sun
Technical discussion of Sun Microsystems products

alt.taiwan.republic
Like *soc.culture.taiwan*, only different

alt.tarot
Your destiny is in the cards

alt.tasteless
Truly disgusting

alt.tasteless.jokes
Sometimes insulting rather than disgusting or humorous

alt.test
Alternative subnetwork testing

alt.test.my.new.group
Thank you for sharing

alt.test.test
Like we really needed another

alt.thinking.hurts
So don't do that

alt.thrash
Thrashlife

alt.timewasters
A pretty good summary of making the list of *alt* groups

alt.toolkits.xview
The X Window System XView toolkit

alt.toys.hi-tech
Optimus Prime is my hero

alt.toys.transformers
From robots to vehicles and back again

alt.transgendered
Boys will be girls and vice-versa

alt.travel.road-trip
Ever go to Montreal for pizza–from Albany?

alt.true-crime
Criminal acts around the world

alt.tv.animaniacs
Steven Spielberg's Animaniacs!

alt.unix.wizards.free
Like *comp.unix.wizards*, only unmoderated

alt.usage.english
English grammar, word usages, and related topics

alt.usage.german
Questions and answers about the German language

alt.usenet.kooks
I have a theory about why we have such crazy theories

alt.usenet.offline-reader
Getting your fix offline

alt.uu.comp.os.linux.questions
USENET University helps with LINUX

alt.uu.future
Does USENET University have a viable future?

alt.uu.lang.russian.misc
Learning Russian at the USENET University

alt.vampyres
Discussion of vampires and related writings, films, etc.

alt.video.laserdisc
LD players and selections available for them

alt.visa.us
Discussion/information on visas pertaining to U.S.

alt.war
Not just collateral damage

alt.war.civil.usa
Discussion of the U.S. Civil War (1861-1865)

alt.war.vietnam
Discussion of all aspects of the Vietnam War

alt.wedding
Til death or our lawyers do us part

alt.winsock
Windows Sockets

alt.wired
Wired magazine

alt.wolves
Discussing wolves and wolf-mix dogs

alt.women.attitudes
The different attitudes that women have

alt.zen
It is

alt.zima
A clear malt beverage, better with lime

alt.zines
Small magazines, mostly noncommercial

Bionet

There is a newsgroup hierarchy for topics interesting to biologists called *bionet* originating from *net.bio.net* and currently carried at over a third of the sites participating in the Arbitron readership survey. Contact *biosci-help@net.bio.net* for more details.

bionet.agroforestry
Discussion of agroforestry

bionet.announce
Announcements of widespread interest to biologists[†]

bionet.biology.computational
Computer and mathematical applications[†]

bionet.biology.grasses
Discussion of the biology of grasses: cereal, forage, turf, etc.

bionet.biology.n2-fixation
Research issues on biological nitrogen fixation

bionet.biology.tropical
Discussions about tropical biology

bionet.biophysics
The science and profession of biophysics

bionet.celegans
Research discussion of the model organism Caenorhabditis elegans

bionet.cellbiol
Disucssions about cell biology

bionet.cellbiol.cytonet
The cytoskeleton, plasma membrane, and cell wall

bionet.chlamydomonas
Discussions about the green alga chlamydomonas

bionet.drosophila
Discussions about the biology of fruit flies

bionet.general
General BIOSCI discussion

bionet.genome.arabidopsis
Information about the Arabidopsis project

bionet.genome.chromosomes
Mapping and sequencing of eucaryote chromosomes

bionet.immunology
Discussions about research in immunology

bionet.info-theory
Discussions about biological information theory

bionet.jobs
Scientific Job opportunities

bionet.jobs.wanted
Requests for employment in the biological sciences

bionet.journals.contents
Contents of biology journal publications[†]

bionet.journals.note
Advice on dealing with journals in biology

bionet.metabolic-reg
Kinetics and thermodynamics at the celluar level

bionet.microbiology
Discussion of issues related to the science and profession of microbiology

bionet.molbio.ageing
Discussions of cellular and organismal ageing

bionet.molbio.bio-matrix
Computer applications to biological databases

bionet.molbio.embldatabank
Info about the EMBL nucleic acid database

bionet.molbio.evolution
How genes and proteins have evolved

bionet.molbio.gdb
Messages to and from the GDB database staff

bionet.molbio.genbank
Info about the GenBank nucleic acid database

bionet.molbio.genbank.updates
Hot off the presses![†]

bionet.molbio.gene-linkage
Discussions about genetic linkage analysis

bionet.molbio.genome-program
Discussion of Human Genome Project issues

bionet.molbio.hiv
Discussions about the molecular biology of HIV

bionet.molbio.methds-reagnts
Requests for information and lab reagents

bionet.molbio.proteins
Research on proteins and protein databases

bionet.molbio.rapd
Research on randomly amplified polymorphic DNA

bionet.molbio.yeast
The molecular biology and genetics of yeast

bionet.molec-model
Discussion of the physical and chemical aspects of molecular modelling

bionet.mycology
Discussions about filamentous fungi

bionet.neuroscience
Research issues in the neurosciences

bionet.organisms.urodeles
Discussions among research scientists using urodele amphibians in any biological field

bionet.organisms.zebrafish
Discussions about research using the model organism Zebrafish (Danio rerio)

bionet.parasitology
Research discussions in parasitology

bionet.photosynthesis
Discussions about research on photosynthesis

bionet.plants
Discussion about all aspects of plant biology

bionet.population-bio
Technical discussions about population biology

bionet.prof-society.biophysics
Biophysical Society official announcements[†]

bionet.protista
Discussion on ciliates and other protists

bionet.sci-resources
Information about funding agencies, etc[†]

bionet.software
Information about software for biology

bionet.software.acedb
Discussions by users of genome DBs using ACEDB

bionet.software.gcg
Discussions about using the ACEDB software

bionet.software.sources
Software source relating to biology[†]

bionet.structural-nmr
Exploring the structure of macromolecules using NMR

bionet.users.addresses
Who's who in biology

bionet.virology
Discussions about research in virology

bionet.women-in-bio
Discussions about women in biology
bionet.xtallography
Discussions about protein crystallography

bit

bit is a collection of newsgroups distributed by a collection of sites that choose to carry them. The *bit* newsgroups are redistributions of the more popular BitNet LISTSERV mailing lists. Contact Jim McIntosh *jim@american.edu* for more information.

biz

biz is a distribution of newsgroups carried and propagated by sites interested in the world of business products around them—in particular, computer products and services. This includes announcements of new products, fixes and enhancements, reviews, and postings of demo software.

biz.americast
AmeriCast announcements
biz.americast.samples
Samples of AmeriCast[†]
biz.books.technical
Technical bookstore and publisher advertising and info
biz.clarinet
Announcements about ClariNet

biz.clarinet.sample
Samples of ClariNet newsgroups for the outside world
biz.comp.hardware
Generic commercial hardware postings
biz.comp.mcs
MCSNet[†]
biz.comp.services
Generic commercial service postings
biz.comp.software
Generic commercial software postings
biz.comp.telebit
Support of the Telebit modem
biz.comp.telebit.netblazer
The Telebit Netblazer
biz.config
Biz USENET configuration and administration
biz.dec
DEC equipment and software
biz.dec.decathena
DECathena discussions
biz.dec.decnews
The *DECNews* newsletter[†]
biz.dec.ip
IP networking on DEC machines
biz.digex.announce
Announcements from Digex[†]
biz.digital.announce
DEC news and announcements[†]
biz.digital.articles
DEC newsletter, catalog, and journal[†]
biz.jobs.offered
Position announcements
biz.misc
Miscellaneous postings of a commercial nature
biz.next.newprod
New product announcements for the NeXT
biz.oreilly.announce
New product announcements from O'Reilly & Associates[†]
biz.pagesat
For discussion of the Pagesat Satellite USENET newsfeed

biz.sco.announce
  SCO and related product
  announcements[†]

biz.sco.binaries
  Binary packages for SCO XENIX, UNIX,
  or ODT[†]

biz.sco.general
  Q&A, discussions, and comments on
  SCO products

biz.sco.magazine
  To discuss SCO magazine and its
  contents

biz.sco.opendesktop
  ODT environment and applications tech
  info, Q&A

biz.sco.sources
  Source code ported to an SCO operating
  environment[†]

biz.sco.wserver
  SCO widget server questions, answers,
  and discussion

biz.stolen
  Postings about stolen merchandise

biz.stortek.forum
  Storage Technology Corp.

biz.tadpole.sparcbook
  Discussions on the SPARCbook portable
  computer

biz.test
  biz newsgroup test messages

biz.univel.misc
  Discussions and comments on Univel
  products

biz.zeos.announce
  Zeos product announcements[†]

biz.zeos.general
  Zeos technical support and general
  information

INDEX

About the Author

Mark Harrison has been involved in computer networking since 1980, when he had a college job answering email for Radio Shack's computer service department. He has worked in several areas of computing, including multilingual human interfaces and compiler design, and now works in the telecommunications industry as a senior architect for Advanced Intelligent Network (AIN) products at DSC Communications Corporation. He lives in Richardson, Texas, with his wife and two children, both of whom have USENET accounts. His interests include juggling, playing classical music, and collecting rare books.

Colophon

Our look is the result of reader comments, our own experimentation, and feedback from distribution channels. Distinctive covers complement our distinctive approach to technical topics, breathing personality and life into potentially dry subjects.

The image on the cover of *The USENET Handbook* is adapted from the 1973 Dover Publications translation of *The Book of Trades (Ständebuch)*, by Hans Sachs and Jost Amman. The *Ständebuch* was originally published in Nuremberg in 1568 with the full title of *Eygentliche Beschreibung Aller Stände auff Erden (Exact Description of All Ranks on Earth)*.

Hans Sachs, the author of the verses in the Standebuch, was a shoemaker by trade, but he wrote over 6000 songs, poems, and plays. His verses were slightly preachy, and were intended to give gentle moral instruction. Sachs is the central figure in Richard Wagner's 1867 opera, *Meistersinger von Nürnberg*.

Sachs intended the *Ständebuch* to praise work in trades and crafts of all kinds, and to warn against idleness. The woodcut designs of Jost Amman were instrumental in creating a new genre of craft art. Art of this genre depicts craftspeople and workers both as the aesthetic subject and as an instructional element.

The woodcut adapted for this cover portrays four singers in performance. Sachs' verse translates as: "THE SINGERS are performing a four-part work (tenor, discant, alto, bass) with a fine courtly text; their harmony gives joy to the heart; Amphion invented song."

Edie Freedman designed this cover. The cover layout was produced with Photoshop 2.5 using the ITC Garamond font.

The inside layout was designed by Jen Niederst and implemented by Mike Sierra in FrameMaker 4.0 running on the X Window System platform. The text and heading fonts are ITC Garamond Light and Garamond Book Italic. The illustrations that appear in the book are a combination of figures created by Chris Reilley and Hanna Dyer, and wood engravings from the Dover Pictorial Archive and the Ron Yablon Graphic Archives, and were created in Adobe PhotoShop and Aldus Freehand. This colophon was written by Clairemarie Fisher O'Leary.

USING UNIX AND X

Books from O'Reilly & Associates, Inc.

SPRING/SUMMER 1995

Basics

Our UNIX in a Nutshell *guides are the most comprehensive quick reference on the market—a must for every* UNIX *user. No matter what system you use, we've got a version to cover your needs.*

UNIX in a Nutshell: System V Edition

By Daniel Gilly & the staff of O'Reilly & Associates
2nd Edition June 1992
444 pages, ISBN 1-56592-001-5

You may have seen UNIX quick-reference guides, but you've never seen anything like *UNIX in a Nutshell*. Not a scaled-down quick reference of common commands, *UNIX in a Nutshell* is a complete reference containing all commands and options, along with generous descriptions and examples that put the commands in context. For all but the thorniest UNIX problems, this one reference should be all the documentation you need. Covers System V, Releases 3 and 4, and Solaris 2.0.

"This book is the perfect desktop reference.... The authors have presented a clear and concisely written book which would make an excellent addition to any UNIX user's library."
—*SysAdmin*

"Whether you are setting up your first UNIX system or adding your fiftieth user, these books can ease you through learning the fundamentals of the UNIX system."
—Michael J. O'Brien, Hardware Editor,
 ABA/Unix/group Newsletter

SCO UNIX in a Nutshell

By Ellie Cutler & the staff of O'Reilly & Associates
1st Edition February 1994
590 pages, ISBN 1-56592-037-6

The desktop reference to SCO UNIX and Open Desktop®, this version of *UNIX in a Nutshell* shows you what's under the hood of your SCO system. It isn't a scaled-down quick reference of common commands, but a complete reference containing all user, programming, administration, and networking commands.

Contents include:

- All commands and options
- Shell syntax for the Bourne, Korn, C, and SCO shells
- Pattern matching, with *vi, ex, sed*, and *aw*k commands
- Compiler and debugging commands for software development
- Networking with email, TCP/IP, NFS, and UUCP
- System administration commands and the SCO sysadmsh shell

This edition of *UNIX in a Nutshell* is the most comprehensive SCO quick reference on the market, a must for any SCO user. You'll want to keep *SCO UNIX in a Nutshell* close by as you use your computer: it'll become a handy, indispensible reference for working with your SCO system.

Learning the UNIX Operating System

By Grace Todino, John Strang & Jerry Peek
3rd Edition August 1993
108 pages, ISBN 1-56592-060-0

If you are new to UNIX, this concise introduction will tell you just what you need to get started and no more. Why wade through a 600-page book when you can begin working productively in a matter of minutes? It's an ideal primer for Mac and PC users of the Internet who need to know a little bit about UNIX on the systems they visit.

This book is the most effective introduction to UNIX in print. The third edition has been updated and expanded to provide increased coverage of window systems and networking. It's a handy book for someone just starting with UNIX, as well as someone who encounters a UNIX system as a "visitor" via remote login over the Internet.

"Once you've established a connection with the network, there's often a secondary obstacle to surmount.... *Learning the UNIX Operating System* helps you figure out what to do next by presenting in a nutshell the basics of how to deal with the 'U-word.' Obviously a 108-page book isn't going to make you an instant UNIX guru, but it does an excellent job of introducing basic operations in a concise nontechnical way, including how to navigate through the file system, send and receive E-mail and—most importantly—get to the online help...."
—Michael L. Porter, Associate Editor, *Personal Engineering & Instrumentation News*

Learning the vi Editor

By Linda Lamb
5th Edition October 1990
192 pages, ISBN 0-937175-67-6

A complete guide to text editing with *vi*, the editor available on nearly every UNIX system. Early chapters cover the basics; later chapters explain more advanced editing tools, such as *ex* commands and global search and replacement.

"For those who are looking for an introductory book to give to new staff members who have no acquaintance with either screen editing or with UNIX screen editing, this is it: a book on *vi* that is neither designed for the UNIX in-crowd, nor so imbecilic that one is ashamed to use it."
—;login

When You Can't Find Your UNIX System Administrator

By Linda Mui
1st Edition April 1995
156 pages, ISBN 1-56592-104-6

This book is written for UNIX users, who are often cast adrift in a confusing environment. It provides the background and practical solutions you need to solve problems you're likely to encounter—problems with logging in, printing, sharing files, running programs, managing space resources, etc. It also describes the kind of info to gather when you're asking for a diagnosis from a busy sys admin. And, it gives you a list of site-specific information that you should know, as well as a place to write it down.

When You Can't Find Your UNIX System Administrator, part of our new What You Need to Know series, gives you tools for solving problems. The goal of this book is not to make you a guru, but to get you back to the job you'd rather be doing.

Learning the Korn Shell

By Bill Rosenblatt
1st Edition June 1993
363 pages, ISBN 1-56592-054-6

A thorough introduction to the Korn shell, both as a user interface and as a programming language. This book provides a clear explanation of the Korn shell's features, including *ksh* string operations, co-processes, signals and signal handling, and command-line interpretation. *Learning the Korn Shell* also includes real-life programming examples and a Korn shell debugger (*kshdb*).

"Readers still bending back the pages of Korn-shell manuals will find relief in...*Learning the Korn Shell*...a gentle introduction to the shell. Rather than focusing on syntax issues, the book quickly takes on the task of solving day-to-day problems with Korn-shell scripts. Application scripts are also shown and explained in detail. In fact, the book even presents a script debugger written for *ksh*. This is a good book for improving your knowledge of the shell."
—*Unix Review*

MH & xmh: Email for Users & Programmers

By Jerry Peek
3rd Edition April 1995
782 pages, ISBN 1-56592-093-7

There are lots of mail programs in use these days, but MH is one of the most durable and flexible. Best of all, it's available on almost all UNIX systems. It has spawned a number of interfaces that many users prefer. This book covers three popular interfaces: *xmh* (for the X environment), *exmh* (written with tcl/tk), and *mh-e* (for GNU Emacs users).

The book contains; a quick tour through MH, *xmh*, *exmh*, and *mh-e* for new users; configuration and customization information; lots of tips and techniques for programmers—and plenty of practical examples for everyone; information beyond the manual pages, explaining how to make MH do things you never thought an email program could do; and quick reference pages.

In addition, the third edition describes the Multipurpose Internet Mail Extensions (MIME) and how to use it with these mail programs. MIME is an extension that allows users to send graphics, sound, and other multimedia formats through mail between otherwise incompatible systems.

"The MH bible is irrefutably Jerry Peek's *MH & xmh: Email for Users & Programmers*. This book covers just about everything that is known about MH and *xmh* (the X Windows front end to MH), presented in a clear and easy-to-read format. I strongly recommend that anybody serious about MH get a copy."—James Hamilton, *UnixWorld*

Learning GNU Emacs

By Debra Cameron & Bill Rosenblatt
1st Edition October 1991
442 pages, ISBN 0-937175-84-6

An introduction to the GNU Emacs editor, one of the most widely used and powerful editors available under UNIX. Provides a solid introduction to basic editing, a look at several important editing modes (special Emacs features for editing specific types of documents), and a brief introduction to customization and Emacs LISP programming. The book is aimed at new Emacs users, whether or not they are programmers.

"Authors Debra Cameron and Bill Rosenblatt do a particularly admirable job presenting the extensive functionality of GNU Emacs in well-organized, easily digested chapters.... Despite its title, *Learning GNU Emacs* could easily serve as a reference for the experienced Emacs user."
—Linda Branagan, Convex Computer Corporation

The USENET Handbook

By Mark Harrison
1st Edition May 1995 (est.)
250 pages (est.), ISBN 1-56592-101-1

USENET, also called Netnews, is the world's largest discussion forum, encompassing the worldwide Internet and many other sites that aren't formally connected to any network. USENET provides a forum for asking and answering technical questions, arguing politics, religion, and society, or discussing most scientific, artistic, or humanistic disciplines. It's also a forum for distributing free software, as well as digitized pictures and sound.

This book unlocks USENET for you. It's not just a technical book, although it includes tutorials on the most popular newsreaders for UNIX and Windows (*tin*, *nn*, GNUS, and Trumpet). It also explains what goes on on the Net: where to look for information and what to do with it once you get it. And, it gives you an introduction into the culture: Net etiquette, the private language, and some of the history...including some of the more notable practical jokes.

Using UUCP and Usenet

By Grace Todino & Dale Dougherty
1st Edition February 1986
(latest update October 1991)
210 pages, ISBN 0-937175-10-2

Shows users how to communicate with both UNIX and non-UNIX systems using UUCP and *cu* or *tip* and how to read news and post articles. This handbook assumes that UUCP is already running at your site.

"Are you having trouble with UUCP? Have you torn out your hair trying to set the Dialers file? *Managing UUCP and Usenet* and *Using UUCP and Usenet* will give you the information you need to become an accomplished net user. The companion book is *!%@:: A Directory of Electronic Mail Addressing & Networks*, a compendium of world networks and how to address and read them. All of these books are well written, and I urge you to take a look at them." —*Root Journal*

Running Linux

By Matt Welsh & Lar Kaufman
1st Edition February 1995
600 pages, ISBN 1-56592-100-3

Linux is the most exciting development today in the UNIX world—and some would say in the world of the PC-compatible. A complete, UNIX-compatible operating system developed by volunteers on the Internet, Linux is distributed freely in electronic form and for low cost from many vendors. Its software packages include the X Window System (X11R6); TCP/IP networking (including SLIP, PPP, and NFS support); popular software tools such as Emacs and TeX; a complete software development environment including C, C++, Perl, Tcl/Tk, and more; libraries, debuggers, multimedia support, scientific and database applications; and much more.

Running Linux covers topics not addressed in any Linux documentation, including everything you need to understand, install, and use the Linux operating system. This includes a comprehensive installation tutorial, complete information on system maintenance, tools for document development and programming, and guidelines for network administration.

X User Tools

By Linda Mui & Valerie Quercia
1st Edition November 1994
856 pages (CD-ROM included)
ISBN 1-56592-019-8

X User Tools provides for X users what *UNIX Power Tools* provides for UNIX users: hundreds of tips, tricks, scripts, techniques, and programs—plus a CD-ROM—to make the X Window System more enjoyable, more powerful, and easier to use. This browser's book emphasizes useful programs culled from the network, offers tips for configuring individual and systemwide environments, and includes a CD-ROM of source files for all—and binary files for some—of the programs.

Volume 3: X Window System User's Guide

Standard Edition
By Valerie Quercia & Tim O'Reilly
4th Edition May 1993
836 pages, ISBN 1-56592-014-7

The X Window System User's Guide orients the new user to window system concepts and provides detailed tutorials for many client programs, including the *xterm* terminal emulator and window managers. Building on this basic knowledge, later chapters explain how to customize the X environment and provide sample configurations. The *Standard Edition* uses the *twm* manager in most examples and illustrations. Revised for X11 Release 5. This popular manual is available in two editions, one for users of the MIT software, and one for users of Motif. (see below).

"For the novice, this is the best introduction to X available. It will also be a convenient reference for experienced users and X applications developers."
—*Computing Reviews*

Volume 3M: X Window System User's Guide

Motif Edition
By Valerie Quercia & Tim O'Reilly
2nd Edition January 1993
956 pages, ISBN 1-56592-015-5

This alternative edition of the *User's Guide* highlights the Motif window manager for users of the Motif graphical user interface. Revised for Motif 1.2 and X11 Release 5.

Material covered in this second edition includes:

- Overview of the X Color Management System (Xcms)
- Creating your own Xcms color database
- Tutorials for two "color editors": *xcoloredit* and *xtici*
- Using the X font server
- Tutorial for *editres,* a resource editor
- Extensive coverage of the new implementations of *bitmap* and *xmag*
- Overview of internationalization features
- Features common to Motif 1.2 applications: tear-off menus and drag-and-drop

Advanced

UNIX Power Tools

By Jerry Peek, Mike Loukides, Tim O'Reilly, et al.
1st Edition March 1993
1162 pages (includes CD-ROM)
Random House ISBN 0-679-79073-X

Ideal for UNIX users who hunger for technical—yet accessible—information, *UNIX Power Tools* consists of tips, tricks, concepts, and freeware (CD-ROM included). It also covers add-on utilities and how to take advantage of clever features in the most popular UNIX utilities.

This is a browser's book...like a magazine that you don't read from start to finish, but leaf through repeatedly until you realize that you've read it all. You'll find articles abstracted from O'Reilly Nutshell Handbooks®, new information that highlights program "tricks" and "gotchas," tips posted to the Net over the years, and other accumulated wisdom. The goal of *UNIX Power Tools* is to help you think creatively about UNIX and get you to the point where you can analyze your own problems. Your own solutions won't be far behind.

The CD-ROM includes all of the scripts and aliases from the book, plus *perl*, GNU *emacs*, *pbmplus* (manipulation utilities), *ispell*, *screen*, the *scs* preadsheet, and about 60 other freeware programs. In addition to the source code, all the software is precompiled for Sun3, Sun4, DECstation, IBM RS/6000, HP 9000 (700 series), SCO Xenix, and SCO UNIX. (SCO UNIX binaries will likely also run on other Intel UNIX platforms, including Univel's new UNIXware.)

"This substantial volume (1,100-plus pages) is about the power use of existing UNIX tools, with a CD distribution of others. It goes into the kind of wonderful detail that most administrators will relish. Take *find* for example. Most people use it only to find a file by name or age, but this book shows you how to do things such as finding all the root-owned executables with the set-user ID bit on that have been deposited in the last four months. (Naturally, this would be very handy for catching potenetial security holes.) You'll learn a lot from this book. I recommend it highly."—Bruce Hunter, *Open Systems Today*

Making TEX Work

By Norman Walsh
1st Edition April 1994
522 pages, ISBN 1-56592-051-1

TeX is a powerful tool for creating professional-quality typeset text and is unsurpassed at typesetting mathematical equations, scientific text, and multiple languages. Many books describe how you use TeX to construct sentences, paragraphs, and chapters. Until now, no book has described all the software that actually lets you build, run, and use TeX to best advantage on your platform. Because creating a TeX document requires the use of many tools, this lack of information is a serious problem for TeX users.

Making TEX Work guides you through the maze of tools available in the TeX system. Beyond the core TeX program there are myriad drivers, macro packages, previewers, printing programs, online documentation facilities, graphics programs, and much more. This book describes them all.

The Frame Handbook

By Linda Branagan & Mike Sierra
1st Edition November 1994
542 pages, ISBN 1-56592-009-0

A thorough, single-volume guide to using the UNIX version of FrameMaker 4.0, a sophisticated document production system. This book is for everyone who creates technical manuals and reports, from technical writers and editors who will become power users to administrative assistants and engineers. The book contains a thorough introduction to Frame and covers creating document templates, assembling books, and Frame tips and tricks. It begins by discussing the basic features of any text-formatting system: how it handles text and text-based tools (like spell-checking). It quickly gets into areas that benefit from a sophisticated tool like Frame: cross-references and footnotes; styles, master pages, and templates; tables and graphics; tables of contents and indexes; and, for those interested in online access, hypertext. Once you've finished this book, you'll be able to use Frame to create and produce a book or even a series of books.

Exploring Expect

By Don Libes
1st Edition December 1995
602 pages, ISBN 1-56592-090-2

Written by the author of Expect, this is the first book to explain how this new part of the UNIX toolbox can be used to automate Telnet, FTP, passwd, rlogin, and hundreds of other interactive applications. Based on Tcl (Tool Control Language), Expect lets you automate interactive applications that have previously been extremely difficult to handle with any scripting language.

The book briefly describes Tcl and how Expect relates to it. It then describes the Expect language, using a combination of reference material and specific, useful examples of its features. It shows how to use Expect in background, in multiple processes, and with standard languages and tools like C, C++, and Tk, the X-based extension to Tcl. The strength in the book is in its scripts, conveniently listed in a separate index.

"Expect was the first widely used Tcl application, and it is still one of the most popular. This is a must-know tool for system administrators and many others."
—John Ousterhout, John.Ousterhout@Eng.Sun.COM

sed & awk

By Dale Dougherty
1st Edition November 1990
414 pages, ISBN 0-937175-59-5

For people who create and modify text files, *sed* and *awk* are power tools for editing. Most of the things that you can do with these programs can be done interactively with a text editor; however, using *sed* and *awk* can save many hours of repetitive work in achieving the same result.

"*sed & awk* is a must for UNIX system programmers and administrators, and even general UNIX readers will benefit. I have over a hundred UNIX and C books in my personal library at home, but only a dozen are duplicated on the shelf where I work. This one just became number twelve."
—*Root Journal*

Learning Perl

By Randal L. Schwartz, Foreword by Larry Wall
1st Edition November 1993
274 pages, ISBN 1-56592-042-2

Learning Perl is ideal for system administrators, programmers, and anyone else wanting a down-to-earth introduction to this useful language. Written by a Perl trainer, its aim is to make a competent, hands-on Perl programmer out of the reader as quickly as possible. The book takes a tutorial approach and includes hundreds of short code examples, along with some lengthy ones. The relatively inexperienced programmer will find *Learning Perl* easily accessible. Each chapter of the book includes practical programming exercises. Solutions are presented for all exercises.

For a comprehensive and detailed guide to advanced programming with Perl, read O'Reilly's companion book, *Programming perl*.

"All-in-all, *Learning Perl* is a fine introductory text that can dramatically ease moving into the world of *perl*. It fills a niche previously filled only by tutorials taught by a small number of *perl* experts.... The UNIX community too often lacks the kind of tutorial that this book offers."
—Rob Kolstad, *;login*

Programming perl

By Larry Wall & Randal L. Schwartz
1st Edition January 1991
482 pages, ISBN 0-937175-64-1

This is the authoritative guide to the hottest new UNIX utility in years, coauthored by its creator, Larry Wall. Perl is a language for easily manipulating text, files, and processes. Perl provides a more concise and readable way to do many jobs that were formerly accomplished (with difficulty) by programming in the C language or one of the shells. *Programming perl* covers Perl syntax, functions, debugging, efficiency, the Perl library, and more, including real-world Perl programs dealing with such issues as system administration and text manipulation. Also includes a pull-out quick-reference card (designed and created by Johan Vromans).

O'Reilly on the Net—
ONLINE PROGRAM GUIDE

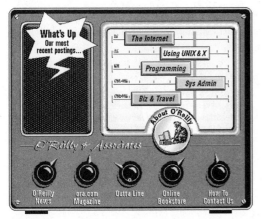

O'Reilly & Associates offers extensive information through various online resources. We invite you to come and explore our little neck-of-the-woods.

Online Resource Center

Most comprehensive among our online offerings is the O'Reilly Resource Center. Here, you'll find detailed information on all O'Reilly products: titles, prices, tables of contents, indexes, author bios, software contents, reviews...you can even view images of the products themselves. With GNN Direct you can now order our products directly off the Net (GNN Direct is available on the Web site only; Gopher users can still use **order@ora.com**). We supply contact information along with a list of distributors and bookstores available worldwide. In addition, we provide informative literature in the field: articles, interviews, excerpts, and bibliographies that help you stay informed and abreast.

To access ORA's Online Resource Center:

Point your Web browser (e.g., `mosaic` or `lynx`) to:

`http://www.com.ora/`

or `http://gnn.com/ora/`

For the plaintext version, `telnet` or `gopher` to:

`gopher.ora.com`

(telnet login: `gopher`)

FTP

The example files and programs in many of our books are available electronically via FTP.

To obtain example files and programs from O'Reilly texts:

`ftp` to:

`ftp.ora.com`

or `ftp.uu.net`
`cd published/oreilly`

Ora-news

An easy way to stay informed of the latest projects and products from O'Reilly & Associates is to subscribe to "ora-news," our electronic news service. Subscribers receive email as soon as the information breaks.

To subscribe to "ora-news":

Send email to:
listproc@online.ora.com

and put the following information on the first line of your message (not in "Subject"):
subscribe ora-news "your name" **of** "your company"

For example enter:

`mail listproc@online.ora.com`

`subscribe ora-news Jim Dandy of`
`    Mighty Fine Enterprises`

Email

Many customer services are provided via email. Here are a few of the most popular and useful.

nuts@ora.com
> For general questions and information.

bookquestions@ora.com
> For technical questions, or corrections, concerning book contents.

order@ora.com
> To order books online and for ordering questions.

catalog@ora.com
> To receive a free copy of our magazine/catalog, *ora.com* Please include a postal address.

Snailmail and Phones

O'Reilly & Associates, Inc.
103A Morris Street, Sebastopol, CA 95472
Inquiries: **707-829-0515, 800-998-9938**
Credit card orders: **800-889-8969** (Weekdays 6 A.M.- 5 P.M. PST)
FAX: 707-829-0104

O'Reilly & Associates—
GLOBAL NETWORK NAVIGATOR™

The Global Network Navigator (GNN)™ is a unique kind of information service that makes the Internet easy and enjoyable to use. We organize access to the vast information resources of the Internet so that you can find what you want. We also help you understand the Internet and the many ways you can explore it.

What you'll find in GNN

There are three main sections to GNN: Navigating the Net, Special GNN Publications, and Marketplace. Here's a look at just some of what's contained in GNN:

Navigating the Net

- The **WHOLE INTERNET USER'S GUIDE & CATALOG**, based on O'Reilly's bestselling book, is a collection of constantly updated links to 1000 of the best resources on the Internet, divided by subject areas.

- The **NCSA MOSAIC "WHAT'S NEW"** page is your best source for the latest Web listings. Browse it like you would a newspaper, then click on the new sites you're most interested in.

Special GNN Publications

- **BOOK STORY**—GNN's newest publication, is the first Internet platform to provide an interactive forum for authors and readers to meet. Book Story serializes books, features author interviews and chats, and allows readers to contact authors with the ease of email.

- **TRAVELERS' CENTER**—This is a great place to visit before your trip begins. The Travelers' Resource Center takes advantage of information that's been on the Internet but hasn't been distilled and compiled in an easy-to-use format—until now. You'll also read feature stories and dispatches from fellow travelers.

- **PERSONAL FINANCE CENTER**—Here is where we bring you a broad spectrum of money management, investment, and financial planning resources on the Internet. There are original features and columns on personal finance, too.

- **GNN SPORTS**—Visit this center for Net coverage of your favorite professional and college teams. (It's better than waiting in line for tickets.) Every week we update the center with articles, interviews, stats, and links to sports resources on the Net.

Marketplace

- **BUSINESS PAGES**—Here's where we've organized commercial resources on the Internet. Choose from a variety of categories like "Business Services," "Entertainment," and "Legal Financial Services."

- **GNN DIRECT**—This is the place to go to read about quality products and services in GNN's collection of catalogs. You can also order online using GNN Direct. Simply browse through product literature, do key word and text searches, and place an order at any time.

Marketing Your Company on GNN

GNN is known as the premier interactive magazine and navigational guide on the Internet. With over 170,000 total subscribers and 8 million document hits every month, GNN attracts a large, dynamic, and growing audience. Because of this, GNN offers exciting opportunities for companies interested in creating a presence on the Internet. We currently offer two programs:

- **TRAFFIC LINKS**—We can link reader traffic from GNN to your Web site. Think of this option as an online form of direct response advertising. GNN staff will work with you to tailor a program to fit your needs. For details about this program, send email to **traffic-links@gnn.com** or call 1-510-883-7220 and ask for our Traffic Link sales representative.

- **BUSINESS PAGES**—Choose from a basic listing (up to 50 words), extended listing (up to 350 words), links from your listing in GNN to your server, or a FAQ (Frequently Asked Questions) document of up to 350 words that's coupled with either a basic or extended listing. For more information, send email to **market@gnn.com** or call 1-510-883-7220.

Get Your Free Subscription to GNN Today

Come and browse GNN! A free subscription is available to anyone with access to the World Wide Web. To get complete information about subscribing, send email to **info@gnn.com**

If you have access to a World Wide Web browser such as Mosaic, Lynx, or NetScape, use the following URL to register online: `http://gnn.com/`

If you use a browser that does not support online forms, you can retrieve an email version of the registration form automatically by sending email to **form@gnn.com** Fill this form out and send it back to us by email and we will confirm your registration.

TO ORDER: **800-889-8969** (CREDIT CARD ORDERS ONLY); **ORDER@ORA.COM**

O'Reilly & Associates—
LISTING OF TITLES

INTERNET

!%@:: A Directory of Electronic Mail
    Addressing & Networks
Connecting to the Internet:
    An O'Reilly Buyer's Guide
The Mosaic Handbook for
    Microsoft Windows
The Mosaic Handbook for
    the Macintosh
The Mosaic Handbook for
    the X Window System Smileys
The Whole Internet User's
    Guide & Catalog
World Wide Web Handbook
    (Summer 95 est.)

SOFTWARE

Internet In A Box
WebSite

WHAT YOU NEED TO KNOW SERIES

Using Email Effectively
Marketing on the Internet
    (Summer 95 est.)
When You Can'T Find Your
    System Administrator

WORKING & LIVING WITH COMPUTERS

Building a Successful Software Business
The Computer User's Survival Guide
    (Summer 95 est.)
The Future Does Not Compute
Love Your Job!

AUDIOTAPES

INTERNET TALK RADIO'S "GEEK OF THE WEEK" INTERVIEWS

The Future of the Internet Protocol,
    4 hours
Global Network Operations, 2 hours
Mobile IP Networking, 1 hour
Networked Information and
    Online Libraries, 1 hour
Security and Networks, 1 hour
European Networking, 1 hour

NOTABLE SPEECHES OF THE INFORMATION AGE

John Perry Barlow, 1.5 hours

USING UNIX

BASICS

Learning the Bash Shell
Learning GNU Emacs
Learning the Korn Shell
Learning the UNIX Operating System
Learning the vi Editor
MH & xmh: Email for Users &
    Programmers
SCO UNIX in a Nutshell
The USENET Handbook (Summer 95 est.)
Using UUCP and Usenet
UNIX in a Nutshell: System V Edition

ADVANCED

Exploring Expect
The Frame Handbook
Learning Perl
Making TeX Work
Programming perl
Running LINUX
sed & awk
UNIX Power Tools (with CD-ROM)

SYSTEM ADMINISTRATION

Computer Security Basics
Computer Crime: A Crimefighter's
    Handbook (Summer 95 est.)
DNS and BIND
Essential System Administration
Linux Network Administrator's Guide
Managing Internet Information Services
Managing NFS and NIS
Managing UUCP and Usenet
Networking Personal Computers
    with TCP/IP (Summer 95 est.)
sendmail
Practical UNIX Security
PGP: Pretty Good Privacy
System Performance Tuning
TCP/IP Network Administration
termcap & terminfo
X Window System Administrator's
    Guide: Volume 8
The X Companion CD for R6

PROGRAMMING

Applying RCS and SCCS
    (Summer 95 est.)
Checking C Programs with lint
DCE Security Programming
    (Summer 95 est.)
Distributing Applications Across DCE
    and Windows NT
Encyclopedia of Graphics File Formats
Guide to Writing DCE Applications
High Performance Computing
Managing Projects with make
Microsoft RPC Programming Guide
Migrating to Fortran 90
Multi-Platform Code Management
lex & yacc
ORACLE Performance Tuning
ORACLE PL/SQL Programming
    (Summer 95 est.)
Porting UNIX Software (Summer 95 est.)
POSIX Programmer's Guide
POSIX.4: Programming for
    the Real World
Power Programming with RPC
Practical C Programming
Practical C++ Programming
    (Summer 95 est.)
Programming with curses
Programming with GNU Software
    (Summer 95 est.)
Software Portability with imake
Understanding and Using COFF
Understanding DCE
Understanding Japanese Information
    Processing
UNIX for FORTRAN Programmers
Using C on the UNIX System
Using csh and tcsh (Summer 95 est.)

BERKELEY 4.4 SOFTWARE DISTRIBUTION

4.4BSD System Manager's Manual
4.4BSD User's Reference Manual
4.4BSD User's Supplementary
    Documents
4.4BSD Programmer's Reference
    Manual
4.4BSD Programmer's Supplementary
    Documents
4.4BSD-Lite CD Companion
4.4BSD-Lite CD Companion:
    International Version

X PROGRAMMING

Volume 0: X Protocol Reference
    Manual, R6
Volume 1: Xlib Programming Manual
Volume 2: Xlib Reference Manual:
Volume 3: X Window System
    User's Guide
Volume. 3M: X Window System
    User's Guide, Motif Ed
Volume. 4: X Toolkit Intrinsics
    Programming Manual
Volume 4M: X Toolkit Intrinsics
    Programming Manual, Motif Ed.
Volume 5: X Toolkit Intrinsics
    Reference Manual
Volume 6A: Motif Programming
    Manual
Volume 6B: Motif Reference Manual
Volume 7A: XView Programming
    Manual
Volume 7B: XView Reference Manual
    Motif Tools
Volume 8: X Window System
    Administrator's Guide
Volume 9: X Programmer's Handbook
    (Summer 95 est.)
PEXlib Programming Manual
PEXlib Reference Manual
PHIGS Programming Manual
    (soft or hard cover)
PHIGS Reference Manual
Programmer's Supplement for Release 6
    (Summer 95 est.)
The X Companion CD for R6
The X Window System in a Nutshell
X User Tools (with CD-ROM)

THE X RESOURCE

A QUARTERLY WORKING JOURNAL FOR X PROGRAMMERS

The X Resource: Issues 0 through 15
    (Issue 15 available 7/95)

TRAVEL

Travelers' Tales Thailand
Travelers' Tales Mexico
Travelers' Tales India
Travelers' Tales: A Woman's World
Travelers' Tales France (6/95 est.)
Travelers' Tales Hong Kong (8/95 est.)
Travelers' Tales Spain (9/95 est.)

FOR INFORMATION: **800-998-9938**, *707-829-0515;* **NUTS@ORA.COM**

O'Reilly & Associates—
INTERNATIONAL DISTRIBUTORS

Customers outside North America can now order O'Reilly & Associates books through the following distributors. They offer our international customers faster order processing, more bookstores, increased representation at tradeshows worldwide, and the high-quality, responsive service our customers have come to expect.

EUROPE, MIDDLE EAST, AND AFRICA
(except Germany, Switzerland, and Austria)

INQUIRIES
International Thomson Publishing Europe
Berkshire House
168-173 High Holborn
London WC1V 7AA, United Kingdom
Telephone: 44-71-497-1422
Fax: 44-71-497-1426
Email: itpint@itps.co.uk

ORDERS
International Thomson Publishing Services, Ltd.
Cheriton House, North Way
Andover, Hampshire SP10 5BE, United Kingdom
Telephone: 44-264-342-832 (UK orders)
Telephone: 44-264-342-806 (outside UK)
Fax: 44-264-364418 (UK orders)
Fax: 44-264-342761 (outside UK)

GERMANY, SWITZERLAND, AND AUSTRIA

International Thomson Publishing GmbH
O'Reilly-International Thomson Verlag
Königswinterer Straße 418
53227 Bonn, Germany
Telephone: 49-228-97024 0
Fax: 49-228-441342
Email: anfragen@ora.de

ASIA *(except Japan)*

INQUIRIES
International Thomson Publishing Asia
221 Henderson Road
#08-03 Henderson Industrial Park
Singapore 0315
Telephone: 65-272-6496
Fax: 65-272-6498

ORDERS
Telephone: 65-268-7867
Fax: 65-268-6727

JAPAN

International Thomson Publishing Japan
Hirakawa-cho Kyowa Building 3F
2-2-1 Hirakawa-cho, Chiyoda-Ku
Tokyo, 102 Japan
Telephone: 81-3-3221-1428
Fax: 81-3-3237-1459

Toppan Publishing
Froebel Kan Bldg. 3-1, Kanda Ogawamachi Chiyoda-Ku
Tokyo 101 Japan
Telex: J 27317
Cable: Toppanbook, Tokyo
Telephone: 03-3295-3461
Fax: 03-3293-5963

AUSTRALIA

WoodsLane Pty. Ltd.
7/5 Vuko Place, Warriewood NSW 2102
P.O. Box 935, Mona Vale NSW 2103
Australia
Telephone: 02-970-5111
Fax: 02-970-5002
Email: woods@tmx.mhs.oz.au

NEW ZEALAND

WoodsLane New Zealand Ltd.
21 Cooks Street (P.O. Box 575)
Wanganui, New Zealand
Telephone: 64-6-347-6543
Fax: 64-6-345-4840
Email: woods@tmx.mhs.oz.au

THE AMERICAS

O'Reilly & Associates, Inc.
103A Morris Street
Sebastopol, CA 95472 U.S.A.
Telephone: 707-829-0515
Telephone: 800-998-9938 (U.S. & Canada)
Fax: 707-829-0104
Email: order@ora.com

TO ORDER: **800-889-8969** (CREDIT CARD ORDERS ONLY); **ORDER@ORA.COM**

Here's a page we encourage readers to tear out...

O'REILLY WOULD LIKE TO HEAR FROM YOU

Please send me the following:

❏ *ora.com*

O'Reilly's magazine/catalog, containing behind-the-scenes articles and interviews on the technology we write about, and a complete listing of O'Reilly books and products.

❏ *Global Network Navigator*™

Information and subscription.

Please print legibly

Which book did this card come from?

_____

Where did you buy this book?
  ❏ Bookstore   ❏ Direct from O'Reilly
  ❏ Bundled with hardware/software   ❏ Class/seminar

Your job description: ❏ SysAdmin   ❏ Programmer
  ❏ Other_____

What computer system do you use?   ❏ UNIX
  ❏ MAC   ❏ DOS(PC)   ❏ Other _____

_____
Name   Company/Organization Name

_____
Address

_____
City   State   Zip/Postal Code   Country

_____
Telephone   Internet or other email address (specify network)

Nineteenth century wood engraving
of the horned owl from the O'Reilly
& Associates Nutshell Handbook®
Learning the UNIX Operating System

O'Reilly & Associates, Inc. 103A Morris Street, Sebastopol, CA 95472-9902

BUSINESS REPLY MAIL
FIRST CLASS MAIL   PERMIT NO. 80   SEBASTOPOL, CA

Postage will be paid by addressee

O'Reilly & Associates, Inc.
103A Morris Street
Sebastopol, CA 95472-9902